RECOGNISING A HUMAN RIGHT TO ABORTION

This book critiques international and regional human rights standards on abortion from a feminist perspective, exploring the progress made and lack thereof on the protection of abortion rights within the EU, UN, Inter-American and African systems. Drawing on the idea that human rights are aspirational tools which can be transformed to make progress on abortion rights from the bottom-up, this book sets out a globally applicable framework and makes recommendations for recognising the human right to abortion. In the face of a growing global backlash against abortion rights, this is a topical, timely and compelling work.

Recognising a Human Right to Abortion

Zoe Tongue

•HART•
OXFORD • LONDON • NEW YORK • NEW DELHI • SYDNEY

HART PUBLISHING
Bloomsbury Publishing Plc
Kemp House, Chawley Park, Cumnor Hill, Oxford, OX2 9PH, UK
1385 Broadway, New York, NY 10018, USA
Bloomsbury Publishing Ireland Limited, 29 Earlsfort Terrace, Dublin 2, D02 AY28, Ireland

HART PUBLISHING, the Hart/Stag logo, BLOOMSBURY and the Diana logo are trademarks of Bloomsbury Publishing Plc

First published in Great Britain 2026

1

A catalogue record for this book is available from the British Library.

A catalogue record for this book is available from the Library of Congress.

ISBN: HB: 978-1-50998-996-6
ePDF: 978-1-50998-998-0
ePub: 978-1-50998-997-3

Typeset by Amnet

For product safety related questions contact productsafety@bloomsbury.com

To find out more about our authors and books visit www.hartpublishing.co.uk. Here you will find extracts, author information, details of forthcoming events and the option to sign up for our newsletters.

Contents

Acknowledgements

THIS MONOGRAPH EMERGED from my PhD thesis, so I must firstly thank Professor Shaun Pattinson for the guidance, care, and support he gave to me as my supervisor. I also wish to thank Dr Anashri Pillay for the further support she provided, Professor Emma Cave and Professor Patrick Capps for creating such a positive viva experience, and everyone else at Durham Law School who helped along the way. I also want to thank my colleagues at the University of Leeds School of Law, and anyone else that I have met at conferences or online over the past few years that has shaped and encouraged my work. Thank you to my parents and grandparents for supporting my academic journey. Endless amounts of love and thanks to Joshua Jowitt, Natalie Tongue, Chloe Longden, Amber Cummings, Anna Barnard-Wright, Annabel Rose, Chloe O'Connor, Evie Garlick, Fiona Hathaway, Lauren Urquhart, Millie Hawes, Chloe Romanis, James Greenwood-Reeves, and Rosie Fox.

Table of Cases

Table of Legislation

Introduction

I. ABORTION IS A MORAL RIGHT

I TAKE AS MY starting point the view that abortion is a fundamental moral right which must be recognised as such by national and international institutions. Many feminist scholars have already established that access to abortion is necessary for human rights, bodily integrity, and substantive gender equality.[1] In the bioethics literature, scholars have framed abortion as a matter of essential healthcare, and Katie Watson advocates for positioning abortion in moral discourse as about the ethics of *access*, rather than continuing to debate the ethical permissibility of abortion.[2] Abortion is, and has always been, a common reproductive experience, regardless of time or place, social acceptability or legislative permissibility.[3] Thus, this book does not engage in discussions of foetal status or personhood, and nor do I seek to debate the morality of abortion. That work has also already been done.[4] In contrast to the prevalent view that moral arguments about abortion *must* relate to foetal life, I follow Watson in recognising

[1] See, eg, Rachel Rebouché, 'Abortion Rights as Human Rights' (2016) 25(6) *Social and Legal Studies* 765; Elisabeth Porter, 'Abortion Ethics: Rights and Responsibilities' (1994) 9(3) *Hypatia* 66; Susan Sherwin, 'Abortion Through a Feminist Ethics Lens' (1991) 30(3) *Dialogue* 327; Sally Markowitz, 'Abortion and Feminism' (1990) 16(1) *Social Theory and Practice* 1; Rosalind Pollack Petchesky, *Abortion and Woman's Choice: The State, Sexuality, and Reproductive Freedom* (Northeastern University Press, 1984).

[2] Elizabeth Chloe Romanis, 'Abortion Access and the Benefits and Limitations of Abortion-Permissive Legal Frameworks: Lessons from the United Kingdom' (2023) 32(3) *Cambridge Quarterly of Healthcare Ethics* 378; Evie Kendal, 'All Abortions are Medically Necessary' (2023) 18(3) *Clinical Ethics* 306; Katie Watson, 'The Ethics of Access: Reframing the Need for Abortion Care as a Health Disparity' (2022) 22 *The American Journal of Bioethics* 22.

[3] See Mary Fissell, *Abortion: A History* (C Hurst & Co Publishers, 2025); Sanhita Ambast, Hazal Atay, and Antonella Lavelanet, 'A Global Review of Penalties for Abortion-Related Offences in 182 Countries' (2023) 8(3) *BMJ Global Health* e010405.

[4] See, eg, Kate Greasley, 'Abortion, Feminism, and 'Traditional' Moral Philosophy' in Andelka M Phillps, Thana C de Campos, and Jonathan Herring (eds), *Philosophical Foundations of Medical Law* (Oxford, Oxford University Press, 2019); Lynn M Morgan and Meredith W Michaels, *Fetal Subjects, Feminist Positions* (University of Pennsylvania Press, 1999); LW Sumner, *Abortion and Moral Theory* (Princeton University Press, 1981); Mary Anne Warren, 'The Moral and Legal Status of Abortion' (1973) 57(1) *The Monist* 43; Judith Jarvis Thomson, 'A Defense of Abortion' (1971) 1(1) *Philosophy and Public Affairs* 47; Philippa Foot, 'The Problem of Abortion and the Doctrine of Double Effect' (1967) 5(5) *Oxford Review* 15.

abortion as a moral good because it is necessary for social, economic, and gender justice.[5]

The arguments I make in relation to abortion are informed not only by feminist scholarship and activism, but by my own positionality. I live in the United Kingdom – England, specifically – where abortion has been legalised on relatively liberal grounds, and there is a dedicated abortion clinic in my city of residence. This is important to me, because I do not want to have children, and nor do I ever want to experience pregnancy or childbirth. I am, at least in the current moment, able to make this decision because of my context, and because I am white, British, and middle-class by virtue of my university education and career. When I think about the privileges I have over my life, body, and reproductive capacity, I think about my grandmother, a working-class woman from a mining town in Northern England. She did not want to have children, but ended up having four, not (at least, directly) because of abortion laws but because she had no real alternatives to getting married and having children. Her husband died, and she became the sole parent to her children when the youngest of them was just two years old. I have the means to be able to choose not to have children, but my grandmother did not. Moreover, while I currently have access to legal abortion services, inequalities in access remain prevalent across the UK, often relating to class and nationality, with migrant women's access to abortion, contraception, and maternity care undermined by hostile government policies and harmful media narratives.[6]

I include this positionality statement because my context affords me reproductive agency, but this is something denied to many people worldwide by restrictive political, legal, and medical frameworks, global injustice, reproductive violence, and inequalities along the intersectional lines of gender, race, class, disability, sexuality, nationality, ethnicity, religion, and other factors. I do not speak for these people, whose experiences are very different to my own, but advocate for a world where reproductive agency is guaranteed for every person.[7] Abortion is a fundamental part of this but is, to state the obvious, heavily contested. It is my argument that current human rights standards do not adequately protect access to abortion, and that recognising a human right to abortion – alongside radical social, cultural, political, economic, and legal change – is necessary to move towards guaranteeing comprehensive access to abortion (alongside other sexual and reproductive health services) for all that need it. The current global landscape for abortion remains far from this ideal.

[5] Katie Watson, 'Abortion as a Moral Good' (2019) 393 *Lancet* 1196.

[6] See Kathryn Cassidy, Rana Amiri, and Gill Davidson, 'Reading for Refusal in UK Maternity Care: Entangling Struggles for Border and Reproductive Justice' (2023) 201(2) *Fennia* 199; Isabelle Whelan, 'The Effect of United Kingdom Immigration Policies on Migrant Access to Sexual and Reproductive Healthcare' (2019) 45(1-2) *BMJ Sex Reprod Healthcare* 1; Gwyneth Lonergan, 'Reproductive Justice and Migrant Women in Great Britain' (2012) 23(1) *Women* 26.

[7] I use the terminology of 'pregnant people' throughout this book to be inclusive of trans, non-binary, and gender expansive people, as well as cisgender women, who are capable of becoming pregnant and therefore need access to abortion.

II. ACCESS TO ABORTION WORLDWIDE

Legal, political, social, cultural, economic, religious, historical, and many other factors shape and constrain access to abortion in any given context. As a result, there are significant worldwide disparities in the provision of safe, legal, and accessible abortion services, and abortion laws vary dramatically. In Canada, abortion has been decriminalised since 1988 when the Supreme Court held that the sections of the criminal code imposing restrictions on abortion were unconstitutional.[8] In recent years, the trend towards decriminalisation has expanded somewhat; as of 2021, abortion has been decriminalised in all jurisdictions of Australia, and abortion is now no longer a criminal offence for the pregnant person in Argentina, Northern Ireland, and Aotearoa (New Zealand).[9] In most of Europe, abortion remains a criminal offence, but has also been legalised on relatively broad grounds.[10] Forty of the 47 countries in Europe provide for abortion on request within the early stages of pregnancy, with most allowing this up to 12 weeks' gestation, though some provide for abortion on request up to 14 (Spain and Romania), 16 (France), or 18 weeks (Norway and Sweden).[11] However, access to abortion is generally very restricted after these points, with legal grounds only covering serious medical risks. The most progressive jurisdictions for later abortions are the UK and the Netherlands, which both allow abortion on broad social grounds up to 24 weeks' gestation, but the law again becomes very restrictive after this gestational cut-off.[12]

There are also a small few European countries which have retained restrictive abortion regimes. Abortion is completely prohibited in the micro-state of Andorra, and this was also the case in Malta until 2023, when abortion was legalised where necessary to save the pregnant person's life.[13] In Poland and Liechtenstein, abortion is legal only where there is a serious risk to the pregnant person's life or health, or in cases of rape or incest.[14] Monaco permits abortion in cases of foetal impairment as well as on those two grounds.[15] Abortion in cases of foetal impairment was previously also permitted in Poland, but this

[8] *R v Morgentaler* [1988] 1 SCR 30.

[9] Termination of Pregnancy Act 2021 [South Australia]; *Ley de Interrupción Voluntaria del Embarazo* No 27.610 2020 [Argentina]; Northern Ireland (Executive Formation etc) Act 2019, s 9 [UK]; Abortion Legislation Act 2020 [Aotearoa].

[10] The vast majority of countries around the world retain criminal offences for abortion. See Ambast, Atay, and Lavelanet, 'A Global Review' (2023) (n 3).

[11] Center for Reproductive Rights, 'European Abortion Laws: A Comparative Overview' (December 2020) https://reproductiverights.org/wp-content/uploads/2020/12/European-abortion-law-a-comparative-review.pdf accessed 9 January 2026.

[12] Abortion Act 1967 [England, Wales, and Scotland]; Abortion (Northern Ireland) Regulations 2020, SI 2020/345; Termination of Pregnancy Act 1984 [Netherlands].

[13] Criminal Code of Malta, Articles 241–243 and 243B.

[14] The Family Planning, Human Embryo Protection and Conditions of Permissibility of Abortion Act of 7 January 1993 [Poland]; Criminal Code of Liechtenstein, Section 96.

[15] Penal Code of Monaco, Article 248.

was declared unconstitutional by the Polish Constitutional Tribunal in 2020.[16] However, social movements and some lawmakers continue to push for legalisation and decriminalisation in these countries. In May 2025, a proposal to legalise abortion on request was approved by Monaco's National Council, but the Head of State Prince Albert II refused to sign the bill, citing the country's Catholic values to justify retaining the existing legal regime.[17] The leader of Poland's coalition government, elected in 2023, made campaign promises around liberalising the country's abortion regime, but a bill that would have legalised abortion on request in early pregnancy was narrowly rejected in the Sejm (the lower house of Poland's Parliament).[18] In early 2025, activists set up their own abortion centre in Warsaw to offer the care that the state had failed to provide.[19] In Malta, the 'Voice for Choice' coalition continues to campaign for more progressive reforms, including decriminalisation.[20]

European powers imposed their historically restrictive abortion laws, and the moral and religious values underpinning them, in the countries they colonised. Britain's Offences Against the Person Acts of 1828, 1837, and 1861 contained criminal offences for abortion with a penalty of life imprisonment, and these laws were applied across the British Empire.[21] Likewise, the Spanish and Portuguese Empires implemented their own criminal abortion offences and introduced Catholicism as the dominant religion within their colonies, thus entrenching these values.[22] Prior to colonisation, Indigenous communities across

[16] Polish Constitutional Tribunal Case K 1/20 (22 October 2020).

[17] Tom Heneghan, 'Monaco rejects abortion bill after prince asserts "place of Catholicism"' (*The Tablet,* 2 December 2025) www.thetablet.co.uk/news/monaco-rejects-abortion-bill-after-prince-asserts-place-of-catholicism/ accessed 9 January 2026.

[18] Owen Dyer, 'Poland Abortion Reform Stalls after Decriminalisation Vote Fails' (2024) 386 *British Medical Journal* 1.

[19] Ada Petriczko, 'We are done waiting': Inside Poland's first abortion centre' (*Context*, 5 May 2025) www.context.news/socioeconomic-inclusion/we-are-done-waiting-inside-polands-first-abortion-centre accessed 9 January 2026.

[20] Times of Malta, 'Activists call for abortion law reform ahead of Valletta rally' (20 September 2025) https://timesofmalta.com/article/activists-call-abortion-law-reform-ahead-valletta-rally.1116528 accessed 9 January 2026.

[21] For discussion of abortion offences in British colonised countries, see, eg, Juanita De Barros, 'Embodied Sources: Abortion, Medicine, and the Law in Early Twentieth-Century British Guiana' in Cassia Roth and Diana Paton (eds), *Intimate Politics: Fertility Control in Global Historical Perspective* (Routledge, 2024); Varsha Chitnis and Danaya Wright, 'Legacy of Colonialism: Law and Women's Rights in India' (2007) 64(4) *Washington & Lee Law Review* 1315.

[22] Abortion was included as an offence in Spain's first Criminal Code (1822) and its subsequent iterations, and in Portugal's two previous Penal Codes (1852 and 1886). For discussion of the role of the Catholic Church and colonial governance on gender and reproduction in countries colonised by Spain and Portugal, see Amélia Polónia and Rosa Capelão, 'Women and Gender in the Portuguese Overseas Empire. Society, Economy, and Politics, 16th–17th Centuries' in Francisco Bethencourt (ed), *Gendering the Portuguese-Speaking World* (Brill, 2021); Amanda Muniz Oliviera, '"Sterilisation Must be Done Against Her Will": Coloniality, Eugenics and Racism in Brazil 2018 – The Case of Janaína Quirino' (2021) 47(1) *Australian Feminist Law Journal* 105; Nora E Jaffary, *Reproduction and Its Discontents in Mexico: Childbirth and Contraception from 1750 to 1905* (University of North Carolina Press, 2016); John Frederick Schwaller, *The History of the Catholic Church in Latin America* (New York University Press, 2011).

the world are known to have used a variety of herbs and plants to induce abortions.[23] While a number of Latin American countries – Argentina, Colombia, and Uruguay – have recently legalised abortion on request, others either only permit abortion in exceptional circumstances (such as to save the pregnant person's life) or prohibit it entirely.[24] In El Salvador, the total criminalisation of abortion has been applied to the extent that women who experience involuntary miscarriage or stillbirths have been prosecuted.[25] In July 2022, for example, a woman was sentenced to 50 years in prison for aggravated homicide after an obstetric emergency which led to the death of her baby.[26] Across Africa, the majority of states limit access to abortion to where the pregnant person's life or health is at risk, where the pregnancy resulted from rape or incest, and in cases of foetal impairment.[27] Similar restrictions limit access to abortion for non-medical reasons in many countries across the Asian continent.[28] Heather Latimer ties the rise of abortion regulation to nineteenth-century colonial ideas about sex, gender, and race, and thus views these regulations as the 'afterlife of reproductive slavery'.[29]

Latimer argues that fertility control, and particularly abortion, was conceptualised in the context of slavery in the United States as a form of resistance, which therefore led to it being seen as illegitimate.[30] Latimer draws on Alys Eve Weinbaum's understanding of 'the slave episteme' which 'enables continued – albeit continuously recalibrated – forms of gendered and racialized exploitation of human reproductive labor'.[31] Latimer also argues that it is because 'reproduction was seen as a racializing process that antiabortionists were worried about white women's procreation after slavery ended',[32] and racialised population concerns have also been identified as underpinning abortion policies and

[23] Tracy X Chen and others, 'Roots, Leaves, and Flowers: A Narrative Review of Herbs and Botanicals Used for Self-Managed Abortion in Asia and the Pacific' (2023) 68(6) *Journal of Midwifery and Women's Health* 710; Heather Latimer, 'Abortion Regulation as the Afterlife of Reproductive Slavery: Or, a Call to Make Abortion Natural Again' (2022) 48(2) *Feminist Studies* 342.

[24] Center for Reproductive Rights, 'The World's Abortion Laws' https://reproductiverights.org/maps/world-abortion-laws/ accessed 9 January 2026.

[25] Elisabeth Malkin, 'They Were Jailed for Miscarriages. Now, Campaign Aims to End Abortion Ban' (The New York Times, 9 April 2018) www.nytimes.com/2018/04/09/world/americas/el-salvador-abortion.html accessed 9 January 2026.

[26] Reuters, 'El Salvador woman's 50-year jail sentence outrages abortion rights group' (4 July 2022) www.reuters.com/world/americas/el-salvador-womans-50-year-jail-sentence-outrages-abortion-rights-group-2022-07-04/ accessed 9 January 2026.

[27] Center for Reproductive Rights, 'The World's Abortion Laws' (n 24).

[28] See Dipika Jain 'Legal Challenges in Expanding the Provider Base for Abortion in Asia' (2025) 168(3) *International Journal of Gynecology and Obstetrics* 1345.

[29] Latimer, 'Abortion Regulation' (2022) (n 23) 342–43.

[30] ibid 343.

[31] Alys Eve Weinbaum, *The Afterlife of Reproductive Slavery* (Duke University Press, 2019) pp 2–3.

[32] Latimer (n 23) 357.

narratives in other settler colonial states such as Australia.[33] These historical roots 'continue to structure how we think about abortion today',[34] at least in the context of European settler colonialism.

In the United States in particular, abortion has remained a highly politicised and deeply controversial issue. In 1973, the US Supreme Court recognised a constitutional protection for abortion in *Roe v Wade* – in the first trimester, access to abortion was required by the right to privacy.[35] This was, however, limited by the subsequent judgment of *Planned Parenthood v Casey*, which allowed states to pass further restrictions and regulations, provided that they did not impose an 'undue burden' on the pregnant person.[36] In June 2022, the US Supreme Court handed down its judgment in *Dobbs v Jackson*, holding that there was no constitutional right to abortion, thus overturning *Roe* and *Casey*.[37] States are now free to impose much more onerous restrictions on abortion. In Texas, for example, abortion is now illegal once the foetal heartbeat is detected (around six weeks' gestation) and Louisiana has made abortion illegal except to save the pregnant person's life.[38] In the two months following *Dobbs*, the estimated number of legal abortions across the US fell by 10,000[39] and 66 abortion clinics had closed by the end of the year.[40] Difficulties with access to abortion in the US long pre-date *Dobbs*, however.[41] In 2023, the number of people having to travel to another state to access abortion care was twice the number of people doing so in 2020 – but there were still 81,000 people travelling out of state for essential healthcare before *Dobbs*.[42]

This lack of access in practice is also true of many countries – even where abortion has been legalised or decriminalised, abortion is not always available to everyone. Geographical, physical, and socio-economic barriers disproportionately affect already marginalised groups, and issues such as conscientious

[33] Erica Miller, '"Too Many": Anxious White Nationalism and the Biopolitics of Abortion' (2015) 30(83) *Australian Feminist Studies* 82.

[34] Latimer (n 23) 364.

[35] *Roe v Wade* 410 US 113 (1973).

[36] *Planned Parenthood v Casey* 505 US 833 (1992).

[37] *Dobbs v Jackson Women's Health* 597 US 215 (2022).

[38] SB 8 (Texas); RS 40: 1061 (Louisiana).

[39] Maggie Koerth and Amelia Thomson-DeVeaux, 'Overturning Roe Has Meant At Least 10,000 Fewer Legal Abortions' (*FiveThirtyEight*, 30 October 2022) https://fivethirtyeight.com/features/overturning-roe-has-meant-at-least-10000-fewer-legal-abortions/ accessed 9 January 2026.

[40] Rachel K Jones, Candace Gibson, and Jesse Philbin, 'The Number of Brick-and-Mortar Abortion Clinics Drops, as US Abortion Rate Rises: New Data Underscore the Need for Policies that Support Providers' (*Guttmacher*, June 2024) www.guttmacher.org/report/abortion-clinics-united-states-2020-2024 accessed 9 January 2026.

[41] See, eg, Elise Andaya, 'The Erosion of Rights to Abortion Care in the United States: A Call for Renewed Anthropological Engagement with the Politics of Abortion' (2017) 31(1) *Medical Anthropology Quarterly* 40; Rachel K Jones and Jenna Jerman, 'How Far Did US Women Travel for Abortion Services in 2008?' (2013) 22(8) *Journal of Women's Health* 706; Marlene Gerber Fried, 'Abortion in the United States: Barriers to Access' (2000) 4(2) *Health and Human Rights Journal* 174.

[42] Guttmacher, 'Fact Sheet: Abortion in the United States' (April 2025) www.guttmacher.org/fact-sheet/induced-abortion-united-states accessed 9 January 2026.

objection, a shortage of trained abortion providers, and the inadequate funding of public healthcare services can also obstruct access. In India and South Africa, for example, despite having relatively liberal abortion laws, a significant proportion of abortions are performed outside of medical institutions due to the inaccessibility of services.[43] Numerous states also impose onerous requirements such as mandatory waiting periods, directive counselling, and ultrasound scans before an abortion is permitted, and these barriers not only delay access to abortion, but also serve to stigmatise abortion seekers.

Where abortion is prohibited or inaccessible, it is an inevitability that pregnant people will resort to clandestine abortion. Not all clandestine abortions are unsafe; safe self-managed early medical abortions using mifepristone and misoprostol will be discussed in chapter four. However, it has been estimated that around 25 million unsafe abortions – amounting to almost one third of all abortions – occur each year, though it is important to note that the actual number is likely to be higher as abortion is underreported due to stigma and fear of criminalisation.[44] Unsafe abortions are much more prevalent in lower-income states due to compounding inequalities and a lack of available resources directed towards healthcare provision.[45] In 2014, researchers estimated that 7.9 per cent of maternal deaths worldwide are abortion-related, though again this may be an underestimation.[46] The greatest percentage of maternal mortality associated with abortion was found in Latin America and Sub-Saharan Africa (9.9 per cent and 9.6 per cent respectively) – lower-income regions where abortion is generally more restricted.[47] Criminalisation is a significant factor in unsafe abortion practices.

These inequalities also come in the context of broader disparities in the provision of sexual and reproductive healthcare, including access to education and information, sexual health services, an unmet need for modern contraceptive methods, contraceptive coercion and forced sterilisation, maternal mortality rates, obstetric violence, and broader gender-based and intersectional inequalities. The ability to make meaningful reproductive decisions requires access to healthcare more broadly, including maternity care and mental health services, and a range of other conditions including food, water, housing, sanitation, social and economic support, safe environmental conditions, and safe working conditions including maternity leave – many of which are not accessible

[43] Susheela Singh and others, 'The incidence of abortion and unintended pregnancy in India, 2015' (2018) 6(1) *Lancet Glob Health* e111; Mary Favier, Jamie MS Greenberg, and Marion Stevens, 'Safe Abortion in South Africa: "We have wonderful laws but we don't have people to implement those laws"' (2018) 143(S4) *International Journal of Gynaecology and Obstetrics* 38.

[44] Bela Ganatra and others, 'Global, Regional, and Subregional Classification of Abortions by Safety, 2010–2014: Estimates from a Bayesian Hierarchical Model' (2017) 390 *Lancet* 2372, 2377, 2379.

[45] ibid 2377.

[46] Lale Say and others, 'Global Causes of Maternal Death: A WHO Systematic Analysis' (2014) *The Lancet Global Health* e323, e331.

[47] ibid e326.

to everyone. Population policies can further undermine reproductive decision-making, ranging from coercive contraceptive practices to forced sterilisation. Leigh Senderowicz highlights issues with contraceptive coercion in family planning programmes operating in the Global South, with people denied their preferred contraception and coerced into an alternative method and people who do not want to use contraception compelled to do so in order to meet targets related to reducing unwanted pregnancies and maternal mortality rates.[48] In some states, population policies have resulted in the non-consensual sterilisation of marginalised groups, for example the targeting of poor and lower caste women for mass coerced sterilisation and unsafe injectable contraceptives in India.[49] While this monograph focuses on abortion, it cannot be framed as *separate* from the other sexual, reproductive, and human rights that ought to be guaranteed for all.

III. REPRODUCTIVE JUSTICE AND PREFIGURATIVE POLITICS

At the International Conference on Population and Development (ICPD) 1994, where the definition of reproductive rights was first formally adopted, a delegation of African American women recognised the gaps in this conception of rights and theorised the reproductive justice framework as an alternative.[50] The SisterSong Women of Colour Reproductive Justice Collective was founded in the US in 1997, and defines reproductive justice as 'the human right to maintain personal bodily autonomy, have children, not have children, and parent the children we have in safe and sustainable communities.'[51] Zakiya Luna and Kristin Luker view reproductive justice requiring both 'a negative right of freedom from undue government interference and a positive right to government action in creating conditions of social justice and human flourishing'.[52] This stands in contrast to the mainstream conception of reproductive rights which, particularly at the time of the ICPD, was restricted to the four key elements of choice, privacy, freedom from governmental interference, and personal autonomy which gives rise to individualised negative rights.[53] The reproductive justice framework retains a human rights foundation which emphasises universality, but takes a broader social justice approach. The framework identifies how broader socio-economic

[48] Leigh Senderowicz, '"I was obligated to accept": A Qualitative Exploration of Contraceptive Coercion' (2019) 239 *Social Science and Medicine* 112531.

[49] Kalpana Wilson, 'For Reproductive Justice in an Era of Gates and Modi: The Violence of India's Population Policies' (2018) 119 *Feminist Review* 89.

[50] Kimala Price, 'What is Reproductive Justice?: How Women of Color Activists Are Redefining the Pro-Choice Paradigm' (2010) 10(2) *Meridians* 42, 56.

[51] SisterSong, 'What is Reproductive Justice?' www.sistersong.net/reproductive-justice accessed 9 January 2026.

[52] Zayika Luna and Kristin Luker, 'Reproductive Justice' (2013) 9 *Annual Review of Law and Social Science* 327, 328.

[53] Angela Hooton, 'A Broader Vision of the Reproductive Rights Movement: Fusing Mainstream and Latina Feminism' (2005) 13(1) *Journal of Gender, Social Policy and The Law* 59, 63.

contexts, including culture and environmental factors, also affect people's reproductive lives.[54] Beyond access to abortion, contraception, and safe parenthood, reproductive justice addresses a range of issues such as gender-based and sexual violence, the provision of healthcare for sexually transmitted infections, control over partner selection and family planning decisions, infertility, and culturally appropriate birthing experiences.[55]

A focus on intersectional oppression and the barriers faced by already marginalised groups is central to the reproductive justice framework. Particular attention is thus afforded to the barriers faced by Black, Indigenous, and People of Colour, people with disabilities, LGBTQ+ people, homeless people, migrants, refugees, and asylum seekers. Reproductive justice scholars have also emphasised the importance of including trans, non-binary, and gender expansive people in demanding 'sexual autonomy and gender freedom for every human being'.[56] Scholars have highlighted the reproductive injustices often faced by Black, Indigenous, and ethnic minority women, such as coercion into using contraception or having abortions, forced sterilisation, and the removal of children.[57] The recognition of the additional barriers faced by already marginalised groups has led reproductive justice scholars and activists to move beyond the 'pro-choice' framing that has been popular in some abortion rights movements. Joan Chrisler has pointed out that social, economic, and political conditions frame the choices available to different people.[58] However, the choice framing assumes that all people capable of becoming pregnant can decide for themselves whether or not to have children, that they all have the resources to pay for sexual and reproductive healthcare, and that they are all afforded control over their bodies, health, and relationships.[59] People capable of becoming pregnant are also unable to exercise true choice 'whenever their livelihood is endangered, public health and education systems are inadequate, and cultural diversity is not respected.'[60] For example, in the absence of widespread access to temporary contraception, abortion has operated as a remedial measure within China's population control programme.[61] Within this context, coupled with the stigma on premarital sex

[54] Loretta J Ross and Rickie Solinger, *Reproductive Justice: An Introduction* (University of California Press, 2017) p 69.

[55] ibid.

[56] ibid p 9.

[57] See, eg, Loretta J Ross, 'African-American Women and Abortion: A Neglected History' (1992) 3(2) *Journal of Health Care for the Poor and Underserved* 274, 275; Leonardo Pegoraro, 'Second-Rate Victims: The Forced Sterilization of Indigenous Peoples in the USA and Canada' (2015) 5(2) *Settler Colonial Studies* 161; Christina Zampas and Adriana Lamačová, 'Forced and Coerced Sterilization of Women in Europe' (2011) 114 *International Journal of Gynaecology and Obstetrics* 163.

[58] Joan C Chrisler (ed) *Reproductive Justice: A Global Concern* (Praeger, 2012) p 53.

[59] ibid p 1.

[60] Sonia Corrêa, *Population and Reproductive Rights* (Zed Books, 2002) p 85.

[61] Kailing Xie, 'Premarital Abortion – What is the Harm? The Responsibilisation of Women's Pregnancy Among China's "Privileged" Daughters' (2019) 8(1) *British Journal of Chinese Studies* 1.

and motherhood outside of marriage, abortion is relatively common amongst young, unmarried women as it is presented as the only option.[62]

In this monograph, I will be presenting an argument for the recognition of an explicit human right to abortion within the international human rights framework. In doing so, I will be moving away from the 'choice' conception of abortion rights by advocating for a feminist transformation of human rights in order to be responsive to gendered, cross-cultural, and socio-economic particularities. I am inspired by the reproductive justice framework, namely in relation to the broader context of reproductive decision-making, intersectionality, and the additional barriers faced by already marginalised groups. However, I will not be explicitly adopting the reproductive justice framework as the foundation of the right to abortion, as this framing goes far beyond this one issue and as Rachel Rebouché identifies, presents a radical agenda for social justice which may be undermined or weakened by its translation into the legal mechanisms of the international human rights framework.[63] Zakiya Luna does, however, view reproductive justice as the 'revolutionary domestication'[64] of human rights norms, and so the progressive values of the reproductive justice conception of reproductive rights will be encompassed in my framework for the right to abortion, as set out in chapter three.

In advocating for a feminist transformation of human rights, I also draw on a prefigurative politics. Prefigurative politics refers to 'the creation of alternative ontologies: alternative ways of being in the world and, one might even dare to say, "alternative worlds"'.[65] This characterises political movements aimed at the creation of these alternative worlds in the present, or in other words, movements aimed at 'building tomorrow today'.[66] 'Prefiguration' literally means to represent something that will happen in the future.[67] Lara Monticelli argues that prefigurative practices 'in the form of alternative production, consumption and food networks, cooperatives, transition towns, intentional and ecological communities, and worker-owned firms are proof that such a transformation, at least on a small scale, is imaginable and realizable.'[68] Monticelli also argues that prefigurative politics is necessary to imagine alternatives to capitalism as the dominant socio-economic and political system,[69] which illustrates prefigurative politics as a counter-hegemonic praxis rather than one which works within

[62] ibid.

[63] Rachel Rebouché, 'Reproducing Rights: The Intersection of Reproductive Justice and Human Rights' (2017) 7(3) *UC Irvine Law Review* 579, 581, 598.

[64] Zakiya Luna, *Reproductive Rights as Human Rights* (New York University Press, 2020) pp 17–18.

[65] Lara Monticelli, *The Future is Now: An Introduction to Prefigurative Politics* (Bristol, Bristol University Press, 2022) p 2.

[66] Paul Raekstad and Sofa Saio Gradin, *Prefigurative Politics: Building Tomorrow Today* (Polity Press, 2020).

[67] Lara Monticelli, 'On the Necessity of Prefigurative Politics' (2021) 167(1) *Thesis Eleven* 99, 106.

[68] Monticelli, *The Future is Now* (2022) (n 65) p.2.

[69] Monticelli, 'On the Necessity' (2021) (n 67).

existing systems. As I will cover in chapter five, some forms of abortion activism, such as self-managed abortion movements, can be understood as prefigurative for rejecting and surpassing the role of medicine and law in abortion provision.

The international human rights framework can be understood as a hegemonic system of power in itself, so this book is not itself an example of prefigurative politics, but draws inspiration from the idea of imagining alternatives capable of real transformation in the present. Davina Cooper explores the potential of 'conceptual prefiguration' which 'acts as if preferred meanings are currently operative, while knowing that they are not, both to reimagine what things could mean and to put new meanings into practice'.[70] Claiming abortion as a fundamental right, in the face of staunch political and legal opposition, is an exercise in conceptual prefiguration. Moreover, in conceptually reimagining the state's relevance for a prefigurative politics, Cooper understands institutions 'as if they could be otherwise'.[71] This idea provides the basis for my argument in favour of a feminist transformation of human rights – an alternative human rights framework capable of supporting aspirational, progressive, and radical claims that echo the work of reproductive justice and prefigurative movements.

IV. A HUMAN RIGHT TO ABORTION

Much has been written on international human rights standards on abortion. This scholarship can be loosely grouped under four themes: tracking the evolving nature of these standards and their limitations;[72] recognising the ways that these standards can be expansively interpreted;[73] arguing that certain rights should be expanded to include abortion;[74] and looking at human rights and abortion in specific contexts.[75] Tatyana A. Margolin argued, prior to much of the recent development of human rights standards on abortion,

[70] Davina Cooper, 'Prefiguring the State' (2017) 49(2) *Antipode* 335, 336.

[71] ibid.

[72] See, eg, Rebecca J Cook and Bernard M Dickens, 'Human Rights Dynamics of Abortion Law Reform' (2003) 1 *Human Rights Quarterly* 1; Christina Zampas and Jaime M Gher, 'Abortion as a Human Right – International and Regional Standards' (2008) 8(2) *Human Rights Law Review* 249; Rachel Rebouché, 'Abortion Rights' (2016) (n 1).

[73] See, eg, Joanna N Erdman, 'Harm Reduction, Human Rights, and Access to Information on Safe Abortion' (2012) 118(1) *International Journal of Gynecology and Obstetrics* 83; Lucía Berro Pizzarossa and Patty Skuster, 'Towards Human Rights and Evidence-Based Legal Frameworks for (Self-Managed) Abortion' (2021) 23(1) *Health and Human Rights Journal* 199.

[74] See, eg, Ronli Sifris, *Reproductive Freedom, Torture, and International Human Rights* (Routledge, 2013).

[75] See, eg, Louise Finer and Johanna B Fine, 'Abortion Law Around the World: Progress and Pushback' (2013) 103(4) *American Journal of Public Health* 585; Ronli Sifris and Suzanne Belton, 'Australia: Abortion and Human Rights' (2017) 19(1) *Health and Human Rights Journal* 209; Lucía Berro Pizzarossa, 'Legal Barriers to Access Abortion Services Through a Human Rights Lens: The Uruguayan Experience' (2018) 26(52) *Reproductive Health Matters* 151.

that establishing 'the right to abortion as a human right is essential' to protect pregnant people either through incorporation into an existing article contained in the Convention on the Elimination of Discrimination Against Women (CEDAW) or as a free-standing clause.[76] Others have argued that the denial of abortion should be recognised as cruel, inhuman, and degrading treatment, pointing to the masculine character of human rights as to why gender-based suffering is not uniformly addressed by treaty bodies.[77] This is currently only the case in a narrow set of circumstances, such as where a pregnant person has been forced to carry a pregnancy to term where the foetus has a fatal impairment, or the pregnancy resulted from rape.[78]

Some scholars have considered the evolution of international human rights standards on abortion as evidence of an emerging right to abortion. For example, Ronli Sifris argued in 2010, prior to the Committee on Economic, Social, and Cultural Rights' more recent comments on the right to sexual and reproductive health, that that the right to health included a right to abortion.[79] In addition, Joanna Erdman and Rebecca Cook noted more recently that human rights standards on abortion have been 'evolving from an exclusive focus on saving women from unsafe abortion to recognizing the broader social effects of criminalization that endanger them'.[80] They argue that 'human rights standards therefore require affirmative legal and policy measures to protect against arbitrary denials of lawful care and to ensure access to services under legal grounds.'[81] The international human rights framework can be interpreted as requiring a procedural right to abortion with substantive elements, both positive and negative, in terms of accessibility and decriminalisation. Thus, Fiona de Londras et al have argued first, that international human rights bodies, while specifying the minimum grounds for the legalisation of abortion, do not specify that a grounds-based approach is to be adopted to meet this requirement; and second, that grounds-based approaches are therefore insufficient to meet human rights obligations.[82] However, as I will argue in chapter one, the expansion of existing human rights to cover abortion and the recently progressive approaches

[76] Tatyana A Margolin, 'Abortion as a Human Right' (2007) 29(2) *Women's Rights Law Reporter* 77, 96, 90.

[77] Isabella Moore, 'Indignity in Unwanted Pregnancy: Denial of Abortion as Cruel, Inhuman and Degrading Treatment' (2019) 23(6) *International Journal of Human Rights* 1010; Sifris, *Reproductive Freedom* (2013) (n 74).

[78] See, eg, HRC, 'General Comment No 36: Article 6 (Right to Life)' (3 September 2019) UN Doc CCPR/C/GC/36, para 8.

[79] Ronli Sifris, 'Restrictive Regulation of Abortion and the Right to Health' (2010) 18 *Medical Law Review* 185.

[80] Joanna N Erdman and Rebecca J Cook, 'Decriminalization of Abortion – A Human Rights Imperative' (2020) 62 *Best Practice and Research: Clinical Obstetrics and Gynaecology* 11, 18.

[81] ibid p 16.

[82] Fiona de Londras, Amanda Cleeve, Maria I. Rodriguez, and Antonella F Lavelanet, 'The Impact of "Grounds" on Abortion-Related Outcomes: A Synthesis of Legal and Health Evidence' (2022) 22(1) *BMC Public Health* 936.

of international human rights bodies have been insufficient in terms of setting out clear obligations to provide comprehensive access to abortion services. The expansion or reinterpretation of existing rights has had a relatively limited impact when it comes to realising gender-based rights.

In this book, I set out the novel argument for recognising a specific and comprehensive right to abortion in the context of a feminist transformation of human rights, which requires the development and recognition of new rights which substantively cover gender-based (and intersectional) issues. In relation to reproductive rights, Melanie M. Lee has argued in favour of the recognition of a human right to reproductive self-determination, and Ricardo Pereira has advanced similar arguments in favour of recognising reproductive self-determination as a sub-category of Indigenous rights, recognising the reproductive autonomy of Indigenous Peoples and the financial, geographic and cultural barriers to healthcare they often face.[83] Kathryn McNeilly has proposed a broad 'right to gender flourishing' which would encompass reproductive and sexual health alongside freedom from gender-based violence, equality and non-discrimination, sexual expression, poverty, and education, among other issues.[84] While McNeilly's proposal responds to a number of feminist critiques of human rights, this 'umbrella right' does not substantively go beyond the gender-based rights set out in CEDAW, except for its moving beyond women to include all 'gendered subjects'.[85] In relation to abortion, non-specificity has been a core limitation of the current international human rights approach, which places relatively weak obligations on states to ensure access to abortion services. In addition, abortion was initially largely excluded from the remit of reproductive rights and numerous states are willing to uphold reproductive rights except when it comes to abortion. Thus, the recognition of broader rights to reproductive self-determination or health would similarly place insufficient pressure on states to legalise and guarantee access to abortion. In contrast, the recognition of a specific human right to abortion would place clearer obligations on states and empower social movements to push for their realisation.

There has been a growing body of literature critiquing and even dismissing human rights as ineffective: for presenting overly romanticised narratives of the emancipatory effects of human rights; for operating merely as a 'palliative' which only helps a limited number of people; for their inability to account for

[83] Melanie M Lee, 'Defining the Agenda: A New Struggle for African-American Women in the Fight for Reproductive Self-Determination' (2000) 6 *Washington and Lee Race and Ethnic Ancestry Journal* 87, 96; Ricardo Pereira, 'Government-Sponsored Population Policies and Indigenous Peoples: Challenges for International Human Rights Law' (2015) 33(4) *Netherlands Quarterly of Human Rights* 437, 457.

[84] Kathryn McNeilly, *Human Rights and Radical Social Transformation* (Routledge, 2018) p 145.

[85] ibid p 146.

everyday experiences of injustice; for failing to support material or distributive equality.[86] Some of these critics recognise that human rights are nonetheless important, as a globally available vocabulary which has brought incalculable benefits and as a radical tool for people living in conditions of oppression.[87] Others, however, conclude that the human rights framework is irredeemable, or that human rights should not be the main tools for working towards global equality.[88] Critical legal scholars are particularly sceptical of the ability of the international human rights system to challenge existing systems of power, imagine radical alternatives, and guarantee freedom.[89] In some contexts, human rights may not the most appropriate or strategic tool for advancing claims relating to freedom and justice, and it is not my argument that human rights ought to be the only or most dominant discourse on abortion. However, human rights provide a powerful and internationally recognised language for challenging injustice and inequality, and the vast majority of states around the world have signed up to international treaties that oblige them to do so.

As I will expand on further in chapter five, abortion activists continue to mobilise human rights claims, and Barbara Sutton and Elizabeth Borland highlight in relation to Argentina's abortion rights campaign that a human right is seen as immediately 'demandable' which also then generates organisational support and international solidarity.[90] They also argue that the human rights framing 'is useful because it allows both broad arguments (abortion rights are part of human rights, which are overarching and international) *and* specific guarantees that can be invoked in particular cases of violation.'[91] Catherine O'Rourke has further explored how feminist activists draw on international law as an important (albeit pragmatic rather than idealist) strategy which is effective for articulating shared feminist values.[92] There are notable limitations to the

[86] Günter Frankenberg, 'Human Rights and the Belief in a Just World' (2014) 12(1) *ICON* 35, 51; Costas Douzinas, *Human Rights and Empire* (Routledge-Cavendish, 2009) p 293; Ratna Kapur, 'Precarious Desires and Ungrievable Lives: Human Rights and Postcolonial Critiques of Legal Justice' (2015) 3(2) *London Review of International Law* 267, 285; David Kennedy, 'International Human Rights Movement: Part of the Problem?' (2002) 15 *Harvard Human Rights Journal* 101, 111; Samuel Moyn, *Not Enough: Human Rights in an Unequal World* (Harvard University Press, 2018) pp 2–3.

[87] Frankenberg, 'Human Rights' (2014) (n 86) 36; Douglass Cassel, 'Does International Human Rights Law Make a Difference?' (2001) 2 *Chicago Journal of International Law* 121, 122; Ratna Kapur, 'Human Rights in the 21st Century: Take a Walk on the Dark Side' (2006) 28 *Sydney Law Review* 665, 683.

[88] Ben Golder, 'Beyond Redemption? Problematising the Critique of Human Rights in Contemporary International Legal Thought' (2014) 2(1) *London Review of International Law* 77, 104; Moyn, *Not Enough* (2018) (n 86) p 220.

[89] Konstantine Eristavi, 'Performing Defiance with Rights' (2021) 32 *Law and Critique* 153, 154; Ratna Kapur, *Gender, Alterity and Human Rights* (Edward Elgar, 2020).

[90] Barbara Sutton and Elizabeth Borland, 'Abortion and Human Rights for Women in Argentina' (2019) 40(2) *Frontiers* 27, 41.

[91] ibid 44.

[92] Catherine O'Rourke, 'Feminist Strategy in International Law: Understanding Its Legal, Normative and Political Dimensions' (2018) 28(4) *European Journal of International Law* 1019.

current human rights framework, hence my argument that a transformation is required alongside the recognition of abortion as a distinct human right, but human rights and other forms of international law remain 'important political resources to support [feminist] mobilization'.[93] This monograph will therefore proceed on basis that a more radical human rights approach is possible, and can be used to prefigure and advance progressive feminist values and rights claims.

V. CHAPTER BREAKDOWN

In chapter one, I begin by addressing the issues with how international human rights bodies have approached abortion thus far. Starting with the initial recognition of reproductive rights at the UN World Conferences on Women and the International Conference on Population and Development 1994, I trace the watered-down recognition of abortion as a human rights issue through to the standards that have subsequently been developed by the Human Rights Committee, Committee on Social, Cultural, and Economic Rights, and Committee on the Elimination of Discrimination Against Women. While the standards of these three bodies have evolved over time, there remain limitations with each Committee's approach. There is no explicit human right to abortion, and I identify three key overarching issues with how abortion is approached by the international human rights framework: that the legalisation or decriminalisation of abortion is recommended in circumstances only where a certain threshold of harm has been reached; the fragmentation of standards on abortion which leaves gaps; and the lack of enforcement and follow-up mechanisms. Finally, I explore the even weaker protections for abortion in each of the three regional treaty bodies – the African Union, Council of Europe, and the Organisation of American States – which have provided little in the way of recognising abortion as a human right.

In chapter two, I then address three key conceptual issues with the international human rights framework which have limited its ability to robustly protect abortion rights: its inadequate approach to gender-based human rights issues; issues with the cross-cultural traction of human rights; and the relatively weaker protection afforded to economic, social, and cultural rights. First, I set out feminist critiques of the international human rights framework and introduce Charlotte Bunch's concept of a feminist transformation of human rights. Building on this idea, I argue that a feminist transformation must take an intersectional approach to gender-based rights, recognising the variable experiences of differently positioned women and inclusive of trans, non-binary, and gender-expansive people. Second, while I reject the iteration of the cultural relativist argument that opposes the idea of universal human rights, I consider the

[93] ibid 1045.

critiques of human rights imperialism. I argue that, while human rights norms must retain some degree of conceptual universality, a feminist transformation of human rights must also embrace pluralism in their application in order to have cross-cultural traction. Finally, I highlight the ways in which economic, social, and cultural rights have been afforded relatively weaker protection than civil and political rights in the international framework, and argue for an integrated approach that would give robust protection to both (overlapping) categories, as is also necessary for both gender-based rights and cross-cultural traction.

Following on from these critiques of the international human rights framework and the argument for a feminist transformation of human rights, chapter three makes the argument for recognising abortion as an explicit human right and sets out the framework for this right. In the first part of this chapter, I draw on feminist perspectives on abortion to frame abortion decisions as relational and embodied, encompassing more than a narrower understanding of bodily autonomy, and access to abortion as necessary for the reproductive citizenship of people capable of becoming pregnant. From this perspective, I set out presumptions in relation to three key issues that are prevalent in law and scholarship: first, legal grounds for abortion and gestational time limits; second, abortion for reasons of foetal sex or impairment; and third, the criminalisation of abortion. These presumptions are then applied in the human rights context, from which I develop a framework for the progressive realisation of the right to abortion. Progressive realisation is important given the worldwide variation in the legalisation of abortion and resources that can be directed towards these services. However, the framework also sets out a minimum core content that all states must meet, progressing in tiers up to full compliance. In doing so, this framework offers a solution to the current limitations with abortion rights standards highlighted in chapter one and offers an example of rights recognition in a transformed human rights framework.

Having established this framework, chapter four goes into more detail on specific issues with the availability and accessibility of abortion: conscientious objection; medically unnecessary restrictions on abortion service provision; access to early medical abortion; and neoliberal healthcare provision. While there are more accessibility issues relating to abortion, the scope of this chapter is limited to those which the international human rights framework has thus far insufficiently addressed. I argue that the international human rights framework's current reliance on mandatory referral mechanisms to regulate conscientious objection is insufficient and set out a framework of recommendations as to how states should respond to conscientious objection. I then set out recommendations for the removal of medically unnecessary regulations such as mandatory waiting periods, ultrasound requirements, counselling, and restrictions on abortion providers. I also make recommendations around the provision of telemedicine for early medical abortion, or the enabling of self-managed abortion where this is not possible, in order to minimise barriers to access in line with the requirements of the framework for the right to abortion set out in chapter three. However, this does not free states from their obligations around providing accessible healthcare facilities, even where private healthcare is the primary mode of delivery.

Finally, this leaves the question of *how* such a right would be effective at pushing states to improve their abortion laws and provision; the recognition of a human right to abortion would not automatically lead to compliance, given international treaty bodies' lack of enforcement and follow-up mechanisms. Chapter five addresses this issue by drawing on the existing work of social movements and national courts. Through processes of vernacularisation, feminist movements translate human rights concepts into ways that resonate in local contexts and put pressure on governments to comply with human rights standards. I look at the examples of Argentina, Ireland, and Northern Ireland where human rights formed part of these recent movements for abortion law reform. In addition, domestic courts can be influential in abortion law reform and in ensuring access to abortion where it is already legalised, as I demonstrate by looking at the Colombian and Argentine courts. Thus, I argue that the human right to abortion could be realised through these alternative avenues and would be significant in bolstering the claims made by abortion law reform movements where there is political resistance. However, I also consider the work of counter-hegemonic rights movements who follow a prefigurative politics and seek to provide better and liberatory abortion care where the state has failed to do so, thus recognising the many avenues which must be taken for real abortion liberation and reproductive justice.

1

Abortion in the International Human Rights Framework

I. INTRODUCTION

ABORTION HAS BEEN increasingly recognised as a human rights issue within the international framework, but most treaties do not include an explicit right to abortion and so human rights standards remain limited in both their approach and their reach. In this chapter, I critique the development of these standards by United Nations (UN) treaty bodies, with a focus on the Human Rights Committee (HRC), Committee on Economic, Social, and Cultural Rights (CESCR), and the Committee on Elimination of Discrimination Against Women (CEDAW Committee), as the three main bodies which have addressed abortion. I start this chapter by setting out the trajectory of the recognition of abortion as a human rights issue at the international level, starting with the four UN World Conferences on Women and the first formal recognition of reproductive rights at the 1994 International Conference on Population and Development (ICPD). I then discuss the evolving approaches of the HRC, CESCR, and CEDAW Committee.

I set out the specific limitations of each respective body's approach, before arguing that their combined approach to abortion is insufficient for three overarching reasons. First, there is a relatively high threshold of harm that must be reached for a human rights violation to be found. Second, the current approach to abortion has developed in a piecemeal manner which leaves gaps in protection, thus applying insufficient pressure on states to provide comprehensive access to abortion. Third, the broader limitations of these human rights bodies' implementation mechanisms have meant that standards on abortion have been ineffective. Yet, even with these limitations, the approach of the UN treaty bodies is still more expansive than that of the regional human rights systems, which have not offered clear guidance in support of comprehensive access to abortion. In the final section of this chapter, I critique the position of abortion within the three regional human rights systems: the African Union, the Council of Europe, and the Organisation of American States. This highlights the inconsistencies and weaknesses of the overall international human rights framework's approach to abortion, which is the starting point for my argument that the recognition of an explicit human right to abortion is necessary to move beyond these limitations.

II. ABORTION AT THE UNITED NATIONS

A. Recognising Reproductive Rights

The four World Conferences on Women organised by the United Nations (Mexico City 1975, Copenhagen 1980, Nairobi 1985, and Beijing 1995) and the ICPD in Cairo 1994 were instrumental to the development of reproductive rights within the international human rights framework. These events were a significant focal point for the global feminist movement to promote the idea of women's rights, as the commitment to universalism within the UN framework was seen as a promising avenue for challenging gender inequality.[1] In the earlier World Conferences on Women, however, abortion received limited attention. The Mexico City Conference established maternal and child health as a priority area, and recognised that one of the causes of maternal mortality and morbidity was 'illegally induced abortion'.[2] Yet, despite recognising that illegal abortion was a maternal health problem, the report that came out of the conference only made a passing reference to the provision of family planning, and did not advocate for the legalisation of abortion.[3] The Copenhagen report only made a vague statement about 'secretly performed abortions' in the context of fertility regulation, and the Nairobi report did not include abortion at all.[4] The dominant human rights approach to reproductive health issues at this time was typically one of population control, whereby maternal mortality (and infant mortality) was viewed as a problem of the number and spacing of a woman's pregnancies, particularly for those in underdeveloped states.[5] In this context, abortion was therefore viewed as an issue stemming from unwanted pregnancies and a lack of contraception, rather than as a common and important aspect of reproductive decision-making.

[1] S Laurel Weldon and others, 'Feminist Waves, Global Activism, and Gender Violence Regimes: Genealogy and Impact of a Global Wave' (2023) *Women's Studies International Forum* 102781, 4.

[2] United Nations, 'Report of the World Conference of the International Women's Year, Mexico City, 19 June – 2 July 1975' (1976) UN Doc E/CONF.66/34, p 28.

[3] ibid p 81.

[4] United Nations, 'Report of the World Conference of the United Nations Decade for Women: Equality, Development and Peace, Copenhagen, 14–30 July 1980' (1980) UN Doc A/COF.94/35, p 32; United Nations, 'Report of the World Conference to Review and Appraise the achievements of the United Nations Decade for Women: Equality, Development and Peace, Nairobi, 15–26 July 1985' (1985) UN Doc A/CONF.116/28/Rev.1.

[5] See, eg, United Nations, 'Report of the World Conference' (1975) (n 2) p 28: 'Where levels of infant and early childhood mortality as well as of foetal mortality are high, their reduction – a desirable end in itself – may also be a prerequisite of the limitation of the number of pregnancies that the average woman will experience, and of the society's adoption of a smaller ideal family size where this is a desired goal.'

The ICPD in 1994 and the Beijing Conference in 1995 transitioned away from the population control approach to reproductive health within the international human rights sphere, and were landmarks in the development of reproductive rights as a distinct concept. The ICPD Programme of Action was the first international human rights document to explicitly recognise reproductive rights as already encompassed within existing human rights and to set out clear objectives for the realisation of these rights.[6] The Programme of Action adopted a broad definition of reproductive healthcare, defined as 'the constellation of methods, techniques and services that contribute to reproductive health and well-being by preventing and solving reproductive health problems.'[7] This required all countries to provide family planning services, comprehensive pregnancy-related healthcare, infertility treatment, sexual health services (including the treatment of sexually transmitted infections), and, although qualified, abortion.[8] The Programme highlighted the importance of education, information, and choice around sexuality, reproductive health, and parenting, and highlighted that reproductive health services should be accessible, affordable, acceptable, and convenient.[9]

While the ICPD delegates did consider abortion to a much greater extent than at the previous conferences, this Programme nonetheless adopted a highly conservative approach to the issue. Abortion was primarily discussed in relation to sex-selective abortion, unsafe abortion as linked to maternal mortality, and the 'current reliance on abortion for fertility regulation' in some countries.[10] Rather than supporting access to abortion as a fundamental aspect of reproductive healthcare, the Programme instead recommended that governments take steps to 'help women avoid abortion'.[11] The key paragraph concerning abortion (paragraph 8.25) emphasised that in 'no case should abortion be promoted as a method of family planning' and that 'every attempt should be made to eliminate the need for abortion.'[12] Recognising unsafe abortion as a public health concern, the Programme encourages governments to expand and improve family planning services in order to prevent unwanted pregnancies and thus reduce recourse to abortion.[13] However, it is (now) widely recognised that the criminalisation of abortion pushes pregnant people towards unsafe abortion practices, but the ICPD did not recognise the legalisation of abortion as a key step towards reducing the maternal mortality and morbidity associated with unsafe abortion. The ICPD took the position that abortion could be eradicated by ensuring access to

[6] United Nations, '*Programme of Action of the International Conference on Population and Development, Cairo,* 5–13 September 1994' (1994) UN Doc A/CONF.171/13 (Annex), Chapter VII.
[7] ibid para 7.2.
[8] ibid para 7.6.
[9] ibid paras 7.5–7.6.
[10] ibid paras 4.15, 7.10, 7.44, 8.19.
[11] ibid para 7.24.
[12] ibid para 8.25.
[13] ibid.

contraception and addressing high-risk sexual behaviour, ignoring the broad and complex reasons why a pregnant person might require an abortion.[14] Instead, the Programme's only support for the provision of safe abortion services was where abortion was already legalised.[15]

Thus, despite its progressive definition of reproductive health and its affirmation of reproductive healthcare as a right, the ICPD failed to recognise the impact of the lack of safe, legal, and accessible abortion services on women. As Marge Berer has argued, the above statements on abortion 'wash their hands of responsibility for the harm that results from unsafe and illegal abortion'.[16] The ICPD entrenched the stigmatisation of abortion by adopting an approach which construed abortion as not only undesirable, but as a practice that governments could and should stamp out. This ignored the reality of abortion decisions and the importance of abortion as part of reproductive decision-making for gender equality, which Rebecca Smyth highlights as an example of 'abortion exceptionalism' – the treatment of abortion as morally and medically distinct from all other healthcare (including other forms of reproductive healthcare).[17] This approach to abortion – referred to by some scholars as the 'Cairo compromise' – resulted from the Catholic Church's opposition to obligations which would have required governments to commit to the legalisation and provision of abortion.[18] The Holy See (the seat of the Vatican) had opposed the inclusion of abortion as a method of family planning, supported by a number of other governments.[19] Malta, for example, opposed any terms in the Programme which could be interpreted as conflicting with its domestic legislation criminalising abortion.[20]

Udi Sommer and Aliza Forman-Rabinovici read the qualifications on abortion as an effort to 'placate both those who called for expanded women's reproductive rights and autonomy on the one hand and forces that opposed abortion on the other' and note the significance of moving abortion 'out of the realm of moral policy and into the realm of public health'.[21] While there was a strong feminist presence at the ICPD, they had to contend with more conservative

[14] ibid paras 8.25, 8.27.

[15] ibid para 8.25.

[16] Marge Berer, 'The Cairo "Compromise" on Abortion and Its Consequences for Making Abortion Safe and Legal' in Laura Reichenbach and Mindy Jane Roseman (eds), *Reproductive Health and Human Rights* (University of Pennsylvania Press, 2011) pp153–54.=

[17] Rebecca Smyth, 'Abortion Exceptionalism in International Human Rights Law' (2024) 46(4) *Human Rights Quarterly* 671, 683; Carole Joffe and Rosalyn Schroeder, 'COVID-19, Health Care, and Abortion Exceptionalism in the United States' (2021) 53(1–2) *Perspectives on Sexual and Reproductive Health* 5.

[18] Joanna N Erdman, 'Abortion in International Human Rights Law' in Sam Rowlands (ed), *Abortion Care* (Cambridge, Cambridge University Press, 2014) p 245; Berer, 'The Cairo "Compromise"' (2011) (n 16).

[19] United Nations General Assembly, 'Overall Review and Appraisal of the Implementation of the Programme of Action of the International Conference on Population and Development' (2 July 1999) UN Doc A/S-21/PV.9, pp 18–19, 41–42.

[20] ibid p 9.

[21] Udi Sommer and Aliza Forman-Rabinovici, *Producing Reproductive Rights* (Cambridge, Cambridge University Press, 2019) pp 173, 180.

forces, including anti-abortion governments and population control advocates.[22] The ICPD therefore pushed forward an 'almost feminist vision'[23] of sexual and reproductive rights, and has been praised for its positioning of gender equality as an integral aspect of reproductive healthcare, despite these setbacks and compromises.[24] However, the ICPD framing of abortion as an unjustifiable practice to be eliminated is where this feminist influence was limited, and meant that the starting point for the formal recognition of reproductive rights was deliberately exclusionary of abortion. Sommer and Forman-Rabinovici acknowledge that a more critical reading of the Programme points to an effort to delegitimise abortion as a reproductive right.[25] As I argue later in this chapter, this starting point has had continuing effects for the recognition of abortion as a human rights issue, as abortion was understood as a negative outlier rather than as a fundamental aspect of reproductive rights.

The following year, the Beijing Conference reaffirmed and built upon the recognition of reproductive rights at the ICPD, including on abortion .[26] The Beijing Platform for Action highlighted that the 'right of all women to control all aspects of their health, in particular their own fertility, is basic to their empowerment.'[27] The Beijing Platform again highlighted the need to 'recognize and deal with the health impact of unsafe abortion as a major public health concern' but added to the text of paragraph 8.25 of the ICPD Programme that governments should 'consider reviewing laws containing punitive measures against women who have undergone illegal abortions'.[28] This addition was significant in light of the failure of the ICPD to recognise criminalisation as a factor of unsafe abortion, and although it was a watered down version of what feminist actors were calling for and thus provided a limited impetus for governments to take action, Rosalind Petchesky considered the addition of this statement to be 'one small step' towards decriminalisation as a human rights norm.[29] Indeed, international human rights bodies subsequently adopted approaches which combined this recognition of criminalisation as harmful with the ICPD's exclusionary approach.

[22] See Leigh Senderowicz and Rishita Nandagiri, 'Thirty Years of "Strange Bedmates": The ICPD and the Nexus of Population Control, Feminism, and Family Planning' (2025) 79(3) *Population Studies* 595.

[23] Rosalind Pollack Petchesky, 'From Population Control to Reproductive Rights: Feminist Fault Lines' (1995) 3(6) *Reproductive Health Matters* 152.

[24] Carmel Shalev, 'Rights to Sexual and Reproductive Health: The ICPD and the Convention on the Elimination of All Forms of Discrimination Against Women' (2000) 4(2) *Health and Human Rights Journal* 38, 40.

[25] Sommer and Forman-Rabinovici, *Producing Reproductive Rights* (2019) (n 21), p 180.

[26] United Nations, 'Beijing Declaration and Platform for Action, adopted at the Fourth World Conference on Women, 4–15 September 1995' (1995) UN Doc A/CONF.177/20/Rev.1.

[27] ibid para 92.

[28] ibid paras 106(j)–(k).

[29] Petchesky, 'From Population Control' (n 23) 154.

B. The Human Rights Committee

The HRC, the treaty body monitoring the implementation of the International Covenant on Civil and Political Rights (ICCPR), has incrementally developed its approach to abortion. The HRC's first significant comment on abortion was in 2000, in a General Comment on the right to the equal enjoyment of rights by men and women (Article 3 ICCPR), in which the Committee stated that the right to life (Article 6) would require States Parties to ensure that women do not undergo life-threatening clandestine abortion.[30] This General Comment also included a recommendation under the right to freedom from torture, cruel, inhuman, and degrading treatment (Article 7) that abortion should be provided where a pregnancy results from rape, and the Committee expressed concerns over compliance with the right to privacy (Article 17) where States Parties impose a duty on medical professionals to report women who have undergone abortions.[31] The HRC has subsequently continued to recognise that restrictions on abortion may violate any of these rights.

In 2005, the HRC heard the first individual complaint relating to abortion to be brought to a United Nations treaty body. *KL v Peru* concerned a KL, a 17-year-old girl who found out that she was pregnant with an anencephalic foetus.[32] Anencephaly is an embryonic developmental impairment which results in the absence of part of the brain, skull, and scalp. Upon being informed that this impairment would be fatal for the foetus and potentially fatal for herself, KL sought to obtain an abortion.[33] Under the Peruvian Criminal Code, therapeutic abortion is permitted only where terminating the pregnancy was the only way to save the life of the pregnant women or to avoid serious and permanent damage to their health.[34] However, despite the risks to her physical and mental health, KL was told by the hospital director that an abortion would be unlawful, and she was forced to continue the pregnancy to term.[35] She gave birth to a baby girl who lived for just four days, during which KL had to breastfeed her.[36] Upon the death of her daughter, KL experienced a state of deep depression.[37]

The HRC noted that KL was forced to endure the 'distress of seeing her daughter's marked deformities and knowing that she would die very soon'.[38] The resulting mental suffering experienced by KL, as a result of the refusal by healthcare professionals to carry out a therapeutic abortion, was found to

[30] HRC 'General Comment No 28: Article 3 (The Equality of Rights Between Men and Women)' (29 March 2000) UN Doc CCPR/C/21/Rev.1/Add.10, paras 10–11.
[31] ibid paras 10–11, 20.
[32] *KL v Peru* (2005) UN Doc CCPR/C/85/D/1153/2003, para 2.1.
[33] ibid para 2.2.
[34] ibid para 2.3.
[35] ibid paras 2.3–2.6.
[36] ibid para 2.6.
[37] ibid para 2.6.
[38] ibid.

amount to cruel, inhuman, and degrading treatment in violation of Article 7.[39] In addition, the HRC found a violation of Article 17, as KL should have been lawfully entitled to a therapeutic abortion under the Criminal Code and the refusal was thus unjustified.[40] In light of these findings, the HRC did not find it necessary to make a determination on Article 6.[41] However, in a dissenting opinion, Hipólito Solari-Yrigoyen stated that this case also revealed a violation of Article 6 as KL's life was placed in grave danger as a result of being refused an abortion.[42] Christina Zampas and Jaime Gher argued that this case was a landmark as it represented 'the first time a UN human rights body held a government accountable for failing to ensure access to abortion services to an individual.'[43] In addition to requiring the Peruvian government to provide an effective remedy for KL, including compensation, the HRC also stated that the government should take steps to avoid similar violations in future, thus requiring Peru to ensure that abortions were accessible in similar cases.[44] This was the first suggestion by the HRC that states ought to ensure access to therapeutic abortion, but this was already a legal ground for abortion in Peru.

In 2011, the HRC heard its second abortion case: *LMR v Argentina*.[45] This case concerned a young woman, LMR, who had a learning disability and had become pregnant from rape.[46] With support from her mother, LMR filed a police report and sought to obtain an abortion, which was legally permitted in cases of rape and for those with learning disabilities under the Argentinian Criminal Code.[47] However, the hospital authorities issued an injunction and initiated judicial proceedings to prevent the abortion from going ahead.[48] The Supreme Court of Buenos Aires ruled that the abortion was lawful, but the hospital again refused to provide it on the basis that LMR's pregnancy was now too far advanced.[49] LMR's family ultimately arranged for her to have an abortion illegally.[50] In a very short ruling, the HRC found violations of Articles 3, 7, and 17 for LMR's mental suffering and the state interference that meant that she was denied the abortion that she was legally permitted to have.[51] As *LMR* concerned access to abortion on a ground which was already legalised domestically, as did *KL*, the HRC did not direct Argentina to amend its abortion law – the issue here was the lengthy judicial process which saw LMR go to three different courts

[39] ibid para 6.3.
[40] ibid para 6.4.
[41] ibid para 6.3.
[42] ibid Appendix.
[43] Christina Zampas and Jaime M Gher, 'Abortion as a Human Right – International and Regional Standards' (2008) 8(2) *Human Rights Law Review* 249, 271.
[44] *KL v Peru* (n 32) para 8.
[45] *LMR v Argentina* (2011) UN Doc CCPR/C/101/D/1608/2007.
[46] ibid paras 2.1–2.3.
[47] ibid.
[48] ibid para 2.4.
[49] ibid paras 2.6–2.7.
[50] ibid para 2.8.
[51] ibid paras 9.2–9.4.

before her abortion was authorised.[52] The requirement that the State Party take steps to prevent future similar violations led the Argentine Supreme Court to affirm that judicial proceedings should not be initiated for abortion requests in cases of rape (see chapter five for a more expansive discussion of this case).[53]

In two later cases concerning Ireland's (at the time) restrictive abortion regime, the HRC demonstrated its increasing willingness to direct States Parties to amend their abortion laws rather than merely ensure access on existing legal grounds. *Mellet v Ireland* and *Whelan v Ireland* both concerned women who had to travel from Ireland to England for abortions in similar situations.[54] Amanda Mellet and Siobhán Whelan received diagnoses of fatal foetal impairments in the 21st and 20th week of their pregnancies, respectively, and were informed that the foetuses they were carrying would most likely die in utero or shortly after birth.[55] Both women travelled to Liverpool for their abortions, at a personal cost of around €3000.[56] Both women were unable to access aftercare and bereavement counselling upon their return to Ireland, which they would have received had they continued their pregnancies until the foetus died or they gave birth to a baby that would not survive.[57]

In *Mellet*, the HRC stated that the applicant's physical and mental distress at being faced with this loss had been exacerbated by a number of factors: being unable to continue receiving medical care and health insurance coverage for her treatment in Ireland, the shame and stigma associated with the criminalisation of abortion, and having to 'choose between continuing her non-viable pregnancy or travelling to another country while carrying a dying fetus, at her personal expense'.[58] The HRC noted that much of this suffering could have been avoided if Amanda Mellet had not been prohibited from undergoing an abortion in her own country under the care of medical professionals she already knew and trusted, thus finding a violation of Article 7.[59] This reasoning and finding was repeated in *Whelan*.[60] The HRC additionally found a violation of Article 17, stating that the interference with Amanda Mellet's decision as to how best to cope with her non-viable pregnancy was unreasonable and arbitrary.[61] In *Whelan*, this reasoning was modified slightly; the HRC found a violation of Article 17 as 'preventing the author from terminating her pregnancy in Ireland caused her mental anguish and constituted an intrusive interference in her decision as to

[52] ibid para 9.4.

[53] F, AL s/ Medida Autosatisfactiva, Expediente Letra "F", No 259, Libro XLVI (2012) Supreme Court of Justice [Argentina], paras 8, 18.

[54] *Mellet v Ireland* (2016) UN Doc CCPR/C/116/D/2324/2013; *Whelan v Ireland* (2017) UN Doc CCPR/C/119/D/2425/2014.

[55] *Mellet* (n 54) paras 2.1–2.2; *Whelan* (n 54) para 2.1.

[56] *Mellet* (n 54) paras 2.3–2.4; *Whelan* (n 54) paras 2.3–2.5.

[57] *Mellet* (n 54) para 2.5; *Whelan* (n 54) para 2.6.

[58] *Mellet* (n 54) para 7.4.

[59] ibid paras 7.4–7.6.

[60] *Whelan* (n 54) paras 7.5–7.7.

[61] *Mellet* (n 54) para 7.8.

how best to cope with her pregnancy, *notwithstanding the non-viability of the fetus.*'[62] This comment suggests that restrictive abortion laws may violate Article 17 even where the viability of the foetus is not an issue. This is significant as the HRC's approach to Article 17 in *KL* and *LMR* has been viewed as primarily an exercise in fulfilling procedural equality, in terms of guaranteeing what the legislature had already permitted.[63] These two cases therefore highlighted the HRC's increasingly expansive understanding of the right to privacy in relation to abortion.

Another point of significance is the finding of a violation of Article 26, equality under the law, in both cases. The HRC considered the position of those who decided to carry a foetus with a fatal impairment until they experienced a miscarriage or stillbirth: they would receive treatment covered by Ireland's healthcare system and their personal health insurance, including aftercare and bereavement support.[64] This was contrasted with the position of those who decided to terminate a non-viable pregnancy and would have to do so outside of Ireland's healthcare system, incurring financial and psychological burdens and being unable to receive post-termination aftercare.[65] The HRC felt that this differential treatment failed to take into account the medical needs and socio-economic circumstances of the applicants, and was not reasonable, objective, or legitimate.[66] However, the claims made by both women as to discrimination under Article 3, concerning equality between men and women, were not separately examined by the HRC, which chose only to consider their position in relation to 'similarly situated'[67] women rather than consider the gendered inequalities perpetuated by Ireland's abortion law. Nonetheless, the HRC took an important step in these cases by explicitly directing Ireland to 'amend its law on voluntary termination of pregnancy [...] to ensure compliance with the Covenant, including ensuring effective, timely and accessible procedures for pregnancy termination in Ireland'.[68] This was therefore a landmark moment in the HRC's jurisprudence, and in the development of human rights standards on abortion more broadly.

The HRC's evolved approach to abortion was set out most clearly in 2019, in one paragraph in its General Comment 36 on the right to life.[69] The HRC stated here that measures regulating abortion must not result in a violation of the right to life, subject pregnant people to physical or mental pain or suffering, or

[62] *Whelan* (n 54) para 7.9 [emphasis added].

[63] Charles Ngwena, 'Access to Safe Abortion as a Human Right in the African Region: Lessons from Emerging Jurisprudence of UN Treaty Monitoring Bodies (2013) 29(2) *South African Journal on Human Rights* 399, 421.

[64] *Mellet* (n 54) para 7.10; *Whelan* (n 54) para 7.11.

[65] ibid.

[66] *Mellet* (n 54) para 7.11; *Whelan* (n 54) para 7.12.

[67] *Mellet* (n 54) para 7.12; *Whelan* (n 54) para 7.12.

[68] *Mellet* (n 54) para 9; *Whelan* (n 54) para 9.

[69] HRC, 'General Comment No 36: Article 6 (Right to Life)' (3 September 2019) UN Doc CCPR/C/GC/36, para 8.

arbitrarily interfere with their right to privacy.[70] The HRC additionally clarified the minimum circumstances in which States Parties must provide safe, legal, and effective access to abortion: where the life and health of the pregnant person is at risk and where carrying the pregnancy to term would cause the pregnant person substantial pain or suffering, particularly where the pregnancy is the result of rape or in cases of fatal foetal impairment.[71] The expansion of the right to life to incorporate suffering was confirmed in three more recent cases concerning girls who were forced to continue pregnancies resulting from rape, finding that forced motherhood in such circumstances violated their right 'to a dignified life and amounted to cruel, inhuman, and degrading treatment'.[72] This recognition that the denial of abortion services amounts to a denial of dignity, a fundamental principle underpinning all human rights, suggests that the HRC could impose more expansive obligations on States in terms of providing access to abortion beyond the minimum circumstances set out by the Committee. However, as these cases all concerned rape, that is yet to be clarified.

Under General Comment 36, States Parties must also ensure that pregnant people do not resort to unsafe abortions by removing criminal sanctions.[73] Beyond the question of abortion legality, the HRC also expanded on the accessibility of abortion services in practice, setting out requirements that governments remove barriers to access including those arising from the conscientious objection of healthcare providers.[74] Abortion must therefore be legalised at the very least in those minimum circumstances, decriminalised to prevent the prosecution of those that terminate their own pregnancies (or those that assist them), and made accessible in practice. The recognition that provision and access must accompany legal change is important in order to make the realisation of these rights possible in practice.

In terms of state accountability, the HRC's Concluding Observations have highlighted their increasing to recognise breaches of these standards and offer recommendations for change. For example, the HRC has made recommendations in relation to El Salvador's total prohibition on abortion which imposes disproportionate criminal penalties, the impacts of conscientious objection and breaches of doctor-patient confidentiality where healthcare professionals have reported pregnant people for abortion offences in Bolivia, and Germany's three-day mandatory waiting period which may act as a barrier to access.[75] While the HRC has avoided making explicit recommendations on gestational time limits

[70] ibid.

[71] ibid.

[72] *Norma v Ecuador* (2025) UN Doc CCPR/C/142/D/3628/2019, para 11.7; *Susana v Nicaragua* (2025) UN Doc CCPR/C/142/D/3626/2019, para 8.5; *Lucía v Nicaragua* (2025) UN Doc CCPR/C/142/D/3628/2019, para 8.5.

[73] ibid.

[74] ibid.

[75] HRC, 'Concluding Observations on the Seventh Periodic Report of El Salvador' (9 May 2018) UN Doc CCPR/C/SLV/CO/7, paras 15–16; HRC, 'Concluding Observations on the Fourth Periodic Report of the Plurinational State of Bolivia' (2 June 2022) UN Doc CCPR/C/BOL/CO/4, paras

for abortion, the Committee has raised concerns in relation to the 'very severe restrictions on abortion for medical reasons after the twentieth week of pregnancy' in India, which does not allow abortion in cases of foetal impairment after this time limit.[76] These more recent documents demonstrate the HRC's recognition of the importance of access to safe, legal abortion services, at least in some circumstances – significant progress since the its first recognition of abortion in 2000.

However, there remain some pressing limitations with the HRC's approach. First, the HRC has avoided directing States Parties to legalise abortion on broader grounds, such as on request or for socio-economic reasons, and has not commented on restrictive gestational time limits for abortion on non-medical grounds. At the time of writing, the statement referred to above in relation to India is the only time that the HRC has explicitly commented on gestational time limits even for medical grounds. The HRC's broader comments on decriminalisation and preventing unsafe abortion would suggest that states should provide access on broader grounds, and within broad gestational time frames so as to minimise barriers to access, but as this is not explicitly required by the treaty body, there is insufficient pressure on States Parties to do so. If a State Party has legalised and made abortion accessible on the specified grounds, but there is a high rate of clandestine abortion for reasons not covered by those grounds, then this ought to be considered to be a continuing violation of human rights by current standards.[77]

Second, the HRC has avoided commenting upon access to abortion as an important facet of gender equality and reproductive autonomy. In *Mellet*, the applicant claimed under Article 26 that the criminalisation of abortion had subjected her to a gender-based stereotype around motherhood as her primary role.[78] As discussed above, the HRC's finding of a violation of Article 26 was not on the basis of gender discrimination, and Article 3 was not expanded upon – which Sarah Cleveland challenged in her dissenting opinion.[79] For Cleveland, Ireland's restrictions on abortion amounted to sex-based discrimination and the HRC's finding of a violation of Article 26 ought to have encompassed issues around gender stereotyping as well as socio-economic inequalities.[80] In a later Concluding Observation on Armenia, the HRC did express general concerns over gender stereotypes around the role of women in the family and recognised intersectional inequalities around access to abortion for women living in rural

16–17; HRC, 'Concluding Observations on the Seventh Periodic Report of Germany' (30 November 2021) UN Doc CCPR/C/DEU/CO/7, paras 18–19.

[76] HRC, 'Concluding Observations on the Fourth Periodic Report of India' (2 September 2024) UN Doc CCPR/C/IND/CO/4, para. 23.

[77] The argument that I will be setting out in later chapters, however, is that restrictions on abortion ought to be understood as violations for many reasons removed other than to prevent unsafe abortion.

[78] *Mellet* (n 54) para 3.19.

[79] *Mellet* (n 54) Annex II.

[80] ibid.

areas, those in poverty, women with disabilities, and women from ethnic or religious minorities.[81] However, acknowledgment of the gendered and intersectional inequalities around access to abortion has not been a consistent feature of the HRC's comments. Without clear recognition of the gendered structural issues surrounding abortion, the HRC's ability to effectively tackle the harms caused by restrictions on abortion is undermined.

Third, and as will be expanded on below, many of the cases concerning abortion heard by the HRC concern minors who have become pregnant from rape, thus meeting the threshold of suffering for the finding of cruel, inhuman, and degrading treatment. Even with the more recent language around the right to live with dignity in the three forced motherhood cases, it is unclear whether the same finding would arise if the applicants were: (a) adult pregnant people; and if (b) their pregnancies resulted from consensual sexual intercourse. The Committee specifically stated that 'forced motherhood interrupts and hinders personal, family, educational and professional goals and severely restricts the lives and futures of *adolescent mothers* and their right to a dignified life.'[82] While restrictions on abortion could have these same impacts on the lives of adult mothers, the Committee specifically emphasises the impact that forced motherhood can have on a child's development.[83] Thus, these cases cannot be read so as to require access to legal abortion services on broad grounds in order to guarantee the right to live a dignified life for all people capable of becoming pregnant.

C. The Committee on Economic, Social, and Cultural Rights

The CESCR, the treaty body monitoring the implementation of the International Covenant on Economic, Social, and Cultural Rights (ICESCR), initially took a much more tentative approach to abortion than the HRC. In 2000, the same year that the HRC issued the first of its General Comment to address abortion, the CESCR adopted General Comment 12 on the right to health (Article 12 ICESCR). Article 12(2)(a) makes reference to infant mortality and the health of the child, and in this General Comment, CESCR stated this was to be understood as requiring measures to improve maternal health as well as child health, including sexual and reproductive health services and access to information and resources in order to access those services.[84] The CESCR also noted the importance of confidential sexual and reproductive health services for adolescents, and the need to ensure an adequate number of hospitals providing sexual and reproductive health services, particularly in rural areas, with doctors adequately

[81] HRC, 'Concluding Observations on the Third Periodic Report of Armenia' (25 November 2021) UN Doc CCPR/C/ARM/CO/3, paras 13(a), 17(b).

[82] *Lucía* (n 72) para 8.5.

[83] ibid.

[84] CESCR, 'General Comment No 14: The Right to the Highest Attainable Standard of Health (Article 12 of the ICESCR)' (11 August 2000) UN Doc E/C.12/2000/4, para 14.

trained to provide those services.[85] However, while including family planning within this discussion of sexual and reproductive health services, the Committee made no explicit mention of abortion in this document. This hesitancy to discuss abortion continued with its General Comment 16, issued in 2005, on the right to the equal enjoyment of rights by men and women (Article 3 ICESCR).[86] Here, the CESCR stated that Article 12 required 'the removal of legal restrictions on reproductive health provisions' which could imply that the decriminalisation of abortion is required, but this was not made explicit.[87]

However, over time the CESCR's approach to abortion has become much more progressive. In 2016, the Committee issued General Comment 22 which was specifically dedicated to expanding on state obligations around the right to sexual and reproductive health as enshrined within Article 12.[88] In relation to abortion, the CESCR recommended that States Parties 'repeal or eliminate' laws that criminalise access to reproductive health services, ensure access to reproductive health services, and take measures to prevent unsafe abortions.[89] While CESCR viewed the prevention of unsafe abortions primarily as a means of lowering maternal mortality and morbidity rates, the Committee did also go on to recognise abortion as integral to gender equality, stating that restrictive abortion laws and the criminalisation of abortion undermines women's 'autonomy and right to equality and non-discrimination in the full enjoyment of the right to sexual and reproductive health'.[90] The CESCR also noted that gender-based stereotypes around motherhood affect the enjoyment of the right to sexual and reproductive health, and recognised the impact of intersectional discrimination in this area, affecting socio-economically disadvantaged women, ethnic minorities and Indigenous populations, migrants, LGBT+ people, and people with disabilities.[91] In recognising these socio-cultural barriers, this document highlighted the importance of addressing intersectional and gender-based discrimination for the full realisation of sexual and reproductive rights.

The CESCR thus set out broad requirements that States Parties 'adopt legal and policy measures to guarantee all individuals access to affordable, safe and effective contraceptives and comprehensive sexuality education, including for adolescents; to liberalize restrictive abortion laws; to guarantee women and girls access to safe abortion services and quality post-abortion care, including by training health-care providers; and to respect the right of women to make

[85] ibid paras 23, 36.

[86] CESCR, 'General Comment No 16: The Equal Right of Men and Women to the Enjoyment of All Economic, Social and Cultural rights (Art 3 of the ICESCR)' (11 August 2005) UN Doc E/C.12/2005/4.

[87] ibid para 29.

[88] CESCR, 'General Comment No 22 on the Right to Sexual and Reproductive Health (Article 12 of the ICESCR)' (2 May 2016) UN Doc E/C.12/GC/22.

[89] ibid para 49(a).

[90] ibid paras 28, 34.

[91] ibid paras 27, 30.

autonomous decisions about their sexual and reproductive health.'[92] Expanding on the provision of sexual and reproductive health services by States Parties, the CESCR emphasised the need for accessibility, availability, affordability, and acceptability.[93] States must make these services, including abortion, readily available, affordable (if not free of charge), and appropriate to the people using them – which requires sensitivity to gender, age, sexuality, and other intersectional characteristics. The CESCR's accessibility standards require the removal of physical, economic, and socio-cultural barriers to services, and States Parties have been directly recommended to take positive measures to ensure equality of access, such as regulating provisions for conscientious objection so that they do not obstruct access to abortion.[94]

In addition, the CESCR requires States Parties to ensure access to the medications on the World Health Organization's (WHO) Model List of Essential Medicines, which includes mifepristone and misoprostol, two medications used to induce abortions in the early stages of pregnancy.[95] The CESCR's General Comment 25 on science and economic, social, and cultural rights adopted in 2020 reiterated the importance of ensuring access to safe and modern methods of abortion, including the above abortion medications, and highlighted that attention should be paid to advancements in best practice for abortion care.[96] Elsewhere I have argued that the CESCR's standards, when taken together, can be interpreted to support telemedical and self-managed abortion, allowing abortion-seekers to take misoprostol and mifepristone at home without medical supervision (issues which will be discussed in more detail in chapter four).[97] The CESCR has increasingly aligned its approach with that of the WHO, and in recent Concluding Observations, has begun to recommend that States Parties revise their abortion laws in line with the requirements from General Comment 22 *and* the WHO's abortion care guidance from 2022.[98]

Unlike the HRC, the CESCR has avoided outlining specific circumstances in which States Parties should legalise abortion. The CESCR has expressed particular concerns over the criminalisation of abortion in some circumstances, such as abortion in cases of rape, but otherwise it opts to advocate for access to

[92] ibid para 28.

[93] ibid paras 12–21.

[94] See, eg, CESCR, 'Concluding Observations on the Initial Report of South Africa' (29 November 2018) UN Doc E/C.12/ZAF/COF/1, paras 65–66; CESCR, 'Concluding Observations on the Sixth Periodic Report of Spain' (25 April 2018) UN Doc E/C.12/ESP/CO/6, paras 43–44.

[95] CESCR, 'General Comment No 22' (2016) (n 88) para 13.

[96] CESCR, 'General Comment No 25 on Science and Economic, Social and Cultural Rights' (30 April 2020) UN Doc E/C.12/GC/25, para 33.

[97] Zoe L Tongue, 'Telemedical and Self-Managed Abortion: A Human Rights Imperative?' (2022) 30(2) *European Journal of Health Law* 158.

[98] See, eg, CESCR, 'Concluding Observations on the Second Periodic Report of Indonesia' (14 March 2024) UN Doc E/C.12/IDN/CO/2, para 59; CESCR, 'Concluding Observations on the Fourth Periodic Report of Kyrgyzstan' (11 October 2024) UN Doc E/C.12/KGZ/CO/4, para 57; CESCR, 'Concluding Observations on the Third Periodic Report of Honduras' (22 October 2024) UN Doc E/C.12/HND/CO/3, para 61(a).

abortion in broader terms.[99] For example, in its 2015 comment on Uganda, the CESCR recommended 'that the State party revise its abortion legislation, including by considering decriminalizing abortion and providing for exceptions to the general prohibition on abortion *in certain cases*.'[100] The lack of specificity in this and similar recommendations can create issues with implementation, particularly in those States Parties that are opposed to abortion and would not interpret tentative recommendations as requiring legalisation even in a minimum set of circumstances. However, this approach also leaves open the possibility for the advocacy of more expansive grounds for legal abortion. In several Concluding Observations issued in 2021 and 2022, the CESCR showed a willingness to direct states to legalise abortion *beyond* the minimum circumstances indicated by the HRC.[101] For example, CESCR recommended that the Bolivian state 'expand the circumstances in which abortion is legally permitted and eliminate restrictive requirements limiting access to abortion.'[102] Moreover, the WHO's abortion care guideline recommends that grounds-based approaches be revised in favour of abortion on request – as the CESCR has recommended that States Parties align their abortion laws with this document, this would suggest that the Committee now also takes this approach.[103] However, unless this is made explicitly clear by the CESCR, there is insufficient pressure on States Parties to provide for abortion on request instead of retaining models that are less supportive of abortion.

D. Special Rapporteurs on the Right to Health

Relevant to the development of CESCR's abortion standards is the work of the Special Rapporteurs for the right to health, two of which have written progressive statements on sexual and reproductive rights, including abortion, which have generally gone beyond those of CESCR. In 2011, five years prior to CESCR's General Recommendation on the issue, Special Rapporteur Anand Grover addressed the right to sexual and reproductive health as a fundamental

[99] See, eg, CESCR, 'Concluding Observations on the Fourth Periodic Report of Ecuador' (14 November 2019) UN Doc E/C.12/ECU/CO/4, paras 51–52; CESCR, 'Concluding Observations on the Initial Report of Bahrain' (4 August 2022) UN Doc E/C.12/BHR/CO/1, paras 44–45.

[100] CESCR, 'Concluding Observations on the Initial Report of Uganda' (8 July 2015) UN Doc E/C.12/UGA/CO/1, para 35 [emphasis added].

[101] CESCR, 'Concluding Observations on the Initial Report of Bahrain' (2022) (n 99) para 45(a); CESCR, 'Concluding Observations on the Sixth Periodic Report of the Democratic Republic of the Congo' (28 March 2022) UN Doc E/C.12/COD/CO/6, para 57(a); CESCR, 'Concluding Observations on the Fifth Periodic Report of Nicaragua' (11 November 2021) UN Doc E/C.12/NIC/CO/5, para 45(a).

[102] CESCR, 'Concluding Observations on the Third Periodic Report of the Plurinational State of Bolivia' (5 November 2021) UN Doc E/C.12/BOL/CO/3, para 55(a).

[103] World Health Organisation, *Abortion Care Guideline* (8 March 2022) www.who.int/publications/i/item/9789240039483 accessed 9 January 2026, pp 26–27.

aspect of the right to health, with a specific focus on abortion.[104] Grover viewed criminal restrictions on abortion as 'impermissible barriers to the realization of women's right to health' which infringed the dignity and autonomy of women by restricting their reproductive decision-making, in addition to generating poor physical and mental health outcomes and thrusting women into the criminal justice system.[105] Grover also noted that safe abortion would not immediately result from decriminalisation.[106] States must therefore create the conditions for accessible services, such as the provision of clinics staffed by trained providers, comprehensive sexual and reproductive health education, and the absence of additional barriers such as mandatory waiting periods.[107] The Special Rapporteur's statement was one of the first UN documents to advocate for the decriminalisation of abortion not only to prevent unsafe abortion and maternal mortality, but also to support reproductive autonomy.

Dr Tlaleng Mofokeng, who was appointed Special Rapporteur for the right to health in 2020, has considered abortion in several of her thematic statements. In a report on sexual and reproductive health amid the COVID-19 pandemic, Mofokeng highlighted that the right to sexual and reproductive health 'guarantees all persons capable of becoming pregnant meaningful control over whether or not to reproduce.'[108] Mofokeng thus recognised access to safe, legal abortion as 'a necessary component of comprehensive health services.'[109] In a subsequent report on violence and the right to health, Mofokeng set out the criminalisation of abortion and denial of abortion services as examples of gender-based violence.[110] The report emphasised the link between criminalisation and unsafe abortion, particularly in regions such as Africa and Latin America where a relatively large percentage of maternal deaths are attributed to unsafe abortion practices.[111] Mofokeng has also reported on the impact of racism on the right to health, and in recognition of how the criminalisation of abortion impacts already marginalised people in particular, recommended the removal of all punitive abortion laws.[112] In addition, Mofokeng highlighted that grounds-based laws

[104] Anand Grover, 'Interim Report of the Special Rapporteur on the Right of Everyone to the Enjoyment of the Highest Attainable Standard of Physical and Mental Health' (3 August 2011) UN Doc A/66/254.

[105] ibid para 21.

[106] ibid para 29.

[107] ibid paras 24, 56.

[108] Tlaleng Mofokeng, 'Report of the Special Rapporteur on the Right of Everyone to the Enjoyment of the Highest Attainable Standard of Physical and Mental Health – Sexual and Reproductive Health Rights: Challenges and Opportunities During the COVID-19 Pandemic' (16 July 2021) UN Doc A/76/172, para 40.

[109] ibid.

[110] Tlaleng Mofokeng, 'Report of the Special Rapporteur on the Right of Everyone to the Enjoyment of the Highest Attainable Standard of Physical and Mental Health – Violence and its Impact on the Right to Health' (14 April 2022) UN Doc A/HRC/50/28, paras 49, 70.

[111] ibid para 50.

[112] Tlaleng Mofokeng, 'Report of the Special Rapporteur on the Right of Everyone to the Enjoyment of the Highest Attainable Standard of Physical and Mental Health – Racism and the Right to Health' (20 July 2022) UN Doc A/77/197, paras 36, 92.

and laws with strict gestational time limits act as barriers to safe, quality abortion care.[113] This comment is particularly progressive, and aligns with CESCR's gradual shift away from a grounds-based approach and is the first human rights document to explicitly critique gestational time limits as barriers to access. This therefore could feed into CESCR's continuously evolving approach in terms of advocating for expansive access to abortion.

E. The Committee on the Elimination of Discrimination Against Women

The Committee on the Elimination of Discrimination Against Women (CEDAW Committee) has, perhaps unsurprisingly, gone further than the HRC or CESCR in connecting restrictions on abortion to gender inequality and discrimination. The Convention on the Elimination of Discrimination Against Women (CEDAW) does not contain any explicit mention of abortion, and there are only limited references to other reproductive rights issues within the treaty – the Convention was adopted in 1979, over a decade before the formal recognition of reproductive rights at the ICPD. However, as with the ICCPR and ICESCR, there are several rights contained in CEDAW that are nonetheless relevant to abortion. Article 12 places obligations on states to eliminate discrimination against women in the field of healthcare, to ensure equal access with men to healthcare services including family planning, and to ensure access to 'appropriate services in connection with pregnancy'. Article 16(e), in the context of equality in marriage and family relations, contains the equal right to 'decide freely and responsibly on the number and spacing of their children and to have access to the information, education and means to enable them to exercise these rights'. The CEDAW Committee has interpreted both rights as encompassing abortion and other reproductive health services.

In 1999, the CEDAW Committee adopted General Recommendation 24 on the right to health.[114] The Committee stated that, where possible, 'legislation criminalizing abortion should be amended, in order to withdraw punitive measures imposed on women who undergo abortion.'[115] There was no explicit recommendation that States Parties liberalise their abortion laws and this statement had been critiqued for failing to issue an 'urgent call to action'.[116] However, this was one of the earliest statements on abortion by a significant treaty body, and the document did contain numerous statements on the provision and accessibility of reproductive health services which could also be applied to abortion. For example, the CEDAW Committee found it 'discriminatory for a State party

[113] ibid para 92.

[114] CEDAW, 'General Recommendation No 24: Article 12 of the Convention (Women and Health)' (1999) UN Doc A/54/38/Rev.1.

[115] ibid para 31(c).

[116] Tatyana A Margolin, 'Abortion as a Human Right' (2007) 29(2) *Women's Rights Law Reporter* 77, 90.

to refuse to provide legally for the performance of certain reproductive health services for women' and recommended that alternatives should be provided where healthcare professionals refuse to perform certain services based on conscientious objection.[117] The Committee also made a number of recommendations around the gender-sensitive delivery of healthcare services, requiring that healthcare services are consistent with rights to 'autonomy, privacy, confidentiality, informed consent and choice' and that barriers to education, information, and access were removed.[118] In particular, the CEDAW Committee emphasised the importance of timely access to sexual and reproductive health services.[119] This includes access to abortion services.

Since then, the CEDAW Committee has taken significant leaps in advocating for abortion provision. In 2011, the CEDAW Committee handed down a decision in its first and, as of yet, only case concerning abortion. *LC v Peru* concerned a girl who had been sexually abused for some years before she became pregnant at the age of 13.[120] LC became depressed and attempted suicide by jumping from a building, resulting in damage to her spinal column which caused paraplegia of her limbs.[121] She was at risk of permanent disability if she did not receive emergency surgery, but this surgery was postponed as her doctors were concerned that it would affect the foetus.[122] LC and her mother requested an abortion, but this was denied despite the risks to her mental and physical health and the fact that therapeutic abortion was permitted under the Penal Code.[123] LC miscarried and eventually received surgery for her spinal injuries three months later, but she was left with a permanent disability, requiring constant care and assistance.[124]

Finding a violation of Article 12, the CEDAW Committee noted that LC should have been entitled to an abortion to avoid serious and permanent harm to her health.[125] The denial of an abortion and the delay to her surgery meant that LC did not have access to effective and accessible medical services, which was all the more serious as she was a minor and a victim of sexual abuse.[126] The CEDAW Committee additionally found a violation of Article 5, which mandates the elimination of social and cultural gender roles, stereotypes, and prejudices, as the decision to refuse LC therapeutic surgery due to her pregnancy was influenced by gender stereotypes which placed the protection of the foetus above the health of the pregnant girl.[127] Violations of Article 2(c), requiring equal legal protection of the rights of women, and 2(f), requiring the modification of

[117] CEDAW, 'General Recommendation No 24' (1999) (n 114) para 11.
[118] ibid para 31.
[119] ibid para 31(c).
[120] *LC v Peru* (2011) UN Doc CEDAW/C/50/D/22/2009, para 2.1.
[121] ibid paras 2.1–2.2.
[122] ibid paras 2.3–2.4.
[123] ibid para 2.5.
[124] ibid paras 2.10–2.11.
[125] ibid para 8.14.
[126] ibid para 8.15.
[127] ibid.

existing laws which constitute discrimination of women, were also found on the basis that the law allowed individual hospitals to arbitrarily decide whether to allow or deny a therapeutic abortion.[128]

As Peru had already legalised therapeutic abortion, the CEDAW Committee stated that it must establish an appropriate framework enabling women to access abortion, recommending that the state review the law to create a mechanism for effective access to prevent future violations.[129] Given that the denial of a therapeutic abortion and the delay to LC's surgery were decisions taken by hospital staff, CEDAW emphasised that the state must enforce General Recommendation 24 with a view of changing attitudes of healthcare providers towards women seeking reproductive health services through education programmes.[130] In addition to ensuring access to abortion on the grounds already legalised, the CEDAW Committee went further and recommended that Peru review the law 'with a view to decriminalizing abortion when the pregnancy results from rape or sexual abuse'.[131] This decision was significant; although it was not the first case at the UN to address abortion on the grounds of rape, as the HRC's decision in *LMR v Argentina* was issued earlier that year, it was the first time a UN treaty body had explicitly recommended that a State Party should decriminalise abortion in cases of rape.

The CEDAW Committee's approach to abortion continued to develop through its Concluding Observations on individual State Party reports, and in 2018, the Committee clarified its position in a lengthy report on abortion in Northern Ireland.[132] In this report, the CEDAW Committee found that the UK government had committed grave and systematic rights violations as a result of the deliberate continuation of the criminalisation of abortion in Northern Ireland, which compelled women to carry pregnancies to full term, travel outside Northern Ireland in order to access safe and legal abortions, or obtain abortion medication illegally.[133] In addition, the CEDAW Committee stated that compelling women to continue their pregnancies to full term in situations of rape or fatal foetal impairment caused mental and physical anguish amounting to gender-based violence.[134] As with *LC v Peru*, the Committee considered the gender stereotypes that inform restrictive abortion laws, finding that Northern Ireland's regime portrayed women's primary role as one of motherhood and created negative stereotypes which stigmatised those who had abortions.[135] The report thus recommended that the state decriminalise abortion in all cases

[128] ibid paras 8.16–8.17.
[129] ibid paras 8.17; 9.2(a).
[130] ibid para 9.2(b).
[131] ibid para 9.2(c).
[132] CEDAW, 'Inquiry Concerning the United Kingdom of Great Britain and Northern Ireland under Article 8 of the Optional Protocol to CEDAW' (6 March 2018) UN Doc CEDAW/C/OP.8/GBR/1.
[133] ibid para 83(b).
[134] ibid para 83(a).
[135] ibid para 73.

and provide access to legal abortion services at least on the following grounds: where there is a risk to the pregnant person's life or health, where the pregnancy results from rape or incest, and where there is a severe or fatal foetal impairment.[136]

Similar recommendations have also been made in subsequent Concluding Observations,[137] which mirrors the minimum circumstances set out by the HRC. In addition, the CEDAW Committee has expanded on socio-economic issues and the accessibility of abortion services. For example, in its Concluding Observations on Ethiopia in 2019, the Committee commented upon the shortage of medical staff qualified to perform abortions and recommended that the state improve access to low cost health services and equip doctors to provide accessible health care for women, including abortions, through the allocation of sufficient budgetary resources.[138] Thus, the approach of the CEDAW Committee can be seen to mirror the combined approaches of the HRC and CESCR in terms of obligations around the minimum circumstances for the legalisation of abortion and accessibility standards.

However, the CEDAW Committee has gone further than these other treaty bodies in relation to the gender-based aspects of abortion, as can already be seen in the comments set out above. Notably, in 2017, the Committee adopted General Comment No 35 on gender-based violence, and stated that 'forced abortion, forced pregnancy, criminalization of abortion, denial or delay of safe abortion and/or post-abortion care [...] may amount to torture or cruel, inhuman or degrading treatment.'[139] The recognition that the forced continuation of pregnancy and the denial of safe abortion can amount to gender-based violence is significant, particularly as the finding of cruel, inhuman, and degrading treatment in relation to abortion has been much more limited by other human rights bodies (such as the European Court of Human Rights, as explored below). Scholars had previously commended CEDAW for showing a greater willingness than other bodies to recognise reproductive rights, and especially abortion, as requiring affirmative state support.[140] While this omission has largely been

[136] ibid para 85.

[137] See, eg, CEDAW, 'Concluding Observations on the Combined Third and Fourth Periodic Reports of Saudi Arabia' (14 March 2018) UN Doc CEDAW/C/SAU/CO/3-4, para 48(b); CEDAW, 'Concluding Observations on the Fourth Periodic Report on Andorra' (13 November 2019) UN Doc CEDAW/C/AND/CO/4, para 36(a); CEDAW, 'Concluding Observations on the Sixth Periodic Report of Namibia' (12 July 2022) UN Doc CEDAW/C/NAM/CO/6, para 42(a).

[138] CEDAW, 'Concluding Observations on the Eighth Periodic Report of Ethiopia' (14 March 2019) UN Doc CEDAW/C/ETH/CO/8, paras 37–38.

[139] CEDAW, 'General Recommendation No 35 on Gender-Based Violence Against Women, updating General Recommendation No 19' (26 July 2017) UN Doc CEDAW/C/GC/35, para 18.

[140] Zampas and Gher, 'Abortion as a Human Right' (2008) (n 43) 251; Barbara Stark, 'The Women's Convention, Reproductive Rights, and the Reproduction of Gender' (2011) 18(2) *Duke Journal of Gender Law & Policy* 261, 271.

corrected in the more recent comments of the HRC and CESCR, this nonetheless remains true in relation to the gendered dimension of abortion.

While the majority of the CEDAW Committee's comments on abortion reiterate State Party obligations to decriminalise abortion, legalise abortion in the minimum circumstances, and ensure access on those grounds, there has been – as with CESCR – movement towards an even more progressive approach in recent years. In its 2022 Concluding Observations on Morocco, the Committee recommended that the state consider decriminalisation 'when it is necessary to protect the woman's health, including her physical, mental and *social well-being*' in accordance with the WHO's definition of reproductive health.[141] Protecting social wellbeing requires a more holistic approach to abortion, as it encompasses factors such as a person's relationships, community, context, and emotional wellbeing.[142] This recommendation suggests that the CEDAW Committee would favour abortion on request or on broader grounds that the minimum circumstances indicated in previous documents, though it is currently an outlier in the Committee's comments.

However, in a number of Concluding Observations issued in 2024, the CEDAW Committee has recommended that several States Parties 'legalize and decriminalize abortion *in all cases*' in order to ensure 'the full realization of [women's] rights, equality and economic and bodily autonomy to make free choices about their reproductive rights'.[143] It may be, therefore, that the CEDAW Committee is following the CESCR in moving away from a grounds-based approach in favour of promoting access to abortion in the broadest sense. The wording of 'in all cases' certainly suggests that the CEDAW Committee is now advocating for abortion at the request of the pregnant person – although the Committee's Concluding Observations on Brazil and Nicaragua from the same year only advocates for decriminalisation, and not legalisation, in all cases.[144] This obfuscation undermines the potential for the CEDAW Committee to place pressure on States Parties to ensure comprehensive access to abortion on grounds beyond the minimum circumstances.

[141] CEDAW, 'Concluding Observations on the Combined Fifth and Sixth Periodic Reports of Morocco' (12 July 2022) UN Doc CEDAW/C/MAR/CO/5-6, para 36(c) [emphasis added].

[142] Ernestina Coast and others, 'Abortion and Well-being: A Narrative Literature Review' 7 *SSM – Qualitative Research in Health* 100508.

[143] See, eg, CEDAW, 'Concluding Observations on the Sixth Periodic Report of the Central African Republic' (20 February 2024) UN Doc CEDAW/C/CAF/CO/6, para 42(c); CEDAW, 'Concluding Observations on the Ninth Periodic Report of Japan' (30 October 2024) UN Doc CEDAW/C/JPN/CO/9, para 42(b); CEDAW, 'Concluding Observations on the Eighth Periodic Report of Chile' (31 October 2024) UN Doc CEDAW/C/CHL/CO/8, para 38(b).

[144] CEDAW, 'Concluding Observations on the Combined Eighth and Ninth Periodic Reports of Brazil' (6 June 2024) UN Doc CEDAW/C/BRA/CO/8-9, para 35(a); CEDAW, 'Concluding Observations on the Combined Seventh to Tenth Periodic Reports of Nicaragua' (14 February 2024) UN Doc CEDAW/C/NIC/CO/7-10, para 40(c).

F. Limitations of the United Nations Approach

As shown above, international human rights standards on abortion have progressively evolved over time. The more recent comments from the CESCR, CEDAW Committee, and Dr Tlaleng Mofokeng demonstrate the recognition of access to abortion as a fundamental requirement of gender-equitable healthcare. However, despite this continual evolution of standards, there are several overarching limitations with the current international human rights approach to abortion. First, there is a tendency, particularly by the HRC, to find that restrictions on abortion violate certain rights based on a relatively high threshold of harm. Lisa Kelly has identified the 'innocent suffering' narrative which tends to arise in abortion rights cases, in which 'an adolescent girl, figured often as a child, is raped, becomes pregnant, and with the support of her parents seeks to terminate the pregnancy' and when this termination is denied, the state is framed as a shameful antagonist.[145] This can be seen in the cases that have reached the HRC and CEDAW: *KL v Peru*, *LMR v Argentina*, and *LC v Peru* all concerned minors and/or victims of rape, and the two Irish cases heard by the HRC were also framed around significant suffering resulting from the loss of the applicants' non-viable foetuses.

While the recent comments from CESCR and CEDAW suggest a departure from this approach, the HRC and CEDAW continue to reference minimum circumstances for the legalisation of abortion – exceptions to general prohibitions on abortion which have been carved out by reference to pain and suffering. The threshold of harm that this sets out implies that restrictions on abortion violate human rights only in relatively rare situations. This, again, is an example of abortion exceptionalism, as these narratives are based upon 'the assumptions that abortion is only acceptable in certain situations' – situations concerned with extreme harm.[146] As Kelly argues, narratives of suffering reinforce conceptions of good versus bad abortions and leave out the majority of abortion experiences, such as 'the experiences of women who desire nonprocreative sex, who have no access to claims of extreme suffering, who seek multiple abortions, who terminate for economic reasons'.[147] This is also made clear by the fact that international human rights bodies have avoided advocating for abortion on request or for social reasons, and even those comments that do suggest support for abortion on broad grounds are tentative.

The shadow of the ICPD, which framed abortion as morally problematic, has instead led international human rights bodies to adopt a public health stance; there is a tendency for these bodies to require decriminalisation or access

[145] Lisa M Kelly, 'Reckoning with Narratives of Innocent Suffering in Transnational Abortion Litigation' in Rebecca J Cook, Joanna N Erdman, and Bernard M Dickens (eds), *Abortion Law in Transnational Perspective* (University of Pennsylvania Press, 2014) p 304.

[146] Smyth, 'Abortion Exceptionalism' (2024) (n 17) 684.

[147] Kelly, 'Reckoning with Narratives' (2014) (n 145) p 305.

to abortion services to prevent unsafe abortion and maternal mortality, instead of drawing 'their main impulse from women's right to reproductive autonomy'.[148] In attempting to approach abortion in a way which is less unpalatable to States Parties, human rights bodies have left themselves with an uneasy tension between their recognition of the gendered inequalities surrounding abortion and the public health justifications for their recommendations.[149] Even under the CEDAW Committee, which has recognised that restrictions on abortion can violate human rights by perpetuating harmful gender-based stereotypes around motherhood, it is not clear whether the mere fact of a restriction on reproductive autonomy, in the absence of a suffering narrative, would be recognised as a violation.

Second, as international human rights standards have evolved gradually, and abortion is not explicitly mentioned within any of the aforementioned treaties, the approaches of the HRC, CESCR, and CEDAW are spread across numerous General Comments, Concluding Observations, and cases. Alice Miller and Mindy Roseman have critiqued this fragmentation which results in issues stretched across multiple bodies and falling under different rights approaches, creating uncertainty and a 'chill' with contentious areas such as sexual and reproductive health.[150] While the HRC and CESCR have summarised their approaches to abortion in relatively recent General Recommendations, much of CEDAW's approach has been developed through state-specific documents. While there are, of course, advantages to this in terms of specificity and responsiveness to contextual issues, there are further problems with the inaccessibility of human rights standards when developed in this way. Inaccessibility means that it becomes harder for civil society groups to hold governments accountable for breaching or failing to protect human rights which require access to abortion. As Mofokeng identified in one of her reports, civil society involvement acts as a guarantee for the effective realisation of the right to health by acting as a mechanism for accountability.[151] The importance of civil society groups for the realisation of human rights, and particularly in relation to contested issues such as abortion, will be explored more expansively in chapter five.

The lack of explicit direction to ensure that abortion services are comprehensively accessible and variation between treaty bodies also creates gaps in standards that may excuse inaction or efforts to restrict access by states opposed to legalising abortion. Magdalena Furgalska and Fiona de Londras have argued that the Polish Constitutional Tribunal's 2020 decision to prohibit abortion for

[148] Ngwena, 'Access to Safe Abortion' (2013) (n 63) 422.

[149] For more of a critique on the public health approach to abortion, see Zoe L Tongue, '"Abortion is Healthcare": The Promise and Pitfalls of Framing Abortion under the Right to Health' in Elizabeth Wicks and Nataly Papadopoulou (eds), *Research Handbook on Human Rights Law and Health* (Edward Elgar, 2025).

[150] Alice M Miller and Mindy J Roseman, 'Sexual and Reproductive Rights at the United Nations: Frustration or Fulfilment?' (2011) 19(38) *Reproductive Health Matters* 102, 104.

[151] Mofokeng, 'Sexual and Reproductive Health Rights' (2021) (n 108) para 89.

foetal impairments was an example of the court taking advantage of the gaps in current international and European human rights standards on abortion.[152] Where these gaps and uncertainties exist, states can claim that restrictive abortion laws nonetheless meet international human rights standards; the Polish Constitutional Tribunal selectively referenced human rights documents in the decision in order to suggest compliance.[153] As Paul Blokker argues, while rights have a protective mechanism, they are 'also "weapons" that are used by different actors for different strategic purposes', and thus can be adopted to pursue anti-abortion political projects.[154] In the absence of clear obligations on states to provide access to abortion, international human rights bodies risk providing legitimacy to the states seeking to maintain or impose restrictions.[155] Despite the progressive evolution of international human rights standards on abortion, particularly in the recent comments on the CESCR and CEDAW, these gaps and uncertainties remain open to exploitation.

Third, there are issues with implementation because of the broader limitations of the international human rights framework. The UN human rights bodies lack strong follow-up and enforcement mechanisms, in part due to a lack of capacity and resources.[156] The primary means of assessing compliance with human rights standards is through state reporting, but there is a significant backlog of overdue state party reports and consequential delays in the review process.[157] In relation to reproductive rights, and abortion specifically, there are limitations as a result of the reservations of some states to certain rights contained in CEDAW. Malta and the Principality of Monaco specifically entered reservations to the Article 16(e) right to decide on the number and spacing of one's children insofar as this contained an obligation to legalise abortion.[158]

[152] Magdalena Furgalska and Fiona de Londras, 'Rights, Lawfare and Reproduction: Reflections on the Polish Constitutional Tribunal's Abortion Decision' (2022) 55(3) *Israel Law Review* 285, 287.

[153] ibid 294–95; Marta Bucholc, 'Abortion Law and Human Rights in Poland: The Closing of the Jurisprudential Horizon' (2022) 14 *Hague Journal on the Rule of Law* 73, 90.

[154] Paul Blokker, 'Using Liberal-Legal Tools for Illiberal Gains: The European Court of Human Rights and Legal Mobilisation by Conservative Right-Wing Actors' (2024) 20 *International Journal of Law in Context* 401, 406.

[155] Furgalska and de Londras, 'Rights, Lawfare and Reproduction' (2022) (n 152) 301.

[156] Alicia Ely Yamin, *When Misfortune Becomes Injustice* (Stanford University Press, 2020) p 149. For treaty body follow-up methods, see: HRC, 'Note by the Human Rights Committee on the Procedure for Follow-up to Concluding Observations' (23 December 2021) UN Doc CCPR/C/161; CEDAW, 'Assessment of the Follow-up Procedure under Article 18 of the CEDAW Convention' (6 November 2019) https://tbinternet.ohchr.org/_layouts/15/TreatyBodyExternal/FollowUp.aspx?Treaty=CEDAW&Lang=en accessed 9 January 2026; CESCR, 'Working Methods Concerning the Committee's Follow-up to Views under the Optional Protocol to the International Covenant on Economic, Social, and Cultural Rights' (2017) UN Doc E/C.12/62/4.

[157] UNHR Office of the High Commissioner, 'Human Rights Committee Holds Twelfth Informal Meeting with States Parties, Discusses Challenges Relating to the Work of the Committee' (18 July 2022) www.ohchr.org/en/press-releases/2022/07/human-rights-committee-holds-twelfth-informal-meeting-states-parties accessed 9 January 2026.

[158] CEDAW, 'Declarations, Reservations, Objections and Notifications of Withdrawal of Reservations Relating to the Convention on the Elimination of All Forms of Discrimination against Women' (10 April 2006) UN Doc CEDAW/SP/2006/2, pp 20–21.

While these states can be held accountable for abortion-related violations under other rights, these reservations do indicate the approach of some governments to treat compliance with human rights standards on abortion as optional.

The lack of clear obligations on states to ensure comprehensive access to abortion, coupled with the lack of effective enforcement mechanisms, means that the direct effect of current human rights standards on abortion is notably limited. For example, in the cases of *KL v Peru* and *LC v Peru* the HRC and CEDAW directed the Peruvian government, respectively, to ensure access to therapeutic abortion and decriminalise abortion in cases of rape. However, Peru's abortion law has not been reformed and the barriers to accessing therapeutic abortions remain.[159] Further, Alicia Ely Yamin highlights that the CEDAW Committee considered Brazil's compliance with recommendations made in the maternal health case *Pimentel v Brazil* to be formally complete before the state had actually fully implemented them.[160] This is not to suggest that international human rights standards on abortion are wholly ineffective, but rather that their direct impact is limited by the approaches of treaty bodies to abortion and broader issues with the framework. The indirect impact of international human rights standards on abortion, in the context of national courts, civil society groups, and other localised methods of accountability, will be discussed in chapter five. However, it is my argument here that if human rights are to have a significant impact on access to abortion worldwide, then clear and robust State Party obligations are required.

III. ABORTION IN THE REGIONAL HUMAN RIGHTS SYSTEMS

Regional human rights systems have the potential to further facilitate the implementation of international human rights standards on abortion within their specific context. S Laurel Weldon and Mala Htun have recognised that regional human rights agreements strengthen international human rights standards on violence against women by emphasising the way these norms apply in more localised contexts.[161] Regional human rights bodies are more likely to have stronger enforcement or follow-up mechanisms – which is important in political contexts where the status of abortion as a human right might be questioned.[162] While

[159] Camila Gianella, 'Despite Legal Exceptions, Access to Abortion Denied in Peru' (*Bill of Health* Blog, 23 October 2023) https://petrieflom.law.harvard.edu/2023/10/23/despite-legal-exceptions-access-to-abortion-denied-in-peru/ accessed 9 January 2026.

[160] Yamin, *When Misfortune* (2020) (n 156) p 149; *Alyne da Silva Pimentel v Brazil* (2011) UN Doc CEDAW/C/49/D/17/2008.

[161] S Laurel Weldon and Mala Htun, 'Feminist Mobilisation and Progressive Policy Change: Why Governments Take Action to Combat Violence Against Women' (2013) 21(2) *Gender and Development* 231, 243–44.

[162] Luisa Cabal and Suzannah Phillips, 'Reproductive Rights Litigation: From Recognition to Transformation' in Malcolm Langford, César Rodrígues-Garavito, and Julieta Rossi (eds), *Social Rights Judgments and the Politics of Compliance* (Cambridge, Cambridge University Press, 2017), p 400.

interventions from regional human rights bodies will have a limited impact in the face of genuine resource limitations, these bodies can nonetheless put additional pressure on governments to incrementally guarantee access to abortion. However, all three regional human rights bodies have addressed abortion to a lesser extent than by the UN human rights bodies, and their potential to facilitate a human right to abortion is therefore very limited at present.

A. The African Union

The Women's Protocol to the African Charter on Human and Peoples' Rights is the only human rights instrument to explicitly indicate a human right to abortion. Under Article 14(2)(c), states are required to 'protect the reproductive rights of women by authorising medical abortion in cases of sexual assault, rape, incest' and where continuing the pregnancy would endanger the life, physical health, or mental health of the pregnant person or the life of the foetus (ie where the foetus has a fatal impairment).[163] The African Commission issued a General Comment in 2014 expanding on the protection of sexual and reproductive rights as required by Article 14.[164] In relation to abortion, the Commission highlighted that the right to safe abortion guaranteed by Article 14(2)(c) encompasses access to family planning and abortion services, including effective modern methods and post-abortion care, and freedom to access information about those services in the circumstances indicated by the Article.[165] The Commission also stated that the criminalisation of pregnant people or the interrogation of them by healthcare professionals, the police, or judicial authorities when accessing therapeutic abortions is a violation of their right to privacy and confidentiality, and may amount to cruel, inhuman, and degrading treatment.[166] This approach broadly aligns with that of the HRC, requiring procedural access as well as legalisation on minimum grounds.

However, while Article 14(2)(c) has been recognised as a landmark for setting out a clearly enforceable obligation on states to guarantee access to abortion on those grounds, its significance is limited by restricting the right to abortion to these exceptional circumstances.[167] In its General Comment, the African Commission emphasised the trauma, mental suffering, and risks to life in order

[163] African Union, *Protocol to the African Charter on Human and Peoples' Rights on the Rights of Women in Africa* (adopted 11 July 2003, entered into force 25 November 2005), Article 14(2)(c).

[164] African Commission on Human and Peoples' Rights, 'General Comment No 2 on Article 14.1(a), (b), (c), and (f) and Article 14.2 (a) and (c) of the Protocol to the African Charter on Human and People's Rights on the Rights of Women in Africa' (28 November 2014) https://achpr.au.int/index.php/ar/node/854 accessed 9 January 2026.

[165] ibid paras 31–33.

[166] ibid paras 32, 34–36.

[167] Charles G Ngwena, 'Inscribing Abortion as a Human Right: Significance of the Protocol on the Rights of Women in Africa' (2010) 32 *Human Rights Quarterly* 783, 785.

to justify the provision of abortion in these circumstances.[168] While maternal mortality and unsafe abortion is a significant problem on the continent, Charles Ngwena argues that this focus 'risks reinforcing the historical treatment of abortion as a criminal act, as well as an unjust stereotype of women as mothers'.[169] As already argued above, the framing of abortion as necessary to prevent suffering in exceptional cases entrenches the belief that only a minority of abortions are morally acceptable. The legalisation of abortion in those circumstances alone will not be enough to combat unsafe abortion, and the law must go further to support those 'seeking abortion as *un*tainted rights-holders'.[170] In this respect, despite the African Union being the only human rights system to recognise an explicit right to abortion, it is much less progressive than the CESCR and CEDAW Committee's approaches.

Moreover, the requirements of Article 14(2)(c) have not been followed by all African states; of the 55 African countries, six prohibit abortion altogether and numerous others only permit abortion to save the pregnant person's life.[171] As with the UN treaty bodies, there are also limitations around enforcement. Six countries are yet to ratify the Women's Protocol (including Mauritania and Egypt, where abortion is completely prohibited), and 22 have not ratified the African Court Protocol to allow cases on violations to be brought.[172] For those individuals living in countries that have ratified both the Women's Protocol and the African Court Protocol, bringing a case is made difficult (beyond the lack of access to resources, legal aid, and legal representation for many women) by the fact that complaints must be referred to the Court by the African Commission, an African intergovernmental organisation, or brought as an inter-state complaint.[173] If a case was to be brought in relation to abortion, Ngwena argues that it would be likely for the Court to defer to the state using 'the cloak of the doctrine of the margin of appreciation, so as not to offend domestic political and religious sensibilities'.[174] This is all the more likely if a case concerned access

[168] African Commission, 'General Comment No 2' (2014) (n 164) paras 37–40.

[169] Ngwena, 'Inscribing Abortion' (2010) (n 167), 786.

[170] Charles G Ngwena, 'Taking Women's Rights Seriously: Using Human Rights to Require State Implementation of Domestic Abortion Laws in African Countries with Reference to Uganda' (2016) 60(1) *Journal of African Law* 110, 135.

[171] Center for Reproductive Rights, 'The World's Abortion Laws' https://reproductiverights.org/maps/worlds-abortion-laws/? accessed 9 January 2026. The United Nations only recognised 54 African countries, but the African Union additionally recognises the Sahrawi Arab Democratic Republic (also known as Western Sahara) as an independent state.

[172] African Union, 'List of Countries Which Have Signed, Ratified/Acceded to the Protocol to the African Charter on Human and People's Rights on the Rights of Women in Africa' (16 October 2019) https://au.int/en/treaties/protocol-african-charter-human-and-peoples-rights-rights-women-africa accessed 9 January 2026; African Union, 'List of Countries Which Have Signed, Ratified/Acceded to the Protocol on the Statute of the African Court of Justice and Human Rights' (18 June 2020) https://au.int/en/treaties/protocol-court-justice-african-union accessed 9 January 2026.

[173] Annika Rudman, 'Women's Access to Regional Justice as a Fundamental Element of the Rule of Law: The Effect of the Absence of a Women's Rights Committee on the Enforcement of the African Women's Protocol' (2018) 18 *African Human Rights Law Journal* 319, 328.

[174] Ngwena (n 167) 813.

to abortion services beyond those limited grounds recognised by Article 14(2)(c). Thus, the lack of implementation and state accountability further undermines the potential of the African Union's right to abortion.

B. The Council of Europe

The European Convention on Human Rights (ECHR)[175] does not contain any specific rights relating to healthcare or reproductive rights, but abortion cases have been considered by the Court under the right to privacy (Article 8) and the right to freedom from torture and cruel, inhuman, and degrading treatment (Article 3). However, the European Court of Human Rights (ECtHR) has never gone so far as to require Member States to legalise abortion in any circumstances. Instead, the ECtHR has only been willing to find violations where access to abortion services on the grounds already legalised by the states is obstructed.[176] In *A, B, and C v Ireland,* the ECtHR distinguished between three applicants who had all travelled to England to access abortion services after becoming pregnant unintentionally.[177] A had a history of depression and alcoholism and felt that continuing her pregnancy would jeopardise her mental health and sobriety.[178] B had taken emergency contraception which had failed.[179] C had a rare form of cancer which was in remission at the time of her pregnancy, but she was unable to access information of the risks the pregnancy would pose to her cancer.[180] All three applicants faced significant delays in accessing abortion as a result of being required to travel abroad, and A and B reported financial difficulties in doing so. The ECtHR determined that A and B had accessed abortion services for health and wellbeing reasons, whereas C feared there was a risk to her life.[181] As Article 40.3.3° of the Irish Constitution only permitted abortion to save the pregnant person's life, a violation was found only in relation to C as there were no processes in place to determine whether she qualified for a legal abortion.[182] The ECtHR's jurisprudence on abortion has therefore established only a procedural right of access under the ECHR Article 8 right to private life, imposing limited obligations on Member States to guarantee access to abortion services on the grounds already legalised domestically.[183]

175 Convention for the Protection of Human Rights and Fundamental Freedoms (Rome, 4 November 1950).

176 See ECtHR, App no 5410/03, *Tysiąc v Poland* (20 March 2007); ECtHR, App no 27617/04, *RR v Poland* (26 May 2011); ECtHR, App no 57375/08, *P and S v Poland* (30 October 2012).

177 ECtHR, App no 25579/05, *A, B, and C v Ireland* (16 December 2010).

178 ibid paras 13–17.

179 ibid paras 18–21.

180 ibid paras 22–26.

181 ibid para 125.

182 ibid para 243.

183 Joanna N Erdman, 'The Procedural Turn: Abortion at the European Court of Human Rights' in Rebecca J Cook, Joanna N Erdman, and Bernard M Dickens (eds), *Abortion Law in Transnational*

This approach has been critiqued for failing to frame abortion as a human right and for failing 'to acknowledge that the option to travel abroad for abortion is not open to everybody and that being forced to travel to another country for a critical health service can entail suffering that rises to the level of cruel and inhuman treatment.'[184] The ECtHR was willing to recognise violations of the ECHR Article 3 right to freedom from torture and cruel, inhuman, and degrading treatment in two other abortion-related cases: in relation to the denial of prenatal testing in *RR v* Poland, and in relation to the denial of an abortion to a minor in *P and S v Poland*.[185] Chiara Cosentino argues that these cases could open up a substantial right to abortion under Article 3, as a non-derogable right to which the margin of appreciation does not apply.[186] While the ECtHR is able to apply the margin of appreciation under Article 8 and defer to the Member State, as it did so in cases such as *A, B, and C,* there is no leeway on Article 3. It could therefore be possible for the ECtHR to find a violation even where there is no procedural right to abortion at stake. Yet, the Court appears to be deliberately avoiding doing so, finding Article 3 violations in relation to reproductive rights issues *only* where this would not confer broader obligations on Member States to uphold reproductive autonomy.[187]

For example, in 2023, the ECtHR handed down its judgment in *ML v Poland,* a case concerning Poland's change in the law to prohibit abortion in cases of foetal impairments.[188] ML was scheduled to have an abortion on the 28 January 2021, but the change to the law came into effect – without warning – on the 27 January 2021.[189] Her appointment was cancelled, and she had to travel to the Netherlands for her abortion.[190] The Court found a violation of ECHR Article 8, but this was on procedural grounds as the timing of the legal change taking effect had been unclear.[191] They did not find a violation of Article 3, despite mentioning human rights standards on foetal impairments at the UN level.[192] This case could also be seen to contradict their earlier decision in *RR*, in which a violation

---

Perspective (University of Pennsylvania Press, 2014); Daniel Fenwick, 'The Modern Abortion Jurisprudence under Article 8 of the European Convention on Human Rights' (2012) 12 *Medical Law International* 249.

[184] Johanna Westeson, 'Reproductive Health Information and Abortion Services: Standards Developed by the European Court of Human Rights' (2013) 122 *International Journal of Gynecology and Obstetrics* 173, 175.

[185] *RR* (n 176); *P and S* (n 176).

[186] Chiara Cosentino, 'Safe and Legal Abortion: An Emerging Human Right? The Long-Lasting Dispute with State Sovereignty in ECHR Jurisprudence' (2015) 15(3) *Human Rights Law Review* 569, 587–88.

[187] See Zoe L Tongue and Lewis Graham, 'YP v Russia: Sterilisation Without Consent, Article 3, and Weak Reproductive Rights at the ECTHR' (*Strasbourg Observers*, 30 September 2022) https://strasbourgobservers.com/2022/09/30/y-p-v-russia-sterilisation-without-consent-article-3-and-weak-reproductive-rights-at-the-ecthr/ accessed 9 January 2026.

[188] ECtHR, App no 40119/21, *ML v Poland* (14 December 2023).

[189] ibid paras 20–22.

[190] ibid paras 23–24.

[191] ibid para 73.

[192] ibid paras 50–51, 83.

of Article 3 was found when a pregnant woman was denied the prenatal testing that would have allowed her to make an abortion decision.[193] In this case, the ECtHR had commented that '[l]ike any other pregnant woman in her situation, she was deeply distressed by information that the foetus could be affected with some malformation' to the extent that her suffering met the threshold for an Article 3 violation to be found.[194] The distress that ML's situation caused her was not recognised in the same way. While *RR* concerned states positive obligations to provide information rather than to provide access to abortion, the implications of such a finding in ML would have required Poland to substantively change its law to avoid similar future violations.[195] This is a direction that the ECtHR appears keen to avoid, as confirmed by another Polish case in 2025 which received largely the same judgment,[196] which seriously limits the potential for advancing abortion rights within the European regional system.

C. The Organisation of American States

The approach of the Organisation of American States towards abortion is yet unclear. Article 4 of the American Convention on Human Rights recognises the right to life as applying 'in general, from the moment of conception'.[197] In the *Baby Boy* case, which challenged the legality of abortion in the US, the Inter-American Commission explicitly highlighted that the words 'in general' were inserted as Article 4 was not intended to limit abortion.[198] This was affirmed by the Inter-American Court in *Artavia Murillo et al v Costa Rica* in the context of a prohibition on IVF treatment.[199] In exploring the status of the embryo/foetus, the Court considered comments from the HRC and CEDAW on abortion and pregnancy, the ECtHR cases rejecting the right to life of the foetus, and Article 14(2)(c) of the African Women's Protocol.[200] The Court concluded that the embryo could not be understood as a person for the purposes of Article 4, but in any event the words 'in general' permitted exceptions to the general rule.[201] Thus, the Court found it disproportionate for Costa Rica to 'aspire to an absolute protection of the embryo' and found the prohibition to violate a number of

[193] *RR* (n 176).
[194] ibid para 159.
[195] For an analysis of the inadmissibility of Article 3 in the *ML* case, see Zoe L Tongue, 'Abortion and the European Court of Human Rights: Avoiding the Question?' (2024) 3 *European Human Rights Law Review* 251.
[196] ECtHR, App no 6030/21, *AR v Poland* (13 November 2025).
[197] Organization of American States, *American Convention on Human Rights* (22 November 1969), Article 4(1).
[198] *White and Potter ('Baby Boy') v the USA,* Inter-Am Comm HR, Case 2141, Report No 23/81 (16 October 1981).
[199] *Case of Artavia Murillo et al v Costa Rica,* Inter-Am Ct HR, Series C 257 (28 November 2012).
[200] ibid paras 224–43.
[201] ibid para 264.

rights protected by the American Convention.[202] This judgment could open up avenues for the Inter-American Court to find that prohibitions on abortion also violate the Convention – particularly as the Inter-American Commission has previously issued precautionary measures to Paraguay to guarantee an abortion to a young pregnant girl.[203]

Patricia Palacios Zuloga therefore argues that the strides made on sexual and reproductive rights by the Inter-American Court suggest that 'the System could be well positioned to support a claim that holds that the criminalisation of abortion is a violation' of the Convention in a future case.[204] However, the Court has subsequently declined to recognise the impact of the criminalisation of abortion when given the opportunity to do so. The case *Manuela v El Salvador* concerned a woman who was an unknown number of weeks pregnant, when she fell heavily and injured her pelvic area, and was later found in her bedroom unconscious and bleeding.[205] She had given birth at home and the baby was found in the septic tank; Manuela could not remember what happened, but thought she gave birth over the toilet.[206] The Court noted that she had previously attempted to seek medical care for several lumps on her neck which were later diagnosed as Hodgkin's lymphoma, and she had severe preeclampsia which could have contributed to premature delivery and foetal death.[207] Manuela had also suffered from a postpartum haemorrhage after the birth.[208] She was arrested for a suspected abortion, but it was later determined that the baby had been born alive and she was sentenced to 30 years imprisonment for aggravated homicide.[209]

The Inter-American Court addressed the fact that the Trial Court had relied heavily on gender stereotypes. As the baby had been born alive, the Trial Court had assumed that Manuela must have committed a crime and they did not take into account the effect of her existing illnesses and the postpartum haemorrhage.[210] Further, the Trial Court assumed that she would have hidden the pregnancy from her family and attempted to end the pregnancy as she had become pregnant outside of marriage and would have been ashamed of this.[211] The Inter-American Court noted the context of the complete criminalisation of abortion in El Salvador, referring to comments by CEDAW and CESCR on the situation, but did not expand upon the broader systemic issues around this. The

[202] ibid paras 311, 317.

[203] Comisión Inter-Americana de Derechos Humanos, 'Resolución 22/2015 Medidas Cautelares No 178/15, Asunto niña Mainumby respecto de Paraguay' (8 June 2015) www.oas.org/es/cidh/decisiones/pdf/2015/MC178-15-ES.pdf accessed 9 January 2026.

[204] Patricia Palacios Zuloaga, 'Pushing Past the Tipping Point: Can the Inter-American System Accommodate Abortion Rights?' (2021) 21(4) *Human Rights Law Review* 899, 913, 933.

[205] *Manuela v El Salvador*, Inter-Am Ct HR, Series C 441 (21 November 2021), paras 49–51.

[206] ibid paras 53, 80.

[207] ibid para 137.

[208] ibid.

[209] ibid para 83.

[210] ibid paras 144, 137.

[211] ibid para 154.

Court instead focused on the issues of pretrial detention, the presumptions that she was guilty because of gender stereotypes, and the shortcomings with the medical care she received. The Court's non-repetition orders were thus limited to the regulation of medical professionals, adapting the pretrial detention regulation, and awareness-raising on gender stereotyping for public officials.[212] Recognising that the sentence Manuela received for infanticide amounted to cruel, inhuman, and degrading treatment in contravention of Article 5 of the American Convention, the Court also required the state to amend the sentence given for infanticide to ensure proportionality.[213]

The Court did not recognise these issues as linked to the total criminalisation of abortion, nor that the same gender stereotypes are applied to people who are prosecuted for having illegal abortions. Smyth argues that the Court should have framed the whole case in this way, but by failing to do so, it 'shied away from providing the resounding critique of El Salvador's abortion legislation that is required to prevent ongoing human rights violations there'.[214] The Court did so again in a more in the subsequent case *Beatriz et al v El Salvador*, which concerned a woman with numerous existing illnesses who was pregnant with an anencephalic foetus.[215] The Medical Committee of the National Maternity Hospital examined her case and possible treatments, including an abortion, but no decision was made. Beatriz eventually made the request for an abortion, but this was refused on the basis that she was now beyond 20 weeks' gestation.[216] At 26 weeks, she underwent a caesarean section, and the newborn died five hours later as a result of the condition.[217]

The Inter-American Court once again avoided commenting on the criminalisation of abortion in El Salvador, instead focusing on the uncertainty that surrounding the bureaucratisation and judicialisation of the *Beatriz* case.[218] The Court concluded that the lack of protocols for effective care in this case led to dehumanising treatment, and while El Salvador has since adopted protocols for pregnancy-related care, including the possibility of abortion in cases of sepsis or ectopic pregnancies, there are significant gaps in what the Court was willing to address.[219] In a concurring judgment, Judge Humberto Antonio Sierra Porto stated that the violations in this case were caused by the criminalisation of abortion in cases of a risk to the life of the pregnant person or foetus, and that the Court should have therefore declared a violation of Article 2 on this basis, requiring El Salvador to take legislative measures to avoid similar future

[212] ibid paras 284–95.
[213] ibid paras 172, 296.
[214] *Beatriz et al v El Salvador*, Inter-Am Ct HR, Series C 549 (22 November 2024); Inter-American Court of Human Rights, '*Beatriz et al v El Salvador* Press Release (English)' https://corteidh.or.cr/docs/comunicados/cp_92_2024_eng.pdf accessed 9 January 2026.
[215] ibid.
[216] ibid.
[217] ibid.
[218] ibid.
[219] ibid.

violations.[220] However, following *Manuela* and *Beatriz*, it seems unlikely that the Court will adopt such an approach in a majority opinion. There are, therefore, significant limitations in the approaches of all three regional human rights systems to abortion, particularly when compared with the UN framework.

IV. CONCLUSION

Over time, and particularly in recent years, restrictions on abortion have been found to violate numerous rights contained in international treaties, and access to abortion services have been considered an important aspect of gender equality. However, international human rights standards on abortion fall short of establishing abortion as a distinct right, thereby creating gaps that can be exploited by anti-abortion governments to avoid providing safe, legal abortion services. The pressure placed on States Parties by human rights bodies, particularly within the regional systems, is insufficient to ensure the realisation of abortion rights standards, particularly as these standards are found across myriad different documents. While comments from the CESCR, CEDAW Committee, and Special Rapporteur Dr Mofokeng suggest a recent move towards a progressive approach, these comments remain outliers. The international human rights framework thus requires a robust approach to abortion, one placing clear obligations on States Parties to provide comprehensive access to services, if it is to fully recognise the importance of abortion for substantive equality and human rights protection.

[220] University of Toronto, 'Concurring and Partially Dissenting Opinion of Judge Humberto Antonio Sierra Porto – Unofficial English Translation' www.law.utoronto.ca/sites/default/files/documents/reprohealth/iacthr_beatriz_opinion_sierra_porto_eng.pdf accessed 9 January 2026.

2

Gender, Culture, and Economy in the International Human Rights Framework

I. INTRODUCTION

ALONGSIDE THE INSUFFICIENT protection currently afforded to abortion within the international human rights framework, there are three broader (and interconnected) conceptual issues that also have a bearing on the development and realisation of abortion rights: (1) the international human rights framework's inadequate approach to gender-based human rights issues; (2) issues with the cross-cultural traction of human rights; and (3) the relatively weaker protection afforded to economic, social, and cultural rights. All three of these issues undermine the current human rights framework's claim to universality, and I adopt Charlotte Bunch's concept of a 'feminist transformation of human rights'[1] to argue that the international human rights framework must be transformed to address them and work towards substantive equality. By addressing each issue in turn, the main argument put forward by this chapter is that a feminist transformation of human rights requires a framework of conceptually universal rights capable of accommodating intersectionality, cultural difference, and diversity. This is necessary for the realisation of a comprehensive human right to abortion, the recognition of which is possible within an aspirational feminist framework.

II. FEMINIST CRITIQUES OF HUMAN RIGHTS

Feminist scholars have long articulated the way in which law and human rights have excluded women's concerns, portraying androcentric norms as universal

[1] Charlotte Bunch, 'Women's Rights as Human Rights: Toward a Re-Vision of Human Rights' (1990) 12(4) *Human Rights Quarterly* 486, 496.

and gender-neutral.[2] Susan Millns, for example, pointed out that it was not enough to grant women the same (purportedly universal) rights already afforded to men, as this ignored the fact that the 'injuries suffered by women may be different to those inflicted upon men'.[3] Further, feminist scholars highlighted that the public/private dichotomy institutionalised by the human rights framework prevented the recognition of issues such as gender-based violence as human rights violations, as this was perpetrated within the home by a private actor rather than by the state.[4] While gender-based issues have been increasingly incorporated into the international human rights framework, as demonstrated in chapter one in relation to abortion, feminist approaches to human rights have not fully addressed gender-based and intersectional human rights issues. Bunch identifies four distinct feminist approaches to human rights (although they generally overlap in practice), and views the first three as important but inadequate.[5] Here I adopt Bunch's model for the purpose of critique, and the fourth approach, which Bunch refers to as the feminist transformation of human rights, informs the remainder of this and the following chapters.

The first and second of the approaches that Bunch identifies focus on taking women's needs into consideration in relation to civil and political rights and the recognition of the 'economic subordination' of women.[6] The feminist movement sought the recognition that civil and political (CP) rights and economic, social, and cultural (ESC) rights applied to women generally, but also sought 'to show how violations of women, like rape, battery and sexual slavery, were manifestations of the abuse of already accepted human rights principles' and how women were particularly affected by poverty.[7] Feminist human rights campaigners thus aimed to realign the liberal underpinnings of the human rights framework in order to meet 'feminist standards of justice' by seeking the reinterpretation of existing rights to include a gender-based dimension.[8] This has broadly been achieved: as established in chapter one, reproductive rights

[2] Hilary Charlesworth, Christine Chinkin, and Shelley Wright, 'Feminist Approaches to International Law' (1991) 85(4) *American Journal of International Law* 613, 644; Frances E Olsen, 'International Law: Feminist Critiques of the Public/Private Distinction' (1993) 25 *Studies in Trasnational Legal Policy* 157; Doris Elisabeth Buss, 'Going Global: Feminist Theory, International Law, and the Public/Private Divide' in Susan B Boyd (ed), *Challenging the Public/Private Divide: Feminism, Law, and Policy* (University of Toronto Press, 1997).

[3] Susan Millns, '"Bringing Rights Home": Feminism and the Human Rights Act 1998' in Susan Millns and Noel Whitty (eds) *Feminist Perspectives on Public Law* (Cavendish Publishing, 1999) p 185.

[4] Gayle Binion, 'Human Rights: A Feminist Perspective' (1995) 17(3) *Human Rights Quarterly* 509, 516; Celina Romany, 'Women as Aliens: A Feminist Critique of the Public/Private Distinction in International Human Rights Law' (1993) 6 *Harvard Human Rights Journal* 87, 87.

[5] Bunch, 'Women's Rights' (1990) (n 1) 493.

[6] ibid 493–95.

[7] Charlotte Bunch, 'Looking Back, Looking Forward: Women's Human Rights in Global Perspective' (2017) 38(3-4) *Women's Rights Law Reporter* 333, 334; Bunch (n 1) 494.

[8] Eileen Hunt Botting, *Wollstonecraft, Mill, and Women's Human Rights* (Yale University Press, 2016) p 9; Rebecca J Cook, 'Women's International Human Rights Law: The Way Forward' in Rebecca J Cook (ed), *Human Rights of Women* (University of Pennsylvania Press, 1994) p 10.

issues, including abortion, have been interpreted (albeit insufficiently) as part of existing rights contained within the International Covenant on Civil and Political Rights (ICCPR) and the International Covenant on Economic, Social, and Cultural Rights (ICESCR). This is also the case with other gendered issues – for example, the Committee on Economic, Social, and Cultural Rights (CESCR) has recognised that the family rights contained in Article 10 ICESCR require the protection of, and remedies for, victims of domestic abuse.[9]

The third approach focused on making legal and political institutions work for women, such as through creation of the Convention on the Elimination of all Forms of Discrimination Against Women (CEDAW).[10] CEDAW takes a substantive approach to gender equality across CP and ESC rights, and therefore represented an important milestone in recognising gender-based rights. At the time, the global feminist movement was focused on the development of universalistic, binding commitments at the international level, and CEDAW was 'the first major initiative to formally institutionalize global feminism'.[11] The World Conferences on Women, discussed in chapter one, were also a significant part of this approach. At the Beijing Conference in 1995, Hilary Clinton – then First Lady to the US President – gave the now well-known affirmation that 'women's rights are human rights' in her speech, and the Platform for Action coming out of this event set out a range of commitments aimed at empowering women and girls and addressing areas of critical concern, including violence against women and economic inequalities.[12] The Vienna Declaration, adopted in 1993 following the UN World Conference on Human Rights, sought to ensure the inclusion of women's rights in mainstream human rights work, emphasising that the eradication of discrimination against women was a priority objective for the international community.[13] While the creation of specific spaces for women's rights was important for the global feminist movement, the process of 'gender mainstreaming' – the awareness of gender issues within *all* international policy-making – became popular within some transnational feminist networks, and this language was soon adopted across the UN.[14]

[9] United Nations General Assembly, *International Covenant on Economic, Social, and Cultural Rights* (16 December 1966, entered into force 3 January 1976) 993 UNTS 3; Committee on Economic, Social, and Cultural Rights, 'General Comment No 16: The Equal Right of Men and Women to the Enjoyment of all Economic, Social, and Cultural Rights (Art 3)' (11 August 2005) UN Doc E/C.12/2005/4, para 27.

[10] Bunch (n 1) 495.

[11] S Laurel Weldon and others, 'Feminist Waves, Global Activism, and Gender Violence Regimes: Genealogy and Impact of a Global Wave' (2023) *Women's Studies International Forum* 102781, 4.

[12] Hilary Rodham Clinton, 'Women's Rights Are Human Rights: Excerpts, Remarks, 5 September 1995' (1996) 24(1/2) *Women's Studies Quarterly* 98; United Nations, 'Beijing Declaration and Platform for Action, adopted at the Fourth World Conference on Women, 4–15 September 1995' (1995) UN Doc A/CONF.177/20/Rev.1.

[13] United Nations, 'World Conference on Human Rights – Vienna Declaration and Programme of Action' (12 July 1993) UN Doc A/CONF.157/23, para 18.

[14] Jacqui True and Michael Mintrom, 'Transnational Networks and Policy Diffusion: The Case of Gender Mainstreaming' (2001) 45(1) *International Studies Quarterly* 27, 30–31.

These three approaches were important steps towards the recognition of gendered human rights issues, the acceptance of a gender equality agenda, and the diffusion of these norms into national policies.[15] The global feminist movement was successful in terms of pushing for the formal recognition of their goals, but this has not translated into substantive gender equality. While Neil Englehart and Melissa Miller show that CEDAW has had a statistically significant positive effect (though varied across different countries) on the advancement of women's rights, Bunch argues that the effectiveness of CEDAW is limited by the fact that it is regarded as a 'convention without teeth' and not taken seriously by many governments.[16] If a binding Convention has not been taken seriously, then this is even more so a problem for the non-binding commitments coming out of the UN Conferences. While the ICPD reflected 'political will'[17] at the time, Leigh Senderowicz and Rishita Nandagiri highlight that the rhetorical shift stemming from the Conference 'has not been accompanied by a commensurate *substantive* shift'.[18] Gülay Calgar similarly notes the difficulties in translating the Beijing commitments into action.[19]

Gender mainstreaming was always contested among feminist actors, but some scholars saw its promise as a process that could make gendered inequalities visible across the board.[20] However, this approach has also proven somewhat ineffective in tackling substantive issues. As gender mainstreaming became more and more institutionalised, the approaches of most human rights bodies, development organisations, and governments were largely procedural and formalistic.[21] Moreover, Jacqui True argues that gender mainstreaming has been deployed to serve political and economic ends, and that it has often reinforced traditional gendered relations.[22] The more formalistic approaches to gender mainstreaming have simply required that policy-makers take into consideration the impact of any given policy on men and women, but this is often clouded by assumptions as to appropriate gender roles and the existence of a rigid gender binary.[23]

[15] ibid 50–51.

[16] Neil A Englehart and Melissa K Miller, 'The CEDAW Effect: International Law's Impact on Women's Rights' (2014) 13(1) *Journal of Human Rights* 22; Bunch (n 1) 496.

[17] Carmel Shalev, 'Rights to Sexual and Reproductive Health: The ICPD and the Convention on the Elimination of All Forms of Discrimination Against Women' (2000) 4(2) *Health and Human Rights Journal* 38, 43.

[18] Leigh Senderowicz and Rishita Nandagiri, 'Thirty Years of "Strange Bedmates": The ICPD and the Nexus of Population Control, Feminism, and Family Planning' (2025) 79(3) *Population Studies* 595, 600.

[19] Gülay Caglar, 'Gender Mainstreaming' (2013) 9(3) *Politics and Gender* 336.

[20] See True and Mintrom, 'Transnational Networks' (2001) (n 14); Sylvia Walby, 'Gender Mainstreaming: Productive Tensions in Theory and Practice' (2005) 12(3) *Social Politics* 321.

[21] Caglar, 'Gender Mainstreaming' (2013) (n 19) 338.

[22] Jacqui True, 'Feminist Problems with International Norms: Gender Mainstreaming in Global Governance' in J Ann Ticklet and Laura Sjoberg (eds), *Feminism and International Relations* (Routledge, 2013) p 75.

[23] ibid p 75.

Instead of challenging structural inequalities, gender mainstreaming can serve to reinforce them.

Niamh Reilly argues that despite the belief that there have been 'genuine improvements in women's legal, economic and social status' that individual women can benefit from, there are continuing 'structural forces at work worldwide that disadvantage women and girls in gender-specific ways.'[24] These structural forces have been insufficiently accounted for within the international human rights framework, and some scholars have argued that feminist struggles aimed at tackling these forces have been obscured or de-radicalised within the UN.[25] Rosa Ehrenreich Brooks, for example, has criticised CEDAW for its failure to identify anything 'fundamentally wrong, or even questionable, in the way social and political relations and structures are organized within the state' which results in an approach amounting to 'just let the women in, and that's that'.[26] Others have questioned whether assimilation into the current international human rights framework is possible, concluding that a change to the foundation structure is required for real inclusion.[27] This leads into the fourth approach of Bunch's model.

Bunch argues that a 'feminist transformation of human rights' is an ongoing process which requires feminists to question what is 'considered a "legitimate" human rights issue' and ask how the human rights framework can become more responsive to women, through a focus on issues such as reproductive rights and gender-based abuse.[28] Bunch leaves this concept somewhat vague, noting that the 'practical applications of transforming the human rights concept from feminist perspectives need to be explored further.'[29] However, the idea of a feminist transformation of human rights has been expanded upon by other commentators, who have suggested that such a transformation would involve more than 'simply refining or reforming existing law' – such as the creation of international regimes focusing on structural abuse, the revision of notions of state responsibility, and challenges to the centrality of the state in international law.[30]

Reilly argues that a feminist transformation of human rights can be achieved through the reinterpretation of human rights in a way which challenges their current biases, all while retaining a commitment to universal human rights principles such

[24] Niamh Reilly, *Women's Human Rights* (Polity Press, 2009) pp 160–61.

[25] Dianne Otto, 'Rethinking Universals: Opening Transformative Possibilities in International Human Rights Law' (1997) 18 *The Australian Year Book of International Law* 1, 26; Anne Orford, 'Feminism, Imperialism, and the Mission of International Law' (2002) 71 *Nordic Journal of International Law* 275, 281; Hilary Charlesworth, 'Not Waving but Drowning: Gender Mainstreaming and Human Rights in the United Nations' (2005) 18 *Harvard Human Rights Law Journal* 1, 2.

[26] Rosa Ehrenreich Brooks, 'Feminism and International Law: An Opportunity for Transformation' (2002) 14 *Yale Journal of Law and Feminism* 345, 351.

[27] Karen Engle, 'International Human Rights and Feminism: When Discourses Meet' (1992) 13 *Michigan Journal of International Law* 517, 523; Eva Brems, 'Enemies or Allies? Feminism and Cultural Relativism as Dissident Voices in Discourse' (1997) 19(1) *Human Rights Quarterly* 136, 138.

[28] Bunch (n 1) 496–97.

[29] ibid 497.

[30] Charlesworth, Chinkin, and Wright, 'Feminist Approaches) (1991) (n 2) 644.

as equality and non-discrimination.[31] This in turn, Reilly argues, requires a 'radical critique' of certain modes hierarchical thinking – including the public/private divide within international law, the prioritisation of civil and political rights, which uncritically accepts neoliberal economics, and the tension between Western hegemony and cultural relativism.[32] Eileen Hunt Botting similarly addresses the combined need for both confronting male bias and tackling cultural bias in the conception of women's rights, arguing that there is a need to examine 'how gender and other cultural differences affect the differential and unjust treatment of women within and across societies.'[33] Hunt Botting argues that this interrogation of injustice can then pave the way for aspirational claims of human rights, to put forward new rights which have not yet been recognised.[34] A feminist transformation of human rights means much more extensive reform of the current human rights framework, and could be prefigurative in its approach. Thus, a feminist transformation of human rights is required to reform the existing human rights framework, addressing its key conceptual issues and recognising gendered rights not yet included in the framework, such as a human right to abortion.

The remainder of this chapter builds on this argument. I argue that this requires a revision of the international human rights framework towards one that is responsive to gender-based issues, has cross-cultural resonance, and substantively protects ESC rights. In terms of how a transformed framework should respond to gender-based human rights issues, I will first consider how feminist theory has often adopted the assumption that all women share experiences of gender inequality and therefore have the same needs and interests. This sets up men and women as two homogenous groups in opposition and fails to appreciate that inequalities are experienced along intersectional lines rather than on the basis of gender alone. An additional shortcoming of this limited construction of 'women's rights' is the exclusion of trans, non-binary, and gender-expansive people who often experience the same or similar rights violations. For the international human rights framework to comprehensively respond to gendered issues, it must adopt a broad and intersectional understanding of gender.

III. RECOGNISING GENDER-BASED RIGHTS

A. From 'Women's Rights' to Intersectionality

The concept and terminology of 'women's rights' can be criticised for suggesting that there exists the single universal category of 'women' which is set in opposition to the single universal category of 'men'. This risks assuming that all

[31] Reilly, *Women's Human Rights* (2009) (n 24) pp 10, 18.
[32] ibid pp 10, 30.
[33] Hunt Botting, *Wollstonecraft* (2016) (n 8) pp 11–12.
[34] ibid p 12.

women, irrespective of any other factors, experience inequality, powerlessness, and human rights violations in the same way, and that all men are similarly positioned in terms of having power. These 'meta-stereotypes' claim that all women share experiences of oppression, and that these experiences are always different from men.[35] This results in sweeping generalisations – for example, assumptions of heterosexuality in Susan Moller Okin's claim that 'a woman's most dangerous environment is the home she lives in.'[36] Further, these claims also suggest that a person's gender is the primary aspect of their identity, rather than their links to other communities.[37] Adetoun Ilumoka looks at the economic position of African women, and argues that for the majority of women in Africa 'whose struggles for basic needs and subsistence *alongside men* prevents them from changing their lives for the better, addressing the problem of poverty is a priority human rights issue'.[38] In critiquing the exclusion of solidarity between women and men within feminist struggles, bell hooks highlights how the shared struggles of Black women and men has been key to anti-racist efforts; many women would not, therefore, see themselves opposed to men.[39]

The framework of intersectionality, developed by Black feminist scholar Kimberlé Crenshaw, understands characteristics such as race, gender, class, sexuality, and disability as interconnected.[40] Experiences of discrimination differ across intersectional lines, so that not all women experience oppression in the same singular way. Crenshaw demonstrated this through considering the experiences of Black women as unique to those of white women and Black men, as their experience is not exclusively or predominantly gender *or* race based, but both.[41] Crenshaw highlights that, for example, race and gender compound rather than being merely additive – Patricia Hill Collins has alternatively described this interconnectedness of oppression based on different characteristics as a 'matrix of domination'.[42] The terminology of intersectionality has been widely adopted and widely misunderstood; Hill Collins and Sirma Bilge thus highlight that intersectionality is fundamentally about viewing gender, race, class, and other characteristics as power relations which build on and mutually shape each

[35] Upendra Baxi, *The Future of Human Rights*, 3rd edn (Oxford, Oxford University Press, 2006) p 157; Tracy E Higgins, 'Anti-Essentialism, Relativism, and Human Rights' (1996) 19 *Harvard Women's Law Journal* 89, 100.

[36] Susan Moller Okin, 'Feminism, Women's Human Rights, and Cultural Differences' (1998) 13(2) *Hypatia* 32, 36.

[37] Inderpal Grewal, '"Women's Rights as Human Rights": Feminist Practices, Global Feminism, and Human Rights in Transnationality' (1999) 3(3) *Citizenship Studies* 337, 341.

[38] Adetoun O Ilumoka, 'African Women's Economic, Social, and Cultural Rights – Towards a Relevant Theory and Practice' in Rebecca J Cook (ed), *Human Rights of Women* (University of Pennsylvania Press, 1994) p 321 [emphasis added].

[39] bell hooks, *Feminist Theory: From Margin to Center* (Routledge, 2015, first pub 1984) p 71.

[40] Kimberlé Crenshaw, 'Demarginalizing the Intersection of Race and Sex: A Black Feminist Critique of Antidiscrimination Doctrine, Feminist Theory, and Antiracist Politics' (1989) 1 *University of Chicago Legal Forum* 139.

[41] ibid 149.

[42] Patricia Hill Collins, *Black Feminist Thought* (Routledge, 2022, first pub 1990) p 25.

other.[43] Intersectionality is therefore an important analytic tool for understanding how gender-related human rights issues are not experienced along the lines of gender alone.

For example, consider CEDAW's requirement that States Parties 'take all appropriate measures *to eliminate discrimination against women* in the field of health care in order to ensure, on a basis of equality of men and women, access to health care services'.[44] While there are inequalities in access to healthcare between men and women, there are also disparities within the category of 'women'. For example, Aboriginal and Torres Strait Islander women are less likely than white Australian women to access reproductive healthcare services due to cultural insensitivity and persistent stereotypes about Aboriginal Peoples; *Dalit* women in India face significant discrimination when attempting to access healthcare services; and in the UK, people with disabilities, particularly disabled women, are more likely to have an unmet need for healthcare services than non-disabled people.[45] An intersectional approach is particularly important in the abortion context, as legal restrictions disproportionately affect people from already marginalised backgrounds.[46]

An important aspect of the intersectionality framework is to consider the power relations and structures underpinning these inequalities, rather than looking at those characteristics alone. In relation to Aboriginal and Torres Strait Islander women, for example, the continual effects of colonialism, displacement, cultural loss, and racialised violence shape those experiences. Barbara Baird highlights that Aboriginal and Torres Strait Islander peoples face difficulties in accessing abortion facilities concentrated in urban centres as they are more likely to live the furthest from those areas.[47] This is in part due to socio-economic disadvantage, but is also a lasting effect of historical restrictions that were imposed on Aboriginal peoples within Australia's towns and cities; in Perth, for example, legislation was in force between 1927 and 1954 prohibiting Aboriginal peoples from entering the city without a permit.[48] Moreover, tens of thousands of

[43] Patricia Hill Collins and Sirma Bilge, *Intersectionality*, 2nd edn (Routledge, 2020) p 2.

[44] United Nations General Assembly, *Convention on the Elimination of All Forms of Discrimination Against Women* (18 December 1979, entered into force 3 September 1981) 1249 UNTS 13, Article 12(2) [emphasis added].

[45] Lisa Morgan and Joey Lynn Wabie, 'Aboriginal Women's Access and Acceptance of Reproductive Health Care' (2012) 10(3) *Pimatisiwin* 312; Nidhi Sadana Sabharwal and Wandana Sonalkar, 'Dalit Women in India: At the Crossroads of Gender, Class, and Caste' (2015) 8(1) *Global Justice: Theory Practice Rhetoric* 44; Dikaios Sakellariou and Elena S Rotarou, 'Access to Healthcare for Men and Women with Disabilities in the UK: Secondary Analysis of Cross-sectional Data' (2017) 7(8) *BMJ Open* 1.

[46] See, eg, Katie Watson, 'The Ethics of Access: Reframing the Need for Abortion Care as a Health Disparity' (2022) 22(8) *Americal Journal of Bioethics* 22.

[47] Barbara Baird, 'Tales of Mobility: Women's Travel and Abortion Services in a Globalized Australia' in Christabelle Sethna and Gayle Davis (eds), *Abortion Across Borders* (John Hopkins University Press, 2019) pp 160–61.

[48] Aborigines Act 1905 (Western Australia); Culture WA, 'Perth's Prohibited Area' https://culture.wa.gov.au/feature/perths-prohibited-area accessed 9 January 2026.

Aboriginal and Torres Strait Islander children were forcibly removed from their families throughout the 1900s as part of the country's assimilation policy, now referred to as the 'Stolen Generations'.[49] These legacies of structurally enacted violence, as well as its present forms, contribute to feelings of distrust and a lack of cultural safety in institutional settings, particularly around reproductive healthcare.[50] Judith Butler thus argues that intersectional issues cannot be separated out from their historical, political, and cultural contexts.[51] The power relations and structures that have shaped socio-cultural meanings and lived experiences of gender and race must also be accounted for. Identities and lived experiences are subjectively constructed within these contexts, so there is no globally or even locally shared experience of intersectional characteristics.

The concept of a 'global sisterhood' is therefore critiqued by Chandra Talpade Mohanty for its 'representation of Woman produced by hegemonic discourses' as 'an arbitrary relation set up in particular cultural and historical contexts.'[52] These representations are typically based on the experiences of white, heterosexual, non-disabled women in the West. Butler similarly questions the 'assumption that there must be a universal basis for feminism, one which must be found in an identity assumed to exist cross-culturally'.[53] Mohanty further critiques the idea of a 'a composite, singular "third-world woman"' by which feminists 'appropriate and colonize the constitutive complexities which characterize the lives of women in these countries.'[54] The universal basis for feminism cannot be found in a monolithic identity of 'woman' – not across *or* within cultures and countries. Mohanty argues in favour of recognition of an 'imagined community' in relation to Third World struggles, which would avoid similar pitfalls through forging 'political rather than biological or cultural bases for alliance'.[55] Global feminism requires a similar approach, recognising shared political values and goals around ending oppression rather than claims to universal experiences; solidarity, not homogeneity.

This also requires the recognition that what have typically been referred to as 'women's rights' are relevant to the trans, non-binary, and gender expansive

[49] Commonwealth of Australia, 'Bringing Them Home: Report of the National Inquiry into the Separation of Aboriginal and Torres Strait Islander Children from Their Families' (1997) https://bth.humanrights.gov.au/sites/default/files/documents/bringing_them_home_report.pdf accessed 9 January 2026.

[50] Morgan and Wabie, 'Aboriginal Women's Access' (2012) (n 45); Jo Spangaro and others, '"They aren't really black fellas but they are easy to talk to': Factors Which Influence Australian Aboriginal Women's Decision to Disclose Intimate Partner Violence During Pregnancy' (2016) 41 *Midwifery* 79; Kate Whitford and others, 'Sexual and Reproductive Health Service Access among Aboriginal and Torres Strait Islander Young People in Regional NSW, Australia' (2024) 1 *Health and Social Care in the Community* 1845971.

[51] Judith Butler, *Gender Trouble* (Routledge, 1999, first pub 1989) p 6.

[52] Chandra Mohanty, 'Under Western Eyes: Feminist Scholarship and Colonial Discourses' (1988) 30 *Feminist Review* 61, 62.

[53] Butler, *Gender Trouble* (1999) (n 51) p 6.

[54] Mohanty, 'Under Western Eyes' (1988) (n 52) 62.

[55] Chandra Talpade Mohanty, *Feminism Without Borders* (Duke University Press, 2006) p 46.

people who also face patriarchal violence or require access to the same services as cisgender women. Trans men and some non-binary and gender-expansive people face difficulties when accessing women-oriented reproductive health services, such as cervical cancer screenings and abortion services.[56] However, recent years have seen the mainstreaming of a particular brand of feminism which is hostile to trans, non-binary, and gender expansive people – and trans women in particular. Self-described 'gender critical' feminists (who are often referred to by others as 'TERFs' – an abbreviation of 'trans-exclusionary radical feminists') reject the inclusion of trans women into the category of 'women', which they see as biologically determined, and seek to exclude trans women from women-only spaces. One of the main claims made by gender critical feminists is that trans rights (such as to self-identify one's gender and use gender-appropriate facilities) encroach upon the rights of non-trans women.[57]

These beliefs are rooted in a supposedly biological understanding of sex. In contrast, Darren Rosenblum views sex as a continuum, arguing that there is no clear divide between 'men' and 'women' as sex/gender is formed through biological *and* cultural factors; chromosomes, gonads, hormones, internal reproductive organs, external genitalia, secondary sexual characteristics, and, importantly, self-identity, are all taken as relevant.[58] Further, Joan Scott argues that gender is a constitutive element of social relationships based on *perceived* differences between the sexes.[59] Scott identifies four interrelated elements to gender: culturally available symbols (such as women represented by Eve and the Virgin Mary in Christian traditions); the interpretation of those symbols which repress any alternative possibilities (typically asserting the binary distinction between male/female and masculine/feminine); social institutions (such as the family) and the organisation of society through segregated labour markets and education; and subjective identity in terms of how gendered identities are substantively constructed with reference to social organisations and historically specific cultural representations.[60] Gender (and sex) is therefore often understood through patriarchal norms which restrict and punish people who deviate from the perceived binary.[61]

[56] Aimee Linfield, 'Reducing Cervical Screening Inequalities for Trans People' (Public Health England Screening, 10 April 2019) https://phescreening.blog.gov.uk/2019/04/10/reducing-cervical-screening-inequalities-for-trans-people/ accessed 9 January 2026; Heidi Moseson and others, 'Abortion Experiences and Preferences of Transgender, Nonbinary and Gender-Expansive People in the United States' (2021) 224(4) *American Journal of Obstetrics and Gynecology* 376.e1.

[57] Sally Hines, 'Trans and Feminist Rights have been Falsely Cast in Opposition' (*The Economist*, 13 July 2018) www.economist.com/open-future/2018/07/13/trans-and-feminist-rights-have-been-falsely-cast-in-opposition accessed 9 January 2026.

[58] Darren Rosenblum, 'Unsex CEDAW, or What's Wrong with Women's Rights?' (2011) 20(2) *Columbia Journal of Gender and Law* 98, 135.

[59] Joan Scott, 'Gender: A Useful Category of Historical Analysis' (1986) 91(5) *American Historical Review* 1053, 1067.

[60] ibid 1067–69.

[61] Griffin Hansbury, 'Don't Take Up Space: How the Patriarchy Works to Undermine Trans Communities from Within' in Jean Petrucelli, Sarah Schoen, and Naomi Snider (eds), *Patriarchy and Its Discontents* (Routledge, 2022).

This understanding of gender takes into account the cultural, historical, and political power relations and structures that have shaped gendered identities, including how our current gender/sex categories were constructed and imposed through colonialism.[62] It also recognises gender as an intersectional 'subject position' which is simultaneously open to change and subjected to emotional, material, and structural constraints.[63] As Sally Hines argues, the positioning of sex as the source of women's oppression precludes any intersectional analysis.[64] Moving towards a genuinely intersectional understanding of gender-based rights issues, and conceptualising feminism as based on shared values and goals rather than universal experiences, therefore requires the inclusion of trans, non-binary, and gender-expansive experiences of disempowerment and oppression. This is all the more important in the context of the connections between restrictions on reproductive rights and trans rights. For example, in the early 2020s, the Texas Governor Greg Abbott was responsible for signing into law *both* restrictions on abortion and a Bill to prevent children from receiving gender affirmative healthcare.[65] Anti-trans and anti-abortion policies often come together, as both would otherwise disrupt socio-culturally constructed understandings of gendered reproductive roles. Protecting 'women's rights' and 'trans rights' is not mutually exclusive, and an intersectional, shared ground for gender-based rights which moves beyond the 'cisgender matrix'[66] is a necessary part of a feminist transformation of human rights.

B. Intersectionality in the International Human Rights Framework

At the UN, some human rights treaties were created to address the particular needs of individual groups – such as CEDAW, the Convention on the Rights of Persons with Disabilities (CRPD), and the International Convention on the Elimination of Racial Discrimination (ICERD).[67] CEDAW and CERD do not explicitly recognise intersectionality in the Convention itself, which can be

[62] María Lugones, 'Toward a Decolonial Feminism' (2010) 25(4) *Hypatia* 742.

[63] Raewyn Connell, 'Gender, Health and Theory: Conceptualizing the Issue, in Local and World Perspective' (2012) 74 *Social Science and Medicine* 1675, 1676–77.

[64] Sally Hines, 'Sex Wars and (Trans) Gender Panics: Identity and Body Politics in Contemporary UK Feminism' (2020) 68(4) *Sociological Review Monographs* 25, 34.

[65] Sneda Dey and Karen Brooks Harper, 'Transgender Texas Kids are Terrified after Governor Orders that Parents be Investigated for Child Abuse' (*The Texas Tribune,* 28 February 2022) www.texastribune.org/2022/02/28/texas-transgender-child-abuse/ accessed 9 January 2026; Shannon Najmabadi, 'Gov Greg Abbott signs into law one of the nation's strictest abortion measures, banning procedure as early as six weeks into pregnancy' (*The Texas Tribune*, 19 May 2021) www.texastribune.org/2021/05/18/texas-heartbeat-bill-abortions-law/ accessed 9 January 2026.

[66] Sandra Duffy, 'Contested Subjects of Human Rights: Trans- and Gender-Variant Subjects of International Human Rights Law' (2021) 84(5) *Modern Law Review* 1041, 1044.

[67] CEDAW (n 44); United Nations General Assembly, *Convention on the Rights of Persons with Disabilities* (13 December 2006, entered into force 3 May 2008) 2515 UNTS 3; United Nations General Assembly, *International Convention on the Elimination of All Forms of Racial Discrimination* (21 December 1965, entered into force 4 January 1969) 195 UNTS 660.

contrasted with CRPD's explicit recognition of the need to include a gender perspective, acknowledging the specific gender-based abuse that women with disabilities may face and the need for gender-sensitive health services.[68] However, international human rights bodies have increasingly adopted an intersectional approach in their General Comments and Concluding Observations.[69] For example, the CEDAW Committee highlighted in its General Recommendation 33 that discrimination against women is compounded by intersecting factors such as

> ethnicity/race, indigenous or minority status, colour, socioeconomic status and/or caste, language, religion or belief, political opinion, national origin, marital and/or maternal status, age, urban/rural location, health status, disability, property ownership and identity as a lesbian, bisexual or transgender woman or intersex person.[70]

Rikki Holtmaat and Paul Post argued back in 2015 that the inclusion of intersectionality by the CEDAW Committee had been gratuitous, ad hoc, and erratic.[71] However, in the decade since then, the Committee has increasingly developed its intersectional approach; in the context of sexual and reproductive healthcare, for example, the Committee has recognised the barriers experienced by women with disabilities, Indigenous women, Black women, and migrant women.[72] Lydia Candelaria González Orta thus praises the Committee for developing an intersectional perspective 'in parallel with the changes in the global women's movement in the last few decades' which have seen the recognition that a focus on gender alone is insufficient.[73] The CESCR has also recognised intersectional issues in recent General Comments on issues such as sexual and reproductive healthcare, workplace equality, and land use.[74]

[68] CRPD (n 67) Preamble, Article 16, Article 25.

[69] See, for analysis on intersectionality in human rights documents: Gauthier de Beco, 'Protecting the Invisible: An Intersectional Approach to International Human Rights Law' (2017) 17(4) *Human Rights Law Review* 633, 636–40; Pok Yin S Chow, 'Has Intersectionality Reached its Limits? Intersectionality in the UN Human Rights Treaty Body Practice and the Issue of Ambivalence' (2016) 16(3) *Human Rights Law Review* 453, 462–67.

[70] CEDAW, 'General Recommendation No 33 on Women's Access to Justice' (23 July 2015) UN Doc CEDAW/C/GC/33, para. 8.

[71] Rikki Holtmaat and Paul Post, 'Enhancing LGBTI Rights by Changing the Interpretation of Convention on the Elimination of All Forms of Discrimination Against Women' (2015) 33(4) *Nordic Journal of Human Rights* 319, 328–30.

[72] See, eg, CEDAW, 'Concluding Observations on the Seventh Periodic Report of Gabon' (1 March 2022) UN Doc CEDAW/C/GAB/CO/7, para 31(c); CEDAW, 'Concluding Observations on the Eighth Periodic Report of Panama' (1 March 2022) UN Doc CEDAW/C/PAN/CO/8, para 38(c); CEDAW, 'Concluding Observations on the Eighth Report of the Dominican Republic' (1 March 2022) UN Doc CEDAW/C/DOM/C/8, para 36(c).

[73] Lydia Candelaria González Orta, 'The Convention on the Elimination of all Forms of Discrimination Against Women (CEDAW): From its Radical Preamble to its Contemporary Intersectional Approach' (2025) 34(1) *Women's History Review* 79, 88.

[74] CESCR, 'General Comment No 22 on the Right to Sexual and Reproductive Health (Article 12 of the ICESCR)' (2 May 2016) UN Doc E/C.12/GC/22, paras 23, 30; CESCR, General Comment No 23 on the Right to Just and Favourable Conditions of Work (Article 7 ICESCR)' (27 April 2016) UN Doc E/C.12/GC/23, paras 31, 47–48; CESCR, 'General Comment No 26 on Land and Economic, Social, and Cultural Rights' (24 January 2023) UN Doc E/C.12/GC/26, paras 13, 16, 18.

However, an intersectional approach has not been adopted by all human rights bodies. In the context of a case concerning sex work, Silvia Steininger has critiqued the European Court of Human Rights (ECtHR) for its 'intersectional blindness' in terms of the lived realities of the applicants.[75] Jens Theilen notes that the ECtHR has considered intersectional factors in some of its case law, but the Court has made efforts to avoid ever referring to 'intersectionality', instead preferring the terminology of 'vulnerability'.[76] In doing so, the ECtHR misses the mark on what an intersectional analysis actually requires – they hide the relevance of gender and intersectional lines of oppression, instead identifying instances of vulnerability based on a narrow categorisation of specific characteristics. For example, in *YP v Russia,* a case concerning non-consensual sterilisation, the ECtHR declined to find a violation of ECHR Article 3 (freedom from torture and cruel, inhuman, and degrading treatment) because of, in part, the lack of additional vulnerabilities.[77] The ECtHR distinguished the case from other cases of non-consensual sterilisation where there was an additional vulnerability – for example, where Roma applicants were sterilised.[78] In other words, gender alone is not taken as relevant to the Court's analysis, and instead of viewing these additional vulnerabilities as intersecting with gender, they have become a *pre-condition* of finding violations of certain rights. Thus, while the Court may be accounting for some intersectional factors in its decisions, they are not adopting an intersectional perspective, which would require them to take a holistic view of intersectional oppression instead of seeing ethnicity and disability, for example, as merely additive characteristics required to cross the Article 3 threshold.

This approach is reflective of a broader issue with how intersectionality has entered human rights discourse; as with gender mainstreaming, there has been a weakening or depoliticisation of what an intersectional lens requires. Theilen argues that the ECHR's approach 'essentializes' vulnerability as a natural part of the applicant's condition, rather than as a structurally produced inequality, a limitation which can also be found in other treaty bodies' engagements with intersectionality.[79] International human rights bodies, as state-centric entities, are hesitant to adopt an intersectional lens which advocates for domestic, let alone global, structural change.[80] In the CEDAW Committee's comments, gender remains the primary category of analysis, with intersectional characteristics mentioned only as an addendum, and the perceived gender/sex binary

[75] Silvia Steininger, 'Sex Work Can't Buy Human Rights' (*Verfassungsblog*, 3 October 2024) https://verfassungsblog.de/ecthr-sex-work-intersectionality/ accessed 9 January 2026.

[76] Jens Theilen, 'Intersectionality's Travels to International Human Rights Law' (2024) 45(2) *Michigan Journal of International Law* 233, 256–57.

[77] ECtHR, App no 43399/13, *YP v Russia* (20 September 2022), para 37.

[78] ECtHR, App no 18968/07, *VC v Slovakia* (8 November 2011), para 179; ECtHR, App no 29518/10, *NB v Slovakia* (12 June 2012), paras 96–97; ECtHR, App no 15966/04, *IG and Ors v Slovakia* (13 November 2012), para 166.

[79] Theilen, 'Intersectionality's Travels' (2024) (n 76) 258.

[80] ibid 259–60.

remains unchallenged even when trans and non-binary people are mentioned. For example, in General Comment 33, the CEDAW Committee acknowledges the intersectional factors that compound inequalities in access to justice, as quoted above, but continues to frame the issue as treating women 'on an equal basis with men'.[81] This does nothing to challenge our socially constructed understanding of gender which produces these inequalities; within international human rights law, gender continues to be framed as simply a question of women reaching the same level as men.[82] Men, in this framing, continue to be homogenised as the people with the power.

Theilen highlights that this lack of structural analysis arises as a result of human rights bodies' framing of themselves as apolitical; intersectionality is rooted in an emancipatory Black feminist politics, which is at odds with the often-depoliticised commitments of human rights law.[83] This is particularly important to consider in relation to abortion – a heavily politicised issue which human rights bodies have attempted to depoliticise in order to advance standards in support of access to it. Abortion decisions take place in the context of broader structures, and difficulties in access are experienced along intersectional lines. Restrictions on abortion perpetuate gendered norms around women's reproductive roles, which are in turn rooted in a perceived gender/sex binary. Without a meaningful intersectional approach which accounts for these structures and inequalities, the international human rights framework is unable to effectively advocate for comprehensive access to abortion. Theilen, however, highlights the possibilities of challenging the institutional contexts that ignore or fail to grapple with structural issues.[84] For those reasons already highlighted above, a feminist transformation of human rights therefore requires an intersectional approach which is conscious of these structures and actively works to challenge them.

IV. THE CROSS-CULTURAL APPLICATION OF HUMAN RIGHTS

A. Cultural Relativism and Human Rights Imperialism

As argued above, identities are constructed within specific cultural settings and historical power relations, such that there is no one global experience of what it means to be, for example, a woman. This has implications for how we frame the universality of human rights norms. Alison Dundes Renteln argues that the presumption of universality presupposes 'that individuals stripped

[81] CEDAW, 'General Recommendation No 33' (n 70) para 8.

[82] Susanne Zwingel, 'International Feminist Strategies: Strengths and Challenges of the Rights-Based Approach' (2013) 9(3) *Politics & Gender* 344, 345.

[83] Theilen (n 76) 268.

[84] ibid 273.

of their cultural and political heritage would be pure rational beings and would thus dutifully select liberal democratic principles of justice.'[85] The cultural relativist position calls into question the universal application of Western norms and rejects claims as to the rightness or wrongness of differing cultural values. This has been simplified as followed: 'norms of morality are relative to a given society; the ethical basis for international human rights is Western; therefore international norms should not be the basis of value judgments in other cultural contexts.'[86]

However, J Oloka-Onyango and Sylvia Tamale distinguish between two broad arguments relating to cultural relativism. They identify the first as emanating from non-Western politicians and scholars, asserting that universal human rights norms are an imperialist interference with religious and cultural beliefs and practices.[87] The second argument comes from Western scholars, who 'evoke the culturalist dimension as both explanation and excuse for inaction or wrong action'.[88] The issue coming from this second argument is that the chief 'defenders of cultural relativism are not from nondominant cultures but are white male intellectuals' who fail to engage with postcolonial concerns.[89] This also risks essentialising cultures, perceiving them as 'unchanging givens' and ignoring the competing assertions of norms or the fact that culture is subject to change and struggle.[90] Uma Narayan thus argues that we should reject the idea that anything can be uncontroversially defined as 'Indian culture' or 'Western culture' or 'African culture'.[91] Cultural values vary not only across nations but within them, and the terminology of 'culture' can be used to refer to values spanning religion, language, ethnicity, nationality, race, and other demographic delineations.[92]

Further, it cannot be assumed that the interests of the dominant group represent the interests of everyone in a given context. What are perceived as commonly accepted cultural values depend on the group(s) with power who decide which cultural values and norms are prioritised. As Jack Donnelly notes, relativism ignores the influence of politics, or conflates politics with culture, thus confusing

[85] Alison Dundes Renteln, *International Human Rights: Universalism Versus Relativism* (Sage, 1990) p 50.

[86] Annie Bunting, 'Theorizing Women's Cultural Diversity in Feminist International Human Rights Strategies' (1993) 20(1) *Journal of Law and Society* 6, 8.

[87] J Oloka-Onyango and Sylvia Tamale, '"The Personal is Political," or Why Women's Rights Are Indeed Human Rights: An African Perspective on International Feminism' (1995) 17(4) *Human Rights Quarterly* 691, 706.

[88] ibid.

[89] Bronwyn Winter, 'Women, the Law, and Cultural Relativism in France: The Case of Excision' (1994) 19(4) *Signs* 939, 959.

[90] Uma Narayan, 'Essence of Culture and a Sense of History: A Feminist Critique of Cultural Essentialism' (1998) 13(2) *Hypatia* 86, 94; Bunting, 'Theorizing Women's Cultural Diversity' (1993) (n 86) 8–9; Jack Donnelly, 'The Relative Universality of Human Rights' (2007) 29(2) *Human Rights Quarterly* 281, 296.

[91] Narayan, 'Essence of Culture' (1998) (n 90) 102.

[92] Sarah Song, 'Feminists Rethink Multiculturalism: Resisting Essentialism and Cross-Cultural Hypocrisy' in Margaret Davies and Vanessa E Munro (eds), *The Ashgate Research Companion to Feminist Legal Theory* (Ashgate, 2013) p 140.

'what a people have been forced to tolerate with what it values.'[93] There is an 'interpretative privilege in cultural formation' and this issue is particularly relevant to feminist theorists who argue that culture often represents the interests of men so 'how and what women choose to accept or reject as part of their culture is often ignored or suppressed'.[94] Thus, in relation to gender-based rights issues, cultural relativism can be used as an excuse for states to avoid reform, masking political beliefs on the rights of people in a society rather than relating to genuine concern over preserving cultural practices.[95] For example, Islam is often presented as incompatible with gender equality, but scholars within that religious context note that the varying interpretations which are elevated and formalised across different states cannot be explained by 'culture' but are shaped by socioeconomic and political developments and, importantly, the exploitation of cultural identities by those in power.[96]

The claim that human rights norms are uniquely Western values has also been challenged by numerous scholars. Oloka-Onyango and Tamale note that such arguments tend to have racist overtones by implying that human rights violations are 'culturally endemic' to non-Western states.[97] This argument also works vice versa, to imply that human rights protection is innate to the West, which is problematic in light of 'the historical reality that Western doctrines of equality and rights coexisted for decades with support for slavery and colonialism'.[98] Upendra Baxi also points to anti-colonial struggles as important expressions of rights-based values, in which people claimed the individual and collective rights that had previously been denied to them.[99] Baxi further argues that no culture is 'devoid of notions about human rights' given that all cultures contain 'beliefs, sentiments, symbols that impart sense to the notion of being human'.[100]

While this form of cultural relativist position is therefore problematic, it is important to engage with the other position that Oloka-Onyango and Tamale outline, in terms of human rights law acting as an imperialist interference. A distinction can be drawn between the claim that rights are inherently Western, and that it happened to be in the West that human rights 'came to fruition in the particular sense of becoming *an important part of the legal and cultural fabric*

[93] Donnelly, 'The Relative Universality' (2007) (n 90) 296.

[94] Arati Rao, 'The Politics of Gender and Culture in International Human Rights Discourse' in Julie Peters and Andrea Wolper (eds), *Women's Rights Human Rights* (Routledge, 1995) p 173; Nancy Kim, 'Toward a Feminist Theory of Human Rights: Straddling the Fence between Western Imperialism and Uncritical Absolutism' (1993) 25 *Columbia Human Rights Law Review* 49, 90.

[95] Cyra Akila Choudhury, 'Beyond Culture: Human Rights Universalism versus Religious and Cultural Relativism in the Activism for Gender Justice' (2015) 30(2) *Berkeley Journal of Gender Law and Justice* 226, 230.

[96] ibid 238; Farida Shaheed, 'Controlled or Autonomous: Identity and the Experience of the Network, Women Living under Muslim Laws' (1994) 19(4) *Signs* 997, 1001.

[97] Oloka-Onyango and Tamale, '"The Personal is Political,"' (1995) (n 87) 706.

[98] Narayan, 'Essence of Culture' (1998) (n 90) 97.

[99] Baxi, *The Future of Human Rights* (2006) (n 35) pp 212–14.

[100] ibid p 25.

and of having real political consequences.'[101] As already noted, the concept of human rights is not specifically Western, and many outside of the West have endorsed the ethical basis for human rights.[102] However, the international human rights framework, as a legal and political institution, has Western liberalism as its foundation and therefore promotes 'a Eurocentric ideal' as universal.[103] Communitarian conceptions of rights, such as those that emerged in Islamic societies and pre-colonial Africa, are thus sidelined.[104]

Consequently, human rights scholarship and practice has tended to assume that non-Western countries perpetuate the worst human rights violations, particularly in relation to gendered issues. Riane Eisler, for example, wrote that '*in many regions of the developing world* (ironically often those with the highest poverty and, correlatively, birth rates), women have no right to reproductive freedom and are defined by both law and custom as literally male controlled mechanisms of reproduction' – ignoring widespread reproductive rights restrictions in higher income countries.[105] Further, issues such as female genital cutting, female infanticide, coercive sterilisation, and sex-selective abortion are often portrayed in ways which reflect imperialist discourse, presenting women as weak and in need of protection from outside influence. Ratna Kapur highlights that the portrayal of women as victims of 'cultural or civilisational backwardness' was used as justification for civilising missions in the colonial era.[106] Taking female genital 'mutilation' as an example, Makau Mutua looks at the language of 'mutilation' in implying 'the wilful, sadistic infliction of pain on a hapless victim, and stigmatizes the practitioners and their cultures as barbaric savages'.[107] Peggy Levitt and Sally Engle Merry contrast the view of female genital cutting as a harmful tradition with 'other forms of surgical bodily modification such as plastic surgery [which have] never been considered a human rights violation.'[108]

[101] Stephen Hopgood, 'Human Rights on the Road to Nowhere' in Stephen Hopgood, Jack Snyder, and Leslie Vinjamuri (Eds) *Human Rights Futures* (Cambridge, Cambridge University Press, 2017) p 286.

[102] Bunting (n 86) 9.

[103] Makau Mutua, 'Savages, Victims, and Saviors: The Metaphor of Human Rights' (2001) 42 *Harvard International Law Journal* 201, 205.

[104] See, eg, Nader Hashemi and Emran Qureshi, 'Islam and Human Rights: A 50 Year Retrospective' (2022) 19(1) *Muslim World Journal of Human Rights* 1; Berdal Aral, 'The Idea of Human Rights as Perceived in the Ottoman Empire' (2004) 26(2) *Human Rights Quarterly* 454; IR Amadi, 'Human Rights in Pre-Colonial Igbo Society of Nigeria: An Analysis' (1991) 46(3) *Africa* 403; Josiah AM Cobbah, 'African Values and the Human Rights Debate: An African Perspective' (1987) 9(3) *Human Rights Quarterly* 309.

[105] Riane Eisler, 'Human Rights: Toward an Integrated Theory for Action' (1987) 9(3) *Human Rights Quarterly* 287, 294. [emphasis added].

[106] Ratna Kapur, 'Human Rights in the 21st Century: Take a Walk on the Dark Side' (2006) 28 *Sydney Law Review* 665, 678.

[107] Mutua, 'Savages, Victims, and Saviors' (2001) (n 103) 225.

[108] Peggy Levitt and Sally Engle Merry, 'Making Women's Human Rights in the Vernacular: Navigating the Culture/Rights Divide' in Dorothy L Hodgson (ed), *Gender and Culture at the Limit of Rights* (University of Pennsylvania Press, 2011) p 85.

African feminist scholars have thus highlighted that the contours of the debate on female genital cutting have ideological underpinnings rooted in colonialism,[109] falsely portraying the issue as one of 'absolute and total cultural conflict' between the right to bodily autonomy and community belonging.[110] While these scholars nonetheless support the feminist project to end female genital cutting, they argue that this must be done through a transnational, multicultural coalition rather than by the imperialist imposition of certain values.[111] Avoiding the imperialist impulses of human rights law must be an integral aspect of a feminist transformation of human rights, requiring collaborative efforts to ensure the cross-cultural traction of rights-based norms and an effort to redress the power asymmetries within the current framework. Thus, the international human rights framework must embrace a pluralistic understanding of human rights and a bottom-up approach to the realisation of universal norms, rather than top-down imposition of rigid values.

B. Conceptual University and Human Rights Pluralism

Anne Phillips argues that feminists must be wary of accepting cultural norms without question, given how dominant constructions of culture can perpetuate gender inequality.[112] However, as highlighted above, it cannot be assumed that gendered interests are the same cross-culturally, and so cultural difference must be accommodated in the human rights framework to ensure that universal human rights norms are applicable and effective in different contexts. Deborah Heikes argues that we nonetheless require a universal foundation capable of defending political and moral concepts in order for the feminist project to succeed; in order for feminist claims to have any traction, there must be 'some manner of determining which are the correct ways of thinking about issues of oppression, justice, equality, and so on.'[113] Thus, cultural traditions or values 'that discriminate against some humans on grounds of race, gender, religion, or other partly interpenetrating variables cannot be permitted' within a rights-based framework.[114] In relation to abortion, which faces widespread

[109] See, eg, Obioma Nnaemeka (ed), *Female Circumcision and the Politics of Knowledge* (Praeger, 2005).

[110] Françoise Lionnet, 'Women's Rights, Bodies, and Identities: The Limits of Universalism and the Legal Debate around Excision in France' in Obioma Nnaemeka (ed), *Female Circumcision and the Politics of Knowledge* (Praeger, 2005) p 102.

[111] See, eg, Ange-Marie Hanckock, 'Overcoming Willful Blindness: Building Egalitarian Multicultural Women's Coalitions' France' in Obioma Nnaemeka (ed), *Female Circumcision and the Politics of Knowledge* (Praeger, 2005).

[112] Anne Phillips, 'Multiculturalism, Universalism, and the Claims of Democracy' in Maxine Molyneux and Shahra Razavi (eds), *Gender Justice, Development, and Rights* (Oxford, Oxford University Press, 2002) p 117.

[113] Deborah K Heikes, *Rationality and Feminist Philosophy* (Continuum, 2010) pp 16–17.

[114] Alan Gewirth, *The Community of Rights* (The University of Chicago Press, 1996) p 68.

opposition globally, entrenching its status as a universal right is integral to ensuring comprehensive access for those that need it and the realisation of other rights such as substantive gender equality. A feminist transformation of human rights would therefore need to retain some universal values, while allowing for a pluralistic adoption of those values – a framework of conceptually universal rights capable of accommodating difference and diversity.[115]

Human rights pluralism could support the cross-cultural traction of universal human rights norms. Michel Rosenfeld argues that comprehensive pluralism can bridge the gap between universalism and cultural relativism.[116] Rosenfeld's understanding of comprehensive pluralism holds one conception of good above all others, but also seeks to accommodate other conceptions.[117] This form of pluralism may include exemptions from generally applicable laws, assistance to do things that the majority can do unassisted, representation of minorities in government bodies, recognition of traditional legal codes by the dominant legal system, or limited self-government rights.[118] Rosenfeld ranks the fundamental norms of comprehensive pluralism (such as tolerance) as 'second-order norms' and norms emanating from remaining conceptions of good as 'first-order norms'.[119] First-order norms would only be accommodated to the extent that they are compatible with second-order norms; comprehensive pluralism thus 'grants priority to second-order norms over first-order norms, such priority only comes into play in the context of an actual conflict among first-order norms.'[120] Rosenfeld considers the protection of Aboriginal rights under the Canadian Constitution as an example of a pluralistic approach to minority rights,[121] and within the international human rights framework, the UN Declaration on the Rights of Indigenous Peoples (UNDRIP) already ascribes rights to Indigenous Peoples to exercise self-determination and self-governance in relation to their internal and local affairs.[122]

The questions of which norms to accommodate, the ranking of norms in this way, and by who are not easily answered, and this approach could therefore perpetuate the same issues in relation to top-down universal imperialism. Further, Giselle Corradi raises two key concerns with legal pluralism: first, that any given legal system may reflect a majority viewpoint to the exclusion of the minority; and second, that 'the adoption of policies that endorse legal pluralism may advance the collective rights of minorities, but may also entail the risk of

[115] ibid p 39; Siobhán Mullally, *Gender, Culture and Human Rights* (Hart, 2006) p xxxii.

[116] Michel Rosenfeld, 'Can Human Rights Bridge the Gap between Universalism and Cultural Relativism – A Pluralist Assessment Based on the Rights of Minorities' (1999) 30(2) *Columbia Human Rights Law Review* 249.

[117] ibid 267.

[118] Song, 'Feminists Rethink Multiculturalism' (2013) (n 92) p 140.

[119] Rosenfeld, 'Can Human Rights Bridge' (1999) (n 116) 270.

[120] ibid 270; 279.

[121] ibid 276.

[122] UN General Assembly, *United Nations Declaration on the Rights of Indigenous Peoples* (2 October 2007) UN Doc A/RES/61/295, Articles 3–4.

violating the individual rights of their members.'[123] In the context of gender-based rights, Sarah Song similarly argues that group-specific rights should not be accommodated where they threaten the agency of individual members of minority cultural groups.[124] While the individualised nature of the Western conception of human rights has been critiqued for failing to accommodate group or communitarian rights, the individualistic element of rights remains important as human rights are intended to protect people from harms caused to them by the cultures, communities, families, or other groups to which they are part of.[125] The protection of individual autonomy is fundamental in the context of abortion, for example, because of its position as heavily contested and restricted in most cultural and legal settings. Thus, to avoid the entrenching of exclusionary power dynamics within pluralistic orders, Alex Green and Jennifer Hendry argue that they must encompass civic equality, individual autonomy, and political legitimacy.[126]

Human rights have been increasingly recognised as a *practice* as well as a legal order, reflecting an understanding of rights as developing over time in dialogue with local, national, regional, or global shifts in values. Corradi refers to this as an 'iterative' process of interactions – including social struggles – by which norms are interpreted.[127] Human rights pluralism viewed in this way entails a more flexible approach than Rosenfeld's conception, reflecting how universal human rights values relating to dignity, equality, freedom, wellbeing, and justice are interpreted and applied from the bottom-up. Abdullahi Ahmed An-Na'im proposes that the universality of human rights must be realised through deliberate strategies to address existing tensions within different cultural settings.[128] He argues that cultural sensitivity and an understanding of the rationale behind cultural values is necessary in order to persuade people that changing religious and customary laws in line with human rights standards is valid and acceptable.[129] This approach looks to the reinterpretation of existing values to correspond with human rights standards through internal, or local, dialogue.[130] For example, Muslim feminists commit 'to the feminist goals of combating patriarchy and transforming the oppressive ideological and material conditions that sustain the subordination of women' while viewing these goals

[123] Giselle Corradi, 'Human Rights and Legal Pluralism: Four Research Agendas' in Giselle Coradi, Eva Brems, and Mark Goodale (eds), *Human Rights Encounter Legal Pluralism* (Hart Publishing, 2017) p 6.

[124] Song (n 92) p 149.

[125] Gewirth, *The Community of Rights* (1996) (n 114) 35.

[126] Alex Green and Jennifer Hendry, *Legal Pluralism: New Trajectories in Law* (Routledge, 2024) p 49.

[127] Corradi, 'Human Rights and Legal Pluralism' (2017) (n 123) p 12.

[128] Abdullahi Ahmed An-Na'im, 'Islam and Human Rights: Beyond the Universality Debate' (2000) 94 *ASIL Proceedings* 95, 100.

[129] Abdullahi Ahmed An-Na'im, 'State Responsibility Under International Human Rights Law to Change Religious and Customary Laws' in Rebecca J Cook (ed), *Human Rights of Women* (University of Pennsylvania Press, 1994) p 177.

[130] ibid p 179.

as compatible with their religion.[131] Accepting that Islamic texts are subject to contestable interpretations, Muslim feminists seek to challenge how dominant patriarchal interpretations are presented as the only possible understandings and instead invoke 'gender positive' readings.[132] This avoids imperialistic readings which view Muslim women as being subjected to gendered Islamophobia.[133]

The contextual application of universal rights concepts will require some translation in settings where there is resistance to the concept or language of human rights. For example, Ilumoka points out that 'freedom and justice has more resonance amongst the "masses"' in Africa whereas the language of rights tends to be used primarily among the political elite.[134] Carolyn Heitmeyer and Maya Unnithan similarly highlight that women in India rarely frame the ability to control their own fertility in the language of reproductive rights.[135] Engle Merry introduced the concept of vernacularisation to explain how civil society organisations translate human rights ideas into the local language in order to realise human rights in a way that resonates.[136] Social movements pursue legal and non-legal avenues in pushing for the realisation of human rights, which can include counter-hegemonic strategies such as protest as well as engagement with human rights mechanisms.[137] While some movements explicitly refer to human rights and international documents, others reframe their claims in alternative terms – including calls for justice or democracy.[138] I return to this point in chapter five to consider how abortion rights movements can effectively translate the human right to abortion to resonate in specific socio-cultural contexts.

Attention to human rights pluralism (both in terms of legal orders and efforts to realise human rights standards) allows for a more accurate and cross-culturally appropriate understanding of human rights. Engle Merry highlights the existing pluralism of the global legal order with its proliferation of treaties, recommendations, guidelines, and other forms of soft law.[139] She also highlights that 'although human rights conventions are technically legally binding on states that ratify them, like most laws they are enforced largely by influence, social and economic pressures, and threats to national

[131] Jasmin Zine, 'Between Orientalism and Fundamentalism: The Politics of Muslim Women's Feminist Engagement' (2006) 3(1) *Muslim World Journal of Human Rights* 1, 15.

[132] ibid 15–16.

[133] ibid 1–2.

[134] Ilumoka, 'African Women's Economic' (1994) (n 38) p 319.

[135] Carolyn Heitmeyer and Maya Unnithan, 'Bodily Rights and Collective Claims: The Work of Legal Activists in Interpreting Reproductive and Maternal Rights in India' (2015) 21 *Journal of the Royal Anthropological Institute* 374, 375.

[136] Sally Engle Merry, *Human Rights and Gender Violence* (The University of Chicago Press, 2006) p 5.

[137] Zoe L Tongue, 'Protest as Counter-Hegemonic Human Rights Work: Lessons from Abortion Rights Movements' *Heidelberg Journal of International Law*, forthcoming.

[138] ibid.

[139] Sally Engle Merry, 'Global Legal Pluralism and the Temporality of Soft Law' (2014) 46(1) *Journal of Legal Pluralism and Unofficial Law* 108, 109.

reputations.'[140] Human rights pluralism can allow for an examination of the 'limits to the ideological power of state law'[141] to which the human rights framework has typically been concerned with, and instead refocuses back on specific and localised actions – including opposition to the state for its rights violations, alternative modes of human rights organising, and the subversion of oppressive state law. Moreover, human rights pluralism recognises that different issues will be prioritised in different localised settings, and may take on the shape or language that is most resonant in that time and place. While human rights law provides a useful basis for this as a 'political technology,'[142] an understanding of grassroots efforts to realise human rights accounts for the cross-cultural application of rights norms without imposing imperialist dialogue on human rights issues. Thus, a feminist transformation of human rights must necessarily be pluralistic in approach.

V. THE IMPORTANCE OF SOCIO-ECONOMIC RIGHTS

A. Socio-Economic Rights in the International Human Rights Framework

Socio-economic rights are central to the cross-cultural realisation of gender-based rights. However, the international human rights framework has typically prioritised civil and political (CP) rights over economic, social, and cultural (ESC) rights. While there is an overlap between these categories and many human rights issues, such as abortion, cut across both, this divide has been entrenched within regional and international human rights systems. The European Convention on Human Rights (ECHR) contains only CP rights, and the European Social Charter, the socio-economic counterpart to the ECHR, was passed by the Council of Europe over 10 years after the ECHR and remains the lesser-known instrument.[143] The American Convention on Human Rights (AHRC) includes one provision that allows for ESC rights – the Article 26 right to progressive development. However, this article is broad, vague, and does not carry the same legal status or obligations as the CP rights contained in the AHRC.[144] Thus, this 'weak obligation' is viewed as a normative compromise by permitting the inclusion of ESC rights without placing them on an equal footing with CP rights.[145]

[140] ibid 108.

[141] Sally Engle Merry, 'Legal Pluralism' (1988) 22(5) *Law and Society Review* 869, 890.

[142] Filippo M Zerilli, 'The Rule of Soft Law' (2010) 56 *Focaal* 3, 8.

[143] Council of Europe, *European Convention for the Protection of Human Rights and Fundamental Freedoms* (4 November 1950, entered into force 3 September 1953) ETS 5; Council of Europe, *European Social Charter* (18 October 1961, entered into force 26 February 1965) ETS 35.

[144] Ludovic Hennebel and Hélenè Tigeoudja, *The American Convention on Human Rights: A Commentary* (Oxford, Oxford University Press, 2022) ch 3.

[145] ibid p 758.

At the UN level, the Universal Declaration of Human Rights (UDHR) contains both categories of rights[146] but during the process to transform the UDHR into binding obligations, ideological disputes arose between Western powers and Eastern Europe. The conception of human rights emerging from Western liberalism prioritised individual rights concerning property and political participation, whereas communist Eastern Soviet states emphasised the importance of socio-economic considerations. The tensions between the East and West in the wake of the Cold War prevented the creation of one unified Covenant, so the UDHR was split into two treaties, the International Covenant on Civil and Political Rights (ICCPR) and the International Covenant on Economic, Social, and Cultural Rights (ICESCR). The drafters of both the UDHR and ICESCR also aimed to differentiate their conception of ESC rights from those of Eastern Europe. For example, Eleanor Roosevelt, in her 1948 Paris speech upon the adoption of the UDHR, said that:

> I think the best example one can give of this basic difference of the use of terms is 'the right to work'. The Soviet Union insists that this is a basic right which it alone can guarantee because it alone provides full employment by the government. But the right to work in the Soviet Union means the assignment of workers to do whatever task is given to them by the government without an opportunity for the people to participate in the decision that the government should do this. [...] We in the United States have come to realize it means freedom to choose one's job, to work or not to work as one desires.[147]

Thus, individual liberal choice was emphasised in relation to ESC rights. Several commentators have linked the historical development of the international human rights framework to the rise of neoliberalism.[148] Where liberalism supported free-market capitalism and state non-interference, neoliberalism modified this economic agenda to view the role of the state as one of facilitator in the operation and expansion of global capitalism.[149] Jessica Whyte argues that neoliberalism and human rights converged as neoliberal thinkers 'mobilised and developed the language associated with [human rights] for their own ends.'[150]

Whyte argues that neoliberals saw the international human rights framework as a threat to market expansion, and in response sought to redefine human

[146] United Nations General Assembly, *Universal Declaration of Human Rights* (10 December 1948) Resolution 217 A (III).

[147] Eleanor Roosevelt, 'The Struggle for Human Rights' (28 September 1948). Available at The Eleanor Roosevelt Papers Project, https://erpapers.columbian.gwu.edu/struggle-human-rights-1948 accessed 9 January 2026.

[148] See, eg, Jessica Whyte, *The Morals of the Market* (Verso, 2019); Susan Marks, 'Four Human Rights Myths' in David Kinley, Wojciech Sadurski, and Kevin Walton (eds), *Human Rights: Old Problems, New Possibilities* (Edward Elgar, 2013); Naomi Klein, *The Shock Doctrine: The Rise of Disaster Capitalism* (Henry Holt, 2007).

[149] Paul O'Connell, 'On Reconciling Irreconcilables: Neo-liberal Globalisation and Human Rights' (2007) 7(3) *Human Rights Law Review* 483, 492.

[150] Whyte, *The Morals of the Market* (2019) (n 148) p 5.

rights to exclude social protections.[151] The rights contained in the UDHR are 'anathema to neo-liberal orthodoxy' given that neoliberals do not view basic needs such as healthcare, housing, or food as human rights.[152] Under neoliberalism, it is the individual – not the state – who is responsible for meeting their own needs, so where 'one might argue that the denial of adequate health care to a particular group emanated from a structural denial of human rights, neoliberals see failures by individual consumers to make adequate provision for their own health-care needs'.[153] This line of thinking was observed by Phillip Alston on his visit to the US, where the poor are demonised, stereotyped as lazy and dishonest, and racially profiled, and internalise these narratives to 'proudly resist applying for benefits to which they are entitled and struggle valiantly to survive against the odds.'[154] In this context, scholars claim that socio-economic rights have been recast as market-friendly, minimalist living standards which are compatible with neoliberalism, standing in opposition to substantive material entitlements.[155]

As a result of this thinking, the ICESCR imposes weaker obligations on states than the ICCPR. The ICCPR requires that each State Party 'undertakes to *respect and to ensure to all individuals* within its territory and subject to its jurisdiction the rights recognized in the present Covenant' including an obligation to take the necessary steps 'to adopt such laws or other measures as may be necessary to give effect to' the rights contained in the Covenant.[156] However, the ICESCR contains a less immediate obligation, requiring that each State Party

> *undertakes to take steps*, individually and through international assistance and co-operation, especially economic and technical, to the maximum of its available resources, with a view to *achieving progressively the full realization of the rights* recognized in the present Covenant by all appropriate means, including particularly the adoption of legislative measures.[157]

Whereas the ICCPR requires that states commit to the realisation of all of the rights contained in the Covenant, the ICESCR only requires states to commit to taking steps towards protecting ESC rights. This allows some states to stroll rather than stride towards full compliance.

Further, the ICCPR states that the rights it contains must be ensured to all 'without distinction of any kind, such as race, colour, sex, language, religion,

[151] ibid p 40.
[152] O'Connell, 'On Reconciling Irreconcilables' (2007) (n 149) 498.
[153] ibid 497.
[154] Philip Alston, 'Statement on Visit to the USA, by Professor Phillip Alston, United Nations Special Rapporteur on extreme poverty and human rights' (15 December 2017) www.ohchr.org/en/statements/2017/12/statement-visit-usa-professor-philip-alston-united-nations-special-rapporteur?LangID=E&NewsID=22533 accessed 9 January 2026, para 37.
[155] Whyte (n 148) pp 99–101; Paul O'Connell, 'The Death of Socio-Economic Rights' (2011) 74(4) *Modern Law Review* 532, 533.
[156] United Nations General Assembly, *International Covenant on Civil and Political Rights* (16 December 1966, entered into force 23 March 1976) 999 UNTS 171, Article 2(1)–(2) [emphasis added].
[157] ICESCR (n 9) Article 2(1) [emphasis added].

political or other opinion, national or social origin, property, birth or other status.'[158] The ICESCR contains the same statement on non-discrimination, but is followed by a limitation: 'Developing countries, with due regard to human rights and their national economy, may determine *to what extent they would guarantee the economic rights* recognized in the present Covenant *to non-nationals*.'[159] This might be explained in terms of the resources required to ensure each set of rights; where CP rights can be framed as negative rights in the sense that they require state non-interference, ESC rights are positive rights as their realisation requires states to take substantive measures.[160] ESC rights are, therefore, seen as expensive rights to guarantee. For example, the right to health (Article 12 ICESCR) requires the infrastructure, equipment, and personnel to provide healthcare for every member of the population, and additionally requires healthcare to be accessible, affordable, and culturally appropriate. Low- and middle-income states may not have the resources available to guarantee every right contained in the ICESCR, and the distinction made between the two categories of rights may be necessary to ensure that states are not held at fault for failing to protect human rights in circumstances where they are unable to.

However, aside from the provision in relation to non-nationals, the ICESCR makes no other clear distinction between low, lower-middle, upper-middle, and high-income states.[161] States with the financial capacity to guarantee all (or most) of the contained rights are not subject to a stronger obligation, nor does the ICESCR require states to ensure that an appropriate proportion of their resources are directed towards the protection of ESC rights. The obligation that states progressively realise ESC rights to the maximum of their *available* resources leaves it to states to decide how much of their resources they want to make available, with the result that ESC rights are granted weak protection even in high-income states with the resource capacity to fully comply. While the Committee on Economic, Social, and Cultural Rights (CESCR) has elaborated in General Comments on the obligations on states to progressively realise ESC rights, including the implementation of national strategies for accountability and cost-effective resource allocation, these documents are not legally binding.[162] This is an issue when faced with States Parties which have the resources to robustly protect ESC rights but lack the political will to do so.

[158] ICCPR (n 156) Article 2(1).

[159] ICESCR (n 9) Article 2(2)–(3) [emphasis added].

[160] Where the infrastructure does not already exist, civil and political rights do also require positive measures. The right to a fair trial under Article 14 ICCPR, for example, would require the existence of an independent judiciary, an appeals system, and access to the courts, amongst other things.

[161] The World Bank classifies economies into these four groups, determined by gross national income per capita. These groupings are imperfect but are useful in relation to this discussion on resource-distribution. See: World Bank Data Team, 'New World Bank Country Classifications by Income Level: 2022–2023' (*World Bank Blogs*, 1 July 2022) https://blogs.worldbank.org/opendata/new-world-bank-country-classifications-income-level-2022-2023 accessed 9 January 2026.

[162] See, eg, CESCR, 'General Comment No 9 on the Domestic Application of the Covenant' (3 December 1998) UN Doc E/C.12/1998/24; CESCR, 'General Comment No. 12 on the Right to Adequate Food (Article 11)' (12 May 1999) UN Doc E/C.12/1999/5, paras 21–28.

For example, in November 2018, the UN Special Rapporteur on extreme poverty and human rights, Phillip Alston, visited the UK and found that, despite residing in the world's fifth largest economy, 14 million people (amounting to one fifth of the population) live in poverty.[163] Alston observed increasing child and pensioner poverty, homelessness and housing insecurity, a falling life expectancy for certain groups, cuts to welfare provision for people with disabilities, and reductions to social services including mental health care.[164] Poverty in the UK had disproportionately affected 'women, racial and ethnic minorities, children, single parents, persons with disabilities and members of other historically marginalized groups'.[165] Alston linked this increasing level of poverty to the welfare reforms and austerity measures put in place by the Conservative Party since entering into Government in 2010, which 'deliberately gutted local authorities and thereby effectively eliminated many social services' despite the fact that the UK had a 'booming economy'.[166] The COVID-19 pandemic and the current 'cost of living crisis' have exacerbated this situation in the few years following Alston's assessment.[167] Cuts to economic support for people with disabilities has meant that families including at least one disabled person are far more likely to experience deep poverty than those without.[168] As Alston noted, the infringement of ESC rights here is the result of political and economic choices, rather than a genuine inability to take those steps.

Efforts have been made to allow for the justiciability of ESC rights in the same way as CP rights. While the splitting of the UDHR into two Covenants was on the understanding that ESC rights would remain judicially unenforceable, in 2013, the Optional Protocol (OP) to the ICESCR came into force, allowing individuals and groups to bring communications on violations to the CESCR, as has been the case under the ICCPR since its inception.[169] The European Committee on Social Rights is likewise able to hear individual complaints, but only since 1998 – much later than the creation of the European Court of Human Rights

[163] HRC, 'Visit to the United Kingdom of Great Britain and Northern Ireland: Report of the Special Rapporteur on Extreme Poverty and Human Rights' (23 April 2019) UN Doc A/HRC/41/39/Add.1, para 3.

[164] ibid paras 3–4.

[165] ibid para 67.

[166] ibid paras 5, 95.

[167] See, eg, Sophie Boobis and Francesca Albanese, 'The Impact of COVID-19 on People Facing Homelessness and Service Provision Across Great Britain' (*Crisis*, 19 November 2020); Charlie Berry and Mike Thompson, 'Shelter Briefing: Cost of Living Crisis and the Housing Emergency' (*Shelter*, 7 September 2022).

[168] Peter Matejic and Tom Clark, 'From Disability to Destitution' (*Joseph Rowntree Foundation*, 2022).

[169] Eibe Riedel, Gilles Giacca, and Christophe Golay, 'The Development of Economic, Social, and Cultural Rights in International Law' in Eibe Riedel, Gilles Giacca, and Christophe Golay (eds), *Economic, Social, and Cultural Rights in International Law* (Oxford, Oxford University Press, 2014) p 7; UN General Assembly, *Optional Protocol to the International Covenant on Economic, Social, and Cultural Rights* (5 March 2009, entered into force 5 May 2013) A/RES/63/117; UN General Assembly, *Optional Protocol to the International Covenant on Civil and Political Rights* (19 December 1966, entered into force 23 March 1976) 999 UNTS 171.

in 1959.[170] However, the use of these mechanisms is much more limited than for their CP counterparts. While the ICCPR and ICESCR have almost equal numbers of States Parties (173 and 171 respectively), the OP to the ICESCR, which is required for the substantive protection of rights by allowing violations to be addressed, has just 26 States Parties compared with 116 States Parties to the equivalent OP to the ICCPR.[171] The European Committee on Social Rights receives far fewer complaints than the ECtHR; it has handed down just over 1100 decisions in comparison to the ECtHR's almost 70,000.[172]

In contrast, the Inter-American and African regional human rights systems have a more progressive track record when it comes to ESC rights. While the only socio-economic right contained in the ACHR is the Article 26 right to progressive development, the Inter-American Court has taken a much more 'integrated' approach to human rights issues, developing the right to life to encompass the conditions of a dignified existence – and thus ruling on socio-economic conditions under this provision.[173] For example, in the case of *Villagrán Morales et al*, which concerned three children living on the streets in Guatemala, the Court found a violation of the right to life not only because the children were tortured and murdered at the hands of state agents, but also for the State's failure to protect them as 'persons who lived in extremely precarious socio-economic conditions and who fought to survive alone'.[174] The State, in failing to prevent them from 'living in misery', had deprived them of 'the minimum conditions for a dignified life'.[175] The Court has continued to develop its conception of a dignified life, implementing measures that uphold ESC rights by expanding upon CP rights.[176]

The African framework likewise takes an integrated approach. The African Charter contains both categories of rights, and explicitly states in its Preamble that 'civil and political rights cannot be dissociated from economic, social and cultural rights in their conception as well as universality'.[177] In addition to rights such as to health and education, the Charter also contains a right to development:

[170] Council of Europe, *Additional Protocol to the European Social Charter Providing for a System of Collection Complaints* (adopted 9 June 1995, entered into force 1 July 1998) ETS No 158.

[171] Office of the UN High Commissioner for Human Rights, 'Status of Ratification' https://indicators.ohchr.org/ accessed 9 January 2026.

[172] Olivier De Schutter and Matthias Sant'Ana, 'The European Committee of Social Rights (the ECSR)' in Gauthier de Beco (ed), *Human Rights Monitoring Mechanisms of the Council of Europe* (Routledge, 2012) p 73; European Social Charter, 'HUDOC' https://hudoc.esc.coe.int/eng accessed 9 January 2026; European Court of Human Rights, 'HUDOC' https://hudoc.echr.coe.int/eng accessed 9 January 2026.

[173] Mónica Feria Tinta, 'Justiciability of Economic, Social, and Cultural Rights in the Inter-American System of Protection of Human Rights Beyond Traditional Paradigms and Notions' (2007) 29(2) *Human Rights Quarterly* 431, 437.

[174] Inter-Am Ct HR, *Villagran-Morales et al v Guatemala,* (19 November 1999), para 184.

[175] ibid para 191.

[176] Feria Tinta, 'Justiciability of Economic, Social, and Cultural Rights' (2007) (n 173) 447.

[177] African Union, *African Charter on Human and Peoples' Rights* (adopted 27 June 1981, entered into force 21 October 1986) OAU Doc CAB/LEG/67/3, rev 5.

all 'shall have the right to their economic, social and cultural development with due regard to their freedom and identity and in the equal enjoyment of the common heritage of mankind.'[178] Scholars have identified the role that this right has played in protecting marginalised groups, including alongside the right to property in relation to the eviction of an Indigenous community from their ancestral land.[179] Thus, while the separateness of CP and ESC rights within the UN and ECHR reinforces the weaker position of the latter, the work of the African and Inter-American regional systems in taking this integrated approach demonstrates the potential for ESC rights to be substantively protected and realised.

B. The Importance of an Integrated Approach

Many human rights violations experienced worldwide relate to socio-economic disadvantage. The failure of international bodies such as the UN and the Council of Europe to place ESC rights on equal footing with CP rights undermines the concept and achievement of the universality of human rights. Eibe Riedel, Gilles Giacca, and Christophe Golay have explained the importance of ESC rights as follows:

> Without minimum claim rights in working life, health protection, and education systems, and without the guarantee of an adequate standard of living, flowing from human dignity, guaranteeing a 'survival kit' that sets a minimum existence protection standard, the overall picture of human rights would be incomplete, missing out crucial dimensions of protection for the most needy, in particular marginalized and disadvantaged persons and groups of persons.[180]

In addition, as already acknowledged by the African Charter, many CP rights cannot be fully realised without their ESC counterparts. James Nickels argues that without sufficient

> protections for subsistence, basic health care and basic education, people in severe poverty will frequently be marginal rightsholders. They will be unlikely to know what rights they have or what they can do to protect them, and their extreme need and vulnerability will make them hard to protect through social political action.[181]

[178] ibid Article 22.
[179] Serges Alain Djoyou Kamga, 'The Right to Development in the African Human Rights System: The *Endorois* case' (2011) 44(2) *De Jure* 381; Serges Alain Djoyou Kamga and Charles Manga Fombad, 'A Critical Review of the Jurisprudence of the African Commission on the Right to Development' (2013) 57(2) *Journal of African Law* 196.
[180] Riedel, Giacca, and Golay, 'The Development of Economic' (2014) (n 169) p 6.
[181] James W Nickels, 'Poverty and Rights' (2005) 55 *The Philosophical Quarterly* 385, 395.

For example, the right to vote and participate in the governance of one's country (Article 21 UDHR) is limited by the powerlessness, exclusion, and deprivation of choice that is often experienced by people in extreme poverty.

The prioritisation of CP rights within the UN and ECHR correlates with the influence of Western liberalism in these systems, whereas those regions that have experienced colonial violence, exploitation, and underdevelopment – with its ongoing effects – view social, economic, and cultural concerns as of fundamental importance. Adamantia Pollis and Peter Schwab argue that the 'cultural patterns, ideological underpinnings, and developmental goals of non-Western and socialist states are markedly at variance' with the portrayal of rights in the UDHR.[182] For former colonised states, experiences of economic exploitation and political authoritarianism have influenced the subsequent development of human rights values; Pollis highlights that the individual liberties of CP rights were 'hardly the values which the colonialists transmitted to the peoples over whom they ruled'.[183] In these states, ESC rights tend to be given precedence as human dignity has become linked to welfare supports, freedom from starvation, and the rights of all people to benefit from economic growth.[184] In the context of the displacement and erasure of cultural values, practices, and customs, cultural rights have likewise become important. Thus, the African Charter explicitly contains, in addition to the right to development discussed above, the right of colonised or oppressed peoples to 'free themselves from the bonds of domination' including political, economic, or cultural domination.[185] Any transformation of the human rights framework must therefore offer strong protections for ESC rights if it is to be genuinely universal and cross-culturally relevant.

In terms of a *feminist* transformation, scholars have also highlighted the importance of ESC rights in addressing gender-based human rights issues, given that major forms of gender inequality operate within the economic, social, and cultural spheres.[186] Reilly, for example, argues that:

> In most societies women are still expected to carry the responsibility of caring for dependent family members (children, elderly, people with disabilities, etc) and accessing basic goods and services on behalf of the family, including food, water, accommodation, healthcare, education etc. The privatization of basic goods and services makes them unaffordable to many and increases the pressures on women to work longer hours in order to earn more income and/or absorb a greater burden of unpaid social care. Further, reduced public and social spending exacerbates female

[182] Adamantia Pollis and Peter Schwab, 'Human Rights: A Western Construct with Limited Applicability' in Adamantia Pollis and Peter Schwab (eds), *Human Rights: Cultural and Ideological Perspectives* (Praeger, 1979) p 14.

[183] Adamantia Pollis, 'Human Rights, Third World Socialism and Cuba' (1981) 9(9/10) *World Development* 1005, 1007.

[184] ibid 1013.

[185] African Union (n 177) Article 20.

[186] Charlesworth, Chinkin, and Wright (n 2) 635; Bunch (n 1) 488.

> poverty and makes girls and women particularly vulnerable to forced migration, forced prostitution, trafficking and a wide range of related abuses.[187]

This is a broad generalisation, and these socio-economic inequalities will not be experienced by all women, but inequalities are deepened by the intersection of gender and socio-economic disadvantage or class. Frances Raday therefore argues that the neoliberal rejection of the redistributive character of ESC rights works to undermine gender equality efforts, by creating 'market conditions which make women's equal opportunity in economic and labor markets in theory axiomatic but in practice unattainable'.[188] The strengthening of protection for ESC rights is therefore of significant importance for the realisation of gender-based rights, including for reproductive rights – as will be explored in chapter three, reproductive decision-making, and the means to exercise it, relates heavily to one's social, economic, and cultural context.

A feminist transformation of human rights must therefore adopt an integrated approach to these two categories of rights. There is already some recognition of this within the UN context; the Vienna Declaration of 1993 stressed that all human rights are 'universal, indivisible, and interdependent and interrelated' and that they must be treated by the international community 'in a fair and equal manner, on the same footing, and with the same emphasis.'[189] The Human Rights Committee has addressed issues of health, such as reproductive rights, under the right to life, and recently expanded its notion of the right to life to mean a 'dignified life'[190] – thus moving towards the approach already taken by the AHRC. However, these efforts will continue to be undermined by the issues explored above – and in particular by the balance that the human rights framework attempts to strike with neoliberal political and economic systems.

Despite the incompatibility of socio-economic rights with neoliberal economic systems which discourage state provision, the CESCR claims a neutral position, stating in its General Comment 3 that

> in terms of political and economic systems the Covenant is neutral and its principles cannot accurately be described as being predicated exclusively upon the need for, or the desirability of a socialist or a capitalist system, or a mixed, centrally planned, or laisser-faire economy, or upon any other particular approach.[191]

[187] Reilly (n 24) p 32

[188] Frances Raday, 'Gender and Democratic Citizenship: The Impact of CEDAW' (2012) 10(2) *ICON* 512, 516, 525.

[189] United Nations (n 16) para 5.

[190] See *Norma v Ecuador* (2025) UN Doc CCPR/C/142/D/3628/2019, para 11.7; *Susana v Nicaragua* (2025) UN Doc CCPR/C/142/D/3626/2019, para 8.5; *Lucía v Nicaragua* (2025) UN Doc CCPR/C/142/D/3628/2019, para 8.5.

[191] CESCR, 'General Comment No 3: The Nature of States Parties' Obligations (Art 2, para 1 of the Covenant)' (14 December 1990) UN Doc E/1991/23, para 8 [emphasis added].

I thus disagree with those scholars who argue that the human rights framework actively supports neoliberalism,[192] and instead argue that the framework has failed to address socio-economic inequalities by remaining neutral on this point. Samuel Moyn similarly argues that human rights have failed to challenge neoliberalism through their failure to meaningfully tackle material inequality – but that it could be theoretically possible for human rights to offer resistance to neoliberal policies.[193]

ESC rights violations cannot be seen as unconnected to political and economic systems, and the deliberate distributions of power and resources within those systems. Alan Gewirth links economic rights to political rights and institutions, arguing that 'the hunger, malnutrition, disease, poverty, and illiteracy that plague millions of human beings throughout the world reflect distributions of power that are unjust' and that these injustices are generated and solidified by the power of the dominant group.[194] Protection for ESC rights within a transformed human rights framework would require, at least progressively, states to take steps towards realising political and economic conditions that support fulfilment. It is generally accepted that certain CP rights, such as the right to vote or the right to own property, require the political background or economic conditions to fulfil those rights.[195] Where certain political and economic circumstances are required to fulfil ESC rights, this must also be acknowledged by the human rights framework. While neoliberal systems discourage state provision of resources, the state is instrumental for the protection of ESC rights, as governments will generally have the institutional capacity to redistribute resources in order to assist those in need. Furthermore, effective rights protection requires addressing widespread structural issues resulting from political and economic choices. Gewirth argues that the duties arising in relation to human rights also apply 'to situations where threats to freedom and well-being arise from social or institutional contexts, such as where economic or political conditions make for unemployment, homelessness, or persecution.'[196] The aim of human rights is thus to equip all people with the ability to protect their rights from 'the hardships of political oppression and severe economic deprivation and to attain their opposites.'[197]

Gewirth also argues that resource concerns should not be used to exempt governments from compliance with the requirements of human rights, as where complete fulfilment is not possible, progressive steps towards compliance must be taken.[198] As already discussed above, the current approach to progressive

[192] See, eg, Whyte (n 148); Marks 'Four Human Rights Myths' (2013) (n 148); Klein, *The Shock Doctrine* (2007) (n 148).
[193] Samuel Moyn, *Not Enough: Human Rights in an Unequal World* (Harvard University Press, 2018) pp 175–76.
[194] Gewirth (n 114) p 227.
[195] ibid p 68.
[196] ibid p 41.
[197] ibid p 228.
[198] ibid p 67.

realisation places insufficient pressure on higher-income states to reach full compliance, who may illegitimately claim resource limitations to avoid doing so. ESC rights do have minimum core obligations – a baseline standard that must be met by all states. In relation to the right to health, for example, all states must provide basic, essential healthcare services.[199] However, international law 'fails to specify the kinds of health services that should be considered to fall within the ambit of minimum core obligations'[200] and leaves their mode of delivery at the state's discretion. Healthcare must be accessible without discrimination within 'a public, private or mixed health insurance system which is affordable for all'.[201] Private for-profit healthcare services can fill the gaps left in state provision, but result in a marked difference in access and quality between private and public-run facilities, thus widening healthcare inequalities.[202] The impact of this on access to abortion services will be explored in chapter four.

Thus, further guidance is required on the minimum core obligations of ESC rights and the steps that states must take towards full compliance. The CESCR's General Comments provide some guidance, but they are ultimately non-binding recommendations and are mostly subject to progressive realisation. In socialist nations, which have typically prioritised the realisation of ESC rights, human rights documents detail more clearly the obligations and duties placed on the state. For example, the right to health contained in the Constitution of Cuba stipulates that '[p]ublic health is a right of all people and it is the State's responsibility to guarantee access to quality medical attention, protection, and recovery services, free of charge.'[203] The Article goes on to specify that the state, 'in order to effectuate this right, institutes a healthcare system at all levels that is accessible to the population and develops prevention and education programs'.[204] In relation to those rights that are not immediately realisable, the Constitution nonetheless specifies how the state will take steps towards it – under the right to shelter, the state 'works to make this right effective through shelter construction programs, with the participation of entities and of the population'.[205]

This example is not intended as wholly enthusiastic praise for Cuba's approach to human rights; Octavio Gómez-Dantés argues that Cuba's health system cannot be considered progressive with its 'limited concern for civil

[199] CESCR, 'General Comment No 14 on the Right to the Highest Attainable Standard of Health (Article 12 ICESCR)' (11 August 2000) UN Doc E/C.12/2000/4, para 12.

[200] Lisa Forman and others, 'What Could a Strengthened Right to Health Bring to the Post-2015 Health Development Agenda?: Interrogating the Role of the Minimum Core Concept in Advancing Global Health Needs' (2013) 13(48) *BMC International Health and Human Rights* 1, 2.

[201] CESCR, 'General Comment No 14' (n 199) para 36.

[202] Rossella De Falco and others, 'Assessing the Human Rights Framework on Private Health Care Actors and Economic Inequality' (2023) 25(2) *Health and Human Rights Journal* 125; Anya Devaja, 'Healthcare Inequalities: The Unintended Consequences of Private Healthcare Policy?' (2013) 105(6) *Bulletin, Royal College of Surgeons England* 272.

[203] Constitution of Cuba Article 72. English translation available at: Constitute Project, 'Cuba 2019' www.constituteproject.org/constitution/Cuba_2019 accessed 9 January 2026.

[204] ibid.

[205] ibid Article 71.

liberties and certain human rights that are considered a core component of a responsive, transparent, and accountable health system.'[206] However, I use this as an example of how binding obligations in relation to ESC rights can be incorporated into human rights treaties – with a clear minimum core content stipulated within the right itself. A system of progressive realisation that imposes clearer and more robust obligations on those states with the resources to meet them would strengthen the position of ESC rights in international human rights law. This will inform my approach to developing a framework for the human right to abortion in the following chapter.

This, however, still leaves the issue of lower-income states being unable to ever achieve full compliance. Lisa Forman et al argue that the failure of international organisations to clarify the obligations on wealthier states to assist lower-income states in meeting minimum core standards undermines the minimum core content of rights.[207] The issue of assistance for states in need in the current human rights framework has also been addressed by Lawrence Gostin and Robert Archer, who consider to what extent governments (where they have the capacity to do so, in addition to fulfilling their obligations to their own citizens) have a responsibility to assist underdeveloped states.[208] They consider the requirement of 'international cooperation' under the UDHR, arguing that the states' commitments to cooperate generate obligations to assist states in need where they can intervene effectively.[209] However, in acknowledging that states must prioritise the needs of their own citizens and are thus more likely to assist where it is in their own interest, Gostin and Archer argue that international assistance is uneven and inadequate.[210] They consider that governments are likely to cooperate in relation to global pandemic responses which may require coordinated vaccination programmes.[211] In contrast, states are less likely to offer assistance in tackling issues such as high maternal mortality rates as it is not in their self-interest to do so.[212] The requirement of 'international cooperation' currently imposes no clear obligations on states to offer consistent assistance. Forman et al thus call for the development of obligations around state assistance, in addition to the further development of the minimum core standards of ESC rights.[213] The development of obligations on higher-income states to help lower-income states would also give greater force to a broader range of rights that are not considered here, such as the right to development, refugee rights,

[206] Octavio Gómez-Dantés, 'The Dark Side of Cuba's Health System: Free Speech, Rights of Patients, and Labor Rights of Physicians' (2018) 4(3) *Health Systems and Reform* 175.

[207] Forman et al, 'What Could a Strengthened Right' (2013) (n 200) 2.

[208] Lawrence O Gostin and Robert Archer, 'The Duty of States to Assist Other States in Need: Ethics, Human Rights, and International Law' (2007) 35(4) *Journal of Law Medicine and Ethics* 526, 527.

[209] ibid 527.

[210] ibid 531.

[211] ibid 530.

[212] ibid 531.

[213] Forman et al (n 200) 8.

and environmental rights – thus strengthening the ability of human rights to respond to broader socio-economic and political inequalities, as well as advancing the realisation of those rights already contained in the ICESCR.

VI. CONCLUSION

In this chapter, I have set out three key conceptual issues within the international human rights framework that must also be addressed for the realisation of the right to abortion and other gender-based rights. I addressed each of these issues by adopting and expanding upon Charlotte Bunch's concept of a feminist transformation of human rights. First, I argued that a feminist transformation of human rights must employ an intersectional approach which recognises gender inequalities as contextual, lending itself to the recognition of gender-based human rights which are inclusive of all women, trans, non-binary, and gender-expansive people. Second, while rejecting cultural relativist claims against universalism, I argued that a feminist transformation of human rights must also address issues of cross-cultural traction. Human rights can remain conceptually universal, while their application is sensitive to cultural difference and inclusive of cultural accommodations. Finally, I argued that a feminist transformation of human rights must also strengthen the protection that is afforded to ESC rights, as these rights are indivisible from CP rights in terms of their importance, are a fundamental part of gender-based rights, and are necessary for cross-cultural traction. The following chapter will demonstrate a feminist transformation of human rights in the context of abortion, thus addressing these three broad conceptual issues and the limitations of current international human rights standards on abortion.

3

A Human Right to Abortion

I. INTRODUCTION

IN THIS CHAPTER, I draw on feminist approaches in order to put forward a framework for the recognition of a human right to abortion. In this monograph, as explained in the Introduction, I adopt the position that abortion is essential healthcare and a human right. Feminist scholars have critiqued the traditional starting point that abortion must be justified or legitimised, and question the 'discursive tropes' that are applied to do so.[1] Thus, I will not be directly addressing anti-abortion arguments, instead choosing to ground my proposed framework for recognising a human right to abortion in intersectional feminist perspectives. I draw on feminist arguments in support of abortion, building the argument that restrictions on abortion are harmful along four fronts: first, that they impact the pregnant person's health and bodily autonomy; second, that they ignore the relational context of pregnancy and abortion decisions; third, that this denial can be recognised as an embodied harm or violation; and fourth, that this embodied harm undermines the citizenship of pregnant people. This has significant implications for human rights, and if abortion is – as I argue it is – necessary for the relational and embodied wellbeing, health, and citizenship status of people capable of becoming pregnant, then abortion is a fundamental right.

Combining this argument with the critiques of the human rights framework's current approach I advanced in the previous two chapters, this requires the recognition of an explicit legal right to abortion by international human rights bodies. To avoid the harms associated with restrictions on access to abortion, such a right must be expansive. However, given the contested position of abortion in global and domestic politics, there are practical limitations – such as resource constraints, opposition to abortion, and global variations in abortion laws – with adopting a human right to abortion that cannot be overlooked.

[1] Katrina Kimport and Monica R McLemore, 'The Problem with "Justifying" Abortion: Why Real Reproductive Justice Cannot Be Achieved by Theorizing the Legitimacy of Abortion' (2022) 9(1) *Women's Reproductive Health* 27; Erica Millar, 'Maintaining Exceptionality: Interrogating Gestational Limits for Abortion' (2022) 31(3) *Social and Legal Studies* 439.

Thus, in this chapter I propose a framework for the progressive realisation of the right to abortion, which starts with minimum core obligations similar to those established by human rights bodies currently, and leads up to full and comprehensive compliance. In the third section of this chapter, I establish three presumptions that will ground the scope of this framework: (1) that abortion should be available on request at least in the early stages of pregnancy, and available on broad grounds throughout the rest of the pregnancy; (2) that disability and sex 'selective' abortion should not be legally prohibited but addressed by states through alternative measures; and (3) that the criminalisation of abortion violates the right to abortion. These presumptions are combined with a socio-economic rights approach which identifies obligations around state provision of abortion care, broader reproductive rights, and the removal of barriers, particularly for pregnant people from marginalised groups. The rights framework established at the end of this chapter would address the conceptual limitations with the international human rights approach framework and its approach to abortion identified in chapters one and two.

II. INCORPORATING FEMINIST PERSPECTIVES ON ABORTION

A. Health and Autonomy

The concept of bodily autonomy occupies much space in feminist thought on abortion, particularly in relation to the impact of pregnancy upon the body. Susan Sherwin, for example, argues that there is a tendency in non-feminist perspectives on abortion to view pregnancy as a 'tolerable burden'.[2] However, far from being a 'mere event'[3] or passive process that one should accept, gestation has significant impacts on the body which range from discomfort to significant and sometimes permanent harm. During pregnancy, many pregnant people experience vitamin deficiencies, nausea, vomiting, and pain in the back, hands, feet, and ankles. Pregnancy can also result in more serious issues such as varicose veins, haemorrhoids, gestational diabetes, urinary tract infections (which can lead to kidney infections), preeclampsia or high blood pressure, damage to the pelvic floor, and loss of bladder control. The latter two can be permanent.

There are then the risks of childbirth itself, which vary depending on socio-demographic status and location, but can result in complications requiring surgery, prolonged issues such as obstetric fistula, and can even be fatal. Many birthing people experience mistreatment and violence within obstetric institutions, ranging from verbal abuse and bullying to physical violence and

[2] Susan Sherwin, 'Abortion Through a Feminist Ethics Lens' (1991) 30(3) *Dialogue* 327, 333.

[3] Catriona Mackenzie, 'Abortion and Embodiment' (1992) 70(2) *Australasian Journal of Philosophy* 155.

non-consensual treatment.[4] Following childbirth, the person may then experience mental health problems such as postnatal depression, and traumatic births can result in post-traumatic stress disorder, depression, or anxiety. Being denied an abortion can also be a dehumanising and distressing experience, which again may lead to mental health issues such as depression or anxiety.[5] Christyne Neff thus argues that the physical effects of an unwanted pregnancy, in presenting risks of serious bodily injury, are similar to the effects of bodily intrusion that would be considered battery in other contexts.[6] While many of these physical impacts may be bearable for someone carrying a *wanted* pregnancy, the risks of bodily intrusion compound with the violation of one's bodily autonomy when one is denied an abortion.

Pregnancy-related risks are exacerbated by intersectional and structural inequalities. Childbirth outcomes vary for ethnic minorities and poorer people in Western countries, with Black women experiencing a higher maternal mortality rate than their white counterparts in the UK and US.[7] There are also significant global disparities in access to safe maternity care: the risks involved in pregnancy are distinctly higher in states where maternal mortality rates are high and resource constraints mean that healthcare is inaccessible or unavailable to many. This includes the US, where the overall maternal mortality rate is significantly higher than other high-income countries, in part caused by a lack of universal affordable healthcare.[8] Issues such as discrimination, living in close proximity to environmental hazards, unsafe working conditions, the unavailability of maternity leave, intimate partner violence, and poverty also increase pregnancy-related risks. Restrictions on abortion in such contexts uphold and perpetuate these inequalities: a 2021 study estimated that if abortion was banned in every state in the US, pregnancy-related deaths would increase by 21 per cent overall, and by a disproportionate 33 per cent for Black women.[9]

[4] See Rachelle Chadwick, *Bodies That Birth: Vitalizing Birth Politics* (Routledge, 2018); Camilla Pickles and Jonathan Herring (eds), *Childbirth, Vulnerability, and Law* (Routledge, 2019).

[5] Diane Greene Foster and others, 'A Comparison of Depression and Anxiety Symptom Trajectories Between Women Who Had an Abortion and Women Denied One' (2015) 45(10) *Psychological Medicine* 2073.

[6] Christyne Neff, 'Woman, Womb, and Bodily Integrity' (1990) 3 *Yale Journal of Law and Feminism* 327, 349.

[7] Allison Felker and others (eds), 'Saving Lives, Improving Mothers' Care: Lessons Learned to Inform Maternity Care from the UK and Ireland Confidential Enquiries into Maternal Deaths and Morbidity 2021–23' (MBRRACE-UK, 11 September 2025) www.npeu.ox.ac.uk/mbrrace-uk/reports/maternal-reports/maternal-report-2021-2023 accessed 9 January 2026; Donna L Hoyert, 'Maternal Mortality Rates in the United States, 2023' (*National Centre for Health Statistics*, 1 May 2025) www.cdc.gov/nchs/data/hestat/maternal-mortality/2023/Estat-maternal-mortality.pdf accessed 9 January 2026.

[8] Munira Z Gunja, Evan D Gumas, and Reginald D Williams II, 'The US Maternal Mortality Crisis Continues to Worsen: An International Comparison' (*The Commonwealth Fund*, 1 December 2022) www.commonwealthfund.org/blog/2022/us-maternal-mortality-crisis-continues-worsen-international-comparison accessed 9 January 2026.

[9] Amanda Jean Stevenson, 'The Pregnancy-Related Mortality Impact of a Total Abortion Ban in the United States: A Research Note on Increased Deaths Due to Remaining Pregnant' (2021) 58(6) *Demography* 2019.

Many feminist scholars take the view that pregnant people should be able to decide for themselves when an abortion would be appropriate, without restriction or interference. Some reject the idea that the foetus has moral status in making this argument: Mary Warren, for example, argued that the foetus has no moral status until it becomes an independent being after birth, so abortion is morally permissible right up until that point.[10] Other scholars argue that even if the foetus had full moral status, this would not trump the pregnant person's right to bodily autonomy. The most well-known iteration of this argument is Judith Jarvis Thomson's 'famous violinist' analogy. The analogy begins with the premise that you wake up and find that the Society of Music Lovers have kidnapped you and plugged your circulatory system into that of an unconscious violinist with a fatal kidney condition.[11] If you unplug yourself, then the violinist will die; this is morally permissible because while the violinist has a right to life, they do not have a right to use your body to keep them alive.[12] Likewise, a foetus, even if it did have full moral status (though Thomson does not accept that it does), does not have the right to the use of a pregnant person's body.[13]

This connection between abortion and bodily autonomy has grounded many feminist arguments in favour of access to abortion, but autonomy in the context of reproduction also goes beyond conceptions of bodily integrity to encompass self-determination over significant personal events, in line with the person's values and beliefs.[14] As Elizabeth Chloe Romanis argues, abortion decisions are thus about more than just bodily autonomy, encompassing decisions that extend beyond the pregnancy itself.[15] These decisions are relational, taking into account a range of different circumstances and factors beyond the pregnancy itself. Thus, it is also necessary to frame abortion through the lenses of relationality, embodiment, and reproductive citizenship in order to account for these complexities, and as such I will use the term 'reproductive agency' rather than 'reproductive autonomy' when discussing a pregnant person's ability to make real decisions over their reproductive life.

B. Relationality

Carol Gilligan, known for her theory of moral development and the ethics of care approach, highlighted in her book *In A Different Voice* how pregnant people are likely to consider their relationship to the foetus, including projections as to

[10] Mary Anne Warren, 'The Moral Significance of Birth' (1989) 4(3) *Ethics and Reproduction* 4, 6.

[11] Judith Jarvis Thomson, 'A Defense of Abortion' (1971) 1(1) *Philosophy and Public Affairs* 47.

[12] ibid 49–50.

[13] ibid 66.

[14] Emily Jackson, *Regulating Reproduction* (Oxford, Hart Publishing, 2001) pp 6–9; Rosamund Scott, *Rights, Duties, and the Body* (Oxford, Hart Publishing, 2002) pp 61–63.

[15] Elizabeth Chloe Romanis, *Biotechnology, Gestation, and the Law* (Oxford, Oxford University Press, 2025) ch 7.

whether they would be able to care for a child once born, in deciding whether or not to have an abortion.[16] Gilligan's work and subsequent feminist thought has raised the important issue that the relational and contextual factors involved in abortion decisions are usually absent from traditional debates on abortion. Theories of relational autonomy highlight that decision-making takes place within one's personal, social, cultural, and historical contexts, and is thus dependent on our relationships with others.[17] What influences an abortion decision cannot always be neatly categorised into a specific reason, as these decisions are made in the context of a complicated multitude of factors – including one's social and environmental circumstances. This can include broader relational considerations such as the pregnant person's desires, religious or cultural values, personal relationships, socio-economic conditions, health and social needs, and many other contextual factors which can shape a decision to continue a pregnancy or not.[18] Janet Hadley, for example, argues that 'the economic pressures of a society marked by poverty, racism, poor housing, and person and institutional injustice and oppression towards women' can influence abortion decisions.[19] Abortion decisions are thus always subjective, and often complex.

This perspective also offers a challenge to the assumption that the pregnant person and foetus are separate entities which, in the context of abortion, are in conflict. In the 1980s, Rosalind Petchesky explored the imagery of an isolated foetus, never portrayed as gestated *within a body*, as a tactic of anti-abortion groups.[20] This presentation of the foetus as a 'free-floating entity' which renders the pregnant person invisible in abortion debates has been widely critiqued in the feminist literature.[21] This is referred to by Elselijn Kingma as the 'containment' view of pregnancy, which treats the pregnant person as a mere container for the foetus, which is construed as a metaphysically separate entity.[22] While some feminist commentators emphasise the relationship between the pregnant person and foetus as two separate but connected entities,[23] Kingma adopts the 'parthood' view which conceptualises the foetus as *a part of* the pregnant person rather than as a separate being.[24] Thus, the pregnant person and foetus are one

[16] Carol Gilligan, *In A Different Voice* (Harvard University Press, 1993, first pub 1982).

[17] Catriona Mackenzie and Natalie Stoljar, *Relational Autonomy* (Oxford, Oxford University Press, 2000) pp 21, 23.

[18] Rosalind Pollack Petchesky, 'Fetal Images: The Power of Visual Culture in the Politics of Reproduction' (1987) 13(2) *Feminist Studies* 263, 288; Sherwin, 'Abortion Through a Feminist Ethics Lens' (1991) (n 2) 329.

[19] Janet Hadley, *Abortion: Between Freedom and Necessity* (Virago, 1996) p 84.

[20] Petchesky, 'Fetal Images' (1987) (n 18) 268.

[21] See Mackenzie, 'Abortion and Embodiment' (1992) (n 3) 136; Sherwin (n 2) 328; Laura M Purdy, 'Are Pregnant Women Fetal Containers?' (1990) 4(4) *Bioethics* 273; Teresa Baron, 'Nobody Puts Baby in the Container: The Foetal Container Model at Work in Medicine and Commercial Surrogacy' (2018) 36(3) *Journal of Applied Philosophy* 491.

[22] Elselijn Kingma, 'Were You a Part of Your Mother?' (2019) 128 *Mind* 609, 609.

[23] Mackenzie (n 3) 136; Sherwin (n 2) 328.

[24] Kingma, 'Were You a Part' (2019) (n 22) 609–10.

entity, not two. Rodante van der Waal and Inge van Nistelrooij take the alternative approach that pregnancy is 'neither one nor two-in-one' as the boundaries between pregnant person and foetus are fluid and relational.[25]

Whether one adopts the 'parthood' or 'fluid' view of pregnancy, these approaches emphasise the relationship between the pregnant person and foetus – a relationship that abortion debates often ignore. It is this relational connection that may give rise to grief upon the ending (either intended or unintended) of a wanted pregnancy for some, but not for others, rather than resting upon the independent moral status of the foetus.[26] Van der Waal and Van Nistelrooij argue that most reproductive care adopts a relational 'severance' between the pregnant person and foetus and the pregnant person and their community, and that this is a form of structural violence.[27] This 'severing' sets up the pregnant person as a threat to their foetus – both in relation to abortion and decisions around (wanted) pregnancy-related healthcare – and in turn positions healthcare professionals' role as one of *protecting* the foetus.[28] This has been recognised as leading to obstetric violence – the mistreatment, abuse, and disrespect experienced by people obtaining reproductive healthcare, which includes forced or non-consensual treatment, physical and verbal abuse, bullying, gaslighting, silencing, discrimination, and other forms of dehumanising treatment.[29] In contrast, an embodied approach to reproduction recognises and respects the pregnant person's subjective experience and knowledge in relation to their reproductive decision-making.

C. Embodiment

Feminist scholars have also worked towards the understanding of pregnancy as an embodied experience.[30] Embodiment, defined as the tangible form of an idea, is applied as a concept for understanding how one experiences the world through their body, thus moving away from the assumed mind and body split.[31] To consider pregnancy as an embodied experience is to recognise that gestation alters the pregnant person's body, and therefore their interactions with their self

[25] Rodante van der Waal and Inge van Nistelrooij, 'Reimagining Relationality for Reproductive Care: Understanding Obstetric Violence as "Separation"' (2022) 29(5) *Nursing Ethics* 1186, 1193.

[26] See Kate Parsons, 'Feminist Reflections on Miscarriage, in Light of Abortion' (2010) 3(1) *International Journal of Feminist Approaches to Bioethics* 1.

[27] Van der Waal and van Nistelrooij, 'Reimagining Relationality' (2022) (n 25).

[28] Zoe L Tongue, 'Locating Abortion and Contraception on the Obstetric Violence Continuum' (2024) 17(1) *International Journal of Feminist Approaches to Bioethics* 1, 3.

[29] ibid 2.

[30] See Mackenzie (n 3); Imogen Tyler, 'Reframing Pregnant Embodiment' in Sara Ahmed and others (eds), *Transformations* (Routledge, 2000); Meredith Nash, *Making 'Postmodern' Mothers* (Palgrave Macmillan, 2012); Elena Neiterman, 'Doing Pregnancy: Pregnant Embodiment as Performance' (2012) 35(5) *Women's Studies International Forum* 372.

[31] Mary Wilde, 'Why Embodiment Now?' (1999) 22(2) *Global Health and Nursing Practice* 25.

and the external world. Iris Marion Young, in her influential essay on pregnant embodiment, wrote that the pregnant person 'experiences her body as herself and not herself.'[32] Young describes this as alienation, or estrangement from one's body.[33] Part of this estrangement comes from the experience of the foetus' movements as the pregnant person's movements; sensations taking place *within* themselves.[34] These bodily sensations are not experienced as separate to oneself, but as part of oneself – thus affecting the pregnant person's sense of self and the way that they move through the world.

Young was discussing a *wanted* pregnancy here, and so the alienation that comes with this embodied experience, carrying with it the bodily risks discussed above, can represent a much more visceral estrangement from one's body when a pregnant person is forced to continue an *unwanted* pregnancy. This loss of control over one's life and identity may be difficult for any pregnant person, but has additional implications for trans, non-binary, and gender expansive people for whom pregnancy (especially unwanted pregnancy) may be dysphoric.[35] Forcing the continuation of pregnancy, and therefore the bodily alterations that come with it, is an *embodied* violation.[36] To recognise this embodied harm is to go beyond merely recognising the lack of desire to have a child, but to recognise the impacts of pregnancy on one's body (beyond the strict bodily autonomy sense) and relational life. As several scholars have noted, abortion is about what makes one's life *liveable*, or about living the lives we want to live.[37] These decisions are embodied, rather than representing an exercise in thought alone.

This approach gives rise to a much more expansive understanding of harm than the threshold of suffering that human rights bodies recognise, and it thus changes the way human rights bodies ought to view the impacts of abortion restrictions. For example, Shaun Pattinson has argued that the mental health implications of an unwanted pregnancy appear serious enough to push people to risk a criminal penalty, their health, or even their life by obtaining an illegal or unsafe abortion.[38] However, the existence of clandestine abortion practices wherever abortion is restricted suggests something more than mental health. While being forced to continue an unwanted pregnancy may impact one's mental health, pregnant people do not seek abortions to avoid depression, or anxiety, or other forms of psychological distress, but to avoid unwanted pregnancy (or a pregnancy they cannot continue due to their own personal and relational

[32] Iris Marion Young, 'Pregnant Embodiment: Subjectivity and Alienation' (1984) 9(1) *Journal of Medicine and Philosophy* 45, 46.

[33] ibid 50.

[34] ibid 48; Adrienne Rich, *Of Woman Born* (Norton, 1995, first pub 1976) p 47.

[35] Juno Obedin-Maliver and Harvey J Makadon, 'Transgender Men and Pregnancy' (2016) 9(1) *Obstetric Medicine* 4.

[36] Tongue, 'Locating Abortion' (2024) (n 28) 13.

[37] Erica Millar, 'Abortion, Decriminalisation and the Medico-Legal Paradigm' (2024) 355 *Social Science and Medicine* 117098, 8; Rishita Nandagiri and others, 'Precarity and Pills in a Pandemic: Online Abortion Care-seeking in Poland During COVID-19' (2025) 8 *SSM* 100663, 10.

[38] Shaun D Pattinson, *Influencing Traits Before Birth* (Ashgate, 2002) p 75.

context) – a visceral intrusion within one's body that affects every aspect of one's life, relationships, and identity. It is this embodied and relational harm that those who have clandestine abortions are seeking to avoid. Restrictions on abortion also enact this embodied harm at a structural level, entrenching gendered stereotypes about pregnancy, abortion, and motherhood which must also be accounted for.

D. Reproductive Citizenship

Feminist scholars have identified that restrictions on abortion are not only, or even primarily, reflective of notions of morality and foetal personhood, but also of biologically essentialist ideas of women as mothers. Mary Boyle, for example, argues that seeking an abortion 'is simultaneously to make a statement about motherhood' whether intentional or not.[39] Women have traditionally been tied to their reproductive roles, generating the expectation that women have an innate maternal instinct, a desire for motherhood, or even a biological *duty* to become mothers, which the decision to have an abortion subverts.[40] In her 1976 book, Adrienne Rich distinguished between mother*ing* versus motherhood, where the former is conceptualised as a relationship of care and the latter is construed as an institution imposed upon women.[41] People capable of becoming pregnant must negotiate the imposition of motherhood through formal and informal structures – by religious and political institutions, law and policy, within reproductive and maternal healthcare delivery, within the media and popular culture, and within one's interpersonal relationships. For Michele Goodwin, restrictions on abortion are therefore connected to the historically entrenched patterns of male power and domination over women.[42] Young discussed how pregnant women are objectified in terms of their proximity to motherhood, and thus pregnant people become 'the subject of the paternal symbolic order'.[43] In this context, abortion is presented as a 'deviant' choice, portraying people that have abortions as morally deficient for rejecting the institutionalised duty of motherhood.[44]

Within Western (and Western colonised) historical contexts, women were a secondary class of citizens denied legal personhood and relegated to the private sphere.[45] Indigenous Peoples and Black women subjected to enslavement experienced specific forms of reproductive and obstetric violence, and other

[39] Mary Boyle, *Re-Thinking Abortion* (Routledge, 1997) p 28.

[40] ibid; Fran Amery, *Beyond Pro-Life and Pro-Choice* (Bristol, Bristol University Press, 2020) p 21; Sally Sheldon, *Beyond Control* (Pluto Press, 1997) p 36; Erica Millar, *Happy Abortions* (Zed, 2017) p 5.

[41] Rich, *Of Woman Born* (1995) (n 34).

[42] Michele Goodwin, *Policing the Womb* (Cambridge, Cambridge University Press, 2020) p 47.

[43] Young, 'Pregnant Embodiment' (1984) (n 32) 53.

[44] Boyle, *Re-Thinking Abortion* (1997) (n 39) pp 29, 39.

[45] See Simone de Beauvoir, *The Second Sex* (Vintage Classic, 2015, first pub 1949).

marginalised groups, including LGBTQ+ and disabled people, have been and continue to be subjected to reproductive injustice.[46] Restrictions on reproductive agency are thus also a continuation of this historical oppression, which affects pregnant people differently along intersectional lines. 'Stratified reproduction' is a term coined by Shellee Colen to describe how some groups of people (based on gender, race, class, and sexuality) are systematically encouraged to reproduce by social, cultural, and political narratives, whereas others are heavily discouraged from doing so.[47] For example, Andréa Becker's study of hysterectomy highlights how some individuals in the US (particularly people of colour and trans and non-binary people) are pushed towards the loss of fertility, whilst others (white cisgender women) are prevented from opting into infertility in the same way.[48]

In this context, restrictions on abortion can therefore be construed as a 'dignitary harm' – one which affects the dignity of women and people capable of gestating as an entire group, by relegating them to the status of 'second class citizens'.[49] This has led some feminist scholars to the concept of 'reproductive citizenship'. Rebecca Smyth, for example, argues that political and legal struggles around abortion 'are part of a much longer and deeper struggle over the conceptual and real-world implications of women realizing their full citizenship'.[50] Turner highlights the importance of citizenship in the context of sexuality, reproduction, and marriage given that the state has a public interest in the family, which thus 'plays a central part in the distribution of citizenship entitlements'.[51] The liberal understanding of citizenship has typically been a formalistic one, focused on legal entitlements to equality and rights on paper and constructing 'all citizens as basically the same and considers the differences of class, ethnicity, gender, etc, as irrelevant to their status as citizens'.[52] Even on this understanding of citizenship, scholars highlight that women are yet to achieve full citizenship, continue to be subjected to gender norms that

[46] See Rodante van der Waal and others, 'Obstetric Violence: An Intersectional Refraction through Abolition Feminism' (2023) 4(1) *Feminist Anthropology* 91; Radi Blas, 'Reproductive Injustice, Trans Rights, and Eugenics' (2020) 28(1) *Sexual and Reproductive Health Matters* 1824318; Dagmar Herzog, *Unlearning Eugenics* (University of Wisconsin Press, 2018).

[47] See Shellee Colen, '"Like a Mother to Them": Stratified Reproduction and West Indian Childcare Workers and Employers in New York' in Faye Ginsburg and Rayna Rapp (eds), *Conceiving the New World Order* (University of California Press, 2015).

[48] Andréa Becker, 'Stratified Reproduction, Hysterectomy, and the Social Process of Opting into Fertility' (2023) 37(4) *Gender and Society* 614.

[49] Zoe L Tongue, 'On Conscientious Objection to Abortion: Questioning Mandatory Referral as Compromise in the International Human Rights Framework' (2022) 22(4) *Medical Law International* 349, 363.

[50] Rebecca Smyth, 'Reproductive Citizenship' (2024) 50(1) *Signs* 189, 191.

[51] Bryan S Turner, 'Citizenship, Reproduction and the State: International Marriage and Human Rights' (2008) 12(1) *Citizenship Studies* 45, 46.

[52] Smyth, 'Reproductive Citizenship' (2024) (n 50) 196; Nira Yuval-Davis, 'Women, Citizenship and Difference' (1997) 57 *Feminist Review* 4, 8.

conflict with rights, and 'lag behind' in terms of economic, political, and social equality.[53]

Smyth argues that a transformative approach to citizenship recognises 'inter-related juridical, political, economic, and cultural practices that determine access to opportunities, resources, and meaningful recognition of one's status as a rights-holder'.[54] This requires an expansive understanding of the relationship between individuals, the state, and society, and the role of the state within this relationship, and also requires an intersectional approach, recognising the needs of different groups, including women and ethnic minorities.[55] This recognition of difference and what Nira Yuval-Davis refers to as the 'politics of belonging'[56] is particularly important given the historical denial of rights and citizenship to women and people of colour in the West.

For example, when the French Declaration on the Rights of Man and of the Citizen was passed in 1789, it applied only to 'active citizens' – defined as French men over the age of 25 who met a poll tax threshold.[57] This excluded *all* women, people of colour, and socio-economically disadvantaged men from holding civil rights, as they were defined as either 'passive citizens' or not citizens at all.[58] The argument that citizenship and civil rights should be extended to women was a key aspect of early Western feminism – in response to the French Declaration, the feminist political activist Olympe de Gouges published her Declaration on the Rights of Woman and of the Female Citizen, advocating for the extension of the French Declaration to women and the recognition of additional gender-based rights.[59] Mary Wollstonecraft similarly argued in her *Vindication of the Rights of Woman* that the moral rights held by men were also held by women, regardless of the conditions of the positive law.[60] The concept of citizenship (in a transformative sense) continues to have relevance for current feminist struggles which are about the 'right to have rights and to determine the scope of those rights'.[61]

Following from this understanding of citizenship, Smyth defines *reproductive* citizenship as 'the ongoing, contested process to realize every individual's

[53] Smyth (n 50) 197; Rosemary Nossiff, 'Gendered Citizenship: Women, Equality, and Abortion Policy' (2007) 29(1) *New Political Science* 61.

[54] Smyth (n 50) 197.

[55] Yuval-Davis, 'Women, Citizenship' (1997) (n 52) 11; Nira Yuval-Davis, 'Intersectionality, Citizenship and Contemporary Politics of Belonging' (2007) 10(4) *Critical Review of International Social and Political Philosophy* 561.

[56] Yuval-Davis, 'Intersectionality' (2007) (n 55).

[57] Jonas Ross Kjærgård, 'The Inequality of Common Utility: Active/passive Citizenship in French Revolutionary Human Rights' in Karen-Margrethe Simonsen and Jonas Ross Kjærgård (eds), *Discursive Framings of Human Rights* (Birkbeck Law Press, 2016).

[58] ibid.

[59] As a result of this publication, Olympe de Gouges was executed for political treason. See Camille Naish, *Death Comes to the Maiden: Sex and Execution 1431–1933* (Routledge, 2013, first pub 1991) ch 4.

[60] Mary Wollstonecraft's *Vindication of the Rights of Woman* (first published 1792) pp 87–88.

[61] Smyth (n 50) 209.

freedom to make decisions about their sexual and reproductive lives, and to have those decisions respected and facilitated'.[62] Reproductive citizenship is undermined by reproductive injustice, reproductive stratification, and (intersectional) gender stereotypes around motherhood, and restrictions on abortion work against the meaningful recognition of a pregnant person's agency and status as a rights-holder. The effects of this are not merely theoretical, but have a marked impact on the rest of the pregnant person's life – a recent study on the long-term impacts of being denied an abortion in Colombia found that those people experienced more health issues, lower educational attainment, reduced labour force participation, and higher rates of single motherhood, poverty, and reliance on government assistance in the 15 years following childbirth.[63] The denial of abortion rights is therefore a denial of the full citizenship of people capable of becoming pregnant. Japa Pallikkathayil thus argues, in the context of *Dobbs v Jackson* overturning the constitutional right to abortion in the first trimester, that democratic equality requires unrestricted access to 'pre-viability' abortion.[64]

However, a transformative approach to reproductive citizenship goes beyond the mere provision of legal entitlements. Turið Hermannsdóttir and Betina Dybbroe view the formation of reproductive citizenship as an embodied process: pregnant people's 'reproductive citizenship and sense of belonging are negotiated within the body: women sense, manage and negotiate their reproductive citizenship and belonging geographically, bodily and relationally'.[65] This sense of reproductive citizenship can be affected by the values underpinning reproductive policies, such as the facilitation of fertility treatments alongside restrictions on abortion in the Danish Faroe Islands placing value on motherhood but not on the right to refuse motherhood.[66] Deborah Lupton also highlights how a neoliberal view of pregnancy holds the pregnant person individually responsible for the optimal development of their foetus, creating a restrictive understanding of reproductive citizenship prefaced on self-regulation.[67] This understanding reflects a narrative of the 'good citizen' being one who 'is procreative within the context of the co-residential heterosexual, gender normative couple'.[68] The transformative approach to reproductive citizenship rejects this focus on procreative duties and self-regulation, and instead considers what is required to

[62] ibid 197.

[63] Juliana Londoño-Vélez and Estefanía Saravia, 'The Impact of Being Denied a Wanted Abortion on Women and Their Children' (2025) 140(2) *Quarterly Journal of Economics* 1061.

[64] Japa Pallikkathayil, 'Abortion and Democratic Equality' (2025) 42(2) *Journal of Applied Philosophy* 473.

[65] Turið Hermannsdóttir and Betina Dybbroe, 'Components of Reproductive Citizenship: Narratives from a Restrictive Abortion Landscape' (2023) 27(8) *Citizenship Studies* 1022, 1033.

[66] ibid 1024.

[67] Deborah Lupton, '"Precious Cargo": Foetal Subjects, Risk and Reproductive Citizenship' (2012) 22(3) *Critical Public Health* 329.

[68] Sasha Roseneil and others, 'Reproduction and Citizenship/Reproductive Citizens' (2013) 17(8) *Citizenship Studies* 901, 903.

enable, support, and respect (relationally) autonomous decision-making around reproduction.

Reproductive citizenship is thus not merely about the ability to act on one's individual preferences, but also requires social supports.[69] As discussed above, reproductive agency is limited by social, economic, and cultural contexts, and in addition to the provision of abortion services, requires states to address these wider limitations so that people capable of becoming pregnant are able to fully exercise their agency over their reproductive lives. As Yuval-Davis argues, '[s]exual and reproductive (or any other) rights, understood as private "liberties" or "choices", are meaningless, especially for the poorest and most disenfranchised, without enabling conditions through which they can be realized'.[70] Abortion is often framed within the Western liberal context as an issue of individual choice, but these decisions are often more complex than this, and many people lack the means to exercise this 'choice' – as reproductive justice scholars likewise emphasise (see Introduction).[71] Many pregnant people are in a precarious situation when it comes to abortion access – for example, in situations of unemployment, lack of housing, intimate partner violence, and many others, the lack of access to abortion 'heightens vulnerability and threatens the limited stability they may have'.[72] Thus, not only is recognition of abortion as a fundamental right essential for the status of people capable of becoming pregnant as rights-holders, but also to ensure full reproductive citizenship through provision of state support – including supports beyond healthcare provision alone. A human right to abortion must therefore encompass expansive state obligations geared towards the realisation of reproductive justice and citizenship, not merely 'choice'.

III. THE SCOPE OF A HUMAN RIGHT TO ABORTION

The remainder of this chapter proceeds from the understanding of abortion as rooted within the relational and embodied experience of an individual pregnant person, and as essential for substantive reproductive citizenship. This understanding requires a pregnant person-centred approach to abortion which calls for comprehensive and expansive access, facilitated and supported by the state. Guaranteeing the right to abortion within a feminist transformation of human rights would place substantive positive obligations on the state to make abortion broadly accessible with minimal delays. This requires addressing multiple issues: the provision of comprehensive sexual and reproductive health education and the combatting of stigma around sex, menstruation, and abortion so

[69] Jackson, *Regulating Reproduction* (2001) (n 14) pp 6–9.

[70] Yuval-Davis (n 52) 15.

[71] See Loretta J Ross and Rickie Solinger, *Reproductive Justice: An Introduction* (University of California Press, 2017); Joan C Chrisler (ed) *Reproductive Justice: A Global Concern* (Praeger, 2012).

[72] Nandagiri and others, 'Precarity and Pills' (2023) (n 37) 10.

that people may identify pregnancy early on; the provision of easily accessible pregnancy testing services; and ensuring the universal accessibility of abortion services with minimal unnecessary barriers. At a wider level, states would also have positive obligations to address structural inequalities relating to health, gender, race, and socio-economic status, among others, which undermine reproductive citizenship.

These obligations must also be responsive to different contextual issues and global inequities, including the marked differences in gender equality and socio-demographic groups facing discrimination based on caste, race, religion, nationality, disability, sexuality and gender identity, and against Indigenous Peoples. There are also significant economic disparities within and across states, with people living in poverty and states lacking the resources to provide comprehensive access to healthcare and other basic services. For states with significant rural populations, there are additional barriers to accessing healthcare services.[73] All of these issues affect access to sexual and reproductive health services, with significant variations worldwide in access to contraception, abortion, sexual and reproductive health education, and pregnancy-related healthcare, and other limitations on reproductive decision-making resulting from population policies and coercive family planning. Historical, political, religious, social, cultural, and economic factors all influence the current regulation of abortion worldwide.

Therefore, I argue that it is necessary to frame a human right to abortion as a socio-economic right which goes beyond the question of legalisation alone, and addresses the broader enabling conditions that are required for the realisation of this right. However, in this global context, it is necessary to recognise that the starting point for each state varies dramatically in terms of opposition to abortion and their ability to provide comprehensive access to abortion services. Thus, a comprehensive right to abortion must also be balanced against these limitations. At the end of this chapter, I set out a framework for the progressive realisation of the right to abortion to identify steps that states must take to work towards the universal provision of abortion services and address structural and intersectional inequalities. Building on the arguments made in chapter two on the limitations of progressive realisation in the current framework, I explicitly indicate the minimum core obligations contained in the right to abortion in line with the approaches taken by socialist constitutions. My framework proceeds of four tiers, to recognise a minimum core content in terms of the grounds on which abortion must be legalised and from there to push states to take steps towards full compliance by gradually liberalising their abortion regimes. I first

[73] See, eg, Lisa R Pruitt and Marta R Vanegas, 'Urbanormativity, Spatial Privilege, and Judicial Blind Spots in Abortion Law' (2015) 30 *Berkeley Journal of Gender Law and Justice* 76; B Subha Sri and TK Sundari Ravindran, 'Medical Abortion: Understanding Perspectives of Rural and Marginalized Women from Rural South India' (2012) 118 *International Journal of Gynecology and Obstetrics* 33.

address three key issues relating to the scope of the right to abortion: gestational time limits and grounds for the legalisation of abortion; 'selective' abortion on the grounds of foetal impairments or foetal sex; and the decriminalisation of abortion. For each of these issues, I set out a policy presumption, informed by the feminist approaches set out above, to be encompassed within my framework.

A. Grounds for Abortion and Gestational Time Limits

As covered in chapter one, international human rights bodies have avoided commenting on gestational time limits, and tend to only set out exceptional circumstances as the grounds on which states must legalise abortion. However, this fails to account for the vast majority of abortion experiences and creates a problematic distinction between 'acceptable' and 'unacceptable' abortions. While some feminist scholars would therefore see all such regulatory barriers removed, it is unlikely that individual states will stop regulating abortion in such a way that relies on gestational time limits and legal grounds, so it is necessary for international human rights law to be responsive to this practical reality. However, given the importance of access to abortion for reproductive citizenship and the status of pregnant people as rights-holders, human rights bodies must encourage states to adopt expansive regulatory responses.

The abortion on request model is viewed by many feminist scholars as preferable to a grounds-based model, which promotes the over-medicalisation of abortion in seeking to place abortion decisions firmly in the hands of doctors, rather than allowing pregnant people to make their own decisions.[74] A review of global abortion laws and policies in 2018 found that 32 per cent of countries already allow abortion on request, highlighting that there already exists some support for abortion without justification worldwide.[75] Almost all European states allow abortion on request, although most also impose gestational time limits for abortion on request, with 12 or 14 weeks as the average, though some states have a later time limit.[76] Elizabeth Chloe Romanis has distinguished between 'abortion-permissive' legal frameworks, in which abortion is legal but overly regulated, and 'abortion-supportive' legal frameworks which enable and protect access.[77] While abortion on request *can* form part of an abortion-supportive

[74] Sheldon, *Beyond Control* (1997) (n 40) p 36; Boyle (n 39) p 45; Ellie Lee, 'Psychologizing Abortion: Women's "Mental Health" and the Regulation of Abortion in Britain' in Anne Morris and Susan Nott (eds), *Well Women* (Routledge, 2018, first pub 2002).

[75] Antonella F Lavelanet and others, 'Global Abortion Policies Database: A Descriptive Analysis of the Legal Categories of Lawful Abortion' (2018) 18(44) *BMC International Health and Human Rights* 1.

[76] Center for Reproductive Rights, 'The World's Abortion Laws' https://reproductiverights.org/maps/worlds-abortion-laws/? accessed 9 January 2026.

[77] Elizabeth Chloe Romanis, 'Abortion Access and the Benefits and Limitations of Abortion-*Permissive* Legal Frameworks: Lessons from the United Kingdom' 32(3) *Cambridge Quarterly of Healthcare and Ethics* 378, 379.

framework, this must also be accompanied by measures to improve ease of access (for example, telemedicine for early medical abortion and the removal of other regulatory barriers, which will be considered in the following chapter).[78]

The early stage of pregnancy is generally taken to be the first 12 weeks' gestation, after which the foetus begins to develop characteristics such as limb movement and rudimentary brain activity. In high-income countries where abortion is both legal and accessible, the majority of abortions already take place before 12 weeks' gestation.[79] In England and Wales, for example, 89 per cent of abortions in 2021 took place at under 10 weeks.[80] This threshold is already adopted as a gestational cut-off point for abortion on request in a number of countries, and could represent an appropriate precautionary threshold for unqualified access to abortion which would accommodate the majority of abortions in legal and accessible contexts. However, there would be significant issues with applying this gestational time limit to all states, given the disparities in access and resources for middle- and lower-income countries.

As Joanna Erdman points out, there are global inconsistencies in how gestational age is measured.[81] Medical professionals may measure gestational age from the pregnant person's last menstrual period (LMP), assuming the pregnant person has kept an accurate record, by developmental age, or by uterine size, and these estimates are routinely off by a few weeks, resulting in variations in access to abortion.[82] Emily Jackson has also critiqued the fictional start date of a pregnancy relied upon in abortion provision, as the date of fertilisation or implantation is unknowable, unless reproductive technologies were used.[83] Even where the pregnant person has kept an accurate record, calculating gestational age by LMP still may mean that the pregnancy start date is estimated at a few weeks earlier than it actually was.[84] Technology such as ultrasound is required for more accurate gestational age estimation, and this requires countries, regions, and individual health facilities to have sufficient resources.

Thus, there is likely to be a pronounced variation in the accuracy of gestational age measurements worldwide, exacerbated by global inequalities in healthcare provision. For example, a study of gestational age estimation in Rajasthan, India found that LMP and fundal height measurement (the size of the pregnant person's stomach) were the most commonly used methods, despite

[78] ibid 382.

[79] Anna Popinchalk and Gilda Sedgh, 'Trends in the Method and Gestational Age of Abortion in High-Income Countries' (2018) 45(2) *BMJ Sexual and Reproductive Health* 95, 99–100.

[80] Department of Health and Social Care, 'Abortion statistics, England and Wales: 2021' www.gov.uk/government/statistics/abortion-statistics-for-england-and-wales-2021/abortion-statistics-england-and-wales-2021 accessed 9 January 2026.

[81] Joanna N Erdman, 'Theorizing Time in Abortion Law and Human Rights' (2017) 19(1) *Health and Human Rights Journal* 29, 42.

[82] ibid.

[83] Jackson (n 14) p 79.

[84] ibid.

their limited accuracy.[85] Providers were often unable to directly offer ultrasound, a more accurate method of measuring gestational age, and where ultrasound was available, this was usually only after the first trimester.[86] Imposing a rigid time limit for abortion on request therefore does not account for the variations in measuring gestational age, and even where gestational age estimation is accurate and the pregnant person requests an abortion within the gestational time frame, there may be delays of weeks until they can obtain one due to capacity or resource constraints.

Moreover, access to abortion within the first 12 weeks requires adequate sexual and reproductive health education, so that all people capable of becoming pregnant can understand the early signs of pregnancy and access pregnancy testing and abortion services without delay. Delays are also likely to be caused by the imposition of additional barriers, distances from abortion providers, socio-economic and other structural and intersectional inequalities. Pregnant people unable to access abortion services within this time limit will also likely travel to a state with an extended time limit to have an abortion or seek alternative means of terminating their pregnancy. For example, Ireland now permits abortion on request up to 12 weeks' gestation but prohibits abortion after this point unless the pregnant person's life or health is at risk or where the foetus has a fatal impairment.[87] However, pregnant people from Ireland continue to travel elsewhere to access abortion services; in 2021, 206 people travelled from Ireland to England and Wales for abortions.[88]

To guarantee access to abortion at this early stage, states should therefore be required to allow abortion on request *at least* up to 12 weeks, accompanied with obligations that states also remove barriers that may cause delays, ensure universal, consistent, and equal access to sexual and reproductive health education and services, and address inequalities in access. In addition, to minimise the potential variations and inconsistencies in measuring gestational age which impact pregnant people's ability to access abortion services in this time frame, states must ensure that accurate means of estimation (such as LMP in conjunction with ultrasound) are provided. Where states are unable to provide universal means of accurate gestational age estimation, it is necessary for those states to set a later gestational time limit for early access to abortion to account for likely misestimates which would obstruct and delay access to abortion. This need not be a legal time limit but could regulated at a regional level to account for in-state variations in resource-allocation. Aside from the difficulties with gestational age estimation, there are variations across states and regions in access to pregnancy testing and abortion and other issues such as the likelihood that people will

[85] Kerry Scott and others, '"I can guess the month … but beyond that, I can't tell" An Exploratory Qualitative Study of Health Care Provider Perspectives on Gestational Age Estimation in Rajasthan, India' (2020) 20(529) *BMC Pregnancy and Childbirth* 1.

[86] ibid.

[87] Health (Regulation of Termination of Pregnancy) Act 2018 [Ireland] ss 9–12.

[88] Department of Health and Social Care (n 80).

discover their pregnancies too late to obtain an abortion before the 12-week limit.

As it is inevitable that some pregnant people will require abortions after this point for a range of reasons, states must also ensure access to later abortions on broad grounds. There are a complex range of reasons as to why a pregnant person might require an abortion at a later stage of pregnancy. Within moral theorising on abortion, concerns are often raised that pregnant people might have later abortions for frivolous reasons, for example where the pregnancy or childbirth would interfere with their holiday arrangements.[89] However, as pointed out by Kate Greasley, late abortions are not, in practice, usually undertaken based on trivial considerations.[90] People are likely to seek an abortion as soon as they are able to, given the physical, mental, relational, and embodied burdens of carrying an unwanted pregnancy. As early abortions are generally safer, particularly where abortion pills are available, pregnant people are unlikely to wait months into the pregnancy to have an abortion, which would require that they undergo surgery.[91]

Rather, pregnant people may require access to abortion as a result of delays in accessing abortion services which take place in the context of rape (due to trauma or distress), intimate partner violence (including coercive and controlling behaviour), existing mental health problems, and being unaware of the pregnancy until a later stage.[92] Adolescents in particular may miss the early signs of pregnancy, seek to hide it from family members or guardians due to the stigmatisation of teenage pregnancy, and then may face difficulties accessing abortion services due to these issues. The lack of access to pregnancy testing and other reproductive healthcare services can cause delays to accessing abortion, and in some states, delays can also result from additional requirements such as mandatory counselling, conscientious objection (including undeclared objection), or significant distance from abortion providers. Where there is a lack of accessible universal healthcare, the cost of abortion services can also cause delays, and people travelling elsewhere for an abortion where it is criminalised or restricted in their own country are likely to have abortions at a relatively later stage due to economic and practical delays.

In addition to late abortions associated with delays, pregnant people may require abortions in cases of previously wanted pregnancies where unexpected events occur. This includes risks to the pregnant person's health or life that present themselves as the pregnancy progresses or based on foetal impairments (to be discussed below), but a pregnant person may also decide to have an abortion due to significant life changes. For example, Diane Green Foster

[89] Sheldon (n 40) p 36.

[90] Kate Greasley, 'In Defense of Abortion Rights' in Kate Greasley and Christopher Kaczor, *Abortion Rights: For and Against* (Cambridge, Cambridge University Press, 2017) p 84.

[91] Jackson (n 14) p 94.

[92] Diane Greene Foster and Katrina Kimport, 'Who Seeks Abortions at or After 20 Weeks?' (2013) 45(4) *Perspectives on Sexual and Reproductive Health* 210, 212–16.

and Katrina Kimport note that people may seek later abortions due to sudden and unexpected changes to their personal circumstances, such as a relationship breakdown or job loss.[93] Geopolitical and environmental events, including war, natural disasters, and epidemics or pandemics, also impact pregnant people's decisions regarding their ongoing pregnancies.[94] In these situations, there may be an increase in rates of unwanted pregnancies, a lack of access to reproductive healthcare services including contraception, pregnancy-related care, and abortion, and the pregnant person may feel unable to continue a pregnancy, give birth, or raise a child in situations of heightened vulnerability and uncertainty.

While some US states have passed laws establishing foetal personhood,[95] the majority of jurisdictions do not ascribe rights to the foetus, but nonetheless impose gestational time limits on later abortion. In Western countries such as the UK, Netherlands, and Australia, foetal viability – the earliest gestational age where the foetus is capable of being born alive – is taken to be a point of moral and legal significance. For example, abortion laws in the UK and the Netherlands distinguish between abortion on broad grounds before 24 weeks gestation, and abortion only on medical grounds after this point.[96] Foetal viability is not a fixed concept but can change over time; the gestational time limit in Britain was initially 28 weeks when the Abortion Act was passed in 1967, but this was reduced to 24 weeks in 1990 due to technological advancements making it possible for a foetus to survive at this point.[97] Politicians in the UK have been arguing for a further reduction to 22 weeks, as extremely premature babies can potentially survive at this point.[98]

Romanis argues, however, that viability is an incoherent legal concept for interpreting 'capable of being born alive' as encompassing a 'newborn capable of only surviving with the aid of intensive care'.[99] Moreover, due to the uncertainty of survival for extremely premature infants, Romanis highlights the lack of clarification as to what 'likely duration of life after birth is sufficient' to

[93] ibid 211.

[94] See Vijayan Pillai, Ya-Chien Wang, and Arati Maleku, 'Women, War, and Reproductive Health in Developing Countries' (2017) 56(1) *Social Work in Health Care* 28, 35; Samantha Loewen, Jessie Pinchoff, Thoai D Ngo, and Michelle J Hindin, 'The Impact of Natural Disasters and Epidemics on Sexual and Reproductive Health in Low- and Middle-income Countries: A Narrative Synthesis' (2022) 157(1) *International Journal of Gynecology and Obstetrics* 11, 16; Ayele Geleto, Jo Taylor, and Tesfalidet Beyene, 'Interruptions in Contraception and Unintended Pregnancy During the COVID-19 Pandemic: A Protocol for Systemic Review and Meta-analysis' (2023) *Women's Health* 19.

[95] Terry McGovern, Ira Memaj, and Lourdes Rivera, 'Fetal Personhood: What Happens When the Rights of the "Fertilized Egg" Supersede the Rights of the Mother' (2025) 388 *BMJ* 372.

[96] Abortion Act 1967 [England, Wales, and Scotland]; Abortion (Northern Ireland) Regulations 2020; Termination of Pregnancy Act 1984 [Netherlands].

[97] Infant Life (Preservation) Act 1929 [England and Wales]; Human Fertilisation and Embryology Act 1990 [United Kingdom], s 37.

[98] Archie Mitchell, 'Nigel Farage calls for parliament to debate stricter abortion limits' (*Independent,* 28 November 2024) www.independent.co.uk/news/uk/politics/farage-abortion-limit-reform-b2655446.html accessed 9 January 2026.

[99] Elizabeth Chloe Romanis, 'Is "Viability" Viable? Abortion, Conceptual Confusion and the Law in England and Wales and the United States' (2020) 7(1) *Journal of Law and the Biosciences* 1, 12.

establish viability.[100] As care for extremely premature infants improves and new reproductive technologies are developed, the point of viability becomes a line that will always need redrawing later.[101] Most importantly, scholars have argued against relying on the concept of foetal viability in abortion law because it is an ambiguous, complex, and fallible concept based on human interpretations of statistical probabilities – probabilities which cannot realistically apply to *all* pregnancies because of the additional considerations as to whether a foetus may or may not survive.[102] This includes some of the social, economic, and environmental factors discussed above, and when considered at the global level, foetal viability is unworkable due to the significant variations in these factors and access to the healthcare and technologies that might help a premature infant survive.

Thus, while many states view abortion as more controversial as the foetus nears birth, there is the need for flexibility. Erica Millar has critiqued gestational time limits which subject later abortions to strict legal and medical regulation, for foreclosing the subjectivity and embodiment of the person wanting an abortion and presenting late abortion as something requiring medical justification.[103] As with abortions at any other time in the pregnancy, there may be myriad reasons as to why someone requires a 'post-viability' abortion. While adoption is often suggested as a more appropriate alternative, this is often not the case – and restrictions on childbirth and parenting decisions undermine reproductive citizenship.[104] Evie Kendal also argues, in contrast to the traditional view of medical necessity that focuses on the life of the pregnant person or viability of the foetus, that abortions for any such reasons should all be considered to be medically necessary because of the harm caused by abortion denial.[105] The Australian state of Victoria has recognised that 'post-viability' abortions may be needed on broader grounds, and so permits abortion after 24 weeks if two doctors agree that abortion is medically appropriate in light of the pregnant persons current and future physical, social, and psychological circumstances:[106] including, but not necessarily limited to, medical issues. This approach may, depending on the specific context of each state, be an appropriate model for the regulation of abortion at a later stage of gestation, provided that 'social,

[100] ibid.

[101] ibid; Leo Han, Maria I Rodriguez, and Aaron B Caughey, 'Blurred Lines: Disentangling the Concept of Fetal Viability from Abortion Law' (2018) 28(4) *Women's Health Issues* 287.

[102] Romanis, 'Is "Viability" Viable?' (2020) (n 99); Erdman, 'Theorizing Time' (2017) (n 81); Samantha Halliday and others, 'The (Mis)use of Fetal Viability as the Determinant of Non-criminal Abortion in the Netherlands and England and Wales' (2023) 31 *Medical Law Review* 538, 539.

[103] Millar (n 1) 440–41.

[104] For a discussion of the limitations of adoption as an alternative and the impacts on the pregnant person, see Lindsey Porter, 'Adoption is Not Abortion-Lite' (2012) 29(1) *Journal of Applied Philosophy* 63; Gretchen Sisson and others, 'Adoption Decision Making Among Women Seeking Abortion' (2017) 27(2) *Women's Health Issues* 136; Malinda L Seymore, 'Adoption as a Substitute for Abortion?' (2024) 95 *Colorado Law Review* 1089.

[105] Evie Kendal, 'All Abortions are Medically Necessary' (2023) 18(3) *Clinical Ethics* 306.

[106] Abortion Law Reform Act 2008 [Victoria, Australia], s 5.

economic, psychological, and medical reasons' are interpreted broadly to offer flexibility and respect for the pregnant person's decision. However, currently in Victoria, access to later abortions is an 'institutional lottery' as individual hospitals place additional restrictions or processes on access to abortions after 20 weeks' gestation,[107] and thus further barriers surrounding the legal grounds for abortion must also be addressed (see chapter four).

As a relational and embodied approach to abortion illustrates, abortion decisions take place in varying social, cultural, political, and historical contexts which cannot be reduced to specific grounds. Therefore, states must ensure that abortion is accessible in the later stages of pregnancy for a wide range of reasons. Demarcating specific grounds as exceptions to a general prohibition on later abortions would likely exclude many pregnant people from accessing abortion care and would, as a result, likely push them towards clandestine abortions or force them to continue unwanted pregnancies in violation of human rights. As Sheelagh McGuiness and Jonathan Montgomery have argued, 'abortion regulations need to move beyond frameworks based on narrow understandings of harm, towards more progressive agendas that take into account the social determinants of health in order to reduce barriers to care.'[108] Law has the potential to exacerbate or alleviate the social determinants of health when it comes to pregnancy and abortion, requiring precaution against an overly restrictive approach.[109] Indeed, a restrictive approach to later abortions has the potential to cause significant embodied and relational harm, while undermining the rights and citizenship of pregnant people requiring abortions at this later stage.

Thus, my first policy presumption is that abortion should be available on request at least in the early stages of pregnancy, and available on broad grounds throughout the rest of the pregnancy – including after any 'viability' threshold.

B. Selective Abortion: Foetal Impairments and Sex Selection

International human rights bodies already require states to legalise abortion in cases of severe or fatal foetal impairments, and it is common for abortion to be permitted on this ground even where it is otherwise restricted (either entirely, or in the later stages of pregnancy). As the Human Rights Committee identified, for example, it is a significant violation of the pregnant person's rights, with no legitimate justification, to be forced to continue a pregnancy where the foetus

[107] Casey Michelle Haining and others, 'The 'Institutional Lottery': Institutional Variation in the Processes Involved in Accessing Late Abortion in Victoria, Australia' (2023) 101 *Women's Stud. Int. Forum* 102822.

[108] Sheelagh McGuinness and Jonathan Montgomery, 'Legal Determinants of Health: Regulating Abortion Care' (2020) 13(1) *Public Health Ethics* 34, 34.

[109] ibid 38.

will die before or shortly after birth.[110] Access to abortion must be guaranteed in cases of fatal foetal impairments at any stage of the pregnancy. However, it is difficult to neatly distinguish fatal from non-fatal impairments. Some non-fatal impairments can have significant health implications and cause pain to the child once born, and it is important that pregnant people are not forced to have children in contexts that would be distressing and difficult for both the parents and child. Fiona de Londras and Máiréad Enright argue that being forced to have a baby with an impairment which is not fatal but nevertheless affects its quality of life can be just as distressing to a pregnant person as being forced to continue a non-viable pregnancy.[111] There is also an issue with forcing pregnant people to have children with non-fatal impairments where this would not be the case, particularly in contexts where people with disabilities face significant stigma and discrimination, and where there is inadequate state support for disabled people and parents of disabled children. The decision to abort a wanted pregnancy on the basis of a foetal impairment is a complex one, and flexibility is required to ensure that pregnant people are able to make a decision based on their specific circumstances. Restricting abortion on the grounds of disability to fatal or severe disabilities, without any flexibility, even in the later stages of pregnancy, would be an inappropriate regulatory response that would undermine reproductive citizenship.

However, foetal impairment grounds for abortion have also been critiqued for perpetuating negative stereotypes towards people with disabilities.[112] Where legislation distinguishes between disabled and non-disabled foetuses in order to justify some abortions, but not others, this sends the message that disabled lives are worth less.[113] This also perpetuates misguided assumptions that disability automatically reduces one's quality of life. McGuinness therefore comments that foetal impairment grounds operate as a weak form of eugenics.[114] This may lead some people to conclude that abortion on the basis of non-fatal foetal impairments ought to be restricted or even prohibited.[115] Feminist scholars have highlighted the importance of reproductive agency and access to abortion in

[110] *Mellet v Ireland* (2016) UN Doc CCPR/C/116/D/2324/2013, para 7.4.

[111] Fiona de Londras and Máiréad Enright, *Repealing the Eighth* (Policy Press, 2018) pp 101, 108.

[112] See, eg, Sheelagh McGuinness, 'Law, Reproduction, and Disability: Fatally "Handicapped"?' (2013) 21(2) *Medical Law Review* 213; Alicia Ouliette, 'Selection against Disability: Abortion, ART, and Access' (2015) 43(2) *Journal of Law, Medicine and Ethics* 211; Marsha Saxon, 'Disability Rights and Selective Abortion' in Lennard J Davis (ed), *The Disability Studies Reader*, 5th edn (Routledge, 2016); *Crowter v Secretary of State for Health and Social Care* [2022] EWCA Civ 1559.

[113] Zoe L Tongue, '*Crowter v Secretary of State for Health and Social Care* [2021] EWHC 2536: Discrimination, Disability, and Access to Abortion' (2022) 30(1) *Medical Law Review* 177, 183.

[114] McGuinness, 'Law, Reproduction, and Disability' (2013) (n 112) 220–25.

[115] See *Crowter* (n 112); Heloise Robinson, 'Discrimination in Abortion Law and the Message the Law is Sending: *R (Crowter) v Secretary of State for Health and Social Care*' (2023) 87(1) *Medical Law Review* 218; Heloise Robinson, 'Prenatal Testing, Disability Equality, and the Limits of the Law' (2023) 29(3) *New Bioethics* 202; Jonathan Herring and Heloise Robinson, 'A Right to Live Without Stigma? Examining Negative Stereotyping, Negative Messages, and Article 8 of the European Convention on Human Rights' (2024) 44(4) *Legal Studies* 685.

these circumstances; Sally Sheldon and Stephen Wilkinson, for example, argue that 'no woman should be forced to carry to term a disabled, or any other, foetus'.[116] While feminist and disability rights arguments around abortion could therefore be constructed as oppositional and 'irreconcilable',[117] I argue that this issue arises out of legislative responses which create narrow exceptions to general restrictions or prohibitions on abortion, as foetal impairment exceptions are 'a symptom of socio-cultural settings which both undervalue disabled people and control the reproductive lives of women and all other people capable of becoming pregnant.'[118] Consequently, this issue requires a nuanced approach that recognises the interconnectedness between reproductive and disability rights. As I have argued elsewhere, '[r]ather than being framed as two separate sets of rights that conflict or require compromise, reproductive justice and disability justice intersect: they are two frameworks that form part of a larger movement towards social justice.'[119]

The Committee on the Rights of People with Disabilities and Committee on the Elimination of Discrimination Against Women issued a joint statement in 2018 on the need to legalise abortion in a manner which respects the reproductive autonomy of pregnant people without perpetuating deep-rooted stereotypes against people with disabilities.[120] Identifying the discriminatory nature of foetal impairment grounds for abortion does not necessitate restrictions on access to abortion for this reason. Instead, a focus on comprehensive access to abortion in the later stages of pregnancy for a broad range of reasons removes the discrepancy between disabled and non-disabled foetuses. As such, the approach proposed above in terms of an expansive, rather than grounds-based, legislative response will also go some way to address disability rights concerns. This is also supported by disability rights scholars; Adrienne Asch and Tom Shakespeare, who identify issues with 'disability-selective' abortion, do not conclude that abortion should be legally restricted.[121] Any alternative approach would infringe the rights of pregnant people, and would not address the stigmatisation of disability.

[116] Sally Sheldon and Stephen Wilkinson, 'Termination of Pregnancy for Reason of Foetal Disability: Are There Grounds for a Special Exception in Law?' (2001) 9 *Medical Law Review* 85, 109.

[117] This argument is also addressed by Keith Sharpe and Sarah Earle, 'Feminism, Abortion and Disability: Irreconcilable Differences?' (2002) 17(2) *Disability and Society* 137, 144.

[118] Tongue, '*Crowter v Secretary of State*' (2022) (n 113) 185.

[119] Zoe L Tongue, 'Foetal Disability and Abortion in the UK: A Reproductive and Disability Justice Perspective' (2026) 34 *Feminist Legal Studies* 51, 64.

[120] CRPD and CEDAW, 'Joint Statement by CRPD and CEDAW: Guaranteeing Sexual and Reproductive Health and Rights for All Women, in Particular Women with Disabilities' (29 August 2019) https://tbinternet.ohchr.org/Treaties/CEDAW/Shared%20Documents/1_Global/INT_CEDAW_STA_8744_E.docx accessed 9 January 2026.

[121] Adrienne Asch, 'Prenatal Diagnosis and Selective Abortion: A Challenge to Practice and Policy' (1999) 89(11) *American Journal of Public Health* 1649, 1655–56; Tom Shakespeare, 'Choices and Rights: Eugenics, Genetics and Disability Equality' (1998) 13(5) *Disability and Society* 665, 672–73.

Rather, Asch and Shakespeare comment on the broader social, cultural, and medical context which encourages pregnant people towards abortion in cases of foetal impairment.[122] The conditions in which abortion decisions are made are also important. A social context in which disabled people are stigmatised and devalued may shape the decision to abort a disabled foetus. Alison Piepmeier has observed how stereotypical attitudes towards people with disabilities arise in discussions around abortion, carrying the assumption that having a child with a disability is undesirable.[123] The language around having a 'healthy child' and the routinisation of prenatal testing can also suggest that abortion is the most medically appropriate route when a foetal impairment is discovered. In the context of Denmark, Laura Heinsen's research has demonstrated how pregnant people do not make active moral decisions around prenatal screening and abortion, as the institutionalised nature of abortion in cases of foetal impairments presents it as a morally appropriate choice.[124] Where pregnant people *do* make active moral decisions, the lack of comprehensive state support for disabled people and other conditions of injustice is likely to be relevant.

These broader contextual issues must therefore also be addressed by the state, alongside allowing for abortion in cases of foetal impairments. Andrea Smith highlights that if our response to these issues lacks nuance by simply facilitating abortion for foetuses with impairments, then 'we never actually focus on changing economic policies that make raising children with disabilities difficult.'[125] Thus, states must also be required to address stigma and structural discrimination against people with disabilities, and to provide material support, including financial assistance, education, and social care, for disabled people and the parents of disabled children. In terms of healthcare institutions, prenatal screening and access to abortion must be presented as an option for pregnant people without being encouraged as the most medically appropriate choice. Pregnant people discovering that the foetus they are carrying has an impairment must be adequately informed about their future child's disability, without feeling coerced, pressured, or influenced into having an abortion. This both supports the pregnant person's rights in enabling autonomous decision-making and addresses the broader issues with disability discrimination, meeting the third and fourth of my policy presumptions around the pregnant person's rights and further support.

[122] ibid.

[123] Alison Piepmeier, 'The Inadequacy of "Choice": Disability and What's Wrong with Feminist Framings of Reproduction' (2013) 39(1) *Feminist Studies* 159, 159–60.

[124] Laura Louise Heinsen, 'Moral Adherers: Pregnant Women Undergoing Routine Prenatal Screening in Denmark' in Ayo Wahlberg and Tine M Gammeltoft (eds), *Selective Reproduction in the 21st Century* (Palgrave Macmillan, 2018); Laura Louise Heinsen, 'Shouldering Death: Moral Tensions, Ambiguity, and the Unintended Ramifications of State-Sanctioned Second-Trimester Selective Abortion in Denmark' (2022) 36(4) *Medical Anthropology Quarterly* 515.

[125] Andrea Smith, 'Beyond Pro-Choice versus Pro-Life: Women of Color and Reproductive Justice' (2005) 17(1) *National Women's Studies Association Journal* 119, 129–30.

In terms of 'selective' abortion practices, abortion on the grounds of sex is often viewed as much more problematic. The termination of (usually) female foetuses has been viewed as morally impermissible by those who otherwise advocate for access to abortion.[126] Mary Anne Warren, for example, who supported access to abortion until birth, coined the term 'gendercide' in relation to sex-selection.[127] So-called 'son preference'[128] can be linked to gender stereotypes and the marginalisation of women in some socio-cultural contexts. However, in states where sex selective abortion is common, this issue is often more complex than simple gender bias on the part of the individual pregnant person. In India, for example, sex selective abortion is linked to the State's two-child policy and the practice of dowry (the giving of gifts, property, or money to the husband's family by the daughter's family upon marriage) which is a significant financial burden, particularly for poorer families.[129] Many people attempt to 'balance' their family by trying to have a son, who will attract dowry, to counter the financial loss of having a daughter.[130] There are also significant repercussions for families unable to pay dowry, with so-called 'dowry deaths' where women have been killed or harassed until they died by suicide in instances where it has not been paid.[131] Prohibiting sex selective abortion thus does little to address its root causes, which relate to socio- economic and gender inequalities and the state's own population policies. India has attempted to prohibit sex selective abortion practices, but this has resulted in opening up a black market for foetal sex identification.[132] Thus, while sex-selective abortion is not to be condoned, states should tackle this practice by addressing broader gender inequalities and avoid implementing population policies that exacerbate these issues, rather than by explicitly prohibiting it. As with foetal impairments, restricting access to abortion does little to address the broader systemic issues involved: attempts to prohibit sex selection in order to uphold gender equality creates a 'double bind' situation whereby prohibition worsens the very social inequalities that it attempts to solve, as it is pregnant people (primarily women) who will suffer the consequences.[133]

[126] Kate Greasley, 'Is Sex-Selective Abortion against the Law?' (2016) 36(3) *OJLS* 535, 540–41.

[127] Mary Anne Warren, *Gendercide: The Implications of Sex Selection* (Rowman & Allanheld, 1985).

[128] See Marie-Claire Robitaille and Ishita Chatterjee, 'Sex-Selective Abortions and Infant Mortality in India: The Role of Parents' Stated Son Preference' (2018) *Journal of Development Studies* 47.

[129] Kumkum Sangari, *Solid:Liquid A (Transnational) Reproductive Formation* (Tulika Books, 2015) Ch 1.

[130] ibid.

[131] Devaki Monani and Felicity Gerry QC, 'Death and the Dowry System: India's Women and Female Children at Global Risk of Gendercide Over Money' (2017) 15(1) *Issues in Legal Scholarship* 1.

[132] Suryatapa Bhattacharya, 'India Targets Illicit Sex-Selective abortions' (*The Wall Street Journal,* 31 January 2016) www.wsj.com/articles/india-targets-illicit-sex-selective-abortions-1454280280 accessed 9 January 2026.

[133] Greasley, 'Is Sex-Selective Abortion' (2016) (n 126) 563.

Thus, my second presumption is that disability and sex 'selective' abortion should not be legally prohibited, and instead states should take measures to address these issues through socio-cultural change and state support.

C. Decriminalisation

Abortion remains a criminal offence in almost all countries. As set out in chapter one, international human rights bodies have recognised the need for the decriminalisation of abortion in addition to legalisation, so that pregnant people seeking abortions outside of the medico-legal system are not criminalised for doing so. Criminalisation has been linked to an increased risk of unsafe abortion, as pregnant people seeking clandestine abortions may be unable to access information on how to safely terminate a pregnancy, or the threat of criminalisation deters them from seeking necessary aftercare where the abortion goes wrong. As those that assist with an illegal abortion, as well as the pregnant person, may also face punitive charges, criminalisation also has a chilling effect on medical professionals who may be reluctant to provide any information on abortion.[134] In Poland, pregnant people are not criminalised for having clandestine abortions, but medical professionals face up to two years in prison for performing an illegal abortion.[135] Between medical professionals who conscientiously object to the provision of abortion, and those that fear facing criminal charges if they provide abortion care, this leaves very few doctors willing to terminate pregnancies even on the legal grounds.[136] This makes it more likely that pregnant people, particularly those without the resources to travel to another country, will seek means of terminating their own pregnancies without accessing healthcare from medical professionals.

Rebecca Cook and Joanna Erdman have argued that criminal abortion laws inflict mental and physical suffering, amount to torture and cruel, inhuman, and degrading treatment, constitute violence against women, and inflict a range of other severe harms and violations.[137] Moreover, people from already marginalised groups are more likely to face more barriers to abortion access and are also more likely to be disproportionately affected by criminalisation of abortion. In El Salvador, where abortion is entirely illegal, people suspected of inducing an abortion are often charged and sentenced to between 30 and 50 years in prison, with the result that people experiencing miscarriages, stillbirths, and obstetric

[134] De Londras and Enright *Repealing the Eighth* (2018) (n 111) p 87.

[135] The Family Planning, Human Embryo Protection and Conditions of Permissibility of Abortion Act 1993, Article 7(2) [Poland].

[136] Tongue, 'On Conscientious Objection' (2022) (n 49) 356, 359.

[137] Joanna N Erdman and Rebecca J Cook, 'Decriminalization of Abortion – A Human Rights Imperative' (2020) 62 *Best Practice and Research: Clinical Obstetrics and Gynaecology* 11, 20.

emergencies are often accused of having an illegal abortion.[138] This overwhelmingly affects poor, working class, and rural people, as most of the women prosecuted are reported by staff at public hospitals.[139] Cora Fernandez Anderson has recognised a similar pattern elsewhere in Latin America.[140] Criminalisation thus exacerbates structural inequalities and reproduces the conditions for 'marginalization and vulnerability'.[141] Rishita Nandagiri, Ernestina Coast, and Joe Strong highlight the 'structural violence' of restrictive and stigmatising abortion regimes, which criminalisation feeds into.[142]

Socio-economically disadvantaged and other marginalised pregnant people, including those without access to the internet and other sources of information on abortion, are more likely to experience delays in obtaining a clandestine abortion, are more likely to have an unsafe abortion, and are then more likely to be criminalised upon seeking aftercare. In circumstances where abortion is morally justifiable (as established throughout this chapter) and should be made legally available and accessible by states, criminalising pregnant people who have illegal abortions is clearly inappropriate as this is due the state's own failure to provide safe, legal access. It is important to note that pregnant people seek clandestine abortions not only in states where abortion is largely prohibited, but also where broader issues and barriers impact comprehensive access.

In addition to the risks of unsafe abortion associated with criminalisation, feminist scholars have identified the gendered dynamics of criminal abortion laws, including the stigmatising of people who have abortions and the perpetuation of gender-based stereotypes around pregnancy and motherhood. Millar argues that the criminalisation of abortion intensified the shaming and stigmatising of women who have abortions, designating them as criminals.[143] This designation is the result, Millar argues, of the continued linking of women's sexuality to reproduction and the maternal identity of pregnant women, which is rejected through the decision to have an abortion.[144] Through rejecting social expectations around motherhood, this shame is converted into ideas of a personal moral failure on the part of women having abortions.[145] Cook similarly argues that criminalisation constructs the social meaning of abortion as

[138] Citizens Coalition for the Decriminalization of Abortion on Grounds of Health, Ethics and Fetal Anomaly, El Salvador, 'From Hospital to Jail: The Impact of Women of El Salvador's Total Criminalization of Abortion' (2014) 22(44) *Reproductive Health Matters* 52, 52–53.

[139] ibid 53–54.

[140] Cora Fernandez Anderson, *Fighting for Abortion Rights in Latin America* (Routledge, 2020) p 60.

[141] McGuinness and Montgomery, 'Legal Determinants of Health' (2020) (n 108) 38.

[142] Rishita Nandagiri, Ernestina Coast, and Joe Strong, 'COVID-19 and Abortion: Making Structural Violence Visible?' (2020) 46(S1) *International Perspectives on Sex and Reproductive Health* 83, 84.

[143] Millar, *Happy Abortions* (2017) (n 40) p 218.

[144] ibid pp 218–19.

[145] ibid.

inherently wrong, thus ascribing deviance to women seeking abortions.[146] Even where abortion has been legalised, the criminalisation of abortion implies that abortion is morally wrong, and so the criminalisation of abortion is a process of gender stereotyping, with wider implications for all people capable of becoming pregnant by treating their bodies as 'societal procreative assets'.[147]

The criminalisation of abortion should therefore be viewed as a tool of undermining reproductive citizenship. Fiona Bloomer, Claire Pierson, and Sylvia Estrada Claudio have argued, for example, that criminalisation 'allows women minimal control over their reproductive lives in most settings' and at worst, completely denies reproductive self-determination.[148] These gendered dimensions have been recognised by CEDAW in characterising the criminalisation of abortion and forced continuation of pregnancy as 'gender-based violence' and elsewhere linking restrictions on abortion to gender stereotypes.[149] The decriminalisation of abortion is necessary as criminalisation unjustifiably stigmatises pregnant people for obtaining abortions that they are or should be legally able to have by reinforcing gender stereotypes. This is important to understand in the context of later abortions which are more heavily regulated, as there may be complex reasons as to why someone may obtain a later abortion and why they were unable to obtain it through the formal healthcare system. These abortions typically take place in conditions of vulnerability, and as Sally Sheldon and Jonathan Lord have argued, are rare cases which call for 'compassion, support and care'.[150]

Historically, the criminalisation of abortion (whilst still reflecting archaic gender stereotypes and reproductive control) had a purpose in preventing harm to pregnant people, as abortion was a dangerous procedure.[151] However, as abortion (when done using safe and evidence-based methods) is now very safe, criminalisation now only has the purpose of foetal protection – and Sheldon argues that it fails in this purpose, as illegal abortions continue to happen.[152] Thus, criminal offences for abortion merely seek to condemn those that have abortions outside

[146] Rebecca J Cook, 'Stigmatized Meanings of Criminal Abortion Law' in Rebecca J Cook, Joanna N Erdman, and Bernard M Dickens (eds), *Abortion Law in Transnational Perspective* (University of Pennsylvania Press, 2014) pp 347, 349.

[147] Charles Ngwena, 'Access to Safe Abortion as a Human Right in the African Region: Lessons from Emerging Jurisprudence of UN Treaty Monitoring Bodies (2013) 29(2) *South African Journal on Human Rights* 399, 424.

[148] Fiona Bloomer, Claire Pierson, and Sylvia Estrada Claudio, *Reimagining Global Abortion Politics: A Social Justice Perspective* (Policy Press, 2018) p 29.

[149] CEDAW, 'General Recommendation No 35 on Gender-Based Violence against Women' (26 July 2017) UN Doc CEDAW/C/GC/35, para 18; *LC v Peru* (2011) UN Doc CEDAW/C/50/D/22/2009, para 8.15; CEDAW, 'Inquiry concerning the United Kingdom of Great Britain and Northern Ireland under Article 8 of the Optional Protocol to CEDAW' (6 March 2018) UN Doc CEDAW/C/OP.8/GBR/1, para 73.

[150] Sally Sheldon and Jonathan Lord, 'Care Not Criminalisation; Reform of British Abortion Law is Long Overdue' (2023) 49(8) *Journal of Medical Ethics* 523, 524.

[151] Sally Sheldon, 'The Decriminalisation of Abortion: An Argument for Modernisation' (2016) 36(2) *Oxford Journal of Legal Studies* 334, 348.

[152] ibid 352–53.

of the law[153] which is a disproportionate response, given the importance of access to abortion for reproductive citizenship and the identifiable and significant harm criminalisation causes to abortion-seekers. Moreover, sending people to prison over illegal abortions serves 'no useful purpose', as a judge stated in a recent English case concerning an illegal abortion after 30 weeks' gestation.[154] While this is outside the scope of this chapter, this feeds into anti-carceral feminist and prison abolitionist approaches which view prison and the criminal justice system as an inappropriate solution for social and economic problems.[155] Thus, even if a state places value on the foetus, foetal protectionism through the criminal law is a rights violation, and decriminalisation is an imperative.

The decriminalisation of abortion would not necessarily amount to the complete deregulation of abortion. Abortion provision is already subject to a range of regulations and processes of informed consent and confidentiality to safeguard pregnant people (and particularly pregnant adolescents and adults lacking mental capacity) from coercion.[156] In Britain, the sections of the Offences Against the Person Act 1861 which cover abortion are generally used to prosecute people who non-consensually terminate (or attempt to terminate) someone else's pregnancy, or those who terminate their own pregnancies at a late stage, as there is little demand to criminalise people having earlier abortions outside the regulatory framework of the Abortion Act 1967.[157] While pregnant people should be exempt from criminal offences (for abortion at any stage of the pregnancy), the criminalisation of non-consensual abortion, whether as a separate offence or under existing criminal offences around bodily harm, may be necessary to safeguard pregnant people's agency and wellbeing.

In Northern Ireland, where abortion has been decriminalised for pregnant people, a new offence was created to cover third parties who terminate a pregnancy, except where it was done to protect the pregnant person from grave permanent harm to their health or from a risk to their life.[158] This covers third parties who provide consensual abortion services outside of medico-legal regulation. In contexts where the only means of having an abortion is outside of formal medical institutions, it would clearly be inappropriate to criminalise third parties who provide these services, even if they are unsafe. States must tackle unsafe abortions through the provision of a range of sexual and reproductive health services including information on and access to abortion and

[153] ibid 354–55.

[154] *R v Foster* [2023] EWCA Crim 1196, para 49 [per Dame Victoria Sharpe].

[155] See, eg, Angela Davis, *Are Prisons Obsolete?* (Seven Stories Press, 2003); Mimi E Kim, 'Anti-Carceral Feminism: The Contradictions of Progress and the Possibilities of Counter-Hegemonic Struggle' (2020) 35(3) *Affilia* 309; Lisa Lowe, 'The Dialectics of Abolition' (2023) 75(2) *American Quarterly* 371.

[156] Jonathan Herring, Emily Jackson, and Sally Sheldon, 'Would Decriminalisation Mean Deregulation?' in Sally Sheldon and Kaye Wellings (eds), *Decriminalising Abortion in the UK* (Policy Press, 2020).

[157] Sheldon (n 151) 339–40.

[158] Abortion (Northern Ireland) Regulations 2020, SI 2020/345, reg 11.

post-abortion care, rather than through punitive deterrents. However, states could create civil or criminal offences, or other forms of regulation, to target individuals who intentionally, recklessly, or negligently provide unsafe abortion services in contexts with recourse to safe abortion methods. The level of regulation will be dependent on each state, but the decriminalisation of abortion should be supported by safeguarding measures and regulatory practices to prevent non-consensual and, where appropriate, unsafe abortions. As will be discussed in the next chapter, any regulatory mechanisms accompanying decriminalisation should not obstruct, prohibit, or target self-managed abortion, which is an important aspect of realising the right to abortion.

Thus, my third presumption is that the criminalisation of abortion violates the right to abortion, so states should decriminalise abortion – although the retention of third party offences may be appropriate in some circumstances.

IV. THE RIGHT TO ABORTION: A FRAMEWORK FOR PROGRESSIVE REALISATION

In this final section of chapter three, I translate the above presumptions into a human right to abortion through a framework for progressive realisation. The scope of this framework is broad, to reflect the feminist approach set out at the start of this chapter and recognising abortion as interconnected to a range of sexual and reproductive health and social justice issues. It is also informed by the ways in which restrictions on and barriers to abortion access perpetuate gendered, racialised, class-based, and other structural inequalities. The framework will consist of four tiers, setting out the steps that states are obligated to take to incrementally work towards full compliance. The first tier, outlining the minimum core content for the right to abortion that all states must meet, largely resembles the approach of the current human rights framework by requiring decriminalisation, the legalisation of abortion in exceptional circumstances, and access to abortion on those grounds. The following tiers require states to additionally legalise abortion on request and later abortion for social, economic, and medical reasons.

Each tier requires states to progressively work towards the provision of universal and consistent access to abortion without delay, and thus the removal of barriers to access. The fourth tier requires states to meet a range of conditions relating to the provision of universal sexual and reproductive health services, pregnancy-related care, comprehensive supports such as those required by other socio-economic rights, and the need to tackle structural inequalities, gender stereotyping, and disability discrimination. States meeting the requirements of the first three tiers must also demonstrate that they are taking steps towards meeting the obligations contained in the fourth tier. Finally, as highlighted in the previous chapter, states which are able to fully comply with the requirements of socio-economic rights are also obligated to offer assistance to states that cannot do so due to resource-constraints. Thus, states able to ensure full or near-full compliance with the right to abortion must also provide assistance to states lacking the resources to implement universally accessible abortion services meeting the conditions required by tier four.

A. The Right to Abortion

Recognising that rights to sexual and reproductive health and agency are a fundamental aspect of gender equality, States Parties must ensure the right to abortion for all people capable of becoming pregnant.

States Parties must recognise this right as part of a wider range of sexual and reproductive rights and as connected to a range of other economic, social, and cultural rights, which are necessary to ensure that all people capable of becoming pregnant are able to freely decide whether or not to have children, how many children, and when they have them.

States Parties have an obligation to meet the minimum core content of this right as set out in the first stage of the framework and must take steps to progress to the following stages until they are able to fully comply with the requirements of the fourth stage. States Parties able to comply with the third and fourth stages have an additional obligation to assist those States Parties unable to meet full compliance.

States Parties must, as part of the requirement to decriminalise abortion, ensure that there are measures in place to obtain informed consent to abortion and to combat unsafe abortion practices. States Parties may retain criminal offences for involuntary terminations of pregnancy, but must have processes to ensure that these offences are applied in good faith.

States Parties must take steps to:

1. Decriminalise abortion and release all people currently facing criminal punishment for performing or having a consensual abortion. In addition, abortion must be legalised where there is a risk to the life or health of the pregnant person, where the pregnancy resulted from a sexual crime, or where the foetus has a serious or fatal impairment. States Parties have an obligation to ensure that abortion on the legal grounds is universally accessible in practice.
2. In addition to the above, legalise abortion on request up to 12 weeks' gestation, provided that accurate methods of estimating gestational age are universally available. States Parties without accurate methods of estimation must ensure processes are in place to provide access to abortion on request up to a later point. States Parties have an obligation to ensure that abortion on the legal grounds is universally accessible in practice with minimal delays. Where delays persist, as result of resource or capacity constraints

and structural inequalities, States Parties should extend the gestational time limit for abortion on request.

3. In addition to the above, legalise abortion in the later stages of pregnancy for social, economic, and medical reasons, so that later abortion is no longer limited to the exceptional circumstances. States Parties have an obligation to ensure that abortion on the legal grounds is universally accessible in practice and address all structural barriers to access. States Parties must also ensure that pregnant people are able to access abortion services as early as possible, without delays.
4. In addition to the above, States Parties must:
   (a) Ensure the universal and consistent provision of a broad range of sexual and reproductive health services, including access to a wide range of contraceptive methods. States Parties must ensure that people capable of becoming pregnant are empowered to avoid unwanted pregnancies.
   (b) Minimise the risk of maternal mortality and unsafe abortion through the provision of comprehensive pregnancy-related care and safe, legal, accessible, and evidence-based abortion services.
   (c) Ensure that medical professionals receive comprehensive training on the safe provision of abortion care, which is sensitive to gender, age, race, caste, disability, sexuality, gender identity, and membership of an indigenous group and is delivered in a culturally appropriate manner.
   (d) Combat abortion stigma, socio-cultural gender stereotypes around pregnancy and motherhood, and religious, moral, or cultural opposition to abortion to the extent that it obstructs abortion provision.
   (e) Provide comprehensive economic and social support to pregnant people and parents, ensuring that a wide range of other socio-economic rights including rights to healthcare, housing, food, water, and sanitation, have been universally fulfilled. Broader social issues, such as gender-based violence, must also be addressed by States Parties.
   (f) Combat disability discrimination and stigma, ensure that parents are able to meet the needs of children with disabilities through the provision of comprehensive support, and ensure that pregnant people receive non-biased information when discovering that the foetus they are carrying has an impairment. Pregnant people must not feel compelled or coerced to have an abortion in such circumstances.
   (g) Address structural and intersectional inequalities in order to ensure that certain groups are not marginalised in accessing sexual and reproductive health services, including abortion. This requires a focus on providing accessible services for poor and rural communities. States Parties must ensure that non-citizens are also able to access abortion services, so not to disadvantage migrants, asylum seekers, and undocumented persons.

The recognition of the right to abortion in a transformed human rights framework would address the issues raised in chapters one and two in relation to the current human rights approach to abortion. The recognition of an explicit right to abortion would resolve much of the problem with the current fragmented approach, by detailing clear obligations and putting pressure on states to make identifiable progress towards full compliance. Moving beyond the current human rights framework's justification for abortion as tied to a relatively high threshold of harm, this approach recognises the forced continuation of an unwanted pregnancy as a violation of pregnant people's rights and requires states to allow abortion on broad grounds. Unsafe abortions are to be addressed through the provision of legal and accessible services, and states must ensure the conditions for people to avoid unwanted pregnancies and have the socio-economic supports in place so that people are not compelled to have an abortion due to their personal contexts, in circumstances where they would otherwise choose to continue the pregnancy. UN treaty bodies such as CESCR have already acknowledged that sexual and reproductive rights are interlinked with other socio-economic rights, and thus this is included as a key aspect of full compliance with the right to abortion.[159]

My framework for the right to abortion is also an example of how a transformed human rights framework which sets out genuinely universal human rights and a more comprehensive approach to progressive realisation can go some way to address the issues relating to intersectional gender-based rights, cross-cultural applicability, and socio-economic rights that I set out in chapter two. It is necessary, however, to further consider socio-economic and cross-cultural issues with the right to abortion, in terms of the regulatory barriers to access which have not been considered in detail in this chapter and in the implementation of this right in domestic contexts. These issues will be addressed in the remaining two chapters.

V. CONCLUSION

Feminist scholars have recognised that abortion decisions are complex, subjective, and relational, and cannot be neatly organised into narrow legal grounds. From a feminist perspective, the harm of restricting abortion is an embodied one which is felt viscerally and affects every aspect of a pregnant person's body, life, and identity. Drawing on this context, and the gendered and racialised stereotypes that influence restrictions on reproductive rights, I argue in line with other feminist scholars that access to abortion is necessary for reproductive citizenship – an integral aspect of the full citizenship of women and people capable of becoming pregnant. The denial of reproductive citizenship is a denial of pregnant

[159] CESCR, 'General Comment No 22 on the Right to Sexual and Reproductive Health (Article 12 of the ICESCR)' (2 May 2016) UN Doc E/C.12/GC/22, paras 7, 10.

people's status as rights-holders – access to abortion is fundamental for full rights realisation.

From this, I recognise that there is a right to abortion which must be recognised within a transformed human rights framework. The scope of this must be expansive: states should avoid imposing grounds-based restrictions or gestational time limits without flexibility and have obligations to create the enabling conditions for reproductive agency, address structural inequalities, and decriminalise abortion. The framework I set out in the final section of this chapter recognises the need for the progressive realisation of the right to abortion, as there are significant global disparities in support for abortion rights and the resources to ensure universal access to abortion, among numerous other relevant issues. The framework for progressive realisation sets out clear obligations, requiring states to meet the minimum core content set out in the first tier, leading up to full compliance in the fourth tier. This framework is, of course, aspirational, but would go some way to move beyond the limitations of the current human rights approach. Each tier of the framework requires the removal of barriers to access – the most pressing barriers and accessibility issues that states must address will be explored in detail in the next chapter.

4

Access to Abortion in Practice

I. INTRODUCTION

IN THE PREVIOUS chapter, I established a framework for the progressive realisation of the right to abortion, which set out the steps that states must take to provide comprehensive, safe, and legal abortion services. At all tiers of the framework, states are required to ensure that abortion services are universally accessible in practice with minimal delays, and the third tier of the framework additionally requires that states address all structural barriers to access. As the right to abortion therefore requires that barriers are removed to ensure that all abortion-seeking pregnant people can access abortion services as early and easily as possible, there are some additional issues to be addressed in relation to the regulation of abortion, once legalised, at the state level. Medically unnecessary regulations imposed upon the provision of abortion services result in delays or difficulties accessing those services, and these barriers compound to have a particular impact on already marginalised groups.

The Committee on Economic, Social, and Cultural Rights (CESCR) identifies four elements required for the provision of comprehensive sexual and reproductive healthcare: availability; accessibility; acceptability; and quality.[1] While these elements are all interrelated, this chapter will address, in particular, how the restrictive regulation of abortion services impacts upon the availability and accessibility of abortion services. This chapter focuses, first, on the insufficient regulation of conscientious objection to the provision of abortion by healthcare professionals which limits the availability of abortion services in some contexts. I then address the medically unnecessary regulatory requirements that obstruct access to abortion, such as mandatory waiting periods, pre-abortion counselling, restrictions imposed on abortion providers, and requirements that the pregnant person attends an abortion facility in person for an early medical abortion. I set out arguments supporting telemedicine for early medical abortion, and the facilitating of self-managed abortion where states have failed to provide comprehensive abortion services, as important measures in minimising barriers and inequalities in accessing abortion services. Finally, I address the

[1] CESCR, 'General Comment No 22 on the Right to Sexual and Reproductive Health (Article 12 of the ICESCR)' (2 May 2016) UN Doc E/C.12/GC/22, paras 11–21.

importance of ensuring the affordability of abortion services, particularly in countries where healthcare is primarily delivered privately. For each section, this chapter concludes with further recommendations to the progressive realisation framework established in the previous chapter. Additional issues relating to the availability and accessibility of abortion services, such as infrastructure and staffing, are mentioned throughout this chapter but are not expanded upon in depth, in favour of a focus on the regulatory issues around abortion provision that have been insufficiently addressed within the current framework.

II. THE AVAILABILITY OF ABORTION SERVICES

The CESCR has stated that the availability of sexual and reproductive healthcare requires that an 'adequate number of functioning health-care facilities, services, goods and programmes should be available to provide the population with the fullest possible range of sexual and reproductive health care', which includes the availability of facilities, services, goods, and essential medicines for abortion care.[2] The legalisation of abortion must therefore be accompanied by the infrastructure and resources to guarantee access to these services for all, and although this may be subject to progressive realisation, steps must be continually taken towards improving abortion provision. The CESCR has also recognised that availability can be undermined by 'ideologically based policies or practices, such as the refusal to provide services based on conscience'.[3] This issue is complex, as healthcare providers with deeply held moral beliefs claim the right to conscientiously object from abortion provision, but this can significantly obstruct access to abortion and would thus violate the right to abortion. In this section, I will focus on these belief-based denials of abortion care as a prominent issue which is currently inadequately addressed by human rights bodies.

A. Belief-Based Denials of Abortion Care

The Current Approach

Many states include conscience-based exemptions within their abortion laws, to enable healthcare providers to conscientiously object to providing abortion services. 'Conscientious objection' (CO) was originally a term used in relation to refusals to participate in military service, which has been afforded protection under the right to freedom of thought, conscience, and religion contained in Article 18 of the International Covenant on Civil and Political Rights (ICCPR).[4]

[2] ibid paras 12–14.
[3] ibid para 14.
[4] HRC, 'General Comment No 22 on Article 18 of the ICCPR' (27 September 1993) UN Doc CCPR/21/Rev.1/Add.4, para 11.

However, CO is now also claimed by healthcare providers with moral opposition to certain treatments or services. This practice emerged within Britain's Abortion Act 1967, which enshrined a legal protection for doctors wishing to avoid providing abortion services.[5] CO most often applies to sexual and reproductive healthcare and other healthcare services that are deemed controversial, such as abortion, emergency contraception, reproductive technologies, and gender-affirming healthcare.[6] CO therefore disproportionately impacts women, people capable of becoming pregnant, and LGBTQ+ individuals, and has the potential to undermine the rights of these groups.

CO has not been explicitly extended to the medical sphere under Article 18, and the European Court of Human Rights (ECtHR) leaves it to individual states to decide whether to allow CO in this context. In *Grimmark v Sweden* and *Steen v Sweden*, the ECtHR dismissed the applications of two midwives over requirements that they provide abortion care as part of their employment at women's clinics as manifestly ill-founded.[7] However, it is also likely that the ECtHR would make a similar finding or apply the margin of appreciation if there was a challenge to a policy allowing CO based on Article 8, and neither has CO been explicitly excluded from the remit of Article 18 ICCPR. International human rights bodies have not indicated that CO provisions, where appropriately regulated, violate human rights standards on sexual and reproductive health. However, the difficult question is *how* to regulate CO in the context of abortion so as not to impede the availability of abortion services, as this could amount to a violation. For example, the European Social Committee has established that the numbers of objecting healthcare providers in Italy violates the right to health for representing a significant barrier to abortion services across the country.[8]

Thus, human rights bodies have so far attempted to strike a balance between the rights of patients and those of the objecting healthcare provider. Anand Grover, the Special Rapporteur on the right to the highest attainable standard of physical and mental health, recommended in his 2011 report that conscience-based exemptions be 'well-defined in scope and well-regulated in use' and that states ensure the availability of alternative services where a doctor objects.[9] The Human Rights Committee (HRC), Committee on the Elimination of

[5] Christian Fiala, Joyce Arthur, and Amelia Martzke, 'Origin of "Conscientious Objection" in Health Care: How Care Denials Became Enshrined Into Law Because of Abortion' (2025) 53(1) *Journal of Law Medicine and Ethics* 89.

[6] See Eileen K Fry-Bowers, 'A Matter of Conscience: Examining the Law and Policy of Conscientious Objection in Health Care' (2020) 21(2) *Policy, Politics and Nursing Practice* 120.

[7] ECtHR, App no 43726/17, *Grimmark v Sweden* (11 February 2020); ECtHR, App no 62309/17, *Steen v Sweden* (11 February 2020).

[8] Complaint no 87/2012, *International Planned Parenthood Federation – European Network (IPPF EN) v Italy* (10 September 2013) CM/ResChS(2014)6; Complaint no 91/2013, *Confederazione Generale Italiana del Lavoro (CGIL) v Italy* (12 October 2015) CM/ResChS(2016)3.

[9] Anand Grover, 'Report of the Special Rapporteur on the Right of Everyone to the Enjoyment of the Highest Attainable Standard of Mental and Physical Health' (3 August 2011) UN Doc A/66/254, para 65(m).

Discrimination Against Women (CEDAW Committee), and CESCR have all expressed concerns over the use of CO provisions in particular states where such provisions are relied on excessively or are unregulated to the point of obstructing access to abortion services.[10] These bodies have recommended that states implement mechanisms for mandatory referrals, requiring objecting healthcare providers to refer the patient to another healthcare provider who does not conscientiously object, and ensure effective means of contesting refusals.[11] In its 2015 Concluding Observations on Slovakia, CEDAW explicitly noted that such a referral mechanism should be implemented while also respecting individual conscientious objectors.[12] The CESCR has also supplemented these comments with the recommendation that there must be an adequate number of non-objecting healthcare providers willing and able to provide abortion services, and that 'such services should be available at all times in both public and private facilities and within reasonable geographical reach'.[13]

Within the current international human rights framework, a compromise position is therefore taken where a mechanism for mandatory referrals is seen as striking a balance between sexual and reproductive rights and the right to freedom of conscience. However, this balance is considered unsatisfactory by both sides of the debate. For proponents of CO, the current human rights approach has been critiqued for affording 'more weight to the woman's right to health than to the health-care provider's right to freedom of conscience'.[14] Carolyn McLeod acknowledges that, while referral may be a compromise for those concerned with ensuring access to abortion, it does not represent a true compromise for anti-abortion doctors who genuinely believe abortion to be murder.[15] Sara Fovargue and Mary Neal have argued along these lines, that requirements placed on healthcare professionals to inform the patient of their conscientious objection and refer them to another doctor entails complicitly in the objected practice.[16] For those concerned with how CO obstructs access to abortion, these existing human rights standards are not expansive enough to cover all situations

[10] See, eg, HRC, 'Concluding Observations on the Seventh Periodic Report of Colombia' (17 November 2016) UN Doc CCPR/C/COL/CO/7, paras 20–21; CESCR, 'Concluding Observations on the Sixth Periodic Report of Poland' (26 Oct 2016) UN Doc E/C.12/POL/CO/6, paras 46–47; CEDAW, 'Concluding Observations on the Combined Seventh and Eighth Periodic Report of Poland' (14 November 2014) UN Doc CEDAW/C/POL/CO/7-8, paras 36–37; CEDAW, 'Concluding Observations on the Combined Seventh and Eighth Periodic Reports of Romania' (24 July 2017) UN Doc CEDAW/C/ROU/CO/7-8, paras 32–33.

[11] ibid.

[12] CEDAW, 'Concluding Observations on the Combined Fifth and Sixth Periodic Reports of Slovakia' (25 November 2015) UN Doc CEDAW/C/SVK/CO/5-6, para 31(d).

[13] CESCR, 'General Comment No 22 (2016) (n 1) para 14.

[14] Meghan Grizzle Fischer, 'The United Nations and the Right to Conscientious Objection in the Health-Care Field' (2016) 21(1) *Texas Review of Law and Politics* 201, 232.

[15] Carolyn McLeod, 'Referral in the Wake of Conscientious Objection to Abortion' (2008) 23(4) *Hypatia* 30, 34–35.

[16] Sara Fovargue and Mary Neal, '"In Good Conscience": Conscience-Based Exemptions and Proper Medical Treatment' (2015) 23(2) *Medical Law Review* 221, 241.

where CO places other human rights in jeopardy, and more guidance from human rights bodies is therefore needed.[17] Fiona de Londras et al, for example, note that 'conscientious objection operates to erect barriers to, and interrupt continuity of, abortion care, with significant implications for pregnant people's human rights.'[18] As I have argued elsewhere, the mandatory referrals approach adopted by international human rights bodies is inadequate at addressing the issues posed by widespread CO, the misuse of conscience exemptions, and the overall harms of being denied legal abortion care based on a healthcare provider's personal beliefs.[19] From the perspective of upholding the right to abortion, the starting point must therefore be to consider the harms caused by the widespread practice of CO.

The Harms of Conscientious Objection

The unfettered use of CO provisions creates widespread issues in abortion provision, often acting as a barrier to access even where abortion has been legalised. The impact of this is heightened in countries with already restrictive laws. For example, Poland only permits abortion where the life or health of the pregnant person is at risk, or in cases of rape.[20] However, abortion on these legal grounds is, in practice, largely unavailable due to the widespread use of CO. Doctors in Poland can refuse to perform non-compulsory healthcare services, such as abortion, if those services are incompatible with the individual's conscience.[21] The law also sets out requirements that an objecting doctor must give advance notice to their supervisor, indicate to the patient that their objection is conscientious, and originally required the objector to refer the patient to another doctor.[22] However, in 2015, the Polish Constitutional Tribunal held that the referral requirement was a limitation on freedom of conscience and was therefore unconstitutional.[23] Doctors thus no longer have the obligation to refer, but in relation to abortion, this requirement was largely unenforced even prior to the Tribunal's ruling. In *RR v Poland* and *P and S v Poland*, the ECtHR criticised the lack of procedural mechanisms in place to ensure that CO did not interfere with the patient's

[17] Christina Zampas, 'Legal and Ethical Standards for Protecting Women's Human Rights and the Practice of Conscientious Objection in Reproductive Healthcare Settings' (2013) 123 *International Journal of Gynecology and Obstetrics* S63, S63; Christina Zampas and Ximena Andión-Ibañez, 'Conscientious Objection to Sexual and Reproductive Health Services: International Human Rights Standards and European Law and Practice' (2012) 19 *European Journal of Health Law* 231, 255.

[18] Fiona de Londras and others, 'The Impact of 'Conscientious Objection' on Abortion-Related Outcomes: A Synthesis of Legal and Health Evidence' (2023) 129 *Health Policy* 104716, 10.

[19] Zoe L Tongue, 'On Conscientious Objection to Abortion: Questioning Mandatory Referral as Compromise in the International Human Rights Framework' (2022) 22(4) *Medical Law International* 349.

[20] The Family Planning, Human Embryo Protection and Conditions of Permissibility of Abortion Act of 7 January 1993 [Poland], Article 4a. The ground for foetal impairment was declared unconstitutional in Polish Constitutional Tribunal Case K 1/20 (22 October 2020).

[21] Doctor and Dentist Professions Act of 5 December 1996 [Poland], Article 39.

[22] ibid.

[23] Polish Constitutional Tribunal Case K 12/14 (7 October 2015).

interest, which enabled doctors to obstruct access to prenatal diagnostic and therapeutic abortion services.[24] Further, *Tysiąc v Poland* highlights how doctors also evade these requirements by refusing to provide abortion services without invoking the CO provision.[25] The applicant, Alicja Tysiąc, had severe myopia (a visual impairment) which doctors concluded would likely worsen following the delivery of the foetus she was carrying.[26] They recommended sterilisation after the birth, due to the risk that pregnancy would have on her eyesight, but refused to certify for an abortion despite her condition meeting the legal criteria for therapeutic abortion.[27]

The volume of healthcare professionals in Poland who invoke CO, or obstruct access to abortion without invoking this provision, thus creates a significant barrier to abortion services. Institutional CO is also widespread, where senior doctors in public hospitals object on behalf of all staff and prevent any abortions being carried out in that facility.[28] Doctors that do not have a genuine objection may nevertheless refuse to provide abortion services for fear of harassment by the Church or of damaging their careers if they are situated in an anti-abortion workplace.[29] The ECtHR has also identified how the criminalisation of people providing illegal abortions has a chilling effect on doctors, who have to decide whether the requirements for a legal abortion have been met in each individual case.[30] The scale of CO in Poland has ultimately resulted in the near-complete removal of abortion services from public hospitals.[31] Doctors who do want to provide abortion services tend to do so only in private practices, where institutional CO can be avoided and prosecutions relating to abortion are rare due to the limited governmental and religious control in the commercial sphere.[32] The impact of CO in this context is the removal of already-limited abortion services from public health facilities, creating a divergence in the ability to obtain an abortion on the basis of socio-economic status.

Abortion provision in Italy similarly suffers due to a high rate of CO. Italy's abortion law is more liberal than in Poland, permitting abortion within the first 90 days (around 12 weeks) for health, social, economic, or family reasons, and after this point where the pregnant person's life or health is at risk or if the foetus has a serious impairment.[33] However, obtaining an abortion is

[24] ECtHR, App no 27617/04, *RR v Poland* (26 May 2011), paras 174–76; ECtHR, App no 57375/08, *P and S v Poland* (30 October 2012), paras 92–93, 106, 107.

[25] ECtHR, App no 5410/03, *Tysiąc v Poland* (20 March 2007).

[26] ibid paras 8–10.

[27] ibid.

[28] Silvia De Zordo and Joanna Mishtal, 'Physicians and Abortion: Provision, Political Participation and Conflicts on the Ground – The Cases of Brazil and Poland' (2011) 21(3S) *Women's Health Issues* S32, S34; *P and S* case (n 24) para 59.

[29] De Zordo and Mishtal, 'Physicians and Abortion' (2011) (n 28) S33–S34.

[30] *RR* (n 24) paras 192–93.

[31] Agata Chełstowska, 'Stigmatisation and Commercialisation of Abortion Services in Poland: Turning Sin into Gold' (2011) 19(37) *Reproductive Health Matters* 98, 98–99.

[32] ibid 98, 102–03.

[33] Law 194 of the Italian Republic 1978, Articles 4, 6.

difficult in practice as CO is so widespread. In 2020, 67 per cent of gynaecologists conscientiously objected to the provision of abortion services.[34] This, again, has a particular impact on the availability of abortion in public hospitals, of which many are affiliated with the Catholic Church. In Catholic hospitals or hospitals where the senior directors object to abortion, institutional CO means that abortion services are unavailable even where individual doctors may be willing to provide them.[35] Further, many hospitals which do not have institutional CO are nevertheless staffed only by objectors.[36] While the law requires regional health departments and hospitals to implement procedures to guarantee abortion services, the high percentage of objectors limits the ability of institutions to organise personnel so as to ensure timely access to abortion.[37] Elena Caruso highlights that some regions of Italy have just one doctor willing to provide abortion services, while others have none at all, requiring pregnant people in those regions to travel elsewhere to access abortion services.[38] In 2022, only 61 per cent of Italian healthcare facilities with obstetrics and gynaecology departments provided abortion services, but there is significant regional variation: in some regions this was only 30 per cent, while in others it was 70 per cent.[39] Thus, as with Poland, CO creates a significant barrier to the comprehensive delivery of abortion services across Italy, despite its more liberal law.

The misuse of CO provisions is also common, with two prominent uses of CO provisions for non-conscientious reasons. First, CO provisions are used by healthcare providers wishing to avoid the potential disadvantages to themselves associated with providing abortion services. As highlighted above in relation to Poland, the stigmatisation and criminalisation of abortion acts as a deterrent for healthcare providers who would not otherwise object. In the Italian context, the career disadvantages of being willing to provide abortion services manifest in an increased workload as non-objectors, who represent a minority of gynaecologists, are required to perform most abortions.[40] Agustina Ramón Michel et al

[34] Ministro della Salute, 'Relazione del Ministro della Salute sulla attuazione della legge contenente norme per law tutela sociale della maternitá e per l'interruzione volontoria di gravidanza (legge 194/78) – dati definitivi 2020' (2022) www.salute.gov.it/imgs/C_17_pubblicazioni_3236_allegato.pdf accessed 9 January 2026.

[35] Wendy Chavin, Laurel Swerdlow, and Jocelyn Fifield, 'Regulation of Conscientious Objection to Abortion: An International Comparative Multiple-Case Study' (2017) 19(1) *Health and Human Rights Journal* 55, 59–60.

[36] ibid 59.

[37] Law 194 (n 33), Article 9; Chavin, Swerdlow, and Fifield, 'Regulation of Conscientious Objection' (2017) (n 35) 59; Francesca Minerva, 'Conscientious Objection in Italy' (2015) 41(2) *Journal of Medical Ethics* 170, 171.

[38] Elena Caruso, 'Abortion in Italy: Forty Years On' (2020) 28 *Feminist Legal Studies* 87, 91–92.

[39] Ministro della Salute, 'Relazione del Ministro della Salute sulla attuazione della legge contenente norme per law tutela sociale della maternitá e per l'interruzione volontoria di gravidanza (legge 194/78) – dati definitivi 2022' (2024) www.salute.gov.it/new/sites/default/files/imported/C_17_pubblicazioni_3493_allegato.pdf accessed 9 January 2026.

[40] Chavin, Swerdlow, and Fifield (n35) 60; Tommaso Autorino, Francesco Mattioli, and Letizia Mencarini, 'The Impact of Gynecologists' Conscientious Objection on Abortion Access' (2020) 87 *Social Science Research* 1, 6.

refer to the use of CO in these contexts as a 'defensive use' as healthcare providers invoke CO to avoid personal disadvantage.[41] This problem is worsened where healthcare providers lack comprehensive understanding of their state's abortion laws and regulations, or where resource limitations incentivise the use of CO.[42]

Second, healthcare professionals often misuse CO provisions in order to deliberately obstruct access to abortion. Lauren Fink et al identify a spectrum of conscientious objection from extreme objectors, who oppose abortion and actively prevent patients from accessing those services by refusing to refer and by giving inaccurate legal and medical information, to partial objectors, who refuse to provide abortions on an ad-hoc basis.[43] They situate moderate objectors, those that conscientiously object and are willing to refer patients or provide accurate information, somewhere between them.[44] CO to referral can also be categorised as complete or selective, and healthcare professionals who completely object to providing abortion services may completely or selectively object to referral. Selective objection also hinders abortion provision, as healthcare professionals may refuse to provide abortions beyond a certain gestational time limit or on certain grounds, despite their legality. For example, healthcare professionals in Brazil will often invoke CO for abortion on the grounds of rape where they do not feel that enough proof has been given, and a study of CO in Mexico and Bolivia revealed gestational age and foetal viability to be a key factor.[45] This selective objection is also used by healthcare professionals to reinforce traditional sexual and gender roles and reinforce stigmatising attitudes around unwanted pregnancies, such as through invoking CO where the pregnant person did not use contraception.[46]

The misuse of CO provisions in this way amounts to the imposition of personal beliefs on patients, and an attempt to circumvent the legalisation of

[41] Agustina Ramón Michel and others, 'Regulating Conscientious Objection to Legal Abortion in Argentina: Taking into Consideration Its Uses and Consequences' (2020) 22(2) *Health and Human Rights Journal* 271, 274.

[42] De Zordo and Mishtal (n 28) S35; Jane Harries and others, 'Conscientious Objection and its Impact on Abortion Service Provision in South Africa: A Qualitative study' (2014) 11(16) *Reproductive Health* 1, 4; Laura Florence Harris and others, 'Conscientious Objection to Abortion Provision: Why Context Matters' (2018) 13(5) *Global Public Health* 556, 560.

[43] Lauren R Fink and others, '"The Fetus Is My Patient, Too": Attitudes Toward Abortion and Referral Among Physician Conscientious Objectors in Bogotá, Colombia' (2016) 42(2) *International Perspectives on Sexual and Reproductive Health* 71, 74–75.

[44] ibid.

[45] Debora Diniz, Alberto Madeiro, and Cristião Rosas, 'Conscientious Objection, Barriers, and Abortion in the Case of Rape: A Study Among Physicians in Brazil' (2014) 22(43) *Reproductive Health Matters* 141, 146–47; Stephanie Andrea Küng and others, '"We Don't Want Problems": Reasons for Denial of Legal Abortion Based on Conscientious Objection in Mexico and Bolivia' (2021) 18(44) *Reproductive Health* 1, 6.

[46] Michel and others, 'Regulating Conscientious Objection' (2020) (n 41) 274; Emily Freeman and Ernestina Coast, 'Conscientious Objection to Abortion: Zambian Healthcare Practitioners' Beliefs and Practices' (2019) 221 *Social Science and Medicine* 106, 107.

abortion.[47] As Charles Ngwena identifies, CO can become a 'Trojan horse for popular patriarchal and religious prejudices that deny women's reproductive agency'.[48] Thus, the lack of sufficient regulation of CO can create anti-abortion medical cultures in lieu of anti-abortion laws and policies, and to the same effect. This has significant impacts on abortion seekers. Christian Fiala and Joyce Arthur argue that there is a continuum of harm associated with CO.[49] Where CO provisions are misused, CO can obstruct access to abortion and leave even those needing emergency terminations without abortion services.[50] There have been recent cases in Poland and Italy where pregnant people have died as a result of being denied life-saving abortions.[51] However, Fiala and Arthur also argue that even where the impacts of CO are relatively minimal, refusals to provide abortion care are still harmful as they stigmatise pregnant people seeking abortions and cause delays.[52] Faced with a healthcare professional who is objecting, pregnant people may be treated disrespectfully or judged for attempting to obtain an abortion.[53] A recent study on CO in Britain highlighted the stress and emotional impact of being denied abortion care, even when the pregnant person eventually obtained an abortion, and one in Germany highlights how healthcare providers may be hostile to patients seeking an abortion even if they do not invoke the CO provision.[54]

Returning to the feminist approach to abortion that I articulated in the last chapter, CO feeds into gendered stereotypes that lead to the denial of pregnant people's embodied agency and reproductive citizenship. McLeod argues that CO in the reproductive healthcare context is always harmful because these

[47] Ana Cristina González Vélez and Laura Gil Urbano, 'Improper Use of Conscientious Objection to Abortion/Authors' Response' (2016) 42(2) *International Perspectives on Sexual and Reproductive Health* 221; Verónica Undurraga and Michelle Sadler, 'The Misrepresentation of Conscientious Objection as a New Strategy of Resistance to Abortion Decriminalisation' (2019) 27(2) *Reproductive Health Matters* 17.

[48] Charles G Ngwena, 'Conscientious Objection to Abortion and Accommodation Women's Reproductive Health Rights: Reflection on a Decision of the Constitutional Court of Colombia from an African Regional Human Rights Perspective' (2014) 58 *Journal of African Law* 183, 209.

[49] Christian Fiala and Joyce H Arthur, 'There is no Defence for "Conscientious Objection" in Reproductive Health Care' (2017) 216 *European Journal of Obstetrics & Gynecology and Reproductive Biology* 254, 255.

[50] ibid.

[51] See, eg, BBC News, 'Italy abortion row as woman dies after hospital miscarriage' (20 October 2016) www.bbc.co.uk/news/world-europe-37713211 accessed 9 January 2026; Adam Easton, BBC News, 'Doctors found guilty over death of pregnant woman in Poland' (17 July 2025) www.bbc.co.uk/news/articles/c1lj145jy5zo accessed 9 January 2026.

[52] Fiala and Arthur, 'There is no Defence' (2017) (n 49) 255.

[53] Christian Fiala and Joyce H Arthur, '"Dishonourable Disobedience" – Why Refusal to Treat in Reproductive Healthcare is Not Conscientious Objection' (2014) 1 *Woman – Psychosomatic Gynaecology and. Obstetrics* 12, 13.

[54] Becky Self, Clare Maxwell, and Valerie Fleming, 'The Missing voices in the Conscientious Objection Debate: British Service Users' Experiences of conscientious Objection to Abortion' (2023) 24(1) *BMC Medical Ethics* 1; Robin Krawutschke, Tania Pastrana, and Dagmar Schmitz, 'Conscientious Objection and Barriers to Abortion Within a Specific Regional Context – An Expert Interview Study' (2024) 25(1) *BMC Medical Ethics* 1.

denials 'have meaning against a certain social background' which includes stereotypes around women's sexuality and that 'good women are maternal and do not put the lives of children, especially their own offspring, at risk'.[55] These norms intersect with race and class stereotypes, and Chelsey Yang has highlighted the disproportionate impact that CO has on people of colour and socio-economically disadvantaged people in the US.[56] I have thus argued elsewhere that CO is 'a form of violence enacted on the gendered body' and can be understood as a 'dignitary harm', in that the practice, in the context of harmful gender stereotypes, treats people capable of becoming pregnant as second-class citizens.[57] In order to reorient the focus on these harms, rather than the moral beliefs of healthcare providers, Fiala and Arthur have adopted the term 'belief-based denial of abortion care'.[58] For the remainder of this section, I adopt this terminology in the context of international human rights regulation, in order to emphasise the impact of belief-based refusals on the provision and availability of abortion services.

Regulating Belief-Based Denials of Abortion Care

McLeod argues that the regulation of belief-based denials must reflect a proper balancing of the competing interests of healthcare provider and patient, rather than a compromise position such as the one currently taken by the international human rights framework.[59] Balancing freedom of conscience with the right to abortion requires full consideration of the harms of denying abortion care, as articulated in this and the previous chapter, and the human rights violations likely to arise as a result of widespread denials. States must therefore be careful about allowing or supporting belief-based denials of abortion care, as pregnant people must be able to easily access safe, legal, and non-judgmental abortion services without additional delays and obstacles.

Some scholars thus argue that belief-based denials should never be permitted in the healthcare context. Fiala and Arthur argue that belief-based denials are never acceptable as the legal provisions are routinely abused, undermine standards of non-judgmental healthcare, violate pregnant people's right to health, and result in the stigmatising of abortion providers.[60] To this end, they argue

[55] Carolyn McLeod, 'Harm or Mere Inconvenience? Denying Women Emergency Contraception' (2010) 25(1) *Hypatia* 11, 12, 18.

[56] Chelsey Yang, 'The Inequity of Conscientious Objection: Refusal of Emergency Contraception' (2020) 27(6) *Nursing Ethics* 1408.

[57] Zoe L Tongue, 'Locating Abortion and Contraception on the Obstetric Violence Continuum' (2024) 17(1) *International Journal of Feminist Approaches to Bioethics* 1, 9; Tongue, 'On Conscientious Objection' (2022) (n 19) 363.

[58] See Christian Fiala and Joyce Arthur, 'How to Discourage Belief-based Denial of Abortion Care' (2025) 30(4) *European Journal of Contraception and Reproductive Health Care* 221.

[59] Carolyn McLeod, *Conscience in Reproductive Health Care: Prioritizing Patient Interests* (Oxford, Oxford University Press, 2020) pp 8–9.

[60] Fiala and Arthur, '"Dishonourable Disobedience"' (2014) (n 53).

that belief-based denials are an unethical abandonment of professional obligations (which they refer to as 'dishonourable disobedience') and should therefore be eliminated from the reproductive healthcare sphere.[61] Udo Schuklenk and Ricardo Smalling similarly take the view that a 'society that grants medical professionals a conscientious objection-based opt-out will have to accept suboptimal health outcomes' and that refusing to allow belief-based denials is the most efficient means of ensuring that access to healthcare services such as abortion is not undermined.[62] This would not mean forcing all anti-abortion doctors to be involved with abortion treatment – they argue that people who object to abortion should not be allowed to enter medical fields such as obstetrics and gynaecology.[63] This is already the case in Sweden, Finland, and Iceland.[64]

However, this may be ineffective elsewhere. In Italy, such a policy would likely lead to a shortage of obstetrics and gynaecology staff given the numbers of objecting healthcare providers. Further, healthcare providers may enter those fields with an undeclared objection to abortion and ostensibly refuse to provide abortions for other reasons. Moreover, bans on CO are met with concerns for certain groups of objectors – in the European context, this is typically of Catholic healthcare providers with religious moral objections to abortion. For example, Irene Domenici has expressed concerns over the de facto exclusion of Catholics from the midwifery profession in Sweden, which the ECtHR seemed to accept in *Grimmark* and *Sweden*.[65] Thus, alternative proposals tend to relate to administrative efforts aimed at striking a balance, such as 'matching' patients with morally compatible doctors, frameworks based on fiduciary duty, and requirements that healthcare institutions manage objecting staff through registration of their objections, distinguishing between legitimate and illegitimate reasons for an objection, or by setting quotas.[66] Concerned with ensuring comprehensive service delivery alongside permitting CO, Daniel Rodger and Bruce Blackshaw suggest the use of quotas to limit, but not entirely prohibit, the

[61] ibid 18–20.

[62] Udo Schuklenk and Ricardo Smalling, 'Why Medical Professionals Have No Moral Claim to Conscientious Objection Accommodation in Liberal Democracies' (2017) 43(4) *Journal of Medical Ethics* 234, 273, 240.

[63] ibid 239.

[64] See Christian Fiala and others, 'Yes We Can! Successful Examples of Disallowing "Conscientious Objection" in Reproductive Health Care' (2016) 21(3) *European Journal of Contraception and Reproductive Health Care* 201.

[65] Irene Domenici, 'Antigone Betrayed? The European Court of Human Rights' Decisions on Conscientious Objection to Abortion in the Cases of *Grimmark v Sweden* and *Steen v Sweden*' (2021) 28 *European Journal of Health Law* 26, 47.

[66] See, eg, Holly Fernandez Lynch, *Conflicts of Conscience in Health Care: An Institutional Compromise* (Massachusetts Institute of Technology Press, 2020) Ch 3; McLeod, *Conscience in Reproductive Health Care* (2020) (n 59) Ch 5; Nathan Gamble and Toni Saad, 'A Taxonomy of Conscientious Objection in Healthcare' (2022) 17(1) *Clinical Ethics* 63; Francesca Minerva, 'Conscientious Objection, Complicity in Wrongdoing, and a Not-So-Moderate Approach' (2017) 26(1) *Cambridge Quarterly of Healthcare Ethics* 109.

number of medical trainees entering fields such as gynaecology and obstetrics.[67] This would be a long-term solution, by imposing quotas at the point that medical trainees enter their specialist pathways rather than excluding already-trained doctors from their field.[68] They propose two instances where the quota system would be appropriate: first, in states such as Italy where existing CO practices significantly obstruct access to abortion; and second, through the use of employment quotas in states without current provision for CO in order to avoid disrupting existing abortion services.[69] Francesca Minerva similarly proposes a 'ratio' system, for example of one objector to nine non-objectors, in any given institution or region.[70]

Given the worldwide variation in the prevalence of belief-based denials and how they impact access to abortion services, it would be inappropriate for the international human rights framework to prescribe a blanket approach. The international human rights framework must, instead, impose a duty on states to ensure that, where belief-based denials are permitted, they must be regulated in a way which guarantees unobstructed access to abortion services in line with the obligations set out in the previous chapter. The means by which this is achieved ought to be reviewed at the national level, in order to assess specific contextual issues and any potential consequences of adopting particular regulations. As Laura Florence Harris et al argue, CO policies seldom take into account the context of reproductive healthcare delivery, and it is this context that leads belief-based denials to function as a barrier to abortion access.[71] They also argue that policies must take account of the economic, social, and political pressures on healthcare providers which may lead to the defensive use of CO provisions, as mentioned above.[72] These pressures shape both the ability of healthcare professionals, in the context of available resources and their workload, to provide abortion services and have an impact upon dominant attitudes towards abortion.[73] Thus, in addition to the regulation of belief-based, states must adopt policies aimed at improving the allocation of resources to reproductive healthcare services and ensure that healthcare professionals who do not object to providing abortions are informed of the relevant regulations, have the support of their colleagues, and any other relevant workplace conditions are met.[74] Further, as noted in the recent statement by the International Federation

[67] Daniel Rodger and Bruce P Blackshaw, 'Quotas: Enabling Conscientious Objection to Coexist with Abortion Access' (2021) 29 *Health Care Analysis* 154, 155.

[68] ibid 160–61.

[69] ibid 155.

[70] Minerva, 'Conscientious Objection' (2017) (n 66) 116.

[71] Laura Florence Harris and others, 'Conscientious Objection to Abortion Provision: Why Context Matters' (2018) 13(5) *Global Public Health* 556, 557.

[72] ibid.

[73] ibid 560–61.

[74] ibid 562.

of Gynecology and Obstetrics (FIGO), CO should not be implemented by entire institutions, as this creates systemic obstacles to abortion care.[75]

This approach may also justify support for the conscientious *provision* of abortion services by healthcare providers in contexts where abortion remains restricted. Alberto Giublini et al, for example, have argued in favour of allowing healthcare providers to follow their conscience in the provision of illegal abortion services based on what is in the patient's best medical interests.[76] Within the framework of the right to abortion, the failure of a state to comply with its human rights obligations ought not to preclude healthcare providers from treating their patients in line with accepted professional standards. The framing of this as an issue of the healthcare provider's conscience, as well as the patient's rights, is important in recognising the fact that abortion providers are also motivated by their deeply held beliefs.[77] States must therefore ensure that the availability of abortion services includes the enabling conditions for the conscientious provision of abortion care, particularly where belief-based denials are permitted, such that freedom of conscience is protected equally.

This will, in turn, require the comprehensive training of medical students on abortion, as well as attempts to tackle abortion stigma in healthcare settings. McLeod argues that training on abortion must also emphasize that abortion provision is morally necessary.[78] Abortion stigma is prevalent in medical schools and healthcare settings, with Erica Millar highlighting that abortion is often portrayed as 'abnormal' in comparison to 'normal healthy pregnancies'.[79] States must recognise that gender stereotypes, myths, and abortion stigma can underpin many healthcare providers' moral objections to abortion, and these must also be addressed. Article 5 of CEDAW requires states

> modify the social and cultural patterns of conduct of men and women, with a view to achieving the elimination of prejudices and customary and all other practices which are based on the idea of the inferiority or the superiority of either of the sexes or on stereotyped roles for men and women.[80]

[75] FIGO, 'Conscientious Objection: A Barrier to Care' (19 October 2021) /www.figo.org/resources/figo-statements/conscientious-objection-barrier-care accessed 9 January 2026.

[76] Alberto Giublini and others, 'Conscientious Commitment, Professional Obligations and Abortion Provision after the Reversal of *Roe v Wade*' (2024) 50 *Journal of Medical Ethics* 351.

[77] Lisa Harris, 'The Moral Agency of Abortion Providers: Conscientious Provision, Dangertalk, and the Lived Experience of Doing Stigmatized Work' in Lori d'Agincourt-Canning and Carolyn Ells (eds), *Ethical Issues in Women's Healthcare: Practice and Policy* (Oxford, Oxford University Press, 2019); Bronwen Merner and others, 'Health Providers' Reasons for Participating in Abortion Care: A Scoping Review' (2024) 20 *Women's Health* 1, 20; Jennifer Karlin and Carole Joffe, 'Self-Sourced Medication Abortion, Physician Authority, and the Contradictions of Abortion Care' (2023) 48(4) *Journal of Health, Politics, Policy and Law* 603.

[78] McLeod 'Referral in the Wake' (2008) (n 15) 42.

[79] Erica Millar, 'Abortion Stigma, Abortion Exceptionalism, and Medical Curricula' (2023) 32(3) *Health Sociology Review* 261, 269.

[80] United Nations General Assembly, *Convention on the Elimination of All Forms of Discrimination Against Women,* UN Treaty Series, vol 1249, 18 December 1979.

The Committee has previously found violations of Article 5 in relation to stereotypes concerning pregnancy and motherhood in the context of the denial of abortion and therapeutic surgery to a pregnant minor.[81] Training for all healthcare providers on the importance of sexual and reproductive rights including abortion, and the harms of care denials, is important for combatting these prejudices. The combatting of abortion stigma and gender stereotypes around pregnancy and motherhood is included in the framework for the right to abortion set out in the previous chapter, encompassing such an obligation.

Putting this into a framework that can be adopted alongside the progressive realisation framework for the right to abortion as set out in the previous chapter, the obligation to sufficiently regulate belief-based denials of abortion care must also be progressively realised alongside it. Clayton Ó Néill suggests two relevant considerations that will be taken into account here: first, that an objecting doctor has a range of options to avoid compromising their conscience and has chosen their profession or specialism in light of this; and second, that the breadth of defensible CO is connected to the breadth of abortion provision, so greater restrictions on CO can be justified where there are greater restrictions on abortion provision.[82] In some contexts, the strict regulation of belief-based denials may be unnecessary, whereas in others much more stringent restrictions will be required to protect access to abortion services. Where the higher tiers of the right to abortion have not been met, or where belief-based denials significantly obstruct access to abortion, they must be restricted to a greater extent than in states where the impact is less harmful. The measures that must be taken towards regulating belief-based denials therefore correlate to the extent to which states comply with the right to abortion.

Finally, there are some situations where belief-based denials should not be permitted at all. In many countries, belief-based denials are permitted except where necessary to save the life of the pregnant person.[83] However, in Italy and Poland, the deaths of pregnant women from sepsis have occurred in the context of objecting healthcare providers refusing to intervene in miscarriage complications.[84] States must therefore impose a clear obligation on healthcare providers to intervene and provide abortion care where there is a serious risk to the pregnant person's life or health. Given the potential risks of abortion complications, particularly where unsafe clandestine abortion is common, healthcare providers should also never be permitted to deny a patient post-abortion care – which is often life-saving.[85]

[81] *LC v Peru* (2011) UN Doc CEDAW/C/50/D/22/2009, para 8.15.

[82] Clayton Ó Néill, *Religion, Medicine and the Law* (Routledge, 2019) p 186.

[83] See, eg, Abortion Act 1967, s 4 [England, Wales, and Scotland].

[84] BBC News, 'Italy abortion row' (n 52); Easton, 'Doctors found guilty' (n 52).

[85] See Carolyn Curtis, 'Meeting Health Care Needs of Women Experiencing Complications of Miscarriage and Unsafe Abortion: USAID's Postabortion Care Program' (2007) 52(4) *Journal of Midwifery and Women's Health* 368.

B. Recommendations on Regulating Belief-Based Denials of Abortion Care

1. Where States Parties allow conscientious objection to abortion, it must be regulated to ensure that access to abortion services in line with the right to abortion is not obstructed. States Parties have a duty to implement procedural mechanisms to assess if and how conscientious objection should be regulated to this effect. Where States Parties have only met the earlier tiers of the right to abortion, and abortion has therefore only been legalised on a limited basis, or where conscientious objection obstructs access to legal abortion services, more restrictive measures will be necessary to ensure that conscientious objection does not operate to prevent any abortion services from being carried out.
2. States Parties must not permit conscientious objection where an abortion is necessary to save the life of or prevent serious harm to the pregnant person, or in relation to post-abortion healthcare. Institutional objections, where senior management objects on behalf of all staff members, must also not be permitted.
3. Alongside providing for conscientious objection, all States Parties must ensure that abortion services are sufficiently staffed and resourced, and that healthcare professionals are properly trained and have sufficient understanding of the relevant regulations. Medical trainees should be given gender-sensitive education on abortion (and contraception), and States Parties must take steps towards a socio-cultural understanding of abortion (and contraception) as a human right and necessary healthcare service. This is particularly important in relation to later abortions, in order to address selective objection to abortions past a certain gestational time limit, and to enable the conscientious provision of abortion care.

III. THE ACCESSIBILITY OF ABORTION SERVICES

The CESCR recognises three components of accessibility for sexual, and reproductive healthcare: physical accessibility; affordability; and information accessibility.[86] Healthcare 'facilities, goods, information and services related to sexual and reproductive health care must be available within safe physical and geographical reach for all, so that persons in need can receive timely services and information' – requiring states to take positive measures to address any relevant barriers to access, such as those experienced by people with disabilities or those living rurally.[87] Essential sexual and reproductive health goods and services must be provided freely or affordably, so that socio-economically disadvantaged people

[86] CESCR (n 1) paras 15–19.
[87] ibid para 16.

are not burdened by health expenses.[88] Information accessibility means 'the right to evidence-based information on all aspects of sexual and reproductive health' including abortion and post-abortion care.[89] The principle of accessibility is further undermined by medically unnecessary regulations on services, and the lack of access to safe, modern methods of abortion (such as abortion medication). Moreover, within a transformed human rights framework, socio-economic rights will pose questions for politico-economic frameworks that are opposed to state welfare provision – namely, neoliberal frameworks. However, these issues have not, as of yet, been widely discussed by international human rights bodies and will thus be the focus of this section.

A. Medically Unnecessary Regulations

Numerous states impose additional regulatory requirements on abortion services, such as mandatory waiting periods, pre-abortion counselling, ultrasound scans, and requirements for in-person visits to an abortion facility. These requirements are unnecessary on medical, social, psychological, or other heath-based grounds (referred to as 'medically unnecessary' throughout this section for ease) and create additional barriers to accessing abortion services. Germany, for example, has mandatory pre-abortion counselling requirements for all abortions other than for medical reasons or in cases of rape, with a minimum three-day waiting period between the counselling and the abortion procedure.[90] In some cases, counselling (and associated requirements) serves the explicit function of deterring the pregnant person from having an abortion. In Russia, pre-abortion counsellors are instructed to convince the pregnant person of 'the immorality and cruelty of abortion.'[91] As of 2022, Hungary requires the pregnant person to listen to the foetal heartbeat before they can have an abortion.[92]

The World Health Organization (WHO) has noted that such measures are medically unnecessary, and therefore contribute to the prevalence of unsafe abortions by imposing barriers to access.[93] The CEDAW Committee has also recommended, in line with WHO guidance, that states should ensure access to

[88] ibid para 17.

[89] ibid para 18.

[90] German Criminal Code, §218a(1).

[91] Ministry of Health and Social Development of the Russian Federation, *Guidelines on Psychological Pre-Abortion Counselling*, 15-0/10/2-9162 (13 October 2010) https://abortion-policies.srhr.org/documents/countries/02-Russian-Federation-Methodical-Letter-Pre-Abortion-Counseling-Ministry-of-Health-and-Social-Development-2010.pdf accessed 9 January 2026.

[92] Decree 29/2022 (IX 12) of the Minister of the Interior on the Amendment of the Decree 32/1992 (XII 23) NM on the Implementation of Act LXXIX of 1992 on the Protection of Fetal Life (Hungarian Official Gazette No 147 of 2022).

[93] WHO, *Safe Abortion: Technical & Policy Guidance For Health Systems* (WHO, 29 June 2015) https://wkc.who.int/resources/publications/i/item/safe-abortion-technical-policy-guidance-for-health-systems accessed 9 January 2026, p.4.

safe abortion without subjecting pregnant people to mandatory counselling and waiting periods.[94] This forms part of the broader existing standards on ensuring timely access to sexual and reproductive health services alongside the removal of barriers such as cost, distance from abortion providers, and unnecessary administrative burdens.[95] However, while the CESCR has recommended that states refrain from implementing mandatory waiting periods, it only takes issue with '*biased* counselling' and the dissemination of medically unsound information.[96] While voluntary and non-directive pre-abortion counselling should be available as an option, mandatory counselling requirements may cause delays in accessing abortion services and therefore act as a medically unnecessary barrier to abortion. As Leah Hoctor and Adriana Lamačková argue, these requirements undermine abortion seekers' human rights, while reinforcing abortion stigma and harmful gender stereotypes.[97]

Moreover, these hurdles amount to a significant barrier for socio-economically disadvantaged people and pregnant people living rurally, by requiring multiple trips to an abortion facility, which is a particular issue in countries such as the US where, in many regions, abortion providers are sparsely located.[98] Barriers such as living rurally, being low-income, and facing hurdles such as mandatory counselling compound to create a significant obstacle to accessing safe, legal abortion services. These regulations could also delay an abortion beyond the gestational time limit, for example preventing a pregnant person from accessing an early abortion on request by delaying the procedure until after 12 weeks. In a study of the impacts of barriers to accessing abortion in two US states, Jenna Jerman et al found three main consequences: abortions obtained at a later gestational age; negative mental health outcomes; and attempts by pregnant people to end their own pregnancies through medication, home remedies, or physical trauma.[99] However, in the US, where regulations such as mandatory ultrasound viewing requirements are in place in number of states, these laws have also been found to have a coercive effect on subsequent abortion decisions. Studies on the impact of such a law in Wisconsin found a small but significant

[94] CEDAW (n 12) para 30(c); CEDAW, 'Concluding Observations on the Combined Seventh and Eighth Periodic Reports of Germany' (9 March 2017) UN Doc CEDAW/C/DEU/CO/7-8, para 38(b).

[95] See, eg, CESCR (n 1), paras 12–19; CEDAW, 'General Recommendation No 24 on Article 12 (Women and Health)' (1999) UN Doc CEDA/A/54/38/Rev.1, paras 21, 23.

[96] CESCR (n 1) para 41; CESCR, 'Concluding Observations on the Third Periodic Report of Slovakia' (14 November 2019) UN Doc E/C.12/SVK/CO/3, para 42(b).

[97] Leah Hoctor and Adriana Lamačková, 'Mandatory Waiting Periods and Biased Abortion Counseling in Central and Eastern Europe' (2017) 139(2) *International Journal of Gynaecology and Obstetrics* 253, 255–56.

[98] Jordan A Parsons and Elizabeth Chloe Romanis, *Early Medical Abortion, Equality of Access, and the Telemedical Imperative* (Oxford, Oxford University Press, 2021) pp 42–43, 51; Rachel K Jones and Jenna Jerman, 'Abortion Incidence and Service Availability in the United States, 2014' (2017) 49(1) *Perspectives on Sexual and Reproductive Health* 17.

[99] Jenna Jerman and others, 'Barriers to Abortion Care and Their Consequences for Patients Traveling for Services: Qualitative Findings from Two States' (2017) 49(2) *Perspectives on Sexual and Reproductive Health* 95, 98.

increase in the likelihood that a pregnant person would continue their pregnancy after viewing the ultrasound, regardless of the certainty of their initial abortion decision.[100] Mandatory ultrasound requirements have therefore been found to impact the decisional agency of pregnant people and, because pregnant people of colour are more heavily surveilled in the US, the effects of these laws are heightened by race.[101]

The imposition of these requirements forms part of what has been termed 'abortion exceptionalism' in the US context, as abortion is uniquely subject to onerous regulations where other procedures are not.[102] While the exceptional or differential treatment of any given medical procedure is not *necessarily* unjustified, abortion is often treated unfairly through the imposition of additional requirements. As abortion is safe, particularly in the early stages, these additional regulations are not medically required to protect the health of the pregnant person, but rather serve an anti-abortion function. In the US, the constitutional right to abortion established in *Roe v Wade* (prior to *Dobbs v Jackson*) was qualified by *Planned Parenthood v Casey*, in which the Supreme Court established the 'undue burden' standard for abortion restrictions. Restrictions or regulations which amount to a substantial obstacle to accessing abortion services pre-viability are unconstitutional; however, this is a relatively high threshold and the effect of this has been to allow medically unnecessary regulations which aim to dissuade pregnant people from having abortions.[103] This resulted in Targeted Regulation of Abortion Providers (TRAP) laws which both aim to dissuade pregnant people from having abortions and impose onerous health and safety requirements on abortion providers. 30 states have 'informed consent' requirements which involve giving pregnant people medically inaccurate materials and information on alternatives to abortion, with some states requiring that pregnant people are urged to choose an alternative such as adoption.[104] Some of those states also include requirements that pregnant people be informed of the risks to themselves, despite the lack of causation between abortion and long-term health outcomes.[105] Additionally, 29 states impose counselling requirements followed by mandatory waiting periods.[106] As Jordan Parsons and Elizabeth Chloe Romanis argue, while these requirements are not deemed an undue burden as they 'do not literally prevent a person from choosing abortion', they nevertheless

[100] Ushma D Upadhyay and others, 'Evaluating the Impact of a Mandatory Pre-Abortion Ultrasound Viewing Law: A Mixed Methods Study' (2017) 12(7) *PLoS One* 0178871.

[101] Katrina Kimport, Nicole E Johns, and Ushma D Upadhyay, 'Coercing Women's Behavior: How a Mandatory Viewing Law Changes Patients' Preabortion Ultrasound Viewing Practices' (2018) 43(6) *Journal of Health Politics and Policy Law* 941, 956.

[102] Ian Vandewalker, 'Abortion and Informed Consent: How Biased Counseling Laws Mandate Violations of Medical Ethics' (2012) 19(1) *Michigan Journal of Gender and Law* 1, 6.

[103] Reva B Siegel, 'Why Restrict Abortion? Expanding the Frame on *June Medical*' (2021) 8 *Supreme Court Review* 17.

[104] Parsons and Romanis, *Early Medical Abortion* (2021) (n 99) pp 34–35, 171–72.

[105] ibid.

[106] ibid.

interfere with that decision by making accessing abortion services a stressful and difficult experience.[107] This is particularly the case where TRAP laws have led to the closure of abortion clinics, increasing the distances that pregnant people must travel for abortion services in many states.[108] Moreover, now that both *Roe v Wade* and *Planned Parenthood v Casey* have been overturned by the recent *Dobbs v Jackson* decision, states are able to pass more onerous restrictions.[109]

Anti-abortion actors have increasingly claimed that these regulations serve the purpose of protecting women's health, even though they are medically unnecessary and can be harmful to pregnant people left without access to safe, legal abortion services. These requirements are enacted as an intentional barrier to abortion, by attempting to prevent pregnant people from accessing services through indirect means.[110] They add to socio-cultural stereotypes of abortion as wrong and harmful through the claimed aims of foetal protection and women's health. This is particularly an issue where significant numbers of healthcare professionals morally object to abortion, as pre-abortion counselling can become directive. For example, Jabulile Mary-Jane Jace Mavuso highlights how non-directive counselling requirements in South Africa have become coercive in an anti-abortion environment, as healthcare providers portray abortion as irresponsible and dangerous.[111] Mavuso highlights how mandatory counselling in an anti-abortion context can therefore produce or exacerbate psychological harm by stigmatising unintended pregnancy and the abortion decision, and by framing motherhood as the only safe and ethical option.[112]

Linda Greenhouse and Reva Siegel critiqued the application of the 'undue burden' standard in *Planned Parenthood v Casey* as a context-insensitive rule, a critique which also applies to the way in which the current international human rights framework treats barriers to abortion access.[113] As indicated in chapter one, international human rights bodies do not require the removal of abortion regulations unless they would cause a certain degree of harm, such as preventing therapeutic abortion or resulting in unsafe abortion. Yet, as highlighted throughout this section, medically unnecessary regulations that do not universally prevent access to safe, legal abortion services are nevertheless harmful to pregnant people through obstructing or delaying access to abortion or resulting in embodied harm. These regulations are thus in conflict with the right to abortion, as states must not make it difficult or stigmatising for pregnant people to access the abortion services to which they have a right to. In line with the

[107] ibid pp 36–37.

[108] See Linda Greenhouse and Reva B Siegel, '*Casey* and the Clinic Closings: When "Protecting Health" Obstructs Choice' (2016) 125 *Yale Law Journal* 1428.

[109] *Dobbs v Jackson Women's Health* 597 US 215 (2022).

[110] Parsons and Romanis (n 98) p 36.

[111] Jabulile Mary-Jane Jace Mavuso, 'Understanding the Violation of Directive Anti-abortion Counselling [and Cisnormativity]: Obstruction to Access or Reproductive Violence?' (2021) 35(3) *Agenda* 69, 70.

[112] ibid 73.

[113] Greenhouse and Siegel, '*Casey* and the Clinic Closings' (2016) (n 108) 1478.

requirements to remove barriers to access and address structural inequalities set out in the previous chapter, states must therefore remove or refrain from adopting medically unnecessary regulations which represent barriers to abortion access, including (but not limited to) mandatory counselling, waiting periods, and ultrasound requirements.

B. Access to Early Medical Abortion

Ensuring that pregnant people can easily access abortion services without medically unnecessary delays or barriers will also require that states provide access to medical abortion pills, particularly in the early stages of pregnancy. Medical abortion refers to the use of two medications, mifepristone and misoprostol, to induce a miscarriage, which is less invasive than surgical abortion methods.[114] WHO includes both medications on its model list of essential medicines ('where permitted under national law and where culturally acceptable') and recommends medical abortion as a safe and effective method up to 24 weeks gestation.[115] Early medical abortion refers to the use of mifepristone followed by misoprostol up to 12 weeks gestation, to be distinguished from medical abortion after this point which requires subsequent doses of misoprostol.[116] Early medical abortion is therefore the most straightforward method of abortion. Abortion service delivery must be responsive to the different needs of individual pregnant people, so surgical abortion (including through vacuum aspiration in the early stages of pregnancy) should also be provided as an option.[117] However, early medical abortion should be provided routinely to ensure that abortion services can be delivered in a simple and timely manner. In addition, states should not impose medically unnecessary restrictions on the provision of early medical abortion, such as by restricting who can dispense the medications and requiring the medications to be taken in-person. The CESCR already indicates that states should guarantee access to the medicines on the WHO's model list, and that the provision of quality abortion care ought to include abortion medication.[118] However, this ought to be expanded to recognise the importance of telemedicine and self-managed abortion for guaranteeing access more broadly.

[114] Parsons and Romanis (n 98) pp 2–5.
[115] WHO, *22nd Model List of Essential Medicines* (WHO, 30 September 2021) www.who.int/publications/i/item/WHO-MHP-HPS-EML-2021.02 accessed 9 January 2026, p 50; WHO, *Safe Abortion* (2015) (n 93).
[116] ibid; Parsons and Romanis (n 98) pp 4–5.
[117] WHO, *22nd Model List* (2021) (n 115) p 3; Parsons and Romanis (n 98) pp 3–4.
[118] CESCR (n 1) paras 13, 49.

Telemedicine for Early Medical Abortion

States should also provide telemedicine for early medical abortion (TEMA) to ensure that safe, legal abortion services are universally accessible. TEMA entails a remote consultation with a healthcare professional, and the abortion medication is then posted to the pregnant person to be taken at home.[119] The pregnant person would receive information on how to safely take the medication, any potential risks or side-effects, and the availability of post-abortion care if necessary.[120] The risks of having an early medical abortion at home, when provided with this information and access to post-abortion care, are equivalent to the already minimal risks of taking abortion medication in a medical facility under supervision.[121] However, of the states that do provide abortion medication for early abortions, few of those provide access via telemedicine. Yet, where TEMA has been implemented, it has been shown to be safe, effective, and preferred by many pregnant people.

In March 2020, temporary regulations were put in place to permit TEMA up to 10 weeks gestation in England and Wales and up to 12 weeks gestation in Scotland for the duration of the COVID-19 pandemic.[122] Studies on the use of TEMA in Britain during this period have demonstrated high satisfaction rates among pregnant people using the service.[123] Additionally, a study comparing access to abortion before and after the change in regulations found that access had improved as waiting times decreased, and that there was no evidence of

[119] Abigail RA Aiken and others, 'Effectiveness, Safety and Acceptability of No-test Medical Abortion (Termination of Pregnancy) Provided via Telemedicine: A National Cohort Study' (2021) 128(9) *BJOG* 1465; British Pregnancy Advisory Service, 'Pills by Post – Abortion Pill Treatment at Home' www.bpas.org/abortion-care/abortion-treatments/the-abortion-pill/remote-treatment/ accessed 9 January 2026.

[120] ibid.

[121] See, eg: Aiken and others, 'Effectiveness, Safety and Acceptability' (2021) (n 119); Margit Endler and others, 'Telemedicine for Medical Abortion: A Systematic Review' (2019) 126(9) *BJOG* 1094; John Joseph Reynolds-Wright and others, 'Adherence to Treatment and Prevalence of Side Effects When Medical Abortion is Delivered via Telemedicine: A Prospective Observational Cohort Study During COVID-19' (2021) 48(3) *BMJ Sexual and Reproductive Health* 185; Elizabeth Chloe Romanis and others, 'Safeguarding and Teleconsultation for Abortion' (2021) 398(1) *Lancet* 555.

[122] Department of Health and Social Care, 'The Abortion Act 1967 – Approval of a Class of Places' (30 March 2020) https://assets.publishing.service.gov.uk/government/uploads/system/uploads/attachment_data/file/876740/30032020_The_Abortion_Act_1967_-_Approval_of_a_Class_of_Places.pdf accessed 9 January 2026; Scottish Government Chief Medical Officer, 'Abortion – COVID-19 – approval for mifepristone to be taken at home and other contingency measures' (31 March 2020) www.sehd.scot.nhs.uk/cmo/CMO(2020)09.pdf accessed 9 January 2026.

[123] Nicola Boydell and others, 'Women's Experiences of a Telemedicine Abortion Service (Up to 12 Weeks) Implemented During the Coronavirus (COVID-19) Pandemic: A Qualitative Evaluation' (2021) 128(11) *BJOG* 1752; John Joseph Reynolds-Wright and others, 'Telemedicine Medical Abortion at Home Under 12 Weeks' Gestation: A Prospective Observational Cohort Study During the COVID-19 Pandemic' (2021) 47(4) *BMJ Sexual and Reproductive Health* 246; Marielle E Meurice and others, 'Client Satisfaction and Experience of Telemedicine and Home Use of Mifepristone and Misoprostol for Abortion up to 10 weeks' Gestation at British Pregnancy Advisory Service: A Cross-sectional Evaluation' (2021) 104(1) *Contraception* 61.

increased risks.[124] TEMA is safe and effective, so requirements that a pregnant person attends a facility in person to obtain abortion medication are medically unnecessary. Further, as telemedicine enables abortion services to become more efficient, thereby reducing delays, the adoption of TEMA would enable states to meet the requirement of ensuring access to abortion services as early as possible.

Requiring people to attend a healthcare facility in person to take abortion medication creates accessibility barriers for people from marginalised groups, imposing a particular burden on socio-economically disadvantaged people, people living rurally or significant distances from abortion facilities, and people with disabilities.[125] Attending a facility to take abortion medication may require a pregnant person to rely on costly or physically inaccessible public transport and incur the additional costs of childcare or taking time off work.[126] In the US and Canada, for example, the costs of travelling to an abortion facility may be significant for pregnant people having to travel to a different state to access an abortion.[127] Further, as abortion facilities tend to be concentrated in urban areas, this has an impact on indigenous populations who are more likely to be socio-economically disadvantaged and live the furthest from those areas.[128] In India, the reliance on private healthcare providers which, again, operate mostly in urban areas means a lack of access to safe, legal abortion services for pregnant people who live rurally or are socio-economically disadvantaged, which increases the likelihood of unsafe abortion practices.[129] The use of TEMA can improve accessibility by circumventing these geographical and socio-economic barriers and thus can address some of the structural inequalities in access faced by marginalised groups. Parsons and Romanis further argue that the use of telemedicine in low- and middle-income countries can potentially lessen inequalities in global health outcomes by making services available in regions with limited facilities.[130] TEMA cannot be a substitute for easily accessible abortion facilities

[124] Aiken and others (n 119) 1469.

[125] Sydney Calkin, 'Towards a Political Geography of Abortion' (2019) 69 *Political Geography* 22, 23, 27.

[126] ibid 23.

[127] Lisa R Pruitt and Marta R Vanegas, 'Urbanormativity, Spatial Privilege, and Judicial Blind Spots in Abortion Law' (2015) 30 *Berkeley Journal of Gender, Law and Justice* 76; Christabelle Sethna and Marion Doull, 'Spatial Disparities and Travel to Freestanding Abortion Clinics in Canada' (2013) *Women's Studies International Forum* 38.

[128] Sethna and Doull, 'Spatial Disparities' (2013) (n 127) 56–57; Barbara Baird, 'Tales of Mobility: Women's Travel and Abortion Services in a Globalized Australia' in Christabelle Sethna and Gayle Davis (eds), *Abortion Across Borders* (John Hopkins University Press, 2019) pp 160–61; Heather Wurtz, 'Indigenous Women of Latin America: Unintended Pregnancy, Unsafe Abortion, and Reproductive Health Outcomes' (2012) 10(3) *Pimatisiwin* 271, 273.

[129] B Subha Sri and TK Sundari Ravindran, 'Medical Abortion: Understanding Perspectives of Rural and Marginalized Women from Rural South India' (2012) 118(S1) *International Journal of Gynaecology and Obstetrics* 33; Susheela Singh and others, 'The Incidence of Abortion and Unintended Pregnancy in India, 2015' (2018) 6(1) *Lancet Global Health* e111; Ryo Yokoe and others, 'Unsafe Abortion and Abortion-Related Death Among 1.8 Million Women in India' (2019) 9(4) *BMJ Global Health* 1.

[130] Parsons and Romanis (n 98) p 76.

as pregnant people should be able to choose an in-person medical abortion or early surgical abortion if necessary, and access to safe abortion in the later stages of pregnancy will require visiting an abortion facility. However, while these issues therefore remain for surgical or later medical abortions, and must be separately addressed by states, they are largely avoidable in relation to early medical abortion if provided by telemedicine.

The provision of telemedicine is also important in relation to the acceptability of abortion services. Studies have demonstrated that the home use of abortion medication is acceptable and has high satisfaction rates among pregnant people using this service.[131] In addition to ease of access, pregnant people often prefer to have an early medical abortion through telemedicine due to the flexibility, comfort, and privacy that it enables.[132] In situations of abuse, coercion, or control from an intimate partner or family members where the pregnant person may be unable to safely disclose an unwanted pregnancy or abortion, accessing abortion medication through telemedicine may be easier to keep secret than a visit to a facility.[133] Further, for trans men and pregnant gender minorities, obtaining an abortion poses additional difficulties such as being misgendered by abortion providers, which may again lend preference to telemedicine.[134] TEMA is therefore important for the acceptability of abortion provision as it enables ease of access to abortion services, greater privacy and comfort, and the minimising of risks that may come with visiting an abortion facility for some people. Telemedicine may not always be the preferred method of obtaining an early medical abortion, as some people may not have a safe, private home environment or access to the internet.[135] However, with the option of both in-person (provided that facilities are physically accessible) and remote early medical abortion, access to safe and acceptable abortion services would be improved.

The comments of human rights bodies such as the CESCR and CEDAW on the accessibility and acceptability of sexual and reproductive health services can lend (limited) support for the adoption of telemedicine. CESCR requires that States provide access to the medicines on the WHO model list, including mifepristone and misoprostol for abortion services, and has commented that the accessibility of sexual and reproductive health services requires that facilities

[131] Aiken and others (n 119); Reynolds-Wright and others (n 121).

[132] Aiken and others (n 119); Sarah J Betstadt, Katrina J Heyrana, and Natalie S Whaley, 'Telemedicine for Medication Abortion: The Time is Now' (2020) 9(5) *Current Obstetrics and Gynecology Reports* 66; Hazal Atay and others, 'Why Women Choose At-Home Abortion via Teleconsultation in France: Drivers of Telemedicine Abortion During and Beyond the COVID-19 Pandemic' (2021) 47(4) *BMJ Sexual and Reproductive Health* 285.

[133] Abigail RA Aiken and others, 'Barriers to Accessing Abortion Services and Perspectives on Using Mifepristone and Misoprostol at Home in Great Britain' (2018) 97(2) *Contraception* 177; Romanis and others (n 121) 556.

[134] Heidi Moseson and others, 'Abortion Experiences and Preferences of Transgender, Nonbinary, and Gender-expansive People in the United States' (2021) 224(4) *American Journal of Obstetrics and Gynaecology* 376.e1.

[135] Parsons and Romanis (n 98) p 77.

are within 'within safe physical and geographical reach for all'.[136] Recognising that some groups, such as people with disabilities and people who live rurally, face additional barriers in accessing facilities, CESCR also requires that positive measures are implemented to ensure substantive equality in access.[137] CEDAW has made similar recommendations in relation to ensuring timely access to healthcare services and the removal of barriers.[138] Although these comments are referring to access to healthcare facilities, Sydney Calkin has critiqued the assumption that accessibility requires a pregnant person's physical presence in an abortion facility.[139] The positive measures taken to remove barriers, such as those outlined above, and ensure access to abortion could therefore include the implementation of TEMA. Additionally, both CEDAW and CESCR have commented on the acceptability of sexual and reproductive health services as requiring sensitivity to the needs and characteristics of individuals.[140] Andrés López Cabello and Ana Cecilia Gaitan interpret such comments to mean that non-therapeutic restrictions on abortion which contradict patient autonomy are unacceptable under international human rights standards.[141] Telemedicine is therefore a means of meeting these existing human rights standards that abortion must be timely, accessible, and acceptable.

However, as human rights bodies do permit some non-therapeutic restrictions on abortion, there is currently insufficient pressure on states to implement abortion service delivery in a way which ensures ease of access for pregnant people in varying contexts. Restrictions on the home use of abortion medication are medically unnecessary, contradict standards of acceptability, and operate as a barrier to access. Regulations that require abortion medication to be taken in a healthcare facility rather than at home are often not in place out of legitimate safety concerns, but in a similar vein to the US TRAP laws claim the purpose of protecting pregnant people's health in order to make it harder to access abortion services. Further, these overly protective regulations reinforce gendered stereotypes and concerns that pregnant people would make reckless or frivolous abortion decisions if they were to take this medication without direct supervision. Parsons and Romanis argue that there is a 'telemedical imperative' where implementing telemedical abortion services is safe, effective, and acceptable.[142] This should be adopted within the international human rights framework. Where it is possible to safely implement abortion service delivery via telemedicine, restrictions on the home use of abortion medication undermine the right to

[136] CESCR (n 1) para 16.
[137] ibid para 16; 24.
[138] CEDAW (n 95) paras 21; 23–24.
[139] Calkin, 'Towards a Political Geography' (2019) (n 125) 23.
[140] CESCR (n 1) para 20; CEDAW (n 95) para 22.
[141] *Andrés López Cabello and Ana Cecilia Gaitán, 'Safe Abortion in Women's Hands: Autonomy and a Human Rights Approach to COVID-19 and Beyond' (2021) 23(1) Health and Human Rights Journal 191, 192–93.*
[142] Parsons and Romanis (n 98) pp 76–87.

abortion. States must therefore take steps to provide for TEMA in order to meet the obligations of ensuring access to abortion as early as possible, removing barriers to access, and addressing structural inequalities.

Furthermore, implementing TEMA is an immediate step that can be taken towards meeting States' other obligations under the right to the abortion where full compliance is not possible. For example, telemedicine would be an effective initial response to tackling the widespread regional disparities in access to abortion resulting from CO in a country such as Italy. This would also reduce the workload burdens on non-objecting doctors, as telemedicine is a more efficient means of abortion service delivery. Additionally, telemedicine is an easier route to providing abortion services in states lacking the resources to set up abortion facilities and can therefore assist States in progressively realising the right to abortion where they are unable to fully comply due to socio-economic limitations. Full compliance with the right to abortion will require additional measures, beyond TEMA, to ensure that abortion services are universally accessible without socio-economic and regional disparities. This will require the availability of abortion facilities, comprehensively trained personnel, and the funding of abortion services to ensure that they are affordable to all. However, the provision of telemedicine will improve accessibility in the short term where progression towards universal access to in-person services is slower. Thus, a 'coherent public health and human rights approach would confer an unfettered endorsement to essential medical abortion medicines'.[143]

Self-Managed Abortion

Supporting access to early medical abortion should not stop at formal medical access, particularly in contexts where abortion remains legally restricted or inadequately provided. Scholars have increasingly critiqued the positioning of abortion within a medico-legal framework, recognising the potential of self-managed abortion not only as an avenue to care where legal abortion is prohibited but also as a more supportive alternative to formal abortion care. The term 'self-managed abortion' is used to refer to abortion outside of legal and medical settings using the abortion pill misoprostol on its own or alongside mifepristone – and to distinguish between this method and unsafe abortion, as self-managed abortion is as safe and effective as TEMA when abortion pills are taken following accurate information.[144] The use of misoprostol, a drug developed for the

[143] Katrina Perehudoff, Lucía Berro Pizzarossa, and Jelle Stekelenburg, 'Realising the Right to Sexual and Reproductive Health: Access to Essential Medicines for Medical Abortion as a Core Obligation' (2018) 18(8) *BMC International Health* 1, 5.

[144] See, eg, Joanna N Erdman, Kinga Jelinska, and Susan Yanow, 'Understandings of Self-Managed Abortion as Health Inequity, Harm Reduction and Social Change' (2018) 26(54) *Reproductive Health Matters* 13; Mariana Prandini Assis and Sara Larrea, 'Why Self-Managed Abortion is so Much More Than a Provisional Solution for Times of Pandemic' (2020) 28(1) *Sexual and Reproductive Health Matters* 37; Lucía Berro Pizzarossa and Rishita Nandagiri, 'Self-Managed

treatment of gastrointestinal ulcers, was discovered to be an effective abortifacient by women in Brazil in the 1980s against the backdrop of abortion prohibitions, limited access to contraception, and high rates of unintended pregnancies.[145] As the drug was relatively cheap and could be obtained from pharmacies without a prescription, knowledge of misoprostol's use as an abortifacient spread through informal networks across Latin America and beyond.[146] Significantly, the increasing use of misoprostol as a method of clandestine abortion correlated with a reduction in maternal mortality and morbidity in this region.[147] Thus, Cordelia Freeman notes that interviewees often describe misoprostol as 'magic' for its significance in the transformation of abortion both within and outside of the medical sphere.[148]

Freeman argues that the real 'magic' of misoprostol really lies in how it has been 'taken up by feminist actors in tandem with empathetic care, accessible information, and autonomy'.[149] As Lucía Berro Pizzarossa and Rishita Nandagiri highlight, self-managed abortion is supported by a 'constellation of actors'[150] including networks that facilitate the movement of abortion pills globally and safe abortion hotlines such as *Socorristas en Red* in Argentina and *Samsara* in Indonesia.[151] Women on Web, one of the most prominent online providers of abortion medication and information on taking the pills safely, provides safe access to abortion for pregnant people living in countries where abortion is legally restricted or inaccessible.[152] Women on Waves, its sister organisation, sails a ship to countries where abortion is illegal in order to provide abortion and contraceptive services and information, and has also used drones to deliver abortion medication to pregnant people in Northern Ireland and Poland.[153] Providing information on their safe use alongside access to misoprostol is what makes self-managed abortion safe and effective, and the provision of pre- and

Abortion: A Constellation of Actors, A Cacophony of Laws?' (2021) 29(1) *Sexual and Reproductive Health Matters* 1.

[145] Fiona Bloomer, Claire Pierson, and Sylvia Estrada Claudio, *Reimagining Global Abortion Politics* (Policy Press, 2018) p 37; Kinga Jelinska and Susan Yanow, 'Putting Abortion Pills into Women's Hands: Realizing the Full Potential of Medical Abortion' (2018) 97 *Contraception* 86, 86; Sarah H Costa and Martin P Vessey, 'Misoprostol and Illegal Abortion in Rio de Janeiro, Brazil' (1993) 341(8855) *Lancet* 1258.

[146] Bloomer, Pierson, and Claudio, *Reimagining Global Abortion Politics* (2018) (n 145) p 37; Silvia De Zordo, 'The Biomedicalization of Illegal Abortion: The Double Life of Misoprostol in Brazil' (2016) 23(1) *História, Ciências, Saúde-Manguinhos* 19.

[147] Jelinska and Yanow, 'Putting Abortion Pills into Women's Hands' (2018) (n 145) 86.

[148] Cordelia Freeman, *Magic Misoprostol: Reproductive Justice and Abortion Liberation in Latin America* (Bristol, Bristol University Press, 2025) p 2.

[149] ibid p 3.

[150] Berro Pizzarossa and Nandagiri, 'Self-Managed Abortion' (2021) (n 144).

[151] Socorristas en Red, '¿Cómo hacerse un aborto seguro con medicamentos?' http://socorristasenred.org/ accessed 9 January 2026; Samsara, 'Samsara Hotline' https://samsara.or.id/samsara-hotline/ accessed 9 January 2026.

[152] Women on Web, 'Abortion with Pills' www.womenonweb.org/en/abortion-pill accessed 9 January 2026.

[153] Women on Waves, 'Who Are We? www.womenonwaves.org/en/page/650/who-are-we accessed 9 January 2026.

post-abortion counselling and support by these networks reduces the risks of harm or incomplete abortion.[154] Operating in effectively the same way as a formal telemedicine system, obtaining a clandestine early medical abortion through these routes is just as safe as having an early medical abortion within the medico-legal system.[155]

While self-managed abortion may be conceived of as an interim solution to minimise the harms associated with clandestine abortion until abortion is safe, legal, and accessible, self-management provides, for many pregnant people, a better alternative to the possible indignities of formal settings.[156] This is particularly relevant in spaces where barriers such as widespread conscientious objection, medically unnecessary regulatory requirements, and the stigmatising attitudes of healthcare professionals make accessing abortion services a difficult and psychologically harmful experience. Obstetric violence, a term created in the Latin American context to encompass the mistreatment and abuse experienced by birthing people, is also experienced in relation to abortion – manifesting as refusals to provide abortion treatment, the reporting of patients suspected of illegal abortions to the police, and physical and verbal abuse towards patients who want or have had an abortion.[157] In contrast to the judgment and stigma that abortion seekers may face in medical settings, self-managed abortion is often accompanied with care and support. For example, in Latin America, abortion *acompañantes* 'go through the process with the person having the abortion, either in person or virtually, while many also run sessions on the law and group therapy-style support groups'.[158] Freeman highlights that these groups follow a feminist model of care, prioritising emotional support and respect, premised upon the idea that everyone has the right to reproductive self-determination.[159] Thus, Mariana Prandini Assis and Sara Larrea argue that self-managed abortion is far from a last resort, but is the best option for many pregnant people across the world.[160]

[154] Raquel I Drovetta, 'Safe Abortion Information Hotlines: An Effective Strategy for Increasing Women's Access to Safe Abortions in Latin America' (2015) 23(45) *Reproductive Health Matters* 47; Caitlin Gerdts and Inna Hudaya, 'Quality of Care in a Safe-Abortion Hotline in Indonesia: Beyond Harm Reduction' (2016) 106(11) *American Journal of Public Health* 2071.

[155] Drovetta, 'Safe Abortion Information Hotlines' (2015) (n 154); Gerdts and Hudaya, 'Quality of Care' (2016) (n 154); Rebecca Gomperts and others, 'Provision of Medical Abortion using Telemedicine in Brazil' (2014) 89(2) *Contraception* 129; Abigail RA Aiken and others, 'Self Reported Outcomes and Adverse Events After Medical Telemedicine: Population-Based Study in the Republic of Ireland and Northern Ireland' (2017) 357 *BMJ* 1.

[156] Erdman, Jelinska, and Yanow, 'Understandings of Self-Managed Abortion' (2018) (n 144) 14; Mariana Prandini Assis and Joanna N Erdman, 'Abortion Rights Beyond the Medico-Legal Paradigm' (2021) *Global Public Health* 1, 8.

[157] Tongue, 'Locating Abortion' (2024) (n 57); Sara Larrea, Mariana Prandini Assis, and Camila Ochoa Mendoza, '"Hospitals Have Some Procedures that Seem Dehumanising to Me": Experiences of Abortion-Related Obstetric Violence in Brazil, Chile and Ecuador' (2021) 35(3) *Agenda* 54.

[158] Freeman, *Magic Misoprostol* (2025) (n 148) p 50.

[159] ibid p 52.

[160] Prandini Assis and Larrea (n 144) 38.

The discovery of misoprostol's use as an abortion pill by women in Brazil and current self-managed abortion practices challenge the assumptions of law and human rights that abortion is best placed in the hands of registered healthcare professionals. The framing of abortion through public health narratives which focus on 'dangerous backstreet abortions' was successful in many ways, moving abortion from a moral issue to one which could be justified on medical grounds.[161] However, early medical abortions require less professional skill than they used to – and Freeman notes that some abortion *acompañantes* in Latin America have been the ones to deliver training to healthcare providers on the safe use of misoprostol.[162] Thus, numerous scholars are critical of overly medicalised approaches, which can act as a barrier to accessing abortion care.[163] This is important for human rights standards on abortion, particularly as the WHO also supports abortion 'self-care' using misoprostol and mifepristone.[164] As I have argued elsewhere, self-managed abortion is important for both accessibility and acceptability, and therefore ought to be supported under the right to abortion.[165]

Criminal offences add significant risk to self-managed abortion. As discussed in the previous chapter, decriminalisation is necessary to ensure that pregnant people are not stigmatised and placed at risk for terminating their own pregnancies. However, countries that decriminalise abortion for the pregnant person often retain criminal offences for third parties, intended to protect pregnant people from negligent or non-consensual abortion.[166] While intended to prevent harm, these offences reflect the public health approach which views all clandestine abortions as unsafe and fail to account for the realities of self-management, which is rarely an individual act.[167] These offences mean that many abortion support groups have to work underground. As Freeman notes, abortion *acompañantes* in Latin America 'have to develop strategies to conceal their activism and abortion care, from both legal authorities and 'unfriendly' healthcare professionals'.[168] In 2022, two years after the legalisation of abortion in Argentina, four members of the *Socorristas en Red* network were arrested

[161] Zoe L Tongue, 'Abortion is Healthcare': The Promise and Pitfalls of Framing Abortion under the Right to Health' in Elizabeth Wicks and Nataly Papadopoulou (eds), *Research Handbook on Human Rights Law and Health* (Edward Elgar, 2025) pp 168–70.

[162] Freeman (n 148) pp 67–68.

[163] See, eg, Prandini Assis and Erdman, 'Abortion Rights' (2021) (n 156); Jessie Hill, 'De-Medicalizing Abortion' (2022) 22(8) *American Journal of Bioethics* 57; Erica Millar, 'Abortion, Decriminalisation and the Medico-Legal Paradigm' (2024) 355 *Social Science and Medicine* 1.

[164] WHO, 'WHO Guideline on Self-care Interventions for Health and Well-being, 2022 Revision' (28 June 2022) www.who.int/publications/i/item/9789240052192 accessed 9 January 2026, p 46.

[165] Zoe L Tongue, 'Telemedical and Self-Managed Abortion: A Human Rights Imperative?' (2022) 30(2) *European Journal of Health Law* 158.

[166] See, eg, Abortion (Northern Ireland) Regulations 2020, SI 2020/345, reg 11.

[167] Rishita Nandagiri and Lucía Berro Pizzarossa, 'Transgressing Biomedical and Legal Boundaries: The "Enticing and Hazardous" Challenges and Promises of a Self-Managed Abortion Multiverse' (2023) 100 *Women's Studies International Forum* 1, 6.

[168] Freeman (n 148) p 110.

and detained for the 'illegal practice of medicine'.[169] In Poland, where abortion remains highly restricted but criminalised only for third parties, activist Justyna Wydrzyńska was charged in 2021 for helping a pregnant woman obtain abortion pills.[170] The criminalisation of those that assist self-managed abortion creates risks and obstacles that undermine access to a safe, effective, and often preferable avenue to abortion care.

In addition to the criminalisation of clandestine abortion, states often restrict self-managed abortion by other means. This can include restrictions on the distribution of abortion medication by pharmacies and customs regulations restricting imports, leading to the unavailability of affordable, reliable, and legitimate sources of abortion medication.[171] This is also complicated by the fact that, as Sydney Calkin highlights, good-quality abortion medications become labelled as fake, dangerous, or illegitimate when they illicitly cross a border.[172] Calkin explores the manufacture of abortion medication in India by reverse-engineering the medication to bypass intellectual property constraints, which is then offered cheaply and without prescription to abortion seekers worldwide.[173] These pills are legally produced, but can become subject to strict legal regulation in other countries. For example, Brazil's criminal regulation of the possession and distribution of misoprostol under drug control laws represents a 'new form of abortion criminalization'.[174] In Brazil, where abortion is permitted only in exceptional circumstances and 200,000 pregnant people are hospitalised for abortion-related complications each year on average, the use of misoprostol for self-managed abortion has also been limited through its removal from pharmacies.[175] A number of states, such as Brazil, South Korea, Iran, and Spain, have also attempted to prevent access to abortion pills online by blocking the Women on Web and Women on Waves websites for the whole country.[176]

[169] Raquel Irene Drovetta, Cordelia Freeman, and Agustina Rúa, 'Self-care for Abortion Activists and Providers: Lessons of Law and Risk from Argentina' (2023) 49 *BMJ Sexual and Reproductive Health* 308.

[170] Amnesty International, 'Poland: Decision to retry activist prosecuted for aiding an abortion gives hope that charges against Justyna can be withdrawn' (13 February 2025) www.amnesty.org/en/latest/news/2025/02/poland-decision-to-retry-activist-prosecuted-for-aiding-an-abortion-gives-hope-that-charges-against-justyna-can-be-withdrawn/ accessed 9 January 2026.

[171] Jelinska and Yanow, 'Putting Abortion' (2018) (n 145) 87.

[172] Sydney Calkin, *Abortion Pills Go Global: Reproductive Freedom Across Borders* (University of California Press, 2023) pp 25–26.

[173] ibid pp 26–27.

[174] Mariana Prandini Assis and Joanna N Erdman, 'In the Name of Public Health: Misoprostol and the New Criminalization of Abortion in Brazil' (2021) 8(1) *Journal of Law and the Biosciences* 1, 4, 7.

[175] Bruno Baptista Cardosa, Fernanda Morena dos Santos Barbeiro Vieira, and Valeria Saraceni, 'Abortion in Brazil: What do the Official Data Say?' (2020) 36 (Suppl 1) *Cadernos de Saúde Pública* 1; Jelinska and Yanow (n 145) 87.

[176] Joana Varon and others, 'On the Blocking of Abortion Rights Websites: Women on Waves & Women on Web' (OONI, 29 October 2019) https://ooni.org/post/2019-blocking-abortion-rights-websites-women-on-waves-web/ accessed 9 January 2026; Women on Web, 'Spain censors information about abortion amid Covid-19 lockdown' (17 January 2020) www.womenonweb.org/en/page

Restricting access to abortion medication increases the likelihood of unsafe abortion practices. Where states are unable to or have failed to implement measures to ensure comprehensive access to abortion services, it is particularly inappropriate for those states to take measures to prevent access to abortion through alternative means. Many of the people and groups supporting self-managed abortion do so because they cannot wait for the laws to change.[177] Supporting the right to abortion must therefore require states to remove regulatory restrictions on access to abortion medication, facilitate the market (or, at least, refrain from interfering with cross-border mobility) to ensure the accessibility and affordability of the drugs, and ensure that pregnant people have access to evidence-based information on self-managed abortion.[178] Joanna Erdman has also highlighted the 'Uruguay Model' of information provision as an effective harm reduction strategy.[179] Prior to the legalisation of abortion on request within the first 12 weeks, healthcare professionals in Uruguay could provide pregnant people with evidence-based information of the risks of different clandestine abortion methods and indicate safer abortion methods such as the use of misoprostol.[180] The pregnant person would then be able to access post-abortion care for any complications, with assured confidentiality.[181] The provision of information through the formal healthcare system ensures its accessibility to pregnant people without access to the internet or without knowledge of alternative information providers.

It is necessary for a human rights approach to foster an enabling environment for self-managed abortion not only as a harm reduction strategy, but as a means of increasing universal access to abortion services where states are unable or unwilling to provide them. Lucía Vázquez-Quesada et al argue that supporting self-managed abortion is a fundamental means of addressing the current inequities in access to abortion services globally.[182] They consider the impact of an active policy supporting self-managed abortion in countries such as India, where the majority of abortions already take place outside the medico-legal system despite abortion being legal, and view this as a means of increasing universal healthcare coverage.[183] The facilitating of self-managed abortion cannot, however, be a substitute for states' own obligations to take

/20230/spain-censors-information-about-abortion-amid-covid-19-lockdown accessed 9 January 2025.

[177] Freeman (n 148) p 109.

[178] Lucía Berro Pizzarossa and Patty Skuster, 'Toward Human Rights and Evidence-Based Legal Frameworks for (Self-Managed) Abortion: A Review of the Last Decade of Legal Reform' (2021) 23(1) *Health and Human Rights Journal* 199, 208; Lucía Vázquez-Quesada and others, 'Abortion Self-Care: A Forward-Looking Solution to Inequitable Access' (2020) 46 (Suppl 1) *International Perspectives on Sexual and Reproductive Health* 91, 93.

[179] Joanna N Erdman, 'Access to Information on Safe Abortion: A Harm Reduction and Human Rights Approach' (2011) 34 *Harvard Journal of Law and Gender* 413.

[180] ibid 420–21.

[181] ibid.

[182] Vázquez-Quesada and others, 'Abortion Self-Care' (2020) (n 178) 93.

[183] ibid 90, 93.

steps towards the comprehensive provision of abortion services (for example, through implementing formal telemedicine services). Erdman likewise emphasises that self-managed abortion as a harm reduction strategy cannot discharge states of their responsibility to address the prevalence of unsafe abortion.[184]

Finally, the facilitating of self-managed abortion could also open up avenues for those states able to comply with the right to abortion to assist those that are unable to due to resource-limitations. As indicated in chapter two, a strengthening of socio-economic rights in the international human rights framework places a moral imperative on states to assist other states to comply with human rights. Tamara Hervey and Sally Sheldon have already argued that the European Union's rules could permit an accredited doctor to prescribe abortion medication by telemedicine to a pregnant person in a different member state.[185] At the global level, Women on Web demonstrates the effectiveness of a telemedical abortion service operating worldwide, and the example of Indian abortion pill manufacturers shows the potential for cross-border support for self-managed abortion. Deirdre Duffy refers to the cross-border mobility of abortion pills and information as 'abortion trail activism' which opens up an accessibility politics beyond individual state-controlled laws and borders.[186] This cannot be fully realised through state action, given the political praxis of an activism that seeks to overcome state inequities, but it could be supported by cross-border abortion provision if states avoid restricting or criminalising the importing or exporting of abortion medication, and decriminalise abortion in order to permit self-management. This would be an easy and cost-effective means of state assistance which could make significant improvements in abortion provision, by guaranteeing access to reliable information and safe drugs until states are able to provide this without assistance.

C. The Neoliberal-isation of Healthcare

As outlined in the introductory chapter, scholars have recognised limitations of law and medicine for reproductive justice, while others have argued that human rights must embrace a challenge to the medicalised model of abortion care.[187] However, de-medicalisation does not mean the removal of abortion from the healthcare sphere – rather, medicalisation refers to the medical power

[184] Erdman, 'Access to Information' (2011) (n 179) 451.

[185] Tamara Hervey and Sally Sheldon, 'Abortion by Telemedicine in the European Union' (2019) 145(1) *International Journal of Gynaecology and Obstetrics* 125.

[186] Deirdre Duffy, *Abortion Trail Activism: The Global Infrastructures for Abortion Access* (Oxford, Bloomsbury, 2024) pp 59–60.

[187] See Pizzarossa and Skuster (n 178); Tongue (n 161); Cabello and Gaitan (n 141); Amirala S Pasha and Roma Sonik, 'Their Body, Our Choice: Organized Medicine's Responsibility to De-Medicalize Abortion' (2024) 26(1) *Health and Human Rights Journal* 137.

that is typically exercised over patients in the abortion context.[188] Alongside self-managed abortion, abortion must be accessible through formal healthcare channels – out of preference, for post-abortion care, or for surgical abortions that do require some medical skill. However, the accessibility of formal healthcare can be constrained by neoliberal economic policies which make abortion and other reproductive health services prohibitively expensive.

In the US, healthcare is largely privately provided, and costs are covered out of pocket, by private health insurance, or by government programmes such as Medicaid and Medicare for some individuals.[189] However, there are restrictions on private insurance coverage for abortion services, and the use of federal funds to pay for abortions has been banned since 1976, with exceptions only for life-saving abortions or in cases of rape.[190] A large proportion of abortion seekers pay out-of-pocket due to this lack of coverage, and this expenditure can be 'financially catastrophic' for those earning a median US income or less.[191] Out-of-pocket payments for abortion currently range between $600 to $1000, before additional expenses relating to travel, lost wages, childcare, and other costs.[192] In Australia, Barbara Baird has highlighted the unusual ratio of private to public care for abortion in comparison to other healthcare services, where most of the country's abortion services are provided through for-profit private clinics.[193] These clinics are concentrated in urban areas, and often, abortion is only accessible in public facilities for medical reasons.[194] This means that those living remotely or rurally, socio-economically disadvantaged people, those without access to Medicare (the Australian public health insurance scheme), and Aboriginal people are significantly disadvantaged when it comes to accessing abortion services in Australia.[195] Similar inequalities are prevalent in the US context, and Katie Watson has thus framed the lack of access to abortion as a health disparity issue.[196]

The neoliberalisation of healthcare means that social protection is sidelined by market-driven logic, and health is viewed as an issue of individual choice

[188] Tongue, 'Abortion is Healthcare' (n 161) pp 177–78; Millar, 'Abortion, Decriminalisation' (n 163) 1.

[189] See Leiyu Shi and Douglas A Singh, *Essentials of the US Health Care System*, 6th edn, (Jones & Bartlett Learning, 2023) Ch 6.

[190] Samuel L Dickman, Kari White, and Daniel Grossman, 'Affordability and Access to Abortion Care in the United States' (2021) 181(9) *JAMA Internal Medicine* 1157.

[191] Rachel K Jones, Ushma D Upadhyay, and Tracy A Weitz, 'At What Cost? Payment for Abortion Care by US Women' (2013) 23(3) *Women's Health Issues* 173; Sarah CM Roberts and others, 'Out-of-Pocket Costs and Insurance Coverage for Abortion in the United States' (2014) 24(2) *Women's Health Issues* 211; Carmela Zuniga, Terri-Ann Thompson, and Kelly Blanchard, 'Abortion as a Catastrophic Health Expenditure in the United States' (2020) 30(6) *Women's Health Issues* 416.

[192] Dickman, White, and Grossman, 'Affordability and Access' (2021) (n 191); Jones, Upadhyay, and Weitz, 'At What Cost?' (2013) (n 192).

[193] Barbara Baird, *Abortion Care is Health Care* (Melbourne University Press, 2023) pp 25, 32.

[194] ibid p 42.

[195] ibid p 83.

[196] Katie Watson, 'The Ethics of Access: Reframing the Need for Abortion Care as a Health Disparity' (2022) 22(8) *American Journal of Bioethics* 22.

and responsibility.[197] Dino Numerato, Karel Čada, and Petra Honová argue that neoliberal ideology thus has implications for health-related citizenship.[198] As articulated in the previous chapter, reproductive citizenship can be undermined by social, economic, and cultural contexts, and social supports are necessary to ensure full citizenship and agency over one's reproductive life. However, the neoliberalisation of healthcare places the social and economic responsibility for the exercise of reproductive agency onto the individual. This manifests in the framing of abortion as a private 'choice' which individuals are free to make (where legalised), provided that they require no additional support from the state. For example, Madeleine Belfrage critiques sexual and reproductive health programmes which 'promote "responsible" reproductive conduct through individualized neoliberal self-steering agency'.[199] Neoliberal rights-based discourse, which similarly frames abortion as an individual right or freedom, constructs some individuals 'as more deserving of those rights than others, specifically those who adhere to neoliberal ideals of responsibility and rationality'.[200] This framing ignores the impact of, and perpetuates, structural race- and class-based inequalities in access to reproductive healthcare and the exercise of reproductive agency.

A key aspect of my framework for the right to abortion is the obligation to address structural and intersectional inequalities and the provision of social and economic support. The right to abortion, as with any other social, economic, and cultural right, cannot be fully supported within a neoliberal politico-economic system. Thus, within a transformed human rights framework, states must take steps towards realising the economic conditions for comprehensive access to abortion and all other reproductive healthcare services. While the expectation that states alter their political and economic systems is a radical one, there are smaller, more practicable steps that states can take to guarantee the right to abortion – for example, ensuring that medical and surgical abortion is accessible through public healthcare provision in urban and rural settings, and where private healthcare is currently the dominant model, ensuring that abortion and reproductive healthcare is covered by public and private insurance programmes. In India, where unsafe and self-managed abortion is prevalent due the lack of abortion services in publicly funded healthcare facilities, the state of Madhya Pradesh has made a concerted effort to improve access to safe abortion services through public healthcare.[201] 71 per cent of public healthcare

[197] Dino Numerato, Karel Čada, and Petra Honová, 'Citizenship, Neoliberalism and Healthcare' in Jonathan Gabe, Mario Cardano, and Angela Genova (eds), *Health and Illness in the Neoliberal Era in Europe* (Emerald Publishing, 2020) p 75.

[198] ibid.

[199] Madeleine Belfrage, 'Revolutionary Pills? Feminist Abortion, Pharmaceuticalization, and Reproductive Governance' (2023) 25(1) *International Feminist Journal of Politics* 6, 9.

[200] Maeve Eberhardt, 'The Social Meaning of Abortion and the Perils of a Neoliberal Rights-Based Discourse' (2023) 17(3) *Gender and Language* 250, 267.

[201] Sushanta K Banerjee and others, 'An Exploration of the Socio-Economic Profile of Women and Costs of Receiving Abortion Services at Public Health Facilities of Madhya Pradesh, India' (2017) 17 *BMC Health Services Research* 223.

facilities in Madhya Pradesh now offer abortion services, in comparison to less than one-third in all other states.[202] There are ongoing issues with informed consent requirements and a lack of abortion facilities in rural areas, which lead to clandestine abortion practices, but the measures taken in Madhya Pradesh have increased access to abortion and post-abortion care for socio-economically disadvantaged pregnant people by reducing the financial burden of seeking care.[203] These measures are thus important for addressing complications and mortality associated with unsafe abortion.[204] This provides a clear example of the importance and possibility of making abortion services accessible and affordably through public healthcare provision, even against a backdrop of neoliberalisation.

D. Recommendations to Ensure Access to Abortion Services

1. States Parties must remove or refrain from implementing medically unnecessary regulatory requirements. States must not impose restrictions such as mandatory counselling, waiting periods, ultrasound viewing requirements (or similar), or requirements that a pregnant person must attend an abortion facility in person for an early medical abortion.
2. States Parties must ensure that that accurate, evidence-based information on abortion is universally available, including the provision of information on self-managed abortion in the absence of full compliance with the right to abortion.
3. States Parties must provide access to a range of abortion methods, including early medical abortion. States Parties must therefore ensure that the medications recommended for safe early medical abortion by the World Health Organization, as indicated in their Model List of Essential Medicines, are made available. Further, States Parties should ensure that early medical abortion services can be routinely provided through telemedicine where feasible, or alternative measures to improve the universal delivery of abortion services. States Parties in compliance with the right to abortion should facilitate the cross-border provision of abortion medication in order to assist those States Parties unable to fully comply due to resource-limitations.

[202] Manas Ranjan Pradhan and others, 'Abortion Care-Seeking and Reproductive Rights Violation in Health Facilities: Evidence from Six States of India' (2022) 11(1) *International Journal of Reproduction, Contraception, Obstetrics and Gynecology* 221, 222.

[203] ibid; Banerjee and others, 'An Exploration' (2017) (n 201); Sarika Chaturvedi and others, 'Availability and Distribution of Safe Abortion Services in Rural Areas: A Facility Assessment Study in Madhya Pradesh, India' (2015) 8(1) *Global Health Action* 26346.

[204] Banerjee and others (n 201).

4. States Parties must not restrict or criminalise the distribution of abortion medication by third-parties in such a way that would increase the likelihood of unsafe abortion practices or prevent universal access to abortion services.
5. The provision of telemedicine and the facilitating of self-managed abortion are not substitutes for the fulfilment of States Parties obligations under the right to abortion. States Parties must continue to take steps towards ensuring comprehensive access to abortion services through setting up accessible public abortion facilities, ensuring that healthcare professionals are trained to provide abortion, and that abortion services are affordable for all, with no detrimental financial impact on the service user. Where States Parties rely on private healthcare provision, in whole or in part, public and private insurance must cover abortion and other reproductive health services.

IV. CONCLUSION

This chapter has expanded on the requirements set out in the framework for progressively realising the right to abortion which require states to remove barriers to abortion services, including structural and intersectional inequalities. Some of the key regulatory issues which limit the availability and accessibility of abortion include belief-based denials of abortion care, medically unnecessary regulations, restrictions on early medical abortion, and the lack of affordable, publicly provided services. In relation to belief-based denials the current international human rights framework recommends implementing a mandatory referral mechanism to balance freedom of conscience with access to abortion. However, the effectiveness of this is limited where belief-based denials are widespread, which consequently has a significant impact on the availability of abortion services. The regulation of belief-based denials is context-dependent, so I set out broad recommendations imposing a duty on states to regulate belief-based denials to ensure that access to abortion services is not obstructed.

Secondly, this chapter considered the impact of medically unnecessary regulatory requirements such as mandatory pre-abortion counselling, waiting periods, restrictions on abortion providers, and ultrasound viewing requirements. These requirements, though they may not completely obstruct access to abortion, create barriers for some pregnant people, particularly for socio-economically disadvantaged people, those living rurally or in regions without abortion facilities, and other marginalised groups. I set out recommendations that states must remove or refrain from implementing medically unnecessary regulatory requirements, and work towards universal access to abortion services by providing TEMA in addition to in-person services. For states unwilling or unable to provide comprehensive access to abortion services including TEMA, self-managed abortion should not be restricted as this may represent the safest or most accessible option for many pregnant people. Self-managed abortion cannot be taken to excuse states from their obligations to provide accessible abortion services through formal healthcare, however, and this requires ensuring robust public provision or affordable routes to private healthcare, including full insurance coverage. Without measures to address these issues, the right to abortion – as a socio-economic right necessary for reproductive citizenship – cannot be fulfilled.

5

Realising the Right to Abortion

I. INTRODUCTION

THUS FAR, I have argued that a robust framework for the right to abortion is necessary, within a broader feminist transformation of human rights, to address the significant inequalities in access to abortion worldwide. In the previous chapters, I set out a framework for the right to abortion and recommendations for addressing specific issues with the availability and accessibility of abortion services. This leaves one final question: what would be the practical significance of recognising a right to abortion in the international human rights framework, given its relatively weak mechanisms for enforcement? In this chapter, I answer this question by considering the potential for realising the right to abortion in domestic contexts through three key avenues: abortion law reform movements; national courts; and prefigurative social movements. These local actors can respond to specific socio-economic, cultural, or gender-based issues, as well as broader issues around sexual and reproductive rights in local context, where international human rights bodies cannot. This chapter therefore grounds the right to abortion in a bottom-up approach to human rights realisation.

First, I explore to concept of the vernacularisation of human rights – the translation of universal human rights concepts to local contexts – and highlight the importance of informal feminist movements (as well as formal non-governmental organisations) in translating the right to abortion, particularly where there is political or cultural resistance to reproductive rights. I consider the recent changes to abortion law in Argentina, Ireland, and Northern Ireland as case studies for how human rights norms were (explicitly or implicitly) adopted by feminist movements to push for these changes, including in non-legal strategies such as protest. Second, I explore the importance of the national courts for realising the right to abortion, as a strategy to complement abortion rights activism and effect legal change where political avenues are closed off, with a focus on the courts in Colombia and Argentina as examples of varying degrees of judicial action on the right to health and abortion. The right to abortion could be progressively realised through these alternative avenues, while also offering increased leverage to existing abortion rights movements.

Finally, I look to abortion rights movements that are focused not on law reform, but on guaranteeing access to abortion outside of the limits of law and medicine. This includes the networks for self-managed abortion discussed in the previous chapter, which can be understood as an example of the 'revolutionary domestication'[1] of human rights norms. Here, I return to the concepts of reproductive justice and prefigurative politics discussed in the Introduction – movements engaging in justice-oriented, prefigurative activism challenge the current constraints on access to abortion in more expansive ways than a focus on law reform alone. Their advocacy for 'non-reformist reforms'[2] is needed alongside the human rights approach in order to shape global abortion politics, address abortion stigma, and facilitate access before comprehensive state action can be envisaged.

II. IMPLEMENTING HUMAN RIGHTS NORMS

The recognition and expansion of gender-based rights in the current international human rights framework was, as covered in chapters one and two, the result of organised feminist activism. The Vienna World Conference on Human Rights in 1993, the Cairo International Conference on Population and Development in 1994, and the Beijing World Conference on Women in 1995 were key platforms for the recognition of women's and reproductive rights. Significant numbers of civil society organisations attended each of these conferences, and the successful organisation of transnational feminist networks around these events initiating the recognition of gender-based rights within the international framework.[3] This includes the framing of sexual and reproductive health as a human rights issue, and efforts to push for the inclusion of abortion as a reproductive right, which would not have been possible without transnational feminist activism because of the resistance from anti-abortion states.[4]

Non-governmental organisations (NGOs), including women's rights and feminist organisations, have been increasingly recognised as having an important role to play in human rights realisation. NGOs have both a formal role within human rights mechanisms, through submitting shadow reports to treaty monitoring bodies and as part of the Universal Periodic Review, and an informal one through lobbying governments and bringing judicial claims to implement

[1] Zakiya Luna, *Reproductive Rights as Human Rights* (New York University Press, 2020) pp 17–18.

[2] Cordelia Freeman, *Magic Misoprostol: Reproductive Justice and Abortion Liberation in Latin America* (Bristol, Bristol University Press, 2025) pp 156.

[3] Alicia Ely Yamin, *When Misfortune Becomes Injustice* (Stanford University Press, 2020) pp 79–84.

[4] Rosalind Pollack Petchesky, 'From Population Control to Reproductive Rights: Feminist Fault Lines' (1995) 3(6) *Reproductive Health Matters* 152; Maud Anne Bracke, 'Contesting "Global Sisterhood": The Global Women's Health Movement, the United Nations and the Different Meanings of Reproductive Rights (1970s–80s)' (2023) *Gender and History* 811.

human rights standards.[5] Specifically, these organisations can identify gaps between ratification and implementation, and in shadow reports will comment upon the failures of the state to meet certain human rights standards. NGOs may bring human rights cases to domestic courts or make test complaints to international treaty bodies. There are, however, limitations to what NGOs and transnational advocacy networks can do. First, the avenues for formal participation are limited. While significant numbers of NGOs were able to engage with the World Conferences, ordinarily their formal role is limited to that of engaging in the treaty body reporting process and Universal Periodic Review by submitting shadow reports. Fiona McGaughey has thus argued that NGOs ought to be given more of a voice in the review process in order to 'facilitate validation, dignity, and self-respect for those who have witnessed human rights violations, or advocate on their behalf.'[6] However, this is currently lacking. Second, for NGOs wishing to be physically present to lobby and engage with treaty bodies, there are limitations in terms of financial resources, knowledge of the system, and access. Some domestic organisations are self-sufficient and are able to engage with treaty bodies, but others are dependent on international NGOs for funding and to facilitate access to the UN.[7]

Third, this difference in access and influence can present an issue when it comes to disagreements within a transnational advocacy network as it can lead to the exclusion of minoritised viewpoints. Within the women's health movement surrounding the 1990's Conferences, there were contrasting and conflicting approaches to sexual and reproductive rights. In particular, groups from the Global South were keen to avoid the dominant framing from Western feminist groups of a universal experience.[8] Global South-based groups were ultimately influential in the framing of reproductive rights at the UN – the Women's Global Network for Reproductive Rights, based in the Philippines, and the Latin American Feminist Encuentros, a series of feminist conferences in the region began in 1981, were key to the development of transnational feminist exchanges.[9] However, there were nonetheless those present at the ICPD who felt that the framing of reproductive rights which was adopted remained Western-centric, thus developing the reproductive justice approach, though this has not been adopted at the international level.

There are also limitations in terms of which civil society organisations or movements are recognised by international human rights bodies. While 'old'

[5] Fiona McGaughey, 'Advancing, Retreating or Stepping on Each Other's Toes? The Role of Non-Governmental Organisations in United Nations Human Rights Treaty Body Reporting and the Universal Periodic Review' (2017) 35 *Australian Year Book of International Law* 187.

[6] ibid 213.

[7] Fiona McGaughey, 'From Gatekeepers to GONGOs: A Taxonomy of Non-Governmental Organisations Engaging with United Nations Human Rights Mechanisms' (2018) 36(2) *Netherlands Quarterly of Human Rights* 111, 121.

[8] Bracke, 'Contesting "Global Sisterhood"' (2023) (n 4) 818.

[9] ibid; Sonia E Alvarez and others, 'Encountering Latin American and Caribbean Feminisms' (2002) 28(2) *Signs* 537.

civil society privileges and interactions with formal advocacy mechanisms and state institutions, including international human rights bodies, 'new' civil society has a much more indirect relationship with the state, and often prioritises the construction of new rights claims and avenues for claiming them.[10] 'New' civil society is often made up of looser communities of activists, which organise themselves in a non-routinised and extra-institutional manner.[11] The result of this is a lack of international recognition of these movements, which continue to 'sit on the fringes of international law'.[12] I have argued elsewhere that protest should, for example, be specifically recognised as part of the feminist human rights work that has been done in the abortion context.[13] These and similar movements can be considered 'counter-hegemonic' in offering an alternative to traditional human rights norms and mechanisms.[14] However, this does and should not mean that they are irrelevant to the formal human rights framework; they form a central part of the vernacularisation process which is integral to human rights realisation, understood as constructed at the local level by grassroots actors.

These movements can push for state compliance with treaties such as CEDAW, and in the absence of mechanisms to allow treaty bodies to hold state parties directly accountable for human rights violations. International treaties also give normative leverage to activists, and thus international human rights standards and feminist movements can magnify the effect of one another.[15] In the face of domestic resistance, international human rights norms can be an attractive source of legitimacy.[16] However, the idea that human rights norms 'diffuse' across the world and lead to change has been considered a 'delusion', as local movements or actors adopt a 'situated approach to norm engagement' which may involve continual interpretation and negotiation.[17] Susanne Zwingel has recognised 'global norm creation and appropriation as an open process of negotiation in which various actors are involved' with no qualitative difference between local, national,

[10] Paul Grady and Simon Robins, 'Rethinking Civil Society and Transitional Justice: Lessons from Social Movements and "New" Civil Society' (2017) 21(7) *International Journal of Human Rights* 956, 957; Zoe L Tongue, 'Protest as Counter-Hegemonic Human Rights Work: Lessons from Abortion Rights Movements' *Heidelberg Journal of International Law* [forthcoming].

[11] Tongue, 'Protest as Counter-Hegemonic Human Rights Work' (n 10).

[12] Florian Kriener, 'The International Law of Protest' (2024) 117 *ASIL Proceedings* 323, 323.

[13] Tongue (n 10).

[14] See, on counter-hegemonic movements, Shaimaa Abdelkarim, 'Subaltern Subjectivity and Embodiment in Human Rights Practices' (2022) 10(2) *London Review of International Law* 243; Konstantine Eristavi, 'Performing Defiance with Rights' (2021) 32 *Law and Critique* 153; Kathryn McNeilly, 'After the Critique of Rights: For a Radical Democratic Theory and Practice of Human Rights' (2016) 27 *Law and Critique* 269.

[15] S Laurel Weldon and Mala Htun, 'Feminist Mobilisation and Progressive Policy Change: Why Governments Take Action to Combat Violence Against Women' (2013) 21(2) *Gender and Development* 231, 245.

[16] Kate Hunt, 'Social Movements and Human Rights Language in Abortion Debates' (2021) 20(1) *Journal of Human Rights* 72, 75.

[17] Lars Engberg-Pederen, Adam Fejerskov, and Signe Marie Cold-Ravnkilde, *Rethinking Gender Equality in Global Governance: The Delusion of Norm Diffusion* (Palgrave Macmillan, 2019) pp 2–4.

or international actors in the production of norms.[18] Zwingel thus rejects the 'international-to-domestic cause-effect logic' which assumes that, in the context of gender equality, CEDAW's norms trickled down to trigger domestic change.[19] Similarly, the relationship between feminist movements and international human rights is not simply a 'boomerang effect' where activists reach out to treaty bodies to put pressure on the state, but is a more complex process of human rights translation and influencing of international standards.[20] As discussed in chapter two, the process of vernacularisation is a complex and multidirectional one. Understanding this non-linear relationship is important for recognising that social movements have been central to the naming of human rights violations, leading to their subsequent recognition by international bodies.[21] Sally Engle Merry and Peggy Levitt also recognise that the organisations they studied were part of a mutually constitutive transnational process in which human rights ideas circulate between local, regional, and international levels.[22]

Moreover, in some contexts, human rights discourse has little traction in the local vernacular. Here, vernacularisation requires adapting or expanding on the content of a specific human right to respond to local issues, or by avoiding reference to human rights at all by translating human rights norms to fit with other values. Feminist movements often modify or reframe rights in order to facilitate their acceptance.[23] If adopting the language of human rights would hinder progress on gender-based issues, movements can adopt alternative framings while retaining a commitment to the conceptual foundations of gender-based rights. In Argentina, activists have directly referenced international human rights standards on abortion (which will be discussed in more detail in the following section), gender-based violence, and the rights of people with disabilities, to indicate just a few examples, to push for reforms.[24] In other contexts, reference to these norms may be less impactful. In one of Engle Merry's studies of human rights vernacularisation, she considers a group of women in Gujarat who drew inspiration for framing their opposition to domestic violence from international human rights documents such as CEDAW but did not cite or refer to these

[18] Susanne Zwingel, 'How Do Norms Travel? Theorizing International Women's Rights in Transnational Perspective' (2012) 56 *International Studies Quarterly* 115, 115.

[19] ibid.

[20] On the 'boomerang effect' theory of transnational activism, see Margaret E Keck and Kathryn Sikkink, *Activists Beyond Borders* (Cornell University Press, 2014) p 36.

[21] Sally Engle Merry and Peggy Levitt, 'The Vernacularization of Women's Human Rights' in Stephen Hopgood, Jack Snyder, and Leslie Vinjamuri (eds) *Human Rights Futures* (Cambridge, Cambridge University Press, 2017) p 216.

[22] Peggy Levitt and Sally Engle Merry, 'Making Women's Human Rights in the Vernacular: Navigating the Culture/Rights Divide' in Dorothy L Hodgson (ed), *Gender and Culture at the Limit of Rights* (University of Pennsylvania Press, 2011) p 90.

[23] ibid p 91.

[24] See, eg, Barbara Sutton and Elizabeth Borland, 'Abortion and Human Rights for Women in Argentina' (2019) 40(2) *Frontiers* 27; Gráinne de Búrca, *Reframing Human Rights in a Turbulent Era* (Oxford, Oxford University Press, 2021) Ch 4.

documents in their advocacy.[25] This group is still engaging in the vernacularisation of human rights, but in a way which is further removed from the letter of international human rights documents.

That international human rights standards are influential as a lobbying tool in relation to abortion has already been noted by scholars,[26] but the role that feminist movements could play in implementing a human right to abortion is worth elaborating on. For example, where there is socio-cultural or religious resistance to abortion, abortion rights movements can do what international human rights bodies cannot; they can be better positioned to undergo the work of changing attitudes to abortion and prominent socio-cultural stereotypes around motherhood and pregnancy. The right to abortion cannot be realised without 'the ability to create women's rights knowledge and agency that is locally meaningful and transformative'.[27] As Zwingel argues, human rights implementation requires 'a network of actors within and beyond the UN system, a division of labor of human rights realization.'[28] International human rights bodies must therefore be cognisant of the importance of informal social movements for rights realisation, and build dialogue within local settings that goes beyond NGOs – recognising a greater range of actors within grassroots human rights advocacy. For example, Kate Seewald, Susan Banki, and Suyheang Kry have highlighted how feminist Participatory Action Research grounded in CEDAW in Cambodia has created an 'innovative bridge between grassroots realities and high-level rights mechanisms.'[29] Thus, in the following section, I demonstrate the importance of social movements for abortion rights realisation in the context of law reform in Argentina, Ireland, and Northern Ireland. I focus on these regions as three countries which transitioned in recent years from highly restrictive abortion regimes to relatively liberal ones, and where human rights norms were particularly relevant to these transitions.

III. ABORTION RIGHTS MOVEMENTS

A. Argentina's Campaign for Legal, Safe and Free Abortion

In December 2020, Argentina's National Congress passed legislation, the *Ley de Interrupción Voluntaria del Embarazo* (IVE), to decriminalise abortion and

[25] Sally Engle Merry, 'What is Legal Culture? An Anthropological Perspective' (2010) 5(2) *Journal of Comparative Law* 40, 56.

[26] See, eg, Johanna B Fine, Katherine Mayall, and Lilian Sepúlveda, 'The Role of International Human Rights Norms in the Liberalization of Abortion Laws Globally' (2017) 19(1) *Health and Human Rights Journal* 69.

[27] Susanne Zwingel, 'International Feminist Strategies: Strengths and Challenges of the Rights-Based Approach' (2013) 9(3) *Politics and Gender* 344, 345.

[28] ibid 350.

[29] Kate Seewald, Susan Banki, and Suyheang Kry, '"CEDAW is Up in the Sky": Reimagining Participation in Human Rights Advocacy Through Mechanism-Based Feminist Participatory Action Research (FPAR)' (2025) *International Journal of Qualitative Methods* [online first].

allow abortion on request up to 14 weeks' gestation.[30] Prior to this, abortion was criminalised under the Argentine Penal Code of 1984. The Code set out a criminal penalty of up to four years imprisonment for medical professionals who performed abortions (or ten years if the abortion was performed without consent).[31] This penalty could be higher if the abortion resulted in the death of the pregnant person.[32] There was also a penalty of up to four years imprisonment for a pregnant person who caused or consented to someone else causing her abortion.[33] Two exceptions were provided, allowing a medical practitioner to perform an abortion with the consent of the pregnant person if: there was a danger to the life or health of the pregnant person, and this danger could not be avoided by other means; or where the pregnancy resulted from the rape or indecent assault of a person with a mental disability.[34] There was a lack of certainty in relation to both exceptions, as the first ground was unclear as to what constituted a sufficient danger and the wording of the second group suggested that a pregnant person could only have an abortion on the grounds of rape if they also had a mental disability.[35] These issues further obstructed access to abortion, with healthcare professionals hesitant to provide abortion services where there was any doubt as to whether one of the exceptions applied. As a result, the number of clandestine abortions taking place in Argentina each year (prior to legalisation) was calculated between 486,000 and 522,000 – accounting for approximately 40 per cent of all pregnancies in the country.[36] It was also estimated that unsafe abortion accounted for just over 20 pet cent of the country's maternal deaths, while around 49,000 pregnant people were discharged from hospital following abortion-related complications each year.[37]

The National Campaign for the Right to Legal, Safe and Free Abortion formed in 2005 as a collective of movements and organisations working to legalise abortion in Argentina.[38] The IVE Bill was first presented to Congress by the Campaign in 2007 and in subsequent years after this until it was debated for the first time in 2018, and eventually passed in 2020.[39] Employing a human

[30] *Ley de Interrupción Voluntaria del Embarazo* No 27.610 2020 [Argentina], Articles 4, 14–18.

[31] Argentine Penal Code (1984) Article 85.

[32] ibid.

[33] ibid Article 88.

[34] ibid Article 86.

[35] Paola Bergallo, 'The Struggle Against Informal Rules on Abortion in Argentina' in Rebecca J Cook, Bernard M Dickens, and Joanna N Erdman (eds) *Abortion Law in Transnational Perspective* (University of Pennsylvania Press, 2014) p 146.

[36] Cora Fernández Anderson, *Fighting for Abortion Rights in Latin America* (Routledge, 2020) p 60.

[37] ibid p 60; Mariana Romero and Agustina Ramón Michel, 'The Shift From Criminalization to Legalization of Abortion in Argentina' (2022) 328(17) *Journal of the American Medical Association* 1699.

[38] Campaña Nacional por el Derecho al Aborto Legal, Seguro y Gratuito www.abortolegal.com.ar accessed 9 January 2026.

[39] Barbara Sutton, 'Intergenerational Encounters in the Struggle for Abortion Rights in Argentina' (2020) 82 *Women's Studies International Forum* 1, 1; Agostina Allori, 'Assessing the "Green Tide": An International Human Rights Advocacy Analysis of the "National Campaign for Legal, Safe and Free Abortion" of 2018 in Argentina' (2018) 4 *Disrupted* 32, 35.

rights framing was a key aspect in gaining support for the bill from politicians and other state actors, as the Campaign could highlight the state's obligations under international human rights law. Existing international human rights standards require states to decriminalise abortion and address unsafe abortions; the prosecution of doctors and pregnant people for assisting or obtaining illegal abortions and the widespread issue of unsafe abortions as connected to the country's maternal mortality rate could therefore be raised as examples of the Argentine government infringing or failing to comply with human rights requirements.[40] The Human Rights Council had previously found Argentina in violation of several rights in *LMR v Argentina*, and the country's abortion law fell short of meeting human rights standards on the minimum grounds on which abortion must be legalised (where there is a risk to life or health of the pregnant person, where the pregnancy results from rape, and in cases of fatal foetal impairment) and access to abortion on those legal grounds.[41] The Campaign could therefore push for ambitious reform by emphasising the public health issues around unsafe abortion and making specific claims as to what was required of the state by reference to international human rights documents.[42]

This was particularly effective in Argentina because of the resonance of human rights discourse in the local vernacular in light of the country's dictatorship past. Argentina's military dictatorship of 1976–1983 was responsible for countless human rights violations, including forced disappearances, killings, torture, and imprisonment.[43] The dictatorship was also responsible for restrictions on reproductive rights, including further restricting the limited exceptions to the criminal offence of abortion that were contained in the 1922 Penal Code (which the 1984 Code reverted back to). Post-dictatorship, Argentina was influenced by international human rights standards in its transition to democracy, and the desire of the new democratic government to distance themselves from this history of state terrorism created an in-road for human rights ideas to become significant.[44] Many of Argentina's political parties actively promote human rights campaigns and have sought the prosecution of those responsible for and involved in forced disappearances and other rights violations between 1976–1983, and human rights campaigns had been successful on other fronts (including on contraception, LGBT+ rights, and disability rights).[45]

[40] Sutton and Borland, 'Abortion and Human Rights' (2019) (n 24) 44.

[41] *LMR v Argentina* (2011) UN Doc CCPR/C/101/D/1608/2007.

[42] Alba Ruibal and Cora Fernández Anderson, 'Legal Obstacles and Social Change: Strategies of the Abortion Rights Movement in Argentina' (2020) 8(4) *Politics, Groups and Identities* 698, 703.

[43] Sutton and Borland (n 24) 32.

[44] Debora Lopreite, 'Travelling Ideas and Domestic Policy Change: The Transnational Politics of Reproductive Rights/Health in Argentina' (2012) 12(2) *Global Social Policy* 109, 109, 122; Sutton and Borland (n 24) 32.

[45] Lopreite, 'Travelling Ideas' (2012) (n 44) 112–13; Lynn M Morgan, 'Reproductive Rights or Reproductive Justice? Lessons from Argentina' (2015) 17(1) *Health and Human Rights Journal* 136, 142–43; Sutton and Borland (n 24) 45; Omar G Encarción, 'International Influence, Domestic Activism, and Gay Rights in Argentina' (2013) 128(4) *Political Science Quarterly* 687; De Búrca, *Reframing Human Rights* (2021) (n 24) Ch 4.

The Campaign tied abortion rights to this history by framing access to abortion as a 'debt of democracy', as well as through its use of imagery; the key symbol of the movement was a green triangular kerchief, mirroring the white kerchief worn by the Mothers of Plaza de Mayo, a group of mothers of people forcibly disappeared by the dictatorship.[46] The Mothers of Plaza de Mayo had also used human rights campaigning in pressuring the UN and international governments to condemn the dictatorship regime between 1976–1983.[47] As Barbara Sutton and Elizabeth Borland argue, this connection that was drawn to Argentina's past 'highlights the significance of local conditions, historical legacies, and political cultures in the articulation of seemingly universal principles of human rights protection in relation to women'.[48] This demonstrates how local movements adopt 'culturally-specific vernacular rights frames in order to achieve the realisation of human rights'.[49] International human rights standards on abortion bolstered these claims, and informed the content of the IVE Bill. The version now in force explicitly states that its provisions have been framed in accordance with several human rights treaties, including the International Covenant on Civil and Political Rights (ICCPR), International Covenant on Economic, Social, and Cultural Rights (ICESCR), and the Convention on the Elimination of Discrimination Against Women (CEDAW).[50]

In addition, the Campaign adopted an understanding of abortion rights which went beyond existing international human rights standards. The Campaign focused on intersectional social justice issues around the criminalisation of abortion, emphasising that it was poorer people at risk of dying from unsafe abortions, and poorer people that were more likely to face arrest and prosecution when showing up at public health facilities for post-abortion aftercare.[51] Further, one of the Campaign's constituent groups, *Ni Una Menos* (Not One Less), was formed in 2015 as a feminist movement campaigning against gender-based violence, and linked access to abortion to wider feminist struggles in Argentina such as femicides, sexual harassment, gender roles, and trans rights.[52] These movements connected feminist struggles to those experienced by Indigenous communities, workers, people living in poverty, and LGBT+ communities and related all of these struggles to class inequality and poverty.[53] Abortion was therefore conceptualised as part of a broader struggle for

[46] Sutton and Borland (n 24) 37; Sutton, 'Intergenerational Encounters' (2020) (n 39) 3.

[47] Keck and Sikkink, *Activists Beyond Borders* (2014) (n 20) p 17.

[48] Sutton and Borland (n 24) 29.

[49] Tongue (n 10).

[50] IVE Art 3.

[51] Mariela Daby and Mason W Moseley, 'Feminist Mobilization and the Abortion Debate in Latin America: Lessons from Argentina' (2022) 18 *Politics & Gender* 359, 372 Sutton and Borland (n 24) 48–49.

[52] Daby and Moseley, 'Feminist Mobilization' (2022) (n 51) 360.

[53] Verónica Gago, *Feminist International* (Verso, 2020) Ch 1; Mabel Bellucci, 'Women's Struggle to Decide About Their Own Bodies: Abortion and Sexual Rights in Argentina' (1997) 5(10) *Reproductive Health Matters* 99, 104.

gender-based rights and bodily autonomy; as a result, the IVE is inclusive of trans, non-binary, and gender expansive people (the IVE explicitly refers to 'women and people with other gender identities capable of gestation') and also highlights the need for comprehensive sexual and reproductive health education.[54] Beyond a simple transplanting of international human rights standards into the domestic sphere, the Campaign built upon these standards to address contextual issues and priorities around access to abortion.

It is important to highlight here that a constellation of additional factors can point towards or against the legalisation of abortion. In the context of Latin America, scholars have suggested that three factors lend themselves towards abortion law reform: a left-wing government, a President who supports abortion decriminalisation, and the relatively weak presence of the Catholic Church.[55] In addition, attempting to rely on international human rights standards on abortion in a context which is hostile towards the idea of human rights would not have the same impact as it did in the Argentine case. Still, in Argentina, it took years before the IVE Bill was first debated in Congress as previous governments were reluctant to support access to abortion. Also relevant to the eventual success of the Argentine campaign was the impact of transnational support. Sutton and Borland note that the presence of support and increasing attention from non-governmental organisations outside of Argentina conveyed an international pressure for the state to decriminalise abortion.[56]

At the time, only three countries in Latin America (Cuba, Guyana, and Uruguay) had legalised abortion on request, but in other parts of the region, incremental progress was being made on abortion. Chile, for example, criminalised abortion without exception until 2017, when limited exceptions (where the pregnant person's life was at risk, where the foetus would not survive, or in cases of rape where the pregnancy is within the first 12 weeks gestation) were introduced.[57] S Laurel Weldon and Mala Htun highlight how international norms are often spread through 'regional diffusion' as the policies of countries within the same region, particularly those that are similarly socio-culturally situated, are influential to one another.[58] Thus, these developments, even though they were narrow in Chile's case, nonetheless represented a turning tide in relation to abortion in Latin America, and support from other abortion rights movements in the region was therefore key to the success of the reproductive rights claims made elsewhere.[59] The translating of international human rights standards into

[54] IVE Arts 2, 13.

[55] Daby and Moseley (n 51) 362.

[56] Sutton and Borland (n 24) 43.

[57] Ley Núm 21.030, *Regula la Despenalización de la Interrupción Voluntaria del Embarazo en Tres Causales*, 23 September 2017, Diario Oficial [D.O.].

[58] Weldon and Htun, 'Feminist Mobilisation' (2013) (n 15) 244.

[59] The decriminalisation of abortion in Argentina could therefore represent a significant turning point for access to abortion in Latin America, in bolstering the claims of movements in other countries.

the local vernacular in Argentina, with the eventual effect of leading to abortion law reform, was possible because of these contextual specifics. Elsewhere, the vernacularisation of human rights might look very different – the localised, culturally-specific nature of vernacularisation means that this is not an approach that can simply be transplanted elsewhere. However, the IVE is indicative of the indirect impact that international human rights standards can have in the context of a strong local movement.

Finally, it is important to note the interconnected development of reproductive rights standards between Argentina (and Latin America more broadly) and international human rights bodies. Lynn Morgan refers to Argentina as a 'powerhouse of knowledge production in sexual and reproductive rights' and thus critiques the idea of a one-directional flow from reproductive rights movements in the West to Argentina.[60] Cordelia Freeman likewise situates Latin America as 'central to understandings of abortion technologies, forms of abortion care, and, therefore, abortion liberation.'[61] Reproductive rights ideas were advanced in workshops on abortion in Argentina in the late 1980s, prior to their popularisation within the international human rights framework.[62] Argentine feminist movements were a key part of the shaping of women's and reproductive rights norms at the World Conferences on Women, and more recently have influenced the recognition of obstetric violence as a feminist and international human rights issue.[63] In addition, as already discussed in the previous chapter, the use of misoprostol as an abortifacient was discovered and shared by women in Latin America – global progress on reproductive rights and modern abortion methods has been made because of the knowledge and practices emerging within this region.

B. Abortion Rights Activism in Ireland and Northern Ireland

In other contexts, international human rights standards can have a less overt role in abortion law reform, but can be nonetheless influential, albeit indirectly. Prior to 2018, abortion was illegal in Ireland except where the pregnant person's life was at risk. Sections 58 and 59 of the Offences Against the Person Act 1861 (OAPA 1861) criminalised abortion until 2013, when the Protection of Life During Pregnancy Act 2013 was passed, setting out a criminal offence for abortion carrying a 14-years sentence with exceptions for preventing a risk to the life

[60] Morgan, 'Reproductive Rights' (2015) (n 45) 143.

[61] Freeman, *Magic Misoprostol* (2025) (n 2) p 162.

[62] Barbara Sutton and Elizabeth Borland, 'Framing Abortion Rights in Argentina's Encuentros Nacionales de Mujeres' (2013) 39(1) *Feminist Studies* 194, 216–17, 219.

[63] Patrizia Quattrocchi, 'Obstetric Violence Observatory: Contributions of Argentina to the International Debate' (2019) 38(8) *Medical Anthropology* 762.

of the pregnant person, including the risk of suicide.[64] The Eighth Amendment to the Constitution, passed in 1983, equated the life of the foetus with that of the pregnant person in order to preclude exceptions to the criminal offence beyond risk to life.[65] The Eighth Amendment was repealed by referendum in May 2018 with 66.9 per cent voting in favour of repeal, and the Health (Regulation of Termination of Pregnancy) Act 2018 was subsequently passed to allow abortion on request up to 14 weeks' gestation, and after this point where there is a risk to the life or health of the pregnant person or in cases of fatal foetal impairment.[66]

Prior to this, the European Court of Human Rights (ECtHR) found in *A, B, and C v Ireland* that Ireland had failed to comply with its positive obligations to ensure access to a legal abortion where a pregnant person's life was at risk, and that the criminalisation of abortion created a chilling effect on doctors who were reluctant to perform abortions for fear of prosecution.[67] In 2016 and 2017, respectively, the Human Rights Committee (HRC) heard the cases of *Mellet v Ireland* and *Whelan v Ireland*, and found a violation of the right to freedom from cruel, inhuman, and degrading treatment where two women had been left with no choice but to travel to England for an abortion when the foetuses they were carried were diagnosed with fatal impairments.[68] Gráinne de Búrca argues that while abortion law reform in Ireland took place in the context of broader cultural, political, and economic transformations over decades, interactions between domestic abortion rights advocates and international human rights bodies played an important part in the eventual success of the Repeal the 8th Campaign.[69] The *A, B, C* decision had a direct, although limited, impact on abortion law reform in Ireland, as the government implemented the ECtHR's judgment by repealing sections 58 and 59 of the OAPA 1861 and replacing them the Protection of Life During Pregnancy Act 2013. The decisions in *Mellet* and *Whelan* did not have this level of direct impact but were nonetheless significant in lending support to the claims already being made by domestic advocates, changing the way that the denial of abortion was viewed in Ireland.

De Búrca further argues that the act of bringing cases alleging that prohibitions on abortion violate human rights is also an important part of the relationship between domestic activists and international treaty bodies.[70] *A, B, C* was one of several ECtHR cases establishing a procedural right to abortion, and the *Mellet* and *Whelan* decisions were central to the expansion of the HRC's approach to abortion in recognising that the denial of abortion services

[64] Protection of Life During Pregnancy Act 2013, ss 7–9, 22. Prior to this legislation, the Irish Supreme Court had affirmed that an abortion was permissible where there was a risk to the pregnant person's life, including a risk of suicide, in *Attorney General v X* [1992] IESC 1.

[65] Constitution of Ireland, Article 40.3.3°.

[66] Health (Regulation of Termination of Pregnancy) Act 2018, ss 9–12.

[67] ECtHR, App no 25579/05, *A, B, and C v Ireland* (16 December 2010) paras 254–66.

[68] *Mellet v Ireland* (2016) UN Doc CCPR/C/116/D/2324/2013; *Whelan v Ireland* (2017) UN Doc CCPR/C/119/D/2425/2014.

[69] De Búrca (n 24) p 182.

[70] ibid p 181.

could amount to cruel, inhuman, and degrading treatment.[71] These cases not only gave weight to the demands of abortion rights advocates in Ireland, but were also an important part of the regional diffusion of abortion law reform in relation to Northern Ireland. The Abortion Act 1967, which legalised abortion in England, Wales, and Scotland, was never extended to Northern Ireland, and the only exceptions to the criminalisation of abortion here were where the pregnant person's life was at risk or where there was a serious risk of permanent injury to their long-term health.[72] Many of the issues raised in the Irish context also applied to Northern Ireland; the chilling effect of the OAPA 1861 as identified in the case of *A, B, and C* also applied here, with uncertainty as to the narrow exceptions to the criminal offence, and pregnant people had no choice but to travel to Britain for abortions in similar circumstances as in *Mellet* and *Whelan*. Further, following the repeal of the Eighth Amendment in Ireland, activist efforts to decriminalise abortion in Northern Ireland galvanised, and human rights discourse was also deployed here.

In 2018, the Supreme Court handed down its judgment in relation to the Northern Ireland Human Rights Commission (NIHRC)'s judicial review action challenging the region's abortion regime as a violation of the rights to freedom from torture (Article 3) and the right to private life (Article 8) of the European Convention on Human Rights.[73] While the Supreme Court highlighted that Northern Ireland's prohibition on abortion in cases of rape and fatal foetal impairment was a violation of the Article 8, the case was unsuccessful as the NIHRC did not have standing.[74] Further, only a minority of the Supreme Court bench were of the opinion that Northern Ireland's abortion law also amounted to a violation of Article 3.[75] In light of this decision, Lynsey Mitchell argues that human rights had a limited impact because the issues involved in the prohibition of abortion services do not fit the 'paradigmatic rights violation narrative'.[76] However, while this case did not directly lead to abortion law reform, it was influential in supporting the claims made by activists from a human rights perspective.

Further, the CEDAW Committee's 2018 inquiry into abortion in Northern Ireland, which found that the near-total prohibition on abortion was a 'grave and systematic' violation of the Convention, pushed the UK government to step

[71] ibid.

[72] These exceptions were established in a series of cases: *R v Bourne* [1939] 1 KB 687; *Northern Health and Social Services Board v F and G* [1993] NI 268; *Northern Health and Social Services Board v A and others* [1994] NIJB 1; *Western Health and Social Services Board v CMB and the Official Solicitor* (NI High Court, 1995); *Re CH (a minor)* (NI High Court, 1995).

[73] *Northern Ireland Human Rights Commission's Application, Re Judicial Review* [2018] UKSC 27.

[74] ibid paras 102–03.

[75] ibid paras 223–25.

[76] Lynsey Mitchell, 'Reading Narratives of Privilege and Paternalism: The Limited Utility of Human Rights Law on the Journey to Reform Northern Irish Abortion Law' (2021) 72(1) *Northern Ireland Legal Quarterly*. 89, 92.

in and introduce new abortion regulations.[77] It is important to note, however, that this was not of the Committee's own volition. It was several abortion rights organisations based in Northern Ireland which first made the request for a CEDAW Committee inquiry into abortion in 2010, which was eventually confirmed in 2016.[78] Section 9 of the Northern Ireland (Executive Formation etc) Act 2019 repealed sections 58 and 59 of the OAPA 1861, specifically noting that this measure was in line with CEDAW's recommendations.[79] The Abortion (Northern Ireland) Regulations 2020 were then passed to set out grounds for a legal abortion: on request within the first 12 weeks, where there is a risk to the physical or mental health of the pregnant person up to 24 weeks, and after this point where there is a risk to the life or of grave permanent injury to the health of the pregnant person, and in cases of severe or fatal foetal impairment.[80] While there remain significant issues with access to abortion in Northern Ireland, the regulations indicate a more progressive approach to abortion than that of the Abortion Act 1967. Thus, while this was a long process, Máiréad Enright, Kathryn McNeilly, and Fiona de Londras argue that the strategic deployment of international human rights standards laid the groundwork for the decriminalisation of abortion in Northern Ireland.[81]

As De Búrca notes, any causal relationship between international human rights standards and law reform is difficult, if at all possible, to substantiate.[82] The extent to which human rights had an impact on abortion law in the contexts discussed above is impossible to determine, particularly as those changes came after decades of work from activists and in the context of broader social change. However, international human rights standards can be useful in changing socio-cultural attitudes towards abortion (and gender-based rights more broadly) and can play an important role in addressing entrenched attitudes, even if this does not directly translate to the legislative level. Rebecca Smyth highlights how human rights provide a useful means of articulating claims against the state, in the absence of other discourses with the same symbolic and practical force.[83] In the abortion rights campaigns of Ireland and Northern Ireland, international human rights standards were influential as activists had the leverage of international support and could make claims that the state must comply

[77] CEDAW, 'Inquiry Concerning the United Kingdom of Great Britain and Northern Ireland under Article 8 of the Optional Protocol to CEDAW' (6 March 2018) UN Doc CEDAW/C/OP.8/GBR/1, para 1.

[78] Judith Cross, Catherine O'Rourke, and Audrey Simpson, 'The Request for an Inquiry under the CEDAW Option Protocol' in Fiona Bloomer and Emma Campbell, *Decriminalizing Abortion in Northern Ireland: Legislation and Protest* (Oxford, Bloomsbury Publishing, 2022) p 55.

[79] Northern Ireland (Executive Formation etc) Act 2019, s 9(1)–(2).

[80] Abortion (Northern Ireland) Regulations 2020, SI 2020/345, regs 3–7.

[81] Máiréad Enright, Kathryn McNeilly, and Fiona de Londras, 'Abortion Activism, Legal Change, and Taking Feminist Law Work Seriously' (2020) 71(3) *Northern Ireland Legal Quarterly* 7, 23.

[82] De Búrca (n 24) p 187.

[83] Rebecca Smyth, '"Repeal the 8th' in a Transnational Context: The Potential of SRHSs for Advancing Abortion Access in El Salvador' (2020) 124 *Feminist Review* 192, 198.

with the recommendations that had been set out by treaty bodies. International human rights standards need not directly translate up to the macro-political level or be instrumental in judicial decision for them to be significant, as the indirect support of human rights bodies was nonetheless important in both the Irish and Northern Irish contexts.

It is important to once again reiterate that these human rights norms would have been ineffective without the long-standing activism of abortion rights campaigners.[84] In Ireland, once engagement with political and legal mechanisms culminated in the 2018 Referendum, human rights norms and documents became less explicitly relevant, as the Repeal campaign refocused on public attitudes and social change.[85] Their strategies involved public protests and marches, with placards portraying Savita Halapannavar and others who had lost their lives due to the country's restrictive abortion laws, and artistic methods highlighting personal stories and statistics around pregnant people being forced to travel abroad for their abortions.[86] This is reflective of Engle Merry's understanding of vernacularisation even where human rights standards are not explicitly referenced, as the campaign drawing on human rights norms around the right to life and *Mellet* and *Whelan* cases, but citing those documents would have had less traction in the public sphere. Norm diffusion relies upon 'the ability of collective action frames and protest repertoires to resonate with local cultures',[87] so it is my argument that human rights realisation requires vernacularisation as much as it requires formal human rights mechanisms, particularly in relation to staunchly contested rights claims.

Similarly, in Northern Ireland, the organisation Alliance for Choice adopted a strategy of 'educate, agitate, and organize' aimed at framing abortion as about health, welfare, and social justice in order to overcome the morally conservative discourse that dominated the issue.[88] This strategy also involved forging connections with trade union movements, university student officers, the LGBTQ+ movement, Medical Students for Choice, and religious leaders in order to create sufficient pressure on the UK government to take action.[89] There were also

[84] For works on activism in Ireland and Northern Ireland, see Kath Browne and Sydney Calkin, *After Repeal: Rethinking Abortion Politics* (Oxford, Bloomsbury Publishing, 2020); Fiona Bloomer and Emma Campbell, *Decriminalizing Abortion in Northern Ireland: Legislation and Protest* (Oxford, Bloomsbury Publishing, 2022); Fiona Bloomer and Emma Campbell, *Decriminalizing Abortion in Northern Ireland: Allies and Abortion Provision* (Oxford, Bloomsbury Publishing, 2022).

[85] Tongue (n 10).

[86] Niamh NicGhabhann, 'City Walls, Bathroom Stalls and Tweeting the Taoiseach: The Aesthetics of Protest and the Campaign for Abortion Rights in the Republic of Ireland' (2018) 32 *Continuum* 553, 558.

[87] Paolo Gerbaudo, 'Protest Diffusion and Cultural Resonance in the 2011 Protest Wave' (2013) 48 *International Spectator* 86, 87.

[88] Kellie O'Dowd, Judith Cross, and Fiona Bloomer, 'Alliance for Choice New beginnings' in Fiona Bloomer and Emma Campbell (eds), *Decriminalizing Abortion in Northern Ireland: Legislation and Protest* (Oxford, Bloomsbury Publishing, 2022) pp 129, 133.

[89] See Bloomer and Campbell, *Decriminalizing Abortion* (2022) (n 84).

examples of cross-border partnerships here, with Irish activists supporting the Northern Irish movement, and the London-Irish Abortion Rights Campaign which campaigned for abortion access in both Ireland and Northern Ireland.[90] Without these movements which adopted human rights alongside other strategies, politicians in Ireland and the UK would likely not have made moves to legalise or decriminalise abortion.

C. Time, Compromise, and Incomplete Realisation

The contextual adoption of international human rights is necessary for implementing the framework for a human right to abortion as set out in the previous chapters, but this also requires strong grassroots abortion rights movements and human rights advocacy which resonates at the local level. However, my argument is not intended to romanticise activism, or underplay the harms, sacrifices, and compromises often present within the law reform process – this is work that can take a long time, and there are limits to what grassroots movements can achieve when faced with apathetic or anti-abortion governments. Moreover, while abortion rights movements may achieve legalisation, this is not the end of the issue. In Argentina, Ireland, and Northern Ireland, there are ongoing issues with access to abortion services in practice, despite the relatively liberal position now taken in law. In Argentina, official statistics show that 73,487 legal abortions were performed in 2021, which is a substantially lower figure than the estimated numbers of clandestine abortions taking place prior to legalisation.[91] In Ireland, restrictions on abortion after the first 12 weeks of pregnancy have meant that pregnant people continue to travel to other countries to access safe, legal abortion care, while ongoing issues with the full commissioning of abortion services in Northern Ireland has limited access in many parts of the country to the first 10 weeks.[92] The realisation of human rights norms is thus a complex and continuous process, which can also take a long time to achieve – abortion rights campaigns in all three countries were active for decades before law reform was eventually successful, and more is yet to be done. Feminist activists often recognise the limitations of working within legal frameworks; in the context of Northern Ireland, this was a 'reluctant, resistant or pragmatic engagement'

[90] ibid.

[91] Dirección Nacional de Salud Sexual y Reproductiva, 'Implementar IVE-ILE: Ley 27.610: informe annual 2021' (Ministerio de Salud de Argentina, July 2022) https://bancos.salud.gob.ar/recurso/implementar-ive-ile-ley-27610-informe-anual-2021 accessed 9 January 2026, p 34.

[92] Lorraine Grimes and others, '"Still Travelling": Access to Abortion post-12 weeks Gestation in Ireland' (2013) 98 *Women's Studies International Forum* 102709; Amnesty International UK, 'Legal But Not Local: Barriers to Accessing Abortion Services in Northern Ireland' (December 2023) www.amnesty.ie/wp-content/uploads/2023/12/Legal-but-not-local-barriers-to-abortion-access-in-Northern-Ireland.pdf accessed 9 January 2026.

which recognises the limitations and dangers of legal control, but viewed law reform as necessary for harm reduction.[93]

Engle Merry and Levitt have also noted the potential issues with the vernacularisation of human rights where a right is extensively transformed to fit within existing social structures, and becomes less likely to challenge those structures.[94] Human rights discourse can be appropriated, and the dominant interpretation of a right may be problematic. They use the example of abortion, where anti-abortion movements adopt the language of the right to life in relation to the foetus.[95] Kate Hunt's more recent study highlights that the human rights frames which are frequently adopted by pro- and anti-abortion actors are repeated by mainstream media sources.[96] Hunt argues that human rights discourse has traction where the national context is resistant to a movement's idea, so this could be a tool to 'challenge stable policy environments concerning women's reproductive rights from abortion to birth control'.[97] The appropriation of human rights framings by anti-abortion movements could work to undermine access to abortion in states that already comply with reproductive rights standards. This is a particular issue in contexts where rights-based discourse is removed from international human rights standards and has acquired the force of absolutism, to be used as a 'trump card' in the face of opposition.[98]

However, this does not make human rights unfruitful, especially if human rights norms are viewed as dynamic, incomplete, and as 'content-in-motion'[99] to be constructed and reconstructed by civil society. While Zwingel also highlights that it is possible to end up with 'distorted' translations of human rights norms, she advocates for recognition of a '*continuum* rather than a *dichotomy* of women's rights abiding domestic frameworks'.[100] Zwingel acknowledges that 'implementation of women's rights norms into concrete policies typically does not reach the goal envisioned.'[101] However, the solution is not more coercive human rights practices, but a stronger focus on transnational activism which can support human rights realisation in the long term. The vernacularisation of human rights, while ever imperfect or incomplete, must be guided by local community efforts, rather than a top-down approach which risks cultural imperialism and lack of resonance. Viewed in this way, questions of realisation can move beyond critiques of the inadequacy and ineffectiveness of human rights

[93] Enright, McNeilly, and de Londras, 'Abortion Activism' (2020) (n 81) 12, 14.

[94] Engle Merry and Levitt, 'The Vernacularization of Women's Human Rights' (2017) (n 21) p 216.

[95] ibid p 235.

[96] Hunt, 'Social Movements' (2021) (n 16) 73.

[97] ibid 75.

[98] Maree Pardy, 'Under Western Eyes Again? Rights Vernacular and the Gender Culture "clash"' (2013) 19(1) *Australian Journal of Human Rights* 31, 35.

[99] Susanne Zwingel, 'Women's Rights Norms as Content-in-motion and Incomplete Practice' (2017) 2(5) *Third World Thematics* 675.

[100] ibid 677.

[101] ibid 685.

bodies and towards the recognition of human rights as a dynamic and localised practice.

IV. ABORTION RIGHTS IN THE COURTS

Alongside feminist movements putting pressure on state actors, the courts can also play a significant role in the realisation of reproductive rights. Cases challenging reproductive rights violations are often brought as part of the broader strategy of social movements, to be heard at the UN level, by regional human rights bodies, or in front of the national courts. While the UN treaty bodies have limited enforcement mechanisms, regional human rights bodies such as the Inter-American Commission on Human Rights and the European Court of Human Rights have follow-up mechanisms in place which can be advantageous.[102] National courts can often, depending on the country, interpret constitutional rights in line with human rights standards and direct governments to comply with those standards, and are better placed than international bodies to respond to specific contextual problems. In the face of political opposition – or a lack of political will – to the legalisation of abortion, feminist movements may be ineffective in putting pressure on their elected representatives. The realisation of the right to abortion may be more effective through the courts in these politically anti-abortion contexts. In this section, I will expand on how national courts in Colombia and Argentina have developed protections for health rights and reproductive rights, thus providing an avenue for human rights realisation alongside the other strategies adopted by social movements.

A. Colombia's Right to Health

The Colombian Constitution of 1991, which was introduced following a period of significant political violence, introduced fundamental rights including socio-economic rights such as the right to freely decide on the number and spacing of one's children (under the right to found a family, Article 42), gender equality (Article 43), and the right to access services that 'promote, protect, and restore health' (Article 49).[103] The Constitution also established the Constitutional Court (Article 116), and provided that any affected individual could bring a *tutela* (writ of protection) before the Court where the immediate

[102] Luisa Cabal and Suzannah Phillips, 'Reproductive Rights Litigation: From Recognition to Transformation' in Malcolm Langford, César Rodrígues-Garavito, and Julieta Rossi (eds), *Social Rights Judgments and the Politics of Compliance* (Cambridge, Cambridge University Press, 2017) p 422.

[103] Colombian Constitution of 1991, Title II. English translation available at: Constitute Project, 'Colombia's Constitution of 1991 with Amendments through 2015' www.constituteproject.org/constitution/Colombia_2015.pdf?lang=en accessed 9 January 2026.

protection of their fundamental constitutional rights was threatened by the act or omission of any public authority (Article 86).[104] The health rights under Article 49 placed obligations on the state around the organisation of healthcare services, but in practice, the healthcare system was subject to limited regulation or public scrutiny and reforms were passed in a piecemeal manner.[105] *Tutelas* for health rights became the most common form of claims brought before the Court, in light of these significant inequities and inefficiencies in the healthcare system.[106] These claims were individualised, with people requiring access to specific treatments or services and in the majority of cases, the Court was simply enforcing existing policies.[107]

However, there have also been a number of notable cases where the Colombian Constitutional Court has been willing to make progress on health and reproductive rights. In 2006, the Colombian Constitutional Court ruled that the total ban on abortion under the Penal Code of 1981 was unconstitutional and set out that abortion was to be permitted if the pregnancy threatened the life or health of the pregnant person, in cases of sexual crime, or where the foetus had an impairment meaning it was not viable.[108] In 2008, in case T-760/08, in addition to addressing 22 individual *tutela* claims, the Constitutional Court reaffirmed the right to health as a justiciable right and issued a set of structural orders to address the key problems with the healthcare system as a whole.[109] In this decision, the Court highlighted that right to health was a fundamental constitutional right with both negative and positive aspects, the positive aspects of which were not always to be subject to gradual protection but required realisation.[110] In doing so, the Court highlighted the state's international human rights obligations under Article 12 of the ICESCR and the Committee on Economic, Social, and Cultural Rights (CESCR) General Comment 14 on the right to the highest attainable standard of health.[111] The Court noted that CESCR recognised obligations to respect, protect, and fulfil rights, and that the obligation to fulfil requires states 'to adopt appropriate legislative, administrative, budgetary,

[104] ibid Title V, Title II.

[105] Yamin, *When Misfortune Becomes Injustice* (2020) (n 3) p 168.

[106] Aquiles Ignacio Arrieta-Gómez, 'Realizing the Fundamental Right to Health through Litigation: The Colombian Case' (2018) 20(1) *Health and Human Rights Journal* 133, 137.

[107] Alicia Ely Yamin and Oscar Parra-Vera, 'Judicial Protection of the Right to Health in Colombia: From Social Demands to Individual Claims to Public Debates' (2010) 33(2) *Hastings International and Comparative Law Review* 431, 443.

[108] Colombian Constitutional Court, Decision C-355 of 2006. English translation summary available at: Rebecca J Cook, 'Excerpts of the Constitutional Court's Ruling that Liberalized Abortion in Colombia' (2007) 15(29) *Reproductive Health Matters* 160.

[109] Colombian Constitutional Court, Decision T-760 of 2008. English translation summary available at: ESCR-Net, 'Judgment T-760/08 July 31, 2008' www.escr-net.org/sites/default/files/English_summary_T-760.pdf accessed 9 January 2026.

[110] ibid paras 3.3.1–3.3.6.

[111] ibid para 3.3.15.

judicial or other measures towards the full realization of the right to health'.[112] This obligation was taken to mean that the Court had a duty to step in and remove barriers to the realisation of the right to health.[113] Thus, the Court sought to address the inequities in healthcare provision by making orders to the relevant public authorities, including requirements to update health coverage plans, allocate resources to the healthcare system, and regulate private companies, putting follow-up mechanisms in place to ensure compliance.[114]

Following the restructuring of the healthcare system in line with these orders, the number of *tutelas* brought for health rights violations significantly reduced.[115] Alicia Ely Yamin notes that a particular impact of the reforms to health coverage plans was improved access for poorer people, although inequalities in healthcare provision – reflective of broader societal inequalities – still remain.[116] In addition, the Court's intervention in T-760/08 was key to establishing the recognition of a national right to health in line with international human rights standards; in treating international human rights documents as part of the Colombian Constitution, the Court was able to advance the progressive realisation of the (internationally recognised) right to health at the national level.[117] This case therefore highlights the comparatively better position of national courts to promote human rights protection in the absence of more powerful enforcement mechanisms by international treaty bodies.

However, there are potential issues with the justiciability of more controversial rights, such as abortion. Yamin is critical of the failure of the Constitutional Court to engage with reproductive rights in the T-760/08 case, making no reference to the reproductive health dimensions of General Comment 14, nor the fact that individuals had been bringing *tutela* claims in order to access therapeutic abortions in the line with the Court's 2006 judgment.[118] Yamin thus concludes that Court's important role in shaping the political agenda around the right to health was limited by overlooking women's realities in the healthcare sphere.[119] Whilst I agree with Yamin's conclusion, it is also relevant to emphasise that international human rights standards on abortion and reproductive health have developed incrementally and were much less progressive in 2006 and 2008.

The Constitutional Court's 2006 ruling, which legalised abortion in the three exceptional circumstances, was largely in line with international human rights

[112] ibid para 3.4.2.9.3, quoting CESCR, 'General Comment No 14: the Right to the Highest Attainable Standard of Health (Article 12 of the ICESCR)' (11 August 2000) UN Doc E/C.12/2000/4, para 33.

[113] ibid para 3.4.2.9.4.

[114] ibid section III.

[115] Arrieta-Gómez, 'Realizing the Fundamental Right' (2018) (n 106) 139.

[116] Yamin (n 3) p 170.

[117] Katharine G Young and Julieta Lemaitre, 'The Comparative Fortunes of the Right to Health: Two Tales of Justiciability in Colombia and South Africa' (2013) 26 *Harvard Human Rights Journal* 179, 183; Arrieta-Gómez (n 106) 138.

[118] Yamin (n 3) 169.

[119] ibid 173.

standards on abortion at this particular point in time.[120] The Constitutional Court in this case interpreted the Constitution in line with human rights treaties such as the ICESCR, ICCPR, and CEDAW. The Court recognised that the total criminalisation of abortion violated pregnant people's fundamental rights (including the rights to life, health, dignity, bodily autonomy, and gender equality), which were protected by the Constitution in conjunction with those international treaties.[121] Access to abortion was, albeit in very restricted circumstances, held to be a Constitutional requirement; at this point in time, this was a landmark case for the judicial implementation of international human rights standards on abortion. This highlights the importance of progressive international standards alongside efforts to liberalise domestic abortion laws, as these standards provide further legitimacy to national courts.

In 2022, the Constitutional Court decriminalised abortion up to 24 weeks' gestation, permitting abortion on request up until this point.[122] In this case, the Colombian Constitutional Court engaged with the evolving international human rights standards on abortion.[123] The Court accepted that developments had taken place since the 2006 case which were relevant, including the evolution of the right to health in Colombia following T-760/08 and the increasing recognition by international human rights bodies of the need for decriminalisation and access to abortion services.[124] Megan Daigle, Deirdre N Duffy, and Diana López Castañeda highlight that the combined effect of the 2022 and 2006 cases is to make Colombia the most progressive abortion regime in Latin America.[125] Yet they also highlight that ongoing (post-)conflict inequalities will continue to leave abortion inaccessible to many pregnant people, particularly those who are Afro-Colombian, Indigenous, and/or socio-economically deprived.[126] However, the ongoing use of *tutelas* to address barriers in healthcare delivery will likely mean the ongoing role of the Court in improving access to abortion services in Colombia.[127] These cases, around the development of the right to health and establishing abortion as a fundamental right, highlight the importance of the national courts in enforcing and expanding international human rights standards, particularly in the context of persistent resistance to abortion legalisation and structural or resource issues which human rights bodies may be unable to fully address.

[120] C-355/06 (n 108).

[121] Cook, 'Excerpts of the Constitutional Court's Ruling' (2007) (n 108) pp 160–61.

[122] Colombian Constitutional Court, Decision C-055 of 2022.

[123] C-055/22 (n 107).

[124] ibid; Mónica Arango Olaya, 'The Fundamental Right to Abortion in Colombia' (*Oxford Human Rights Hub*, 10 March 2022) https://ohrh.law.ox.ac.uk/the-fundamental-right-to-abortion-in-colombia/ accessed 9 January 2026.

[125] Megan Daigle, Deirdre N Duffy, and Diana López Castañeda, 'Abortion Access and Colombia's Legacy of Civil War: Between Reproductive Violence and Reproductive Governance' (2022) 98(4) *International Affairs* 1423, 1423.

[126] ibid 1446.

[127] Arrieta-Gómez (n 106) 139.

B. Procedural Rights in Argentina

Short of being able to expand access to abortion or protection for human rights, national courts can nonetheless play an important role in upholding procedural guarantees where abortion is already legalised. As the *LMR v Argentina* case highlighted, abortion on the legal grounds at that time were difficult to access, with burdensome administrative processes in place.[128] There was also uncertainty over the specific wording of the rape ground for legal abortion, which suggested a requirement that the pregnant person also had a mental disability, which left many pregnant people unable to access abortion services under this ground.[129] In what Paola Bergallo referred to as the 'procedural turn' in the abortion rights movement, activists brought court cases in order to push for the adoption of clearer guidelines on the legality of abortion and press the state to comply with the recommendations of international human rights bodies.[130] In 2012, the Argentine Supreme Court heard the case *F, AL* which concerned a 15-year-old girl who had become pregnant as a result of rape, and began to experience depression and suicidal ideation as a result of the pregnancy.[131] The Superior Court of Chubut affirmed that girl could have a legal abortion under the rape ground.[132] However, this decision was appealed to the Supreme Court on behalf of the unborn child, challenging the application of the rape ground as the girl did not have a mental disability.[133] The Supreme Court agreed with the decision of the Chubut Court, and established two key changes to Argentina's abortion regime.

First, the Court affirmed that abortion in cases of rape must not be subject to judicial proceedings, noting that the informal rule that court approval was required had been generated from misinformation and had never been a legal requirement.[134] Second, the Court reinterpreted the rape ground so that it would not be limited to pregnant people with mental disabilities.[135] The Court relied on international human rights standards (including those established in in *LMR*) on access to abortion in cases of rape, and noted that international human rights treaties formed part of the constitutional legal order and so the state had a responsibility to comply with them.[136] In addition, the Court noted that limiting abortion on the grounds of rape to women with mental disabilities

[128] *LMR v Argentinal* (n 41).

[129] Bergallo, 'The Struggle Against Informal Rules' (2014) (n 35) p 146.

[130] ibid p 144.

[131] F, AL s/ Medida Autosatisfactiva, Expediente Letra "F", No 259, Libro XLVI (2012) Supreme Court of Justice. English translation available at: Hugo Leal-Neri, '*F, A L* Unofficial Translation' www.law.utoronto.ca/sites/default/files/documents/reprohealth/Case-Argentina_abortion_rape_English.pdf accessed 9 January 2026, paras 1–2.

[132] ibid.

[133] ibid para 3.

[134] ibid paras 8, 18.

[135] ibid paras 9, 17.

[136] ibid paras 7, 12–14.

was unreasonable differential treatment amounting to discrimination – which was also contrary to human rights standards.[137] While the government had not acted in response to the HRC's recommendations in *LMR*, the case still had an impact in the national courts as the Supreme Court was able to hold the state accountable for failing to comply with international human rights standards on accessibility. The Argentine courts, and others, may therefore continue to play a role in guaranteeing the ongoing accessibility of legal abortion services in line with human rights standards.

C. The Limits of Court-Directed Reform

As these examples highlight, national courts can play a key role in the realisation of human rights, which is particularly important for both the legalisation of and continuing access to abortion. However, there are limitations – most obviously, the costs, in both money and time, to bringing a case. Bergallo has highlighted that the Argentine system has enabled litigation on the right to health because of the *beneficio de litigar sin gastos*, a cost waiver if the plaintiffs claim fails, which incentivised private lawyers to work for free where the result of a case was uncertain.[138] In countries where the financial risk of litigation is not minimised in this way, it will be harder for individuals to bring claims – particularly as those experiencing barriers to healthcare or abortion services are more likely to be socio-economically disadvantaged. Global or local non-governmental organisations can sometimes support important cases challenging human rights violations, which mitigates this issue. The Center for Reproductive Rights (CRR) is a global organisation which has been key to bringing abortion cases to human rights bodies and national courts by partnering with local advocacy groups and movements. Many of the landmark human rights cases around abortion have been supported by CRR, including *KL v Peru*, *LC v Peru*, *Mellet* and *Whelan* at the UN level, and *RR v Poland* and *P and S v Poland* at the European Court of Human Rights.[139] The CRR has supported cases in national courts in the US, Latin America (including the recent Colombian Constitutional Court case which decriminalised abortion), and elsewhere, both on abortion and sexual and reproductive healthcare more broadly.[140]

[137] ibid paras 15–16.

[138] Paola Bergallo, 'Argentina – Courts and the Right to Health: Achieving Fairness Despite "Routinization" in Individual Coverage Cases?' in Alicia Ely Yamin and Siri Gloppen (eds), *Litigating Health Rights: Can Courts Bring More Justice to Health?* (Harvard University Press, 2011) p 48.

[139] Center for Reproductive Rights, 'Landmark Cases' https://reproductiverights.org/our-work/landmark-cases/ accessed 9 January 2026; *KL v Peru* (2005) UN Doc CCPR/C/85/D/1153/2003; *LC v Peru* (2011) UN Doc CEDAW/C/50/D/22/2009; *Mellet* (n 68); *Whelan* (n 68); ECtHR, App no 27617/04, *RR v Poland* (26 May 2011); ECtHR, App no 57375/08, *P and S v Poland* (30 October 2012).

[140] ibid.

However, these cases are often strategic, brought where there is a gap in case law and/or the outcome would likely have a significant and far-reaching impact, rather than just achieving a win for the individual applicant in the case. For example, Yamin highlights that *Alyne da Silva Pimentel v Brazil,* the first maternal mortality case to be decided by an international human rights body, was brought because Alyne's death happened at precisely the same time as when CRR were looking to bring a case on maternal health.[141] While these strategic cases are influential on international human rights standards and the protection of human rights in countries beyond those the decisions apply to, this selective approach to supporting cases does mean that many individual rights violations will not be heard. Moreover, Thandiwe Matthews argues that where legal challenges are funded, social movements may be required to 'frame their issues of concern in accordance with the priorities of the donors that fund them' which only perpetuates prevailing power dynamics between grassroots movements and larger NGOs.[142]

The effectiveness of litigation, even with a winning case, is also dependent on the remedies issued by the court. Ciara O'Connell argues that the failure to implement and enforce non-repetition remedies designed to address the 'underlying sociocultural practices that place women in a position of less power' seriously limits the impact of reproductive rights cases.[143] For the courts to effectively protect human rights, this requires directing broader systemic changes – such as the orders around restructuring the healthcare system made by the Colombian Constitutional Court in the T-760/08 case. While inequalities in the healthcare system do remain, the effectiveness of these restructuring orders is evidenced by the reduction in the number of health rights *tutela* claims being brought in subsequent years. However, non-repetition remedies may have limited impact where there is a lack of political will to comply with orders or where there are genuine resource limitations.

Through public interest litigation system in India, the courts have addressed reproductive rights violations and have implemented non-repetition remedies over maternal health issues. For example, in 2010 the Delhi High Court addressed two petitions concerning rights violations around maternal health.[144] The first concerned Shanti Devi, a woman who miscarried and was denied urgently required treatment to remove the foetus by multiple hospitals as she could not prove she was living below the poverty line and eligible for free healthcare.[145] She became pregnant again after this and died from preventable complications

[141] Yamin (n 3) p 170; *Alyne da Silva Pimentel Teixera* (2011) UN Doc CEDAW/C/49/D/17/2008.

[142] Thandiwe Matthews, 'Interrogating the Debates Around Lawfare and Legal Mobilization: A Literature Review' (2023) 15 *Journal of Human Rights Practice* 24, 33.

[143] Ciara O'Connell, 'Litigating Reproductive Health Rights in the Inter-American System: What Does a Winning Case Look Like?' (2014) 16(2) *Health and Human Rights Journal* 116.

[144] *Laxmi Mandal v Deen Dayal Haringar Hospital* (2010) WP(C) 8853/2008; *Jaitun v Maternity Home MCD, Jangpura* (2010) WP(C) 10700/2009 (High Court of Delhi) [combined judgment].

[145] ibid paras 28.2–28.5.

after giving birth at home without the presence of a healthcare professional.[146] The second concerned Fatema, a woman who had given birth under a tree in full public view as she was unable to access maternal health services and was denied financial aid to support her child.[147]

Recognising the systemic issues in access to the public healthcare system, the Court ordered the central and state governments to make improvements to and monitor the implementation of schemes intended to support access to healthcare services for socio-economically disadvantaged people, including ensuring guaranteed access to maternal healthcare services.[148] In public interest litigation judgments, the courts will often implement interim measures and continuously monitor the extent to which the government has taken steps towards fulfilment of the orders, allowing for progressive compliance with orders concerning resource allocation or policy change.[149] However, this has been insufficient in addressing barriers to healthcare services, including reproductive healthcare, as access varies significantly between states, most healthcare institutions are private, and hospitals are concentrated in urban areas, leaving socio-economically disadvantaged people and those living rurally without access.[150] Thus, while the courts have recognised the importance of reproductive rights and have attempted to implement non-repetition remedies, this has not translated into the effective protection of reproductive rights.

Even where a case does have a limited direct impact, judgments supporting the realisation of abortion rights can nonetheless be symbolically important. Yamin highlights that while traditional assessments of the effectiveness of human rights cases focuses on the direct impact, the symbolic effect of litigation is also important.[151] This might include raising awareness over an issue where a case comes with media coverage, as well as changing public attitudes and the agendas of both civil society organisations and political parties.[152] Matthews thus argues that the strategic value of court litigation is not 'to presume the implementation of positive court decisions in the present, but more as an articulation of the strong belief of citizens that their contexts will transform in the future'.[153]A broad range of political and civil society actors are likely to adopt rulings and become involved in the informal monitoring of compliance with

[146] ibid para 28.8.
[147] ibid paras 29.1–29.6.
[148] ibid paras 62–70.
[149] Cabal and Phillips, 'Reproductive Rights Litigation' (2017) (n 102) p 422.
[150] Partners for Law in Development and SAMA Resource Group, *Sexual Health and Reproductive Health Rights in India* (2018) p 78; Linda Sanneving and others, 'Inequity in India: The Case of Maternal and Reproductive Health' (2013) 6(1) *Global Health Action* 1.
[151] Yamin (n 3) p 116.
[152] César Rodríguez-Garavito, 'Beyond the Courtroom: The Impact of Judicial Activism on Socioeconomic Rights in Latin America' (2011) 89 *Texas Law Review* 1669, 1696; Yamin (n 3) pp 116–17.
[153] Matthews, 'Interrogating the Debates Around Lawfare' (2023) (n 142) 36.

a judgment, in turn helping the courts overcome political resistance.[154] In relation to a right to abortion, where political resistance to implementation is likely, this symbolic influence of litigation would be of importance – and could lend additional iterative support to feminist movements putting pressure on governments to legalise abortion. This is not a one-way process whereby abortion rights movements place all their hopes of law reform on the courts, but bringing court cases can be an important part of an abortion rights movement's strategy and civil society involvement in cases can act as a catalyst for political action.[155] The case C-055/22 which decriminalised abortion in Colombia, for example, was brought by Causa Justa, a collective of feminist and human rights organisations working towards abortion rights protection.[156] Legal mobilisation through the courts thus remains an important avenue for the realisation of abortion rights where alternative political routes are closed off or have been ineffective.

However, this avenue can also become closed off where the court becomes a prominent site for abortion rights 'lawfare'. The term 'lawfare' (combining 'law' and 'warfare') is used broadly to describe the 'phenomenon where rights, legislation, and litigation are strategic tools in a broader sociopolitical battle between organized, antagonistic groups' and where the court becomes a key site of contestation.[157] While this term is often used to refer specifically to the use of law as a repressive tool, several scholars have advocated for an understanding of lawfare which is removed from these normative connotations, instead recognising that legal mobilisation and the courts 'can be used constructively or destructively depending on who controls them and for what purposes'.[158] In the abortion context, lawfare can therefore refer to both pro- and anti-abortion rights mobilisation – and it is lawfare precisely because of the 'war' between either position. Viewing the court as a terrain of lawfare, rather than a simple tool for rights implementation, illuminates how some actors can, and do, instrumentalise legal and human rights arguments to reverse abortion rights. This has been the case in Poland and the US in recent years, and in Peru, Camila Gianella and Brenda Álvarez highlight that anti-abortion challenges to abortion guidelines, while unsuccessful, have demonstrated the 'weak innovate capacity' of the courts when faced with anti-abortion arguments – particularly those that claim constitutional or human rights for the foetus.[159] Where domestic courts are susceptible to, or willing to promote, an anti-abortion agenda, abortion rights movements are less likely to pursue judicial intervention, which could have

[154] Rodríguez-Garavito, 'Beyond the Courtroom' (2011) (n 152) 1696.

[155] Yamin (n 3) pp 167–68.

[156] Causa Justa, 'Quiénes Somos' https://causajustaporelaborto.org/quienes-somos-2/ accessed 9 January 2026.

[157] Siri Gloppen, 'Conceptualizing Abortion Lawfare' (2021) 17(3) *Revista Direito GV* 1, 3.

[158] Daniel M Brinks and Guillermo Pérez, 'Legalization, Judicialization, Lawfare: On the Light Side and the Dark Side of the Turn to Law' (2025) 21 *Annual Review of Law and Social Science* 55, 61–62.

[159] Camila Gianella and Brenda Álvarez, 'Judicial Lawfare: Analysis of Legal Arguments against Abortion Rights in Peruvian Courts' (2021) 17(3) *Revista Direito GV* 1, 19.

unintended outcomes. Whether abortion rights lawfare can be effective thus depends very much on the domestic context.

V. PREFIGURING ABORTION RIGHTS

While law reform and engagement with legal institutions is central to many abortion rights movements, some activists and scholars remain suspicious of these mechanisms due to their broader limitations and may even reject this avenue for change. In particular, there is a view that legal, medical, and human rights frameworks cannot guarantee reproductive justice due to inequalities and injustices inherent in these structures. As discussed in the first section of this chapter, 'new' civil society often operates outside of these mechanisms, and counter-hegemonic movements may produce contextual understandings of human rights that are rooted in local identities and reject the norms and power dynamics of formal institutions.[160] Some movements can also be understood as engaging in a 'revolutionary domestication' of human rights concepts – Zakiya Luna's work highlights how reproductive justice organisations in the US have adopted a more radical framing of reproductive rights than international human rights standards.[161] Many abortion rights movements have adopted the idea that abortion is a right or as essential healthcare, but in a way which transcends the limited framing of human rights bodies. This had led to notable progress in countries across Latin America, including Argentina.

However, *counter-hegemonic* abortion movements are critical of rights and healthcare framings which fail to challenge structures of legal and medical control over abortion access, instead viewing their work as a political project aimed at liberation, justice, and the abolition of abortion governance through law.[162] The self-managed abortion movements and *acompañantes* discussed in chapter four take this approach, providing 'autonomous, safe, empathetic, feminist, care-full abortion'[163] in contrast to the restrictive nature of law and medicine, even where abortion is legalised on relatively liberal terms. In Mexico, while abortion activism has often drawn on liberal feminist understandings of choice and bodily autonomy, Madeleine Belfrage highlights how newer generations seek to reclaim an understanding autonomy from the state by removing abortion from the violence of legislative control.[164] Thus, for these activists, reforms aimed at simply reforming harmful hegemonic structures without any broader transformation (which Freeman refers to as 'reformist reforms'[165]) are to

[160] See Tongue (n 10).
[161] Luna (n 1) pp 17–18.
[162] Freeman (n 2) p 156.
[163] ibid p 166.
[164] Madeleine Belfrage, 'Reclaiming Autonomy: The Changing Landscape of Mexican Abortion Activism' (2024) 49(3) *Signs* 535.
[165] Freeman (n 2) p 156.

be rejected. Reformist reforms may be necessary in some contexts as a starting point, but counter-hegemonic movements highlight the importance of thinking about more liberatory futures for abortion care beyond harmful structures of regulation.

In striving for these possibilities, many abortion movements engage in a prefigurative politics. As outlined in the introductory chapter, the term 'prefigurative politics' is used to characterise political movements that embody an imagination of a future progressive society brought into the present. Not all abortion movements engage in the 'new world building' that is central to prefiguration – many are focused on the reform structures in our current world, and Deirdre Duffy argues that prefigurative politics, in contrast, is a 'praxis that pursues social transformation through collective, anti-oppressive ways of relating to each other; strategies that recognize and address co-existing and intersecting injustices; and infrastructures that remove the requirement to seek permission or legitimacy from another actor (ie the State).'[166] Self-managed abortion networks, abortion *acompañantes*, and abortion trail activists are examples of this, and Duffy has recognised their work in prefiguring new, progressive abortion infrastructures which are 'shaped by and emblematize an active critique of both the infrastructures and constructions of abortion formed by and within discourses of reproductive health'.[167] These movements emerge as a counter to hegemonic political, legal, and medical structures, and the vision of abortion liberation enacted by these movements is therefore a transgressive one.[168]

Clearly, then, construing the future of abortion rights within a human rights frame – even a radically transformed one – is not in itself an example of prefigurative politics, as the state and its political, legal, and medical infrastructure remains a key focus of human rights norms. However, the idea of imagining a future progressive society within the present is an important one for progressive human rights norms when construed as aspirational or even utopian values that we wish to strive for. Ruth Levitas understands utopia as 'concerned with what ought to be and the process of conforming the world to that standard.'[169] Utopia is thus a method, rather than an end point – a process of continuous transformation, rather than a blueprint for what, where, when, or how utopia 'is'. This understanding shares similarities with prefigurative politics in that utopia can emerge in the 'everyday' present through movements on small or larger scales, from transnational self-managed abortion movements to individual schools

[166] Deirdre Duffy, *Abortion Trail Activism: The Global Infrastructures for Abortion Access* (Oxford, Bloomsbury Publishing, 2024) p 109.

[167] ibid p 110.

[168] See Freeman (n 2) p 162; Rishita Nandagiri and Lucía Berro Pizzarossa, 'Transgressing Biomedical and Legal Boundaries: The "Enticing and Hazardous" Challenges and Promises of a Self-Managed Abortion Multiverse' (2023) 100 *Women's Studies International Forum* 1; Claire Pierson, *Women's Troubles: Gender and Feminist Politics in Post-Agreement Northern Ireland* (Manchester, Manchester University Press, 2025) Ch 5.

[169] Ruth Levitas, *Utopia as Method* (Palgrave Macmillan, 2013) p 66.

opting for democratic running involving staff and students.[170] My framework for the right to abortion is envisaged as a utopian process for transforming political, legal, and medical power, to ultimately understand abortion as central for the reproductive citizenship and embodied, relational agency of people capable of becoming pregnant.

Anti-abortion politics and restrictive legal and medical approaches remain in our present, and cannot be ignored, but through these processes we might work towards disentangling abortion access from state control and medical gatekeeping. While prefigurative or counter-hegemonic movements reject these institutions entirely, it is my argument that there is the potential for transformative reforms in the present while the institutions of law and medicine remain the primary frames through which states understand abortion (and other contested healthcare services). This does not mean entrenching dominant legal and medical norms, but rather integrating the principles of care and empowerment from self-managed abortion movements into formal abortion care. Sara Larrea and Suzanne Veldhuis argue that for this to be possible 'requires meaningful, horizontal collaborations between [self-managed abortion] activists and biomedical professionals, acknowledging that [self-managed abortion] activists are abortion experts and should be treated as such.'[171] Specifically, they highlight how self-managed abortion movements place emphasis on the 'individual needs, desires, and possibilities of each person' and promote non-judgmental, non-violent, non-discriminatory, and stigma-free care.[172] Elsewhere, I have also highlighted the need for healthcare providers to validate and support the embodied experiences of their patients in accessing all forms of reproductive healthcare and work '*in relation* with' their patients instead of imposing medicalised power.[173] The process of moving away from medicalised power will be slow and context-dependent, and so while human rights bodies can support this through implementing standards for socio-cultural change, the work of prefigurative abortion movements is necessary for real structural transformation.

VI. CONCLUSION

In political contexts where abortion is a polarised issue, abortion rights have a 'pendular character' and can swing back and forth between progressive and

[170] See Zoe L Tongue, 'Ectogestation as Emancipation: A Feminist Science Fiction' in Alex Green, Mitchell Travis, and Kieran Tranter (eds), *Cultural Legal Studies of Science Fiction* (Routledge, 2024) pp 309–10; Davina Cooper, *Everyday Utopias* (Duke University Press, 2013) Ch 7.

[171] Sara Larrea and Suzanne Veldhuis, 'Hegemonic Medicine and Self-Managed Abortion: Reclaiming Latin America Feminists' Contributions to Knowledge and Practice Development' (2025) *Sexual Reproductive Health Matters* [online first].

[172] ibid.

[173] Zoe L Tongue, 'Locating Abortion and Contraception on the Obstetric Violence Continuum' (2024) 17(1) *International Journal of Feminist Approaches in Bioethics* 1, 17.

restrictive regimes.[174] Progress on abortion is non-linear, and abortion is unlikely to become a 'resolved' issue in many of these contexts. Whether progressive abortion law reform is possible depends on a range of socio-political factors, including the political leanings of the current government and their support (or opposition to) abortion, the makeup and scope of the courts, and the influence of religious institutions, pro- or anti-abortion movements, non-governmental and human rights organisations, and other actors. While this pendular nature of abortion means that access remains insecure even where abortion is currently legalised, this also means that prohibitions on abortion are not static. Feminist movements can challenge these prohibitions by translating gender-based human rights concepts into the local vernacular, which is also supported by the work of domestic courts in some contexts. Even in countries currently experiencing roll-backs or continuing hostility towards abortion, the possibility for this to change therefore remains open, as demonstrated by the gradually increasing number of countries in Latin America starting to overcome heavily restrictive regimes. This will take time to achieve, however, making self-managed abortion and prefigurative activism a central and vital aspect of feminist mobilisation for abortion rights. Against this backdrop, it is important for international human rights bodies to explicitly recognise abortion as a human right as this would bolster localised abortion rights movements, national courts, and regional human rights systems in pushing for reform. Entrenching abortion as a human right in the international human rights framework and in national contexts is imperative for challenging the worldwide ongoing resistance to abortion, and support abortion movements in imagining better futures for reproductive justice.

[174] Clara Franco Yáñez, 'Abortion Rights in Latin America: An Unsettled Battle' (2021) 3 *GIGA Focus* 1, 1.

Conclusion

What Can Human Rights Do?

In late 2025, while finishing the writing of this monograph, I watched Together Films' documentary on *Zurawski v Texas*, following a group of women through their legal challenge to the restrictive abortion laws passed by the state of Texas in 2021.[1] Amanda Zurawski, the lead plaintiff, experienced complications during her first pregnancy, which led to sepsis because she was unable to have an abortion while the foetus still had a heartbeat. As a result, she was unable to become pregnant again. Another plaintiff, Samantha Casiano, found out that the foetus she was carrying had anencephaly, a condition where the foetus' skull does not develop, and had no choice but to continue her pregnancy to term, give birth, and watch her daughter suffer and die four hours later. While recounting her story in the District Court, reliving her trauma makes her physically sick, and she could not cope with the thought of experiencing pregnancy and childbirth again. Austin Dennard is an obstetrician and gynaecologist who, at risk of criminalisation, was unable to provide abortion care to another plaintiff, Lauren Miller, who had to travel out of state to have an abortion for a fatal foetal impairment. Austin herself also had to travel out of state for an abortion when she found out that the foetus she was carrying had anencephaly. There was a total number of 22 plaintiffs in the case, all with similar stories.[2] In 2023, the Texas District Court ruled to block the state's abortion ban insofar as it applied to dangerous pregnancy complications.[3] In 2024, this was overruled by the Texas Supreme Court and later that year, Tierra Walker died from preeclampsia, a pregnancy complication that can become life-threatening and only

[1] *Zurawski v Texas* (2024), dir Maisie Crow and Abbie Perrault, Together Films, US.

[2] Center for Reproductive Rights, 'The Plaintiffs and Their Stories: Zurawski v State of Texas' (14 November 2023) https://reproductiverights.org/news/zurawski-v-texas-plaintiffs-stories-remarks/ accessed 9 January 2026.

[3] *Zurawski v Texas* (2023) D-1-GN-000968 (Texas State Trial Court).

ends with the pregnancy.[4] None of the healthcare professionals treating her ever offered her an abortion.[5]

In 2025, a new law was passed intending to clarify when a physician can perform a therapeutic abortion without fear of prosecution, allowing them to exercise their 'reasonable medical judgment' as to whether a pregnancy would create the risk of death or substantial impairment of the pregnant person's major bodily functions.[6] This includes the pregnant person's fertility.[7] While this is, of course, an important step forward and is what the plaintiffs in *Zurawski v Texas* were arguing for, it is yet unclear if this legal clarification will effectively prevent any more of these cruel, painful, and traumatic situations arising. Some healthcare professionals may still fear criminalisation, and those with moral objections to abortion may refuse to offer or provide care under the cover of the law. Texas also allows private citizens to sue others up to $10,000 for wrongful death, if they 'aid or abet' an illegal abortion, which adds a significant financial risk to those healthcare professionals that would otherwise provide abortion care.[8]

I emphasised in chapter one that focusing solely on these kinds of exceptional circumstances is problematic for ignoring the vast majority of abortion experiences, and the broader harms that abortion prohibitions can cause. This remains true – there are many, many people in Texas, other US states, and across the world who suffer because their reproductive agency is taken away by oppressive laws. Legalising abortion only for medical reasons is not, and never will be, enough to guarantee the rights, wellbeing, and citizenship of people capable of becoming pregnant. Nonetheless, this documentary is a reminder of the deeply horrific consequences of abortion prohibitions that do not allow even for these small exceptions – as their lawyer Molly Duane states during the film, this is the absolute minimum required.[9] Thus, my framework for the right to abortion retains these medical circumstances as its minimum core content and, as the example of Texas shows, they must apply broadly enough so that no pregnant person has to risk their health, life, and body or carry a pregnancy to term knowing that their child will not and cannot survive.

Chapter one presented a critique of the current approach to abortion in the international human rights framework for not going far enough to require states to provide comprehensive access to abortion. There are discrepancies between the approaches of the Human Rights Committee (HRC), Committee on Social,

[4] *State v Zurawski* (2024) 690 SW3d 644 (Texas Supreme Court); Kavitha Surana and Lizzie Presser, '"Ticking Time Bomb": A Pregnant Mother Kept Getting Sicker. She Died After She Couldn't Get an Abortion in Texas' (*ProPublica*, 19 November 2025) www.propublica.org/article/texas-abortion-ban-tierra-walker-preeclampsia accessed 9 January 2026.

[5] ibid.

[6] SB.31 (Texas), Section 3.

[7] ibid.

[8] SB.8 (Texas).

[9] Crow and Perrault, *Zurawski v Texas* (2024) (n 1).

Economic, and Cultural Rights (CESCR), and the Committee on the Elimination of Discrimination Against Women (CEDAW Committee), and all three have been reluctant to recognise an obligation on states to provide access to abortion expansively. This is, even more so, the case for the three regional human rights bodies of Africa, America, and Europe. While their approaches are continually evolving, and the CESCR and CEDAW Committee have demonstrated a more progressive view of abortion in recent years, there remains a tendency to focus on those minimum exceptions and a relatively high threshold of harm and suffering for a violation of existing rights to be found. Moreover, the piecemeal and fragmented nature of this evolution has left gaps in protection which, when coupled with the limited follow-up mechanisms of the Committees, places inadequate pressure on states to comply even with these more limited standards.

Addressing these issues requires, as I argued in chapter two, a feminist transformation of human rights capable of supporting aspirational gender-based rights, socio-economic rights, and cross-cultural pluralism in their application. The recognition of an explicit human right to abortion would be part of this conceptually prefigurative project, and by drawing on feminist approaches to abortion in terms of autonomy, relationality, embodiment, and citizenship, chapter three presented a scaffolded framework for the progressive realisation of such a right. Under this framework, states would have clear obligations to meet the minimum core, which mirrors the current international human rights approach, and take steps up the framework's four tiers in order to eventually reach full compliance. Full compliance requires abortion to be provided on expansive grounds, including for later pregnancies, the removal of criminal offences for abortion, comprehensive access in practice, and a range of measures to tackle intersectional and structural inequalities and thus guarantee reproductive agency for all. In chapter four, I addressed specific issues relating to the availability and accessibility of abortion services once legalised that states must also address. This approach would significantly strengthen state obligations to provide and support access to abortion as a fundamental right and moral good, further challenging restrictive legislative frameworks such as that of Texas and other countries worldwide.

This framing requires respect and support for each pregnant person's individual experiences, context, and decision-making. However, it also requires moving beyond abortion as a singular issue, and connecting it to human rights and social justice across the board. In numerous countries, governments are not only backsliding on reproductive rights, but are systematically violating human rights more broadly. In the US, for example, abortion bans have been accompanied by anti-LGBTQ+ legislation, targeted at trans people in particular, and extreme hostility towards migrants through the aggressive enforcement of policies by Immigration and Customs Enforcement (ICE) officers.[10] In 2025, at least

[10] ACLU, 'Mapping Attacks of LGBTQ Rights in US State Legislatures in 2025' (29 December 2025) www.aclu.org/legislative-attacks-on-lgbtq-rights-2025 accessed 9 January 2026; Marianne

32 people died while in ICE detention and US police officers killed over 1,000 people in the same year through excessive force, disproportionately affecting Black and Hispanic communities.[11] Elsewhere, armed conflict, genocide, and violations of international law have led to torture, killing, imprisonment, sexual violence, famine, and many more human rights violations on a mass scale.[12] Across the world, but mostly in the Global South, climate change is taking a devastating toll on global human health, environments, and livelihoods.[13]

All of these issues are connected to reproductive injustice – Maya Pendleton and Alan Dettlaff argue that 'the family policing system, prisons, immigration detention, and other systems that make it dangerous to be a racialized parent' undermine reproductive agency by making pregnancy and parenting unsafe.[14] The effects of climate change likewise affect reproductive decision-making and reproductive health, thus undermining reproductive agency. In relation to Israel's occupation of Gaza, both before and after October 2023, scholars have also highlighted the reproductive violence imposed on Palestinians by Israeli security forces.[15] There are extremely high rates of miscarriage, stillbirth, prematurity, and pregnancy complications due to the physical, mental, and environmental

LeVine, Emmanuel Martinez, and Álvaro Valiño, 'ICE shift in tactics leads to soaring number of at-large arrests, data shows' (*The Washington Post,* 28 December 2025) www.washingtonpost.com/immigration/2025/12/28/ice-deportations-data-trump-arrests/ accessed 9 January 2026.

[11] Maanvi Singh, Coral Murphy Marcos, and Charlotte Simmonds, '2025 was ICE's deadliest year in two decades. Here are the 32 people who died in custody' (*The Guardian,* 4 January 2026) www.theguardian.com/us-news/ng-interactive/2026/jan/04/ice-2025-deaths-timeline accessed 9 January 2026; Police Brutality Center, 'Policing Killings Surpass 1,000 in 2025' (10 October 2025) https://policebrutalitycenter.org/news/police-killings-surpass-1000-in-2025/ accessed 9 January 2026.

[12] United Nations General Assembly, 'Report of the Independent International Commission of Inquiry on the Occupied Palestinian Territory, Including East Jerusalem, and Israel' (11 September 2024) UN Doc A/79/232; United Nations Office of the High Commissioner for Human Rights, 'Report on the Human Rights Situation in Ukraine: 1 June – 30 November 2025' (9 December 2025) https://ukraine.ohchr.org/en/reports/periodic-reports-on-the-human-rights-situation-in-ukraine accessed 9 January 2026; United Nations Office of the High Commissioner for Human Rights, 'Protecting Human Rights in the DRC Amid Escalating Conflict' (10 September 2025) www.ohchr.org/en/stories/2025/09/protecting-human-rights-drc-amid-escalating-conflict accessed 9 January 2026.

[13] Marina Romanello and others, 'The 2025 of the *Lancet* Countdown on Health and Climate Change: Climate Change Action Offers a Lifeline' (2025) 406(10521) *Lancet* 2804; United Nations Office for South-South Cooperation, 'Climate Change and its Impact on the Countries of the Global South' (2025) https://southsouth-galaxy.org/wp-content/uploads/2025/07/Climate-change-and-its-impact-on-the-countries-of-the-Global-South.pdf accessed 9 January 2026.

[14] Maya Pendleton and Alan J Dettlaff, 'Policing Is Reproductive Oppression: How Policing and Carceral Systems Criminalize Parenting and Maintain Reproductive Oppression' (2024) 13(1) *Social Science* 515, 529.

[15] Cordelia Freeman and Hala Shoman, 'No Justice in a Genocide: Sexual and Reproductive Health and Rights in Gaza' (2025) 33(1) *Sexual and Reproductive Health Matters* 1; Nicola Pratt and others, 'Why Palestine is a Feminist Issue: A Reckoning with Western Feminism in a Time of Genocide' (2024) 27(1) *International Feminist Journal of Politics* 226; Laura Ferguson and Sapna Desai, 'Sexual and Reproductive Health and Rights in Palestine – Securing Spaces to Speak Out' (2024) 32(1) *Sexual and Reproductive Health Matters* 1.

impacts of armed conflict and famine.[16] The decimation of hospitals by Israeli forces, increase in hospital bed occupation as a result of injuries, and lack of access to essential medical supplies also creates unsafe conditions for pregnancy and childbirth.[17] Abortion is illegal in Palestine, and access to contraception has also been limited, though many people who menstruate have opted to take contraceptive pills to prevent their periods because of a lack of sanitary products due to Israel's aid blockades.[18] These are all violations of the four tenets that make up reproductive justice: bodily autonomy; the right to have a child; the right to not have a child; and the right to parent safely and sustainably. Because of the scale of this violence, the Palestinian Feminist Collective and Cordelia Freeman and Hala Shoman have thus referred to this as 'reproductive genocide', not merely reproductive injustice.[19]

In 2024, the International Court of Justice (ICJ), the principal court of the United Nations (UN), issued three sets of Provisional Measures in the case of *South Africa v Israel*, finding that there was a 'real and imminent risk' that Israel's military offensive could violate the rights of Palestinians under the Convention on the Prevention and Punishment of the Crime of Genocide (CPPCG) and thus amount to genocide.[20] The ICJ ordered Israel to take action to prevent and punish rights violations and incitement to genocide, stop its military offensive, ensure the unhindered provision of humanitarian aid, and allow UN investigators to access Gaza.[21] The UN Office of the High Commissioner for Human Rights has likewise expressed repeated concerns over gross violations of

[16] Freeman and Shoman, 'No Justice in a Genocide' (2025) (n 15) 3; UNFPA, 'UNFPA warns of catastrophic birth outcomes in Gaza amid starvation, psychological trauma and collapsing healthcare' (*UNFPA in Palestine,* 23 July 2025) https://palestine.unfpa.org/en/news/unfpa-warns-catastrophic-birth-outcomes-gaza-amid-starvation-psychological-trauma-and accessed 9 January 2026; Bilal Irfan and others, 'Is Gaza Still a Place for Newborn Life?' (2025) 406(10505) *Lancet* 803.

[17] ibid.

[18] Freeman and Shoman (n 15) 3; Bettina Böttcher, Mysoon Abu-El-Noor, and Nasser Abu-El-Noor, 'Choices and Services Related to Contraception in the Gaza Strip, Palestine: Perceptions of Service Users and Providers' (2019) 19 *BMC Women's Health* 165; UNFPA, 'From natural process to nightmare: How Gaza's women and girls cope with periods in a war zone' (2 June 2025) www.unfpa.org/news/natural-process-nightmare-how-gaza%E2%80%99s-women-and-girls-cope-their-periods-war-zone accessed 9 January 2026; Linah Alsaafin and Ruwaida Amer, 'No privacy, no water: Gaza women use period-delaying pills amid Israel war' (*Aljazeera*, 31 October 2023) www.aljazeera.com/news/2023/10/31/no-privacy-no-water-gaza-women-use-period-delaying-pills-amid-war accessed 9 January 2026.

[19] Freeman and Shoman (n 15) 4; Palestinian Feminist Collective, 'The Palestinian Feminist Collective Condemns Reproductive Genocide in Gaza' https://palestinianfeministcollective.org/the-pfc-condemns-reproductive-genocide-in-gaza/ accessed 9 January 2026.

[20] Application of the Convention on the Prevention and Punishment of the Crime of Genocide in the Gaza Strip (*South Africa v Israel*), Provisional Measures, Order of 26 January 2024, ICJ Reports 2024, p 3; Application of the Convention on the Prevention and Punishment of the Crime of Genocide in the Gaza Strip (*South Africa v Israel*), Request for the Modification of the Order Indicating Provisional Measures of 26 January 2024, Order of 28 March 2024, ICJ Reports 2024, p 513; Application of the Convention on the Prevention and Punishment of the Crime of Genocide in the Gaza Strip (*South Africa v Israel*), Request for the Modification of the Order of 28 March 2024, Order of 24 May 2024, ICJ Reports 2024, p 649.

[21] ibid.

international human rights and humanitarian law by Israel, and thus stressed the importance of the full and immediate compliance by Israel with the ICJ's orders.[22] Israel, however, rejected the ICJ's conclusions and has to date (at the time of writing) continued its military offensive in violation of the CPPCG, despite previous ceasefire agreements.[23]

In September 2025, the Independent International Commission of Inquiry on the Occupied Palestinian Territory presented its report to the UN Human Rights Council, finding that the 'Israeli authorities and Israeli security forces have the genocidal intent to destroy, in whole or in part, the Palestinians in the Gaza Strip.'[24] The Commission explicitly addressed reproductive violence, including the intentional destruction of reproductive and maternal healthcare centres, as a violation of the CPPCG.[25] In addition to recommendations aimed at Israel, the report also requested that Member States employ 'all means reasonably available to them to prevent the commission of genocide in the Gaza Strip' including stopping arms transfers to Israel, facilitate proceedings and impose sanctions on Israel, and co-operate with the International Criminal Court's investigation.[26] However, numerous states in the West, continue to side with Israel, with the US and numerous European Union states opposing South Africa's ICJ case.[27] Around two dozen countries have stopped arms exports, but the US is by far Israel's largest arms supplier and has provided at least $21.7 billion in military aid since October 2023.[28]

[22] UN OHCHR, 'Six-month update report on the human rights situation in Gaza: 1 November 2023 to 30 April 2024' (8 November 2024) www.ohchr.org/sites/default/files/documents/countries/opt/20241106-Gaza-Update-Report-OPT.pdf accessed 9 January 2026; UN OHCHR, 'Detention in the context of the escalation of hostilities in Gaza (October 2023 – June 2024)' (31 July 2024) www.ohchr.org/sites/default/files/documents/countries/opt/20240731-Thematic-report-Detention-context-Gaza-hostilities.pdf accessed 9 January 2026; UN OHCHR, 'Indiscriminate and disproportionate attacks during the conflict in Gaza (October – December 2023)' (19 June 2024) www.ohchr.org/sites/default/files/documents/countries/opt/20240619-ohchr-thematic-report-indiscrim-disprop-attacks-gaza-oct-dec2023.pdf accessed 9 January 2026.

[23] Observations of the State of Israel on the Request Filed by the Republic of South Africa on 6 March 2024 for the Indication of Additional Provisional Measures and/or the Modification of Measures Previously Indicated (15 March 2024) www.icj-cij.org/sites/default/files/case-related/192/192-20240315-wri-01-00-en.pdf accessed 9 January 2026; Al Jazeera, 'Israel launches deadly strikes in Gaza in new ceasefire violations' (4 January 2026) www.aljazeera.com/news/2026/1/4/israel-launches-deadly-strikes-in-gaza-in-new-ceasefire-violations accessed 9 January 2026.

[24] Human Rights Council, 'Legal Analysis of the Conduct of Israel in Gaza Pursuant to the Convention on the Prevention and Punishment of the Crime of Genocide' (16 September 2025) UN Doc A/HRC/60/CRP.3, para 220.

[25] ibid para 140.

[26] ibid para 256.

[27] Kanishka Singh, 'US criticizes ICJ opinion on Israeli occupation of Palestinian territories' (*Reuters*, 20 July 2024) www.reuters.com/world/us-criticizes-icj-opinion-israeli-occupation-palestinian-territories-2024-07-20/ accessed 9 January 2026; Mared Gwyn Jones, 'Why is the EU mostly silent on South Africa's genocide case against Israel' (*Euro News,* 10 January 2024) www.euronews.com/my-europe/2024/01/12/where-do-eu-countries-stand-on-south-africas-genocide-case-against-israel accessed 9 January 2026

[28] Cate Brown, 'These countries no longer arm Israel. It's not making much difference.' (*The Washington Post*, 16 October 2025) www.washingtonpost.com/world/2025/10/16/israel-weapons-ban-gaza-arms/ accessed 9 January 2025; Matthew Lee, 'US has given at least $21.7 billion in military aid to Israel since war in Gaza began, report says' (*AP News*, 7 October 2025)

In the face of genocide and acquiescence from Western political powers, international law thus appears to be wholly ineffective – the Chief of the UN Relief and Works Agency for Palestine Refugees, Phillipe Lazzarini, has stated that 'Gaza is becoming the graveyard of international humanitarian law'.[29] In 2024, a group of legal scholars offered reflections on the role of international law in Gaza, with some critical of the role of international law given its historical and current hypocrisy when it comes to non-white victims, its silence on settler colonialism, and its ability to only mitigate violence in increasingly small ways.[30] Tor Krever, for example, refers to international law as an 'edgeless sword'.[31] Others, however, reaffirm the importance of international law to humanise victims, increase external pressure, and extend ideas of justice, freedom, and common humanity, demonstrate social collectivity, and provide hope.[32] Human rights and humanitarian law may not be able to *prevent* violence, but Lori Allen argues that every 'reassertion of international legal principles, and every collective demand for Israel's violence to stop, voiced with the authoritative language of international criminal law accusations' still matters.[33] The question of what international law can do is an important one for this monograph, which affirms a commitment to the international human rights framework as a significant tool for progress.

First, the current international legal order, including the human rights framework, is deeply flawed and driven by imperialist impulses. However, it is my argument that human rights remain a necessary language (though not the *only* language) for combatting suffering, violence, and injustice – and so rather than abandoning this framework, it must instead be transformed. In her reflections on international law and Gaza, Souheir Edelbi argues that 'we need to make use of legal tools in more creative, subversive and contrapuntal ways that enable us to reclaim and reimagine what law should be and what it should look like from the standpoint of the oppressed'.[34] This monograph, though on a different focus, is an exercise in this reclamation and reimagining – a conceptual prefiguration of what international human rights could and should be, at least in relation to abortion liberation.

Second, while human rights might be considered an 'edgeless sword', focusing on the limited powers that international human rights bodies have entrenches a top-down, state-centric view of what human rights can do. In chapter five of this monograph, I take a bottom-up approach to human rights realisation,

---

https://apnews.com/article/israel-gaza-war-military-aid-83cebb16b3e504f70112e374a0c74bfc accessed 9 January 2026.

[29] Natalia Sancha, 'UNRWA chief: 'Gaza is becoming the graveyard of international humanitarian law' (*El País*, 1 September 2025) https://english.elpais.com/international/2025-09-01/unrwa-chief-gaza-is-becoming-the-graveyard-of-international-humanitarian-law.html accessed 9 January 2026.

[30] Tor Krever and others, 'On International Law and Gaza: Critical Reflections' (2024) 12 *London Review of International Law* 217.

[31] ibid 232.

[32] ibid.

[33] ibid 241–42

[34] ibid 261.

understanding the implementation of human rights (and other international legal) norms as situational, local, contextual, plural, and always in motion. Human rights realisation is the work taken up by actors across multiple levels, not by legal bodies alone, and social movements create the necessary bridge between international standards and domestic realities. State governments may not condemn genocide in Gaza, but pro-Palestine movements across the world have; state governments may not comply with international human rights standards on abortion, but abortion rights movements work to change that. International legal standards and social movements are mutually constitutive in how human rights ideas are shaped, recognised, and implemented. Law can still fail, however, and so counter-hegemonic activism becomes a particularly important aspect of human rights as a *concept*, rather than a legal practice. Whether through the global Boycott, Divestment, Sanctions movement, which seeks to place pressure on Israel to end its oppression of Palestine through actions including public boycotts of businesses based in Israel,[35] or feminist networks facilitating access to safe abortion outside of medical and legal frameworks, counter-hegemonic social movements offer a grassroots approach to justice and freedom. Human rights, through this lens, belong to the people – not the institutions. This is their continued importance.

For legal scholars, we are at a critical juncture of human rights and humanitarian violations, which international law in its current form is ill-equipped to address – and so a conceptual prefigurative politics is necessary, to imagine a radically different international order capable of condemning violence and supporting real justice. In doing so, we can support those that work towards futures of abortion liberation, of reproductive justice, of freedom for Palestine, of decolonisation, of socio-economic redistribution, and of human rights for all.

[35] See BDS Movement https://bdsmovement.net/ accessed 9 January 2026; Shaimaa Abdelkarim, 'Space-making 'After Rights': Carcerality, Rights-claims, and the Practice of Freedom' (2024) 28 *International Journal of Human Rights* 1394.

Bibliography

Articles

Abdelkarim, Shaimaa, 'Space-making "After Rights": Carcerality, Rights-claims, and the Practice of Freedom' (2024) 28 *International Journal of Human Rights* 1394

Abdelkarim, Shaimaa, 'Subaltern Subjectivity and Embodiment in Human Rights Practices' (2022) 10(2) *London Review of International Law* 243

Aiken, Abigail RA and others, 'Barriers to Accessing Abortion Services and Perspectives on Using Mifepristone and Misoprostol at Home in Great Britain' (2018) 97(2) *Contraception* 177

Aiken, Abigail RA and others, 'Effectiveness, Safety and Acceptability of No-test Medical Abortion (Termination of Pregnancy) Provided via Telemedicine: A National Cohort Study' (2021) 128(9) *BJOG* 1465

Aiken, Abigail RA and others, 'Self Reported Outcomes and Adverse Events After Medical Telemedicine: Population-based Study in the Republic of Ireland and Northern Ireland' (2017) 357 *BMJ* 1

Allori, Agostina, 'Assessing the "Green Tide": An International Human Rights Advocacy Analysis of the "National Campaign for Legal, Safe and Free Abortion" of 2018 in Argentina' (2018) 4 *Disrupted* 32

Alvarez, Sonia E and others, 'Encountering Latin American and Caribbean Feminisms' (2002) 28(2) *Signs* 537

Amadi, IR, 'Human Rights in Pre-Colonial Igbo Society of Nigeria: An Analysis' (1991) 46(3) *Africa* 403

Ambast, Sanhita, Atay, Hazal, and Lavelanet, Antonella, 'A Global Review of Penalties for Abortion-related Offences in 182 Countries' (2023) 8(3) *BMJ Global Health* e010405

Andaya, Elise, 'The Erosion of Rights to Abortion Care in the United States: A Call for Renewed Anthropological Engagement with the Politics of Abortion' (2017) 31(1) *Medical Anthropology Quarterly* 40

An-Na'im, Abdullahi Ahmed, 'Islam and Human Rights: Beyond the Universality Debate' (2000) 94 *ASIL Proceedings* 95

Aral, Berdal, 'The Idea of Human Rights as Perceived in the Ottoman Empire' (2004) 26(2) *Human Rights Quarterly* 454

Arrieta-Gómez, Aquiles Ignacio, 'Realizing the Fundamental Right to Health Through Litigation: The Colombian Case' (2018) 20(1) *Health and Human Rights Journal* 133

Asch, Adrienne, 'Prenatal Diagnosis and Selective Abortion: A Challenge to Practice and Policy' (1999) 89(11) *American Journal of Public Health* 1649

Atay, Hazal and others, 'Why Women Choose At-home Abortion via Teleconsultation in France: Drivers of Telemedicine Abortion During and Beyond the COVID-19 Pandemic' (2021) 47(4) *BMJ Sexual and Reproductive Health* 285

Autorino, Tommaso, Mattioli, Francesco, and Mencarini, Letizia, 'The Impact of Gynecologists' Conscientious Objection on Abortion Access' (2020) 87 *Social Science Research* 1

Banerjee, Sushanta K and others, 'An Exploration of the Socio-economic Profile of Women and Costs of Receiving Abortion Services at Public Health Facilities of Madhya Pradesh, India' (2017) 17 *BMC Health Services Research* 223

Baron, Teresa, 'Nobody Puts Baby in the Container: The Foetal Container Model at Work in Medicine and Commercial Surrogacy' (2018) 36(3) *Journal of Applied Philosophy* 491

Becker, Andréa, 'Stratified Reproduction, Hysterectomy, and the Social Process of Opting into Fertility' (2023) 37(4) *Gender and Society* 614

Belfrage, Madeleine, 'Reclaiming Autonomy: The Changing Landscape of Mexican Abortion Activism' (2024) 49(3) *Signs* 535

Belfrage, Madeleine, 'Revolutionary Pills? Feminist Abortion, Pharmaceuticalization, and Reproductive Governance' (2023) 25(1) *International Feminist Journal of Politics* 6

Bellucci, Mabel, 'Women's Struggle to Decide About Their Own Bodies: Abortion and Sexual Rights in Argentina' (1997) 5(10) *Reproductive Health Matters* 99

Berro Pizzarossa, Lucía and Nandagiri, Rishita, 'Self-Managed Abortion: A Constellation of Actors, A Cacophony of Laws?' (2021) 29(1) *Sexual and Reproductive Health Matters* 1

Berro Pizzarossa, Lucía, 'Legal Barriers to Access Abortion Services Through A Human Rights Lens: The Uruguayan Experience' (2018) 26(52) *Reproductive Health Matters* 151

Berro, Lucía Pizzarossa and Skuster, Patty, 'Toward Human Rights and Evidence-Based Legal Frameworks for (Self-Managed) Abortion: A Review of the Last Decade of Legal Reform' (2021) 23(1) *Health and Human Rights Journal* 199

Betstadt, Sarah J, Heyrana, Katrina J, and Whaley, Natalie S, 'Telemedicine for Medication Abortion: The Time is Now' (2020) 9(5) *Current Obstetrics and Gynecology Reports* 66

Binion, Gayle, 'Human Rights: A Feminist Perspective' (1995) 17(3) *Human Rights Quarterly* 509

Blas, Radi, 'Reproductive Injustice, Trans Rights, and Eugenics' (2020) 28(1) *Sexual and Reproductive Health Matters* 1824318

Blokker, Paul, 'Using Liberal-Legal Tools for Illiberal Gains: The European Court of Human Rights and Legal Mobilisation by Conservative Right-Wing Actors' (2024) 20 *International Journal of Law in Context* 401

Böttcher, Bettina, Abu-El-Noor, Mysoon, and Abu-El-Noor, Nasser, 'Choices and Services Related to Contraception in the Gaza Strip, Palestine: Perceptions of Service Users and Providers' (2019) 19 *BMC Women's Health* 165

Boydell, Nicola and others, 'Women's Experiences of a Telemedicine Abortion Service (Up to 12 weeks) Implemented During the Coronavirus (COVID-19) Pandemic: A Qualitative Evaluation' (2021) 128(11) *BJOG* 1752

Bracke, Maud Anne, 'Contesting 'Global Sisterhood': The Global Women's Health Movement, the United Nations and the Different Meanings of Reproductive Rights (1970s–80s)' (2023) *Gender and History* 811

Brems, Eva, 'Enemies or Allies? Feminism and Cultural Relativism as Dissident Voices in Discourse' (1997) 19(1) *Human Rights Quarterly* 136

Brinks, Daniel M and Pérez, Guillermo, 'Legalization, Judicialization, Lawfare: On the Light Side and the Dark Side of the Turn to Law' (2025) 21 *Annual Review of Law and Social Science* 55

Bucholc, Marta, 'Abortion Law and Human Rights in Poland: The Closing of the Jurisprudential Horizon' (2022) 14 *Hague Journal on the Rule of Law* 73

Bunch, Charlotte, 'Looking Back, Looking Forward: Women's Human Rights in Global Perspective' (2017) 38(3-4) *Women's Rights Law Reporter* 333

Bunch, Charlotte, 'Women's Rights as Human Rights: Toward a Re-Vision of Human Rights' (1990) 12(4) *Human Rights Quarterly* 486

Bunting, Annie, 'Theorizing Women's Cultural Diversity in Feminist International Human Rights Strategies' (1993) 20(1) *Journal of Law and Society* 6

Cabello, Andrés López and Gaitán, Ana Cecilia, 'Safe Abortion in Women's Hands: Autonomy and a Human Rights Approach to COVID-19 and Beyond' (2021) 23(1) *Health and Human Rights Journal* 191

Caglar, Gülay, 'Gender Mainstreaming' (2013) 9(3) *Politics and Gender* 336

Calkin, Sydney, 'Towards a Political Geography of Abortion' (2019) 69 *Political Geography* 22

Cardosa, Bruno Baptista, Morena dos Santos Barbeiro Vieira, Fernanda, and Saraceni, Valeria, 'Abortion in Brazil: What do the Official Data Say?' (2020) 36 (Suppl 1) *Cadernos de Saúde Pública* 1

Caruso, Elena, 'Abortion in Italy: Forty Years On' (2020) 28 *Feminist Legal Studies* 87

Cassel, Douglass, 'Does International Human Rights Law Make a Difference?' (2001) 2 *Chicago Journal of International Law* 121

Cassidy, Kathryn, Amiri, Rana, and Davidson, Gill, 'Reading for Refusal in UK Maternity Care: Entangling Struggles for Border and Reproductive Justice' (2023) 201(2) *Fennia* 199

Charlesworth, Hilary, 'Not Waving but Drowning: Gender Mainstreaming and Human Rights in the United Nations' (2005) 18 *Harvard Human Rights Law Journal* 1

Charlesworth, Hilary, Chinkin, Christine, and Wright, Shelley, 'Feminist Approaches to International Law' (1991) 85(4) *American Journal of International Law* 613

Chaturvedi, Sarika and others, 'Availability and Distribution of Safe Abortion Services in Rural Areas: A Facility Assessment Study in Madhya Pradesh, India' (2015) 8(1) *Global Health Action* 26346

Chavin, Wendy, Swerdlow, Laurel, and Fifield, Jocelyn, 'Regulation of Conscientious Objection to Abortion: An International Comparative Multiple-Case Study' (2017) 19(1) *Health and Human Rights Journal* 55

Chełstowska, Agata, 'Stigmatisation and Commercialisation of Abortion Services in Poland: Turning Sin into Gold' (2011) 19(37) *Reproductive Health Matters* 98

Chen, Tracy X and others, 'Roots, Leaves, and Flowers: A Narrative Review of Herbs and Botanicals Used for Self-Managed Abortion in Asia and the Pacific' (2023) 68(6) *Journal of Midwifery & Women's Health* 710

Chitnis, Varsha and Wright, Danaya, 'Legacy of Colonialism: Law and Women's Rights in India' (2007) 64(4) *Washington & Lee Law Review* 1315

Choudhury, Cyra Akila, 'Beyond Culture: Human Rights Universalism versus Religious and Cultural Relativism in the Activism for Gender Justice' (2015) 30(2) *Berkeley Journal of Gender Law and Justice* 226

Chow, Pok Yin S, 'Has Intersectionality Reached its Limits? Intersectionality in the UN Human Rights Treaty Body Practice and the Issue of Ambivalence' (2016) 16(3) *Human Rights Law Review* 453

Citizens Coalition for the Decriminalization of Abortion on Grounds of Health, Ethics and Fetal Anomaly, El Salvador, 'From Hospital to Jail: The Impact of Women of El Salvador's Total Criminalization of Abortion' (2014) 22(44) *Reproductive Health Matters* 52

Coast, Ernestina and others, 'Abortion and Well-Being: A Narrative Literature Review' 7 *SSM – Qualitative Research in Health* 100508

Cobbah, Josiah AM, 'African Values and the Human Rights Debate: An African Perspective' (1987) 9(3) *Human Rights Quarterly* 309

Connell, Raewyn, 'Gender, Health and Theory: Conceptualizing the Issue, In Local and World Perspective' (2012) 74 *Social Science and Medicine* 1675

Cook, Rebecca J and Dickens, Bernard M, 'Human Rights Dynamics of Abortion Law Reform' (2003) 1 *Human Rights Quarterly* 1

Cook, Rebecca J, 'Excerpts of the Constitutional Court's Ruling that Liberalized Abortion in Colombia' (2007) 15(29) *Reproductive Health Matters* 160

Cooper, Davina, 'Prefiguring the State' (2017) 49(2) *Antipode* 335

Cosentino, Chiara, 'Safe and Legal Abortion: An Emerging Human Right? The Long-Lasting Dispute with State Sovereignty in ECHR Jurisprudence' (2015) 15(3) *Human Rights Law Review* 569

Costa, Sarah H and Vessey, Martin P, 'Misoprostol and Illegal Abortion in Rio de Janeiro, Brazil' (1993) 341(8855) *Lancet* 1258

Crenshaw, Kimberlé, 'Demarginalizing the Intersection of Race and Sex: A Black Feminist Critique of Antidiscrimination Doctrine, Feminist Theory, and Antiracist Politics' (1989) 1 *University of Chicago Legal Forum* 139

Curtis, Carolyn, 'Meeting Health Care Needs of Women Experiencing Complications of Miscarriage and Unsafe Abortion: USAID's Postabortion Care Program' (2007) 52(4) *Journal of Midwifery & Women's Health* 368
Daby, Mariela and Moseley, Mason W, 'Feminist Mobilization and the Abortion Debate in Latin America: Lessons from Argentina' (2022) 18 *Politics & Gender* 359
Daigle, Megan, Duffy, Deirdre N, and Castañeda, Diana López, 'Abortion Access and Colombia's Legacy of Civil War: Between Reproductive Violence and Reproductive Governance' (2022) 98(4) *International Affairs* 1423
De Beco, Gauthier, 'Protecting the Invisible: An Intersectional Approach to International Human Rights Law' (2017) 17(4) *Human Rights Law Review* 633
De Falco, Rossella and others, 'Assessing the Human Rights Framework on Private Health Care Actors and Economic Inequality' (2023) 25(2) *Health and Human Rights Journal* 125
De Londras, Fiona and others, 'The Impact of "Conscientious Objection" on Abortion-Related Outcomes: A Synthesis of Legal and Health Evidence' (2023) 129 *Health Policy* 104716
De Londras, Fiona, 'The Impact of "Grounds" on Abortion-Related Outcomes: A Synthesis of Legal and Health Evidence' (2022) 22(1) *BMC Public Health* 936
De Zordo, Silvia and Mishtal, Joanna, 'Physicians and Abortion: Provision, Political Participation and Conflicts on the Ground – The Cases of Brazil and Poland' (2011) 21(3S) *Women's Health Issues* S32
De Zordo, Silvia, 'The Biomedicalization of Illegal Abortion: The Double Life of Misoprostol in Brazil' (2016) 23(1) *História, Ciências, Saúde-Manguinhos* 19
Devaja, Anya, 'Healthcare Inequalities: The Unintended Consequences of Private Healthcare Policy?' (2013) 105(6) *Bulletin, Royal College of Surgeons England* 272
Dickman, Samuel L, White, Kari, and Grossman, Daniel, 'Affordability and Access to Abortion Care in the United States' (2021) 181(9) *JAMA Internal Medicine* 1157
Diniz, Debora, Madeiro, Alberto, and Rosas, Cristião, 'Conscientious Objection, Barriers, and Abortion in the Case of Rape: A Study Among Physicians in Brazil' (2014) 22(43) *Reproductive Health Matters* 141
Djoyou Kamga, Serges Alain and Fombad, Charles Manga, 'A Critical Review of the Jurisprudence of the African Commission on the Right to Development' (2013) 57(2) *Journal of African Law* 196
Djoyou Kamga, Serges Alain, 'The Right to Development in the African Human Rights System: The *Endorois* Case' (2011) 44(2) *De Jure* 381
Domenici, Irene, 'Antigone Betrayed? The European Court of Human Rights' Decisions on Conscientious Objection to Abortion in the Cases of *Grimmark v Sweden* and *Steen v Sweden*' (2021) 28 *European Journal of Health Law* 26
Donnelly, Jack, 'The Relative Universality of Human Rights' (2007) 29(2) *Human Rights Quarterly* 281
Drovetta, Raquel I, 'Safe Abortion Information Hotlines: An Effective Strategy for Increasing Women's Access to Safe Abortions in Latin America' (2015) 23(45) *Reproductive Health Matters* 47
Drovetta, Raquel Irene, Freeman, Cordelia, and Rúa, Agustina, 'Self-care for abortion activists and providers: lessons of law and risk from Argentina' (2023) 49 *BMJ Sexual and Reproductive Health* 308
Duffy, Sandra, 'Contested Subjects of Human Rights: Trans- and Gender-Variant Subjects of International Human Rights Law' (2021) 84(5) *Modern Law Review* 1041
Dyer, Owen, 'Poland Abortion Reform Stalls After Decriminalisation Vote Fails' (2024) 386 *BMJ* 1
Eberhardt, Maeve, 'The Social Meaning of Abortion and the Perils of a Neoliberal Rights-Based Discourse' (2023) 17(3) *Gender and Language* 250
Ehrenreich Brooks, Rosa, 'Feminism and International Law: An Opportunity for Transformation' (2002) 14 *Yale Journal of Law and Feminism* 345
Eisler, Riane, 'Human Rights: Toward an Integrated Theory for Action' (1987) 9(3) *Human Rights Quarterly* 287

Encarción, Omar G, 'International Influence, Domestic Activism, and Gay Rights in Argentina' (2013) 128(4) *Political Science Quarterly* 687
Endler, Margit and others, 'Telemedicine for Medical Abortion: A Systematic Review' (2019) 126(9) *BJOG* 1094
Engle Merry, Sally, 'Global Legal Pluralism and the Temporality of Soft Law' (2014) 46(1) *Journal of Legal Pluralism and Unofficial Law* 108
Engle Merry, Sally, 'Legal Pluralism' (1988) 22(5) *Law and Society Review* 869
Engle Merry, Sally, 'What is Legal Culture? An Anthropological Perspective' (2010) 5(2) *Journal of Comparative Law* 40
Engle, Karen, 'International Human Rights and Feminism: When Discourses Meet' (1992) 13 *Michigan Journal of International Law* 517
Englehart, Neil A and Miller, Melissa K, 'The CEDAW Effect: International Law's Impact on Women's Rights' (2014) 13(1) *Journal of Human Rights* 22
Enright, Máiréad, McNeilly, Kathryn, and De Londras, Fiona, 'Abortion Activism, Legal Change, and Taking Feminist Law Work Seriously' (2020) 71(3) *Northern Ireland Legal Quarterly* 7
Erdman, Joanna N, 'Access to Information on Safe Abortion: A Harm Reduction and Human Rights Approach' (2011) 34 *Harvard Journey of Law and Gender* 413
Erdman, Joanna N and Cook, Rebecca J, 'Decriminalization of Abortion – A Human Rights Imperative' (2020) 62 *Best Practice and Research: Clinical Obstetrics and Gynaecology* 11
Erdman, Joanna N, 'Harm Reduction, Human Rights, and Access to Information on Safe Abortion' (2012) 118(1) *International Journal of Gynecology and Obstetrics* 83
Erdman, Joanna N, 'Theorizing Time in Abortion Law and Human Rights' (2017) 19(1) *Health and Human Rights Journal* 29
Erdman, Joanna N, Jelinska, Kinga, and Yanow, Susan, 'Understandings of Self-Managed Abortion as Health Inequity, Harm Reduction and Social Change' (2018) 26(54) *Reproductive Health Matters* 13
Eristavi, Konstantine, 'Performing Defiance with Rights' (2021) 32 *Law Critique* 153
Favier, Mary, Greenberg, Jamie MS, and Stevens, Marion, 'Safe Abortion in South Africa: "We Have Wonderful Laws but We Don't Have People to Implement Those Laws' (2018) 143(S4) *International Journal Gynaecology Obstetrics* 38
Fenwick, Daniel, 'The Modern Abortion Jurisprudence under Article 8 of the European Convention on Human Rights' (2012) 12 *Medical Law International* 249
Ferguson, Laura and Desai, Sapna, 'Sexual and Reproductive Health and Rights in Palestine – Securing Spaces to Speak Out' (2024) 32(1) *Sexual and Reproductive Health Matters* 1
Feria Tinta, Mónica, 'Justiciability of Economic, Social, and Cultural Rights in the Inter-American System of Protection of Human Rights Beyond Traditional Paradigms and Notions' (2007) 29(2) *Human Rights Quarterly* 431
Fiala, Christian and Arthur, Joyce H, '"Dishonourable Disobedience" – Why Refusal to Treat in Reproductive Healthcare is Not Conscientious Objection' (2014) 1 *Woman – Psychosomatic Gynaecology and Obstetrics* 12
Fiala, Christian and Arthur, Joyce H, 'There is No Defence for 'Conscientious Objection' in Reproductive Health Care' (2017) 216 *European Journal of Obstetrics & Gynecology and Reproductive Biology* 254
Fiala, Christian and Arthur, Joyce, 'How to Discourage Belief-Based Denial of Abortion Care' (2025) 30(4) *European Journal of Contraception and Reproductive Health Care* 221
Fiala, Christian and others, 'Yes We Can! Successful Examples of Disallowing "Conscientious Objection" in Reproductive Health Care' (2016) 21(3) *European Journal of Contraception and Reproductive Health Care* 201
Fiala, Christian, Arthur, Joyce, and Martzke, Amelia, 'Origin of "Conscientious Objection" in Health Care: How Care Denials Became Enshrined into Law Because of Abortion' (2025) 53(1) *Journal of Law Medicine and Ethics* 89

Fine, Johanna B, Mayall, Katherine, and Sepúlveda, Lilian, 'The Role of International Human Rights Norms in the Liberalization of Abortion Laws Globally' (2017) 19(1) *Health and Human Rights Journal* 69

Finer, Louise and Fine, Johanna B, 'Abortion Law Around the World: Progress and Pushback' (2013) 103(4) *American Journal of Public Health* 585

Fink, Lauren R and others, '"The Fetus Is My Patient, Too": Attitudes Toward Abortion and Referral Among Physician Conscientious Objectors in Bogotá, Colombia' (2016) 42(2) *International Perspectives on Sexual and Reproductive Health* 71

Foot, Philippa, 'The Problem of Abortion and the Doctrine of Double Effect' (1967) 5(5) *Oxford Review* 15

Forman, Lisa and others, 'What Could a Strengthened Right to Health Bring to the Post-2015 Health Development Agenda?: Interrogating the Role of the Minimum Core Concept in Advancing Global Health Needs' (2013) 13(48) *BMC International Health and Human Rights* 1

Foster, Diane Greene and Kimport, Katrina, 'Who Seeks Abortions at or After 20 Weeks?' (2013) 45(4) *Perspectives on Sexual and Reproductive Health* 210

Fovargue, Sara and Neal, Mary, '"In Good Conscience": Conscience-Based Exemptions and Proper Medical Treatment' (2015) 23(2) *Medical Law Review* 221

Frankenberg, Günter, 'Human Rights and the Belief in a Just World' (2014) 12(1) *ICON* 35

Freeman, Cordelia and Shoman, Hala, 'No Justice in a Genocide: Sexual and Reproductive Health and Rights in Gaza' (2025) 33(1) *Sexual and Reproductive Health Matters* 1

Freeman, Emily and Coast, Ernestina, 'Conscientious Objection to Abortion: Zambian Healthcare Practitioners' Beliefs and Practices' (2019) 221 *Social Science and Medicine* 106

Fry-Bowers, Eileen K, 'A Matter of Conscience: Examining the Law and Policy of Conscientious Objection in Health Care' (2020) 21(2) *Policy Politics and Nursing Practice* 120

Furgalska, Magdalena and De Londras, Fiona, 'Rights, Lawfare and Reproduction: Reflections on the Polish Constitutional Tribunal's Abortion Decision' (2022) 55(3) *Israel Law Review* 285

Gamble, Nathan and Saad, Toni, 'A Taxonomy of Conscientious Objection in Healthcare' (2022) 17(1) *Clinical Ethics* 63

Ganatra, Bela and others, 'Global, Regional, and Subregional Classification of Abortions by Safety, 2010–2014: Estimates from a Bayesian Hierarchical Model' (2017) 390 *Lancet* 2372

Geleto, Ayele, Taylor, Jo, and Beyene, Tesfalidet, 'Interruptions in Contraception and Unintended Pregnancy During the COVID-19 Pandemic: A Protocol for Systemic Review and Meta-Analysis' (2023) *Women's Health* 19

Gerbaudo, Paolo, 'Protest Diffusion and Cultural Resonance in the 2011 Protest Wave' (2013) 48 *International Spectator* 86

Gerber Fried, Marlene, 'Abortion in the United States: Barriers to Access' (2000) 4(2) *Health and Human Rights Journal* 174

Gerdts, Caitlin and Hudaya, Inna, 'Quality of Care in a Safe-Abortion Hotline in Indonesia: Beyond Harm Reduction' (2016) 106(11) *American Journal of Public Health* 2071

Gianella, Camila and Álvarez, Brenda, 'Judicial Lawfare: Analysis of Legal Arguments against Abortion Rights in Peruvian Courts' (2021) 17(3) *Revista Direito GV* 1

Giublini, Alberto and others, 'Conscientious Commitment, Professional Obligations and Abortion Provision After the Reversal of *Roe v Wade*' (2024) 50 *Journal of Medical Ethics* 351

Gloppen, Siri, 'Conceptualizing Abortion Lawfare' (2021) 17(3) *Revista Direito GV* 1

Golder, Ben, 'Beyond Redemption? Problematising the Critique of Human Rights in Contemporary International Legal Thought' (2014) 2(1) *London Review of International Law* 77

Gómez-Dantés, Octavio, 'The Dark Side of Cuba's Health System: Free Speech, Rights of Patients, and Labor Rights of Physicians' (2018) 4(3) *Health Systems and Reform* 175

Gomperts, Rebecca and others, 'Provision of Medical Abortion Using Telemedicine in Brazil' (2014) 89(2) *Contraception* 129

González Orta, Lydia Candelaria, 'The Convention on the Elimination of all Forms of Discrimination Against Women (CEDAW): From its Radical Preamble to its Contemporary Intersectional Approach' (2025) 34(1) *Women's History Review* 79
González Vélez, Ana Cristina and Urbano, Laura Gil, 'Improper Use of Conscientious Objection to Abortion/Authors' Response' (2016) 42(2) *International Perspectives on Sexual and Reproductive Health* 221
Gostin, Lawrence O and Archer, Robert, 'The Duty of States to Assist Other States in Need: Ethics, Human Rights, and International Law' (2007) 35(4) *Journal of Law Medicine and Ethics* 526
Grady, Paul and Robins, Simon, 'Rethinking Civil Society and Transitional Justice: Lessons from Social Movements and "New" Civil Society' (2017) 21(7) *International Journal of Human Rights* 956
Greasley, Kate, 'Is Sex-Selective Abortion against the Law?' (2016) 36(3) *OJLS* 535
Greene Foster, Diane and others, 'A Comparison of Depression and Anxiety Symptom Trajectories Between Women Who Had an Abortion and Women Denied One' (2015) 45(10) *Psychological Medicine* 2073
Greenhouse, Linda and Siegel, Reva B, '*Casey* and the Clinic Closings: When "Protecting Health" Obstructs Choice' (2016) 125 *Yale Law Journal* 1428
Grewal, Inderpal, '"Women's Rights as Human Rights": Feminist Practices, Global Feminism, and Human Rights in Transnationality' (1999) 3(3) *Citizenship Studies* 337
Grimes, Lorraine and others, '"Still travelling": Access to Abortion Post-12 Weeks Gestation in Ireland' (2013) 98 *Women's Studies International Forum* 102709
Grizzle Fischer, Meghan, 'The United Nations and the Right to Conscientious Objection in the Health-Care Field' (2016) 21(1) *Texas Review of Law and Politics* 201
Haining, Casey Michelle and others, 'The "Institutional Lottery": Institutional Variation in the Processes Involved in Accessing Late Abortion in Victoria, Australia' (2023) 101 *Women's Studies International Forum* 102822
Han, Leo, Rodriguez, Maria I, and Caughey, Aaron B, 'Blurred Lines: Disentangling the Concept of Fetal Viability from Abortion Law' (2018) 28(4) *Women's Health Issues* 287
Harries, Jane and others, 'Conscientious Objection and its Impact on Abortion Service Provision in South Africa: A Qualitative Study' (2014) 11(16) *Reproductive Health* 1
Harris, Laura Florence and others, 'Conscientious Objection to Abortion Provision: Why Context Matters' (2018) 13(5) *Global Public Health* 556
Hashemi, Nader and Qureshi, Emran, 'Islam and Human Rights: A 50 Year Retrospective' (2022) 19(1) *Muslim World Journal of Human Rights* 1
Heinsen, Laura Louise, 'Shouldering Death: Moral Tensions, Ambiguity, and the Unintended Ramifications of State-sanctioned Second-trimester Selective Abortion in Denmark' (2022) 36(4) *Medical Anthropology Quarterly* 515
Heitmeyer, Carolyn and Unnithan, Maya, 'Bodily Rights and Collective Claims: The Work of Legal Activists in Interpreting Reproductive and Maternal Rights in India' (2015) 21 *Journal of the Royal Anthropological Institute* 374
Hermannsdóttir, Turið and Dybbroe, Betina, 'Components of Reproductive Citizenship: Narratives from a Restrictive Abortion Landscape' (2023) 27(8) *Citizenship Studies* 1022
Herring, Jonathan and Robinson, Heloise, 'A Right to Live Without Stigma? Examining Negative Stereotyping, Negative Messages, and Article 8 of the European Convention on Human Rights' (2024) 44(4) *Legal Studies* 685
Hervey, Tamara and Sheldon, Sally, 'Abortion by Telemedicine in the European Union' (2019) 145(1) *International Journal of Gynaecoly & Obstetrics* 125
Higgins, Tracy E 'Anti-Essentialism, Relativism, and Human Rights' (1996) 19 *Harvard Women's Law Journal* 89
Hill, Jessie, 'De-Medicalizing Abortion' (2022) 22(8) *American Journal of Bioethics* 57
Hines, Sally, 'Sex Wars and (Trans) Gender Panics: Identity and Body Politics in Contemporary UK Feminism' (2020) 68(4) *Sociological Review Monographs* 25

Hoctor, Leah and Lamačková, Adriana, 'Mandatory Waiting Periods and Biased Abortion Counseling in Central and Eastern Europe' (2017) 139(2) *International Journal of Gynaecology and Obstetrics* 253

Holtmaat, Rikki and Post, Paul, 'Enhancing LGBTI Rights by Changing the Interpretation of Convention on the Elimination of All Forms of Discrimination Against Women' (2015) 33(4) *Nordic Journal of Human Rights* 319

Hooton, Angela, 'A Broader Vision of the Reproductive Rights Movement: Fusing Mainstream and Latina Feminism' (2005) 13(1) *Journal of Gender, Social Policy and The Law* 59

Hunt, Kate, 'Social Movements and Human Rights Language in Abortion Debates' (2021) 20(1) *Journal of Human Rights* 72

Irfan, Bilal and others, 'Is Gaza Still a Place for Newborn Life?' (2025) 406(10505) *Lancet* 803

Jain, Dipika, 'Legal Challenges in Expanding the Provider Base for Abortion in Asia' (2025) 168(3) *International Journal of Gynecology and Obstetrics* 1345

Jelinska, Kinga and Yanow, Susan, 'Putting Abortion Pills into Women's Hands: Realizing the Full Potential of Medical Abortion' (2018) 97 *Contraception* 86

Jerman, Jenna and others, 'Barriers to Abortion Care and Their Consequences for Patients Traveling for Services: Qualitative Findings from Two States' (2017) 49(2) *Perspectives on Sexual and Reproductive Health* 95

Joffe, Carole and Schroeder, Rosalyn, 'COVID-19, Health Care, and Abortion Exceptionalism in the United States' (2021) 53(1-2) *Perspectives on Sexual and Reproductive Health* 5

Jones, Rachel K and Jerman, Jenna, 'Abortion Incidence and Service Availability in the United States, 2014' (2017) 49(1) *Perspectives on Sexual and Reproductive Health* 17

Jones, Rachel K and Jerman, Jenna, 'How Far Did US Women Travel for Abortion Services in 2008?' (2013) 22(8) *Journal of Women's Health* 706

Jones, Rachel K, Upadhyay, Ushma D, and Weitz, Tracy A, 'At What Cost? Payment for Abortion Care by US Women' (2013) 23(3) *Women's Health Issues* 173

Kapur, Ratna, 'Human Rights in the 21st Century: Take a Walk on the Dark Side' (2006) 28 *Sydney Law Review* 665

Kapur, Ratna, 'Precarious Desires and Ungrievable Lives: Human Rights and Postcolonial Critiques of Legal Justice' (2015) 3(2) *London Review of International Law* 267

Karlin, Jennifer and Joffe, Carole, 'Self-Sourced Medication Abortion, Physician Authority, and the Contradictions of Abortion Care' (2023) 48(4) *Journal of Health, Politics, Policy and Law* 603

Kendal, Evie, 'All Abortions are Medically Necessary' (2023) 18(3) *Clinical Ethics* 306

Kennedy, David, 'International Human Rights Movement: Part of the Problem?' (2002) 15 *Harvard Human Rights Journal* 101

Kim, Mimi E, 'Anti-Carceral Feminism: The Contradictions of Progress and the Possibilities of Counter-Hegemonic Struggle' (2020) 35(3) *Affilia* 309

Kim, Nancy, 'Toward a Feminist Theory of Human Rights: Straddling the Fence between Western Imperialism and Uncritical Absolutism' (1993) 25 *Columbia Human Rights Law Review* 49

Kimport, Katrina and McLemore, Monica R, 'The Problem with "Justifying" Abortion: Why Real Reproductive Justice Cannot Be Achieved by Theorizing the Legitimacy of Abortion' (2022) 9(1) *Women's Reproductive Health* 27

Kimport, Katrina, Johns, Nicole E, and D Upadhyay, Ushma, 'Coercing Women's Behavior: How a Mandatory Viewing Law Changes Patients' Preabortion Ultrasound Viewing Practices' (2018) 43(6) *Journal of Health Politics, Policy and Law* 941

Kingma, Elselijn, 'Were You a Part of Your Mother?' (2019) 128 *Mind* 609

Krawutschke, Robin, Pastrana, Tania, and Schmitz, Dagmar, 'Conscientious Objection and Barriers to Abortion Within a Specific Regional Context – An Expert Interview Study' (2024) 25(1) *BMC Medical Ethics* 1

Krever, Tor and others, 'On International Law and Gaza: Critical Reflections' (2024) 12 *London Review of International Law* 217

Kriener, Florian, 'The International Law of Protest' (2024) 117 *ASIL Proceedings* 323

Küng, Stephanie Andrea and others, '"We Don't Want Problems": Reasons for Denial of Legal Abortion Based on Conscientious Objection in Mexico and Bolivia' (2021) 18(44) *Reproductive Health Matters* 1
Larrea, Sara and Veldhuis, Suzanne, 'Hegemonic Medicine and Self-Managed Abortion: Reclaiming Latin America Feminists' Contributions to Knowledge and Practice Development' (2025) *Sexual and Reproductive Health Matters* [online first]
Larrea, Sara, Prandini Assis, Mariana, and Ochoa Mendoza, Camila, '"Hospitals Have Some Procedures that Seem Dehumanising to Me": Experiences of Abortion-Related Obstetric Violence in Brazil, Chile and Ecuador' (2021) 35(3) *Agenda* 54
Latimer, Heather, 'Abortion Regulation as the Afterlife of Reproductive Slavery: Or, a Call to Make Abortion Natural Again' (2022) 48(2) *Feminist Studies* 342
Lavelanet, Antonella F and others, 'Global Abortion Policies Database: A Descriptive Analysis of the Legal Categories of Lawful Abortion' (2018) 18(44) *BMC International Health and Human Rights* 1
Lee, Melanie M, 'Defining the Agenda: A New Struggle for African-American Women in the Fight for Reproductive Self-Determination' (2000) 6 *Washington and Lee Race and Ethnic Ancestry Journal* 87, 96
Loewen, Samantha and others, 'The Impact of Natural Disasters and Epidemics on Sexual and Reproductive Health in Low- and Middle-Income Countries: A Narrative Synthesis' (2022) 157(1) *International Journal of Gynecology and Obstetrics* 11
Londoño-Vélez, Juliana and Saravia, Estefanía, 'The Impact of Being Denied a Wanted Abortion on Women and Their Children' (2025) 140(2) *Quarterly Journal of Economics* 1061
Lonergan, Gwyneth, 'Reproductive Justice and Migrant Women in Great Britain' (2012) 23(1) *Women* 26
Lopreite, Debora, 'Travelling Ideas and Domestic Policy Change: The Transnational Politics of Reproductive Rights/Health in Argentina' (2012) 12(2) *Global Social Policy* 109
Lowe, Lisa, 'The Dialectics of Abolition' (2023) 75(2) *American Quarterly* 371
Lugones, María, 'Toward a Decolonial Feminism' (2010) 25(4) *Hypatia* 742
Luna, Zayika and Luker, Kristin, 'Reproductive Justice' (2013) 9 *Annual Review of Law and Social Science* 327
Lupton, Deborah, '"Precious Cargo": Foetal Subjects, Risk and Reproductive Citizenship' (2012) 22(3) *Critical Public Health* 329
Mackenzie, Catriona, 'Abortion and Embodiment' (1992) 70(2) *Australasian Journal of Philosophy* 155
Margolin, Tatyana A, 'Abortion as a Human Right' (2007) 29(2) *Women's Rights Law Reporter* 77
Markowitz, Sally, 'Abortion and Feminism' (1990) 16(1) *Social Theory and Practice* 1
Matthews, Thandiwe, 'Interrogating the Debates Around Lawfare and Legal Mobilization: A Literature Review' (2023) 15 *Journal of Human Rights Practice* 24
Mavuso, Jabulile Mary-Jane Jace, 'Understanding the Violation of Directive Anti-Abortion Counselling [and Cisnormativity]: Obstruction to Access or Reproductive Violence?' (2021) 35(3) *Agenda* 69
McGaughey, Fiona, 'From Gatekeepers to GONGOs: A Taxonomy of Non-Governmental Organisations Engaging with United Nations Human Rights Mechanisms' (2018) 36(2) *Netherlands Quarterly of Human Rights* 111
McGaughey, Fiona, 'Advancing, Retreating or Stepping on Each Other's Toes? The Role of Non-Governmental Organisations in United Nations Human Rights Treaty Body Reporting and the Universal Periodic Review' (2017) 35 *Australian Year Book of International Law* 187
McGovern, Terry, Memaj, Ira and Rivera, Lourdes, 'Fetal Personhood: What Happens When the Rights of the "Fertilized Egg" Supersede the Rights of the Mother' (2025) 388 *BMJ* 372
McGuinness, Sheelagh and Montgomery, Jonathan, 'Legal Determinants of Health: Regulating Abortion Care' (2020) 13(1) *Public Health Ethics* 34
McGuinness, Sheelagh, 'Law, Reproduction, and Disability: Fatally "Handicapped"?' (2013) 21(2) *Medical Law Rev* 213

McLeod, Carolyn, 'Harm or Mere Inconvenience? Denying Women Emergency Contraception' (2010) 25(1) *Hypatia* 11
McLeod, Carolyn, 'Referral in the Wake of Conscientious Objection to Abortion' (2008) 23(4) *Hypatia* 30
McNeilly, Kathryn, 'After the Critique of Rights: For a Radical Democratic Theory and Practice of Human Rights' (2016) 27 *Law Critique* 269
Merner, Bronwen and others, 'Health Providers' Reasons for Participating in Abortion Care: A Scoping Review' (2024) 20 *Women's Health* 1
Meurice, Marielle E and others, 'Client Satisfaction and Experience of Telemedicine and Home Use of Mifepristone and Misoprostol for Abortion up to 10 weeks' Gestation at British Pregnancy Advisory Service: A Cross-Sectional Evaluation' (2021) 104(1) *Contraception* 61
Millar, Erica, '"Too Many": Anxious White Nationalism and the Biopolitics of Abortion' (2015) 30(83) *Australian Feminist Studies* 82
Millar, Erica, 'Abortion Stigma, Abortion Exceptionalism, and Medical Curricula' (2023) 32(3) *Health Sociology Review* 261
Millar, Erica, 'Abortion, Decriminalisation and the Medico-Legal Paradigm' (2024) 355 *Social Science and Medicine* 117098
Millar, Erica, 'Maintaining Exceptionality: Interrogating Gestational Limits for Abortion' (2022) 31(3) *Social and Legal Studies* 439
Miller, Alice M and Roseman, Mindy J, 'Sexual and Reproductive Rights at the United Nations: Frustration or Fulfilment?' (2011) 19(38) *Reproductive Health Matters* 102
Minerva, Francesca, 'Conscientious Objection in Italy' (2015) 41(2) *Journal of Medical Ethics* 170
Minerva, Francesca, 'Conscientious Objection, Complicity in Wrongdoing, and a Not-So-Moderate Approach' (2017) 26(1) *Cambridge Quarterly of Healthcare Ethics* 109
Mitchell, Lynsey 'Reading Narratives of Privilege and Paternalism: The Limited Utility of Human Rights Law on the Journey to Reform Northern Irish Abortion Law' (2021) 72(1) *Norther Ireland Legal Quarterly* 89
Mohanty, Chandra, 'Under Western Eyes: Feminist Scholarship and Colonial Discourses' (1988) 30 *Feminist Review* 61
Moller Okin, Susan, 'Feminism, Women's Human Rights, and Cultural Differences' (1998) 13(2) *Hypatia* 32
Monani, Devaki and Gerry QC, Felicity, 'Death and the Dowry System: India's Women and Female Children at Global Risk of Gendercide Over Money' (2017) 15(1) *Issues in Legal Scholarship* 1
Monticelli, Lara, 'On the Necessity of Prefigurative Politics' (2021) 167(1) *Thesis Eleven* 99
Moore, Isabella, 'Indignity in Unwanted Pregnancy: Denial of Abortion as Cruel, Inhuman and Degrading Treatment' (2019) 23(6) *International Journal of Human Rights* 1010
Morgan, Lisa and Wabie, Joey Lynn, 'Aboriginal Women's Access and Acceptance of Reproductive Health Care' (2012) 10(3) *Pimatisiwin* 312
Morgan, Lynn M, 'Reproductive Rights or Reproductive Justice? Lessons from Argentina' (2015) 17(1) *Health and Human Rights Journal* 136
Moseson, Heidi and others, 'Abortion Experiences and Preferences of Transgender, Nonbinary and Gender-Expansive People in the United States' (2021) 224(4) *American Journal of Obstetrics and Gynecology* 376.e1
Muniz Oliviera, Amanda, '"Sterilisation Must be Done Against Her Will": Coloniality, Eugenics and Racism in Brazil 2018 – The Case of Janaína Quirino' (2021) 47(1) *Australian Feminist Law Journal* 105
Mutua, Makau, 'Savages, Victims, and Saviors: The Metaphor of Human Rights' (2001) 42 *Harvard International Law Journal* 201
Nandagiri, Rishita and Berro Pizzarossa, Lucía, 'Transgressing Biomedical and Legal Boundaries: The "Enticing and Hazardous" Challenges and Promises of a Self-Managed Abortion Multiverse' (2023) 100 *Women's Studies International Forum* 1
Nandagiri, Rishita and others, 'Precarity and Pills in a Pandemic: Online Abortion Care-Seeking in Poland During COVID-19' (2025) 8 *SSM* 100663

Nandagiri, Rishita, Coast, Ernestina, and Strong, Joe, 'COVID-19 and Abortion: Making Structural Violence Visible?' (2020) 46(S1) *International Perspectives on Sexual and Reproductive Health* 83

Narayan, Uma, 'Essence of Culture and a Sense of History: A Feminist Critique of Cultural Essentialism' (1998) 13(2) *Hypatia* 86

Neff, Christyne, 'Woman, Womb, and Bodily Integrity' (1990) 3 *Yale Journal of Law and Feminism* 327

Neiterman, Elena, 'Doing Pregnancy: Pregnant Embodiment as Performance' (2012) 35(5) *Women's Studies International Forum* 372

Ngwena, Charles G, 'Conscientious Objection to Abortion and Accommodation Women's Reproductive Health Rights: Reflection on a Decision of the Constitutional Court of Colombia from an African Regional Human Rights Perspective' (2014) 58 *Journal of African Law* 183

Ngwena, Charles G, 'Inscribing Abortion as a Human Right: Significance of the Protocol on the Rights of Women in Africa' (2010) 32 *Human Rights Quarterly* 783

Ngwena, Charles G, 'Taking Women's Rights Seriously: Using Human Rights to Require State Implementation of Domestic Abortion Laws in African Countries with Reference to Uganda' (2016) 60(1) *Journal of African Law* 110

Ngwena, Charles, 'Access to Safe Abortion as a Human Right in the African Region: Lessons from Emerging Jurisprudence of UN Treaty Monitoring Bodies (2013) 29(2) *South African Journal on Human Rights* 399

Ngwena, Charles, 'Access to Safe Abortion as a Human Right in the African Region: Lessons from Emerging Jurisprudence of UN Treaty Monitoring Bodies (2013) 29(2) *South African Journal on Human Rights* 399

NicGhabhann, Niamh, 'City Walls, Bathroom Stalls and Tweeting the Taoiseach: The Aesthetics of Protest and the Campaign for Abortion Rights in the Republic of Ireland' (2018) 32 *Continuum* 553

Nickels, James W, 'Poverty and Rights' (2005) 55 *The Philosophical Quarterly* 385

Nossiff, Rosemary, 'Gendered Citizenship: Women, Equality, and Abortion Policy' (2007) 29(1) *New Political Science* 61

O'Connell, Ciara, 'Litigating Reproductive Health Rights in the Inter-American System: What Does a Winning Case Look Like?' (2014) 16(2) *Health and Human Rights Journal* 116

O'Connell, Paul, 'On Reconciling Irreconcilables: Neo-liberal Globalisation and Human

O'Connell, Paul, 'The Death of Socio-Economic Rights' (2011) 74(4) *Modern Law Review* 532

O'Rourke, Catherine, 'Feminist Strategy in International Law: Understanding Its Legal, Normative and Political Dimensions' (2018) 28(4) *European Journal of International Law* 1019

Obedin- Maliver, Juno and Makadon, Harvey J, 'Transgender Men and Pregnancy' (2016) 9(1) *Obstetric Medicine* 4

Oloka-Onyango, J and Tamale, Sylvia, '"The Personal is Political," or Why Women's Rights Are Indeed Human Rights: An African Perspective on International Feminism' (1995) 17(4) *Human Rights Quarterly* 691

Olsen, Frances E, 'International Law: Feminist Critiques of the Public/Private Distinction' (1993) 25 *Studies in Trasnational Legal Policy* 157

Orford, Anne, 'Feminism, Imperialism, and the Mission of International Law' 71 *Nordic Journal of International Law* 275

Otto, Diane, 'Rethinking Universals: Opening Transformative Possibilities in International Human Rights Law' (1997) 18 *The Australian Year Book of International Law* 1

Ouliette, Alicia, 'Selection against Disability: Abortion, ART, and Access' (2015) 43(2) *Journal of Law, Medicine and Ethics* 211

Palacios Zuloaga, Patricia, 'Pushing Past the Tipping Point: Can the Inter-American System Accommodate Abortion Rights?' (2021) 21(4) *Human Rights Law Review* 899

Pallikkathayil, Japa, 'Abortion and Democratic Equality' (2025) 42(2) *Journal of Applied Philosophy* 473

Pardy, Maree, 'Under Western Eyes Again? Rights Vernacular and the Gender Culture "Clash"' (2013) 19(1) *Australian Journal of Human Rights* 31

Parsons, Kate, 'Feminist Reflections on Miscarriage, in Light of Abortion' (2010) 3(1) *International Journal of Feminist Approaches to Bioethics* 1

Pasha, Amirala S and Sonik, Roma, 'Their Body, Our Choice: Organized Medicine's Responsibility to De-Medicalize Abortion' (2024) 26(1) *Health and Human Rights Journal* 137

Pegoraro, Leonardo, 'Second-Rrate Victims: The Forced Sterilization of Indigenous Peoples in the USA and Canada' (2015) 5(2) *Settler Colonial Studies* 161

Pendleton, Maya and Dettlaff, Alan J, 'Policing Is Reproductive Oppression: How Policing and Carceral Systems Criminalize Parenting and Maintain Reproductive Oppression' (2024) 13(1) *Social Sciences* 515

Perehudoff, Katrina, Berro Pizzarossa, Lucía, and Stekelenburg, Jelle, 'Realising the Right to Sexual and Reproductive Health: Access to Essential Medicines for Medical Abortion as a Core Obligation' (2018) 18(8) *BMC International Health* 1

Pereira, Ricardo, 'Government-Sponsored Population Policies and Indigenous Peoples: Challenges for International Human Rights Law' (2015) 33(4) *Netherlands Quarterly of Human Rights* 437

Petchesky, Rosalind Pollack, 'Fetal Images: The Power of Visual Culture in the Politics of Reproduction' (1987) 13(2) *Feminist Studies* 263

Petchesky, Rosalind Pollack, 'From Population Control to Reproductive Rights: Feminist Fault Lines' (1995) 3(6) *Reproductive Health Matters* 152

Piepmeier, Alison, 'The Inadequacy of "Choice": Disability and What's Wrong with Feminist Framings of Reproduction' (2013) 39(1) *Feminist Studies* 159

Pillai, Vijayan, Wang, Ya-Chien, and Maleku, Arati, 'Women, War, and Reproductive Health in Developing Countries' (2017) 56(1) *Social Work in Health Care* 28

Pollis, Adamantia, 'Human Rights, Third World Socialism and Cuba' (1981) 9(9/10) *World Development* 1005

Popinchalk, Anna and Sedgh, Gilda, 'Trends in the Method and Gestational Age of Abortion in High-Income Countries' (2018) 45(2) *BMJ Sexual and Reproductive Health* 95

Porter, Elisabeth, 'Abortion Ethics: Rights and Responsibilities' (1994) 9(3) *Hypatia* 66

Porter, Lindsey, 'Adoption is Not Abortion-Lite' (2012) 29(1) *Journal of Applied Philosophy* 63

Prandini Assis, Mariana and Erdman, Joanna N, 'Abortion Rights Beyond the Medico-Legal Paradigm' (2021) *Global Public Health* 1

Prandini Assis, Mariana and Erdman, Joanna N, 'In the Name of Public Health: Misoprostol and the New Criminalization of Abortion in Brazil' (2021) 8(1) *Journal of Law and the Biosciences* 1

Prandini Assis, Mariana and Larrea, Sara, 'Why Self-Managed Abortion is so Much More than a Provisional Solution for Times of Pandemic' (2020) 28(1) *Sexual and Reproductive Health Matters* 37

Pratt, Nicola and others, 'Why Palestine is a Feminist Issue: A Reckoning with Western Feminism in a Time of Genocide' (2024) 27(1) *International Feminist Journal of Politics* 226

Price, Kimala, 'What is Reproductive Justice?: How Women of Color Activists Are Redefining the Pro-Choice Paradigm' (2010) 10(2) *Meridians* 42

Pruitt, Lisa R and Vanegas, Marta R, 'Urbanormativity, Spatial Privilege, and Judicial Blind Spots in Abortion Law' (2015) 30 *Berkeley Journal of Gender Law and Justice* 76

Purdy, Laura M, 'Are Pregnant Women Fetal Containers?' (1990) 4(4) *Bioethics* 273

Quattrocchi, Patrizia, 'Obstetric Violence Observatory: Contributions of Argentina to the International Debate' (2019) 38(8) *Medical Anthropology* 762

Raday, Frances, 'Gender and Democratic Citizenship: The Impact of CEDAW' (2012) 10(2) *ICON* 512

Ramón Michel, Agustina and others, 'Regulating Conscientious Objection to Legal Abortion in Argentina: Taking into Consideration Its Uses and Consequences' (2020) 22(2) *Health and Human Rights Journal* 271

Ranjan Pradhan, Manas and others, 'Abortion Care-Seeking and Reproductive Rights Violation in Health Facilities: Evidence from Six States of India' (2022) 11(1) *International Journal of Reproduction, Contraception, Obstetrics and Gynecology* 221
Rebouché, Rachel, 'Abortion Rights as Human Rights' (2016) 25(6) *Social and Legal Studies* 765
Rebouché, Rachel, 'Reproducing Rights: The Intersection of Reproductive Justice and Human Rights' (2017) 7(3) *UC Irvine Law Review* 579
Reynolds-Wright, John Joseph and others, 'Adherence to Treatment and Prevalence of Side Effects When Medical Abortion is Delivered via Telemedicine: A Prospective Observational Cohort Study During COVID-19' (2021) 48(3) *BMJ Sexual and Reproductive Health* 185
Reynolds-Wright, John Joseph and others, 'Telemedicine Medical Abortion at Home Under 12 weeks' Gestation: A Prospective Observational Cohort Study During the COVID-19 Pandemic' (2021) 47(4) *BMJ Sexual and Reproductive Health* 246
Roberts, Sarah CM and others, 'Out-of-Pocket Costs and Insurance Coverage for Abortion in the United States' (2014) 24(2) *Women's Health Issues* 211
Robinson, Heloise, 'Discrimination in Abortion Law and the Message the Law is Sending: *R (Crowter) v Secretary of State for Health and Social Care*' (2023) 87(1) *Medical Law Review* 218
Robinson, Heloise, 'Prenatal Testing, Disability Equality, and the Limits of the Law' (2023) 29(3) *New Bioethics* 202
Robitaille, Marie-Claire and Chatterjee, Ishita, 'Sex-selective Abortions and Infant Mortality in India: The Role of Parents' Stated Son Preference' (2018) *Journal of Development Studies* 47
Rodger, Daniel and Blackshaw, Bruce P, 'Quotas: Enabling Conscientious Objection to Coexist with Abortion Access' (2021) 29 *Health Care Analysis* 154
Rodham Clinton, Hilary, 'Women's Rights Are Human Rights: Excerpts, Remarks, 5 September 1995' (1996) 24(1/2) *Women's Studies Quarterly* 98
Rodríguez-Garavito, César, 'Beyond the Courtroom: The Impact of Judicial Activism on Socioeconomic Rights in Latin America' (2011) 89 *Texas Law Review* 1669
Romanello, Marina and others, 'The 2025 of the *Lancet* Countdown on Health and Climate Change: Climate Change Action Offers a Lifeline' (2025) 406(10521) *Lancet* 2804
Romanis, Elizabeth Chloe and others, 'Safeguarding and Teleconsultation for Abortion' (2021) 398(1) *Lancet* 555
Romanis, Elizabeth Chloe, 'Abortion Access and the Benefits and Limitations of Abortion-*Permissive* Legal Frameworks: Lessons from the United Kingdom' 32(3) *Cambridge Quarterly of Healthcare Ethics* 378
Romanis, Elizabeth Chloe, 'Is "Viability" Viable? Abortion, Conceptual Confusion and the Law in England and Wales and the United States' (2020) 7(1) *Journal of Law and the Biosciences* 1
Romany, Celina, 'Women as Aliens: A Feminist Critique of the Public/Private Distinction in International Human Rights Law' (1993) 6 *Harvard Human Rights Journal* 87
Romero, Mariana and Ramón Michel, Agustina, 'The Shift From Criminalization to Legalization of Abortion in Argentina' (2022) 328(17) *JAMA* 1699
Rosenblum, Darren, 'Unsex CEDAW, or What's Wrong with Women's Rights?' (2011) 20(2) *Columbia Journal of Gender and Law* 98
Roseneil, Sasha and others, 'Reproduction and Citizenship/Reproductive Citizens' (2013) 17(8) *Citizenship Studies* 901
Rosenfeld, Michel, 'Can Human Rights Bridge the Gap between Universalism and Cultural Relativism – A Pluralist Assessment Based on the Rights of Minorities' (1999) 30(2) *Columbia Human Rights Law Review* 249
Ross, Loretta J, 'African-American Women and Abortion: A Neglected History' (1992) 3(2) *Journal of Health Care for the Poor and Underserved* 274
Rudman, Annika, 'Women's Access to Regional Justice as a Fundamental Element of the Rule of Law: The Effect of the Absence of a Women's Rights Committee on the Enforcement of the African Women's Protocol' (2018) 18 *African Human Rights Law Journal* 319

Ruibal, Alba and Fernández Anderson, Cora, 'Legal Obstacles and Social Change: Strategies of the Abortion Rights Movement in Argentina' (2020) 8(4) *Politics, Groups and Identities* 698

Sabharwal, Nidhi Sadana and Sonalkar, Wandana, 'Dalit Women in India: At the Crossroads of Gender, Class, and Caste' (2015) 8(1) *Global Justice: Theory Practice Rhetoric* 44

Sakellariou, Dikaios and Rotarou, Elena S, 'Access to Healthcare for Men and Women with Disabilities in the UK: Secondary Analysis of Cross-Sectional Data' (2017) 7(8) *BMJ Open* 1

Sanneving, Linda and others, 'Inequity in India: The Case of Maternal and Reproductive Health' (2013) 6(1) *Global Health Action* 1

Say, Lale and others, 'Global Causes of Maternal Death: A WHO Systematic Analysis' (2014) *The Lancet Global Health* e323

Schuklenk, Udo and Smalling, Ricardo, 'Why Medical Professionals Have No Moral Claim to Conscientious Objection Accommodation in Liberal Democracies' (2017) 43(4) *Journal of Medical Ethics* 234

Scott, Joan, 'Gender: A Useful Category of Historical Analysis' (1986) 91(5) *American Historical Review* 1053

Scott, Kerry and others, '"I can guess the month . . . but beyond that, I can't tell" An Exploratory Qualitative Study of Health Care Provider Perspectives on Gestational Age Estimation in Rajasthan, India' (2020) 20(529) *BMC Pregnancy and Childbirth* 1

Seewald, Kate, Banki, Susan, and Kry, Suyheang, '"CEDAW is Up in the Sky": Reimagining Participation in Human Rights Advocacy Through Mechanism-Based Feminist Participatory Action Research (FPAR)' (2025) *International Journal of Qualitative Methods* [online first]

Self, Becky, Maxwell, Clare and Fleming, Valerie, 'The Missing Voices in the Conscientious Objection Debate: British Service Users' Experiences of Conscientious Objection to Abortion' (2023) 24(1) *BMC Medical Ethics* 1

Senderowicz, Leigh and Nandagiri, Rishita, 'Thirty Years of "Strange Bedmates": The ICPD and the Nexus of Population Control, Feminism, and Family Planning' (2025) 79(3) *Population Studies* 595

Senderowicz, Leigh, '"I Was Obligated to Accept": A Qualitative Exploration of Contraceptive Coercion' (2019) 239 *Social Science and Medicine* 112531

Sethna, Christabelle and Doull, Marion, 'Spatial Disparities and Travel to Freestanding Abortion Clinics in Canada' (2013) *Women's Studies International Forum* 38

Seymore, Malinda L, 'Adoption as a Substitute for Abortion?' (2024) 95 *Colorado Law Review* 1089

Shaheed, Farida, 'Controlled or Autonomous: Identity and the Experience of the Network, Women Living under Muslim Laws' (1994) 19(4) *Signs* 997

Shakespeare, Tom, 'Choices and Rights: Eugenics, Genetics and Disability Equality' (1998) 13(5) *Disability & Society* 665

Shalev, Carmel, 'Rights to Sexual and Reproductive Health: The ICPD and the Convention on the Elimination of All Forms of Discrimination Against Women' (2000) 4(2) *Health and Human Rights Journal* 38

Sheldon, Sally and Lord, Jonathan, 'Care Not Criminalisation; Reform of British Abortion Law is Long Overdue' (2023) 49(8) *Journal of Medical Ethics* 523

Sheldon, Sally, 'The Decriminalisation of Abortion: An Argument for Modernisation' (2016) 36(2) *Oxford Journal of Legal Studies* 334

Sherwin, Susan, 'Abortion Through a Feminist Ethics Lens' (1991) 30(3) *Dialogue* 327

Siegel, Reva B, 'Why Restrict Abortion? Expanding the Frame on *June Medical*' (2021) 8 *Supreme Court Review* 17

Sifris, Ronli and Belton, Suzanne, 'Australia: Abortion and Human Rights' (2017) 19(1) *Health and Human Rights Journal* 209

Sifris, Ronli, 'Restrictive Regulation of Abortion and the Right to Health' (2010) 18 *Medical Law Review* 185

Singh, Susheela and others, 'The Incidence of Abortion and Unintended Pregnancy in India, 2015' (2018) 6(1) *Lancet Global Health* e111

Sisson, Gretchen and others, 'Adoption Decision Making Among Women Seeking Abortion' (2017) 27(2) *Women's Health Issues* 136

Smith, Andrea, 'Beyond Pro-Choice versus Pro-Life: Women of Color and Reproductive Justice' (2005) 17(1) *National Women's Studies Association Journal* 119

Smyth, Rebecca, '"Repeal the 8th' in a Transnational Context: The Potential of SRHSs for Advancing Abortion Access in El Salvador' (2020) 124 *Feminist Review* 192

Smyth, Rebecca, 'Abortion Exceptionalism in International Human Rights Law' (2024) 46(4) *Human Rights Quarterly* 671

Smyth, Rebecca, 'Reproductive Citizenship' (2024) 50(1) *Signs* 189

Spangaro, Jo and others, '"They aren't really black fellas but they are easy to talk to": Factors Which Influence Australian Aboriginal Women's Decision to Disclose Intimate Partner Violence During Pregnancy' (2016) 41 *Midwifery* 79

Stark, Barbara, 'The Women's Convention, Reproductive Rights, and the Reproduction of Gender' (2011) 18(2) *Duke Journal of Gender Law & Policy* 261

Stevenson, Amanda Jean, 'The Pregnancy-Related Mortality Impact of a Total Abortion Ban in the United States: A Research Note on Increased Deaths Due to Remaining Pregnant' (2021) 58(6) *Demography* 2019

Subha Sri, B and Sundari Ravindran, TK, 'Medical Abortion: Understanding Perspectives of Rural and Marginalized Women from Rural South India' (2012) 118 *International Journal of Gynecology and Obstetrics* 33

Sutton, Barbara and Borland, Elizabeth, 'Abortion and Human Rights for Women in Argentina' (2019) 40(2) *Frontiers* 27

Sutton, Barbara and Borland, Elizabeth, 'Framing Abortion Rights in Argentina's Encuentros Nacionales de Mujeres' (2013) 39(1) *Feminist Studies* 194

Sutton, Barbara, 'Intergenerational Encounters in the Struggle for Abortion Rights in Argentina' (2020) 82 *Women's Studies International Forum* 1

Theilen, Jens, 'Intersectionality's Travels to International Human Rights Law' (2024) 45(2) *Michigan Journal of International Law* 233

Thomson, Judith Jarvis, 'A Defense of Abortion' (1971) 1(1) *Philosophy and Public Affairs* 47

Tongue, Zoe L, 'Abortion and the European Court of Human Rights: Avoiding the Question?' (2024) 3 *European Human Rights Law Review*

Tongue, Zoe L, '*Crowter v Secretary of State for Health and Social Care* [2021] EWHC 2536: Discrimination, Disability, and Access to Abortion' (2022) 30(1) *Medical Law Review* 177

Tongue, Zoe L, 'Foetal Disability and Abortion in the UK: A Reproductive and Disability Justice Perspective' (2026) 34 *Feminist Legal Studies* 51

Tongue, Zoe L, 'Locating Abortion and Contraception on the Obstetric Violence Continuum' (2024) 17(1) *International Journal of Feminist Approaches to Bioethics* 1

Tongue, Zoe L, 'On Conscientious Objection to Abortion: Questioning Mandatory Referral as Compromise in the International Human Rights Framework' (2022) 22(4) *Medical Law International* 349

Tongue, Zoe L, 'Protest as Counter-Hegemonic Human Rights Work: Lessons from Abortion Rights Movements' *Heidelberg Journal of International Law* [forthcoming]

Tongue, Zoe L, 'Telemedical and Self-Managed Abortion: A Human Rights Imperative?' (2022) 30(2) *European Journal of Health Law* 158

True, Jacqui and Mintrom, Michael, 'Transnational Networks and Policy Diffusion: The Case of Gender Mainstreaming' (2001) 45(1) *International Studies Quarterly* 27

Turner, Bryan S, 'Citizenship, Reproduction and the State: International Marriage and Human Rights' (2008) 12(1) *Citizenship Studies* 45

Undurraga, Verónica and Sadler, Michelle, 'The Misrepresentation of Conscientious Objection as a New Strategy of Resistance to Abortion Decriminalisation' (2019) 27(2) *Reproductive Health Matters* 17

Upadhyay, Ushma D and others, 'Evaluating the Impact of a Mandatory Pre-abortion Ultrasound Viewing Law: A Mixed Methods Study' (2017) 12(7) *PLoS One* 0178871

Van der Waal, Rodante and others, 'Obstetric Violence: An Intersectional Refraction through Abolition Feminism' (2023) 4(1) *Feminist Anthropology* 91
Van der Waal, Rodante and Van Nistelrooij, Inge, 'Reimagining Relationality for Reproductive Care: Understanding Obstetric Violence as "Separation"' (2022) 29(5) *Nursing Ethics* 1186
Vandewalker, Ian, 'Abortion and Informed Consent: How Biased Counseling Laws Mandate Violations of Medical Ethics' (2012) 19(1) *Michigan Journal of Gender and Law* 1
Vázquez-Quesada, Lucía and others, 'Abortion Self-Care: A Forward-Looking Solution to Inequitable Access' (2020) 46 (Suppl 1) *International Perspectives on Sexual and Reproductive Health* 91
Walby, Sylvia, 'Gender Mainstreaming: Productive Tensions in Theory and Practice' (2005) 12(3) *Social Politics* 321
Warren, Mary Anne, 'The Moral and Legal Status of Abortion' (1973) 57(1) *Monist* 43
Warren, Mary Anne, 'The Moral Significance of Birth' (1989) 4(3) *Ethics and Reproduction* 4
Watson, Katie, 'Abortion as a Moral Good' (2019) 393 *Lancet* 1196
Watson, Katie, 'The Ethics of Access: Reframing the Need for Abortion Care as a Health Disparity' (2022) 22(8) *American Journal of Bioethics* 22
Weldon, S Laurel and Htun, Mala, 'Feminist Mobilisation and Progressive Policy Change: Why Governments Take Action to Combat Violence Against Women' (2013) 21(2) *Gender and Development* 231
Weldon, S Laurel and others, 'Feminist Waves, Global Activism, and Gender Violence Regimes: Genealogy and Impact of a Global Wave' (2023) *Women's Studies International Forum* 102781
Westeson, Johanna, 'Reproductive Health Information and Abortion Services: Standards Developed by the European Court of Human Rights' (2013) 122 *International Journal of Gynecology and Obstetrics* 173
Whelan, Isabelle, 'The Effect of United Kingdom Immigration Policies on Migrant Access to Sexual and Reproductive Healthcare' (2019) 45(1-2) *BMJ Sexual and Reproductive Health* 1
Whitford, Kate, and others, 'Sexual and Reproductive Health Service Access Among Aboriginal and Torres Strait Islander Young People in Regional NSW, Australia' (2024) 1 *Health & Social Care in the Community* 1845971
Wilde, Mary, 'Why Embodiment Now?' (1999) 22(2) *Global Health Nursing Practice* 25
Wilson, Kalpana, 'For Reproductive Justice in an Era of Gates and Modi: The Violence of India's Population Policies' (2018) 119 *Feminist Review* 89
Winter, Bronwyn, 'Women, the Law, and Cultural Relativism in France: The Case of Excision' (1994) 19(4) *Signs* 939
Wurtz, Heather, 'Indigenous Women of Latin America: Unintended Pregnancy, Unsafe Abortion, and Reproductive Health Outcomes' (2012) 10(3) *Pimatisiwin* 271
Xie, Kailing, 'Premarital Abortion – What is the Harm? The Responsibilisation of Women's Pregnancy Among China's "Privileged" Daughters' (2019) 8(1) *British Journal of Chinese Studies* 1
Yamin, Alicia Ely and Parra-Vera, Oscar, 'Judicial Protection of the Right to Health in Colombia: From Social Demands to Individual Claims to Public Debates' (2010) 33(2) *HICLR* 431
Yáñez, Clara Franco, 'Abortion Rights in Latin America: An Unsettled Battle' (2021) 3 *GIGA Focus* 1
Yang, Chelsey, 'The Inequity of Conscientious Objection: Refusal of Emergency Contraception' (2020) 27(6) *Nursing Ethics* 1408
Yokoe, Ryo and others, 'Unsafe Abortion and Abortion-Related Death Among 1.8 Million Women in India' (2019) 9(4) *BMJ Global Health* 1
Young, Iris Marion, 'Pregnant Embodiment: Subjectivity and Alienation' (1984) 9(1) *Journal of Medicine and Philosophy*45
Young, Katharine G and Lemaitre, Julieta, 'The Comparative Fortunes of the Right to Health: Two Tales of Justiciability in Colombia and South Africa' (2013) 26 *Harvard Human Rights Journal* 179
Yuval-Davis, Nira, 'Intersectionality, Citizenship and Contemporary Politics of Belonging' (2007) 10(4) *Critical Review of International Social and Political Philosophy* 561

Yuval-Davis, Nira, 'Women, Citizenship and Difference' (1997) 57 *Feminist Review* 4
Zampas, Christina and Andión-Ibañez, Ximena, 'Conscientious Objection to Sexual and Reproductive Health Services: International Human Rights Standards and European Law and Practice' (2012) 19 *European Journal of Health Law* 231
Zampas, Christina and Gher, Jaime M, 'Abortion as a Human Right – International and Regional Standards' (2008) 8(2) *Human Rights Law Review* 249
Zampas, Christina and Lamačová, Adriana, 'Forced and Coerced Sterilization of Women in Europe' (2011) 114 *International Journal of Gynecology and Obstetrics* 163
Zampas, Christina, 'Legal and Ethical Standards for Protecting Women's Human Rights and the Practice of Conscientious Objection in Reproductive Healthcare Settings' (2013) 123 *International Journal of Gynaecology and Obstetrics* S63
Zerilli, Filippo M, 'The Rule of Soft Law' (2010) 56 *Focaal* 3
Zine, Jasmin, 'Between Orientalism and Fundamentalism: The Politics of Muslim Women's Feminist Engagement' (2006) 3(1) *Muslim World Journal of Human Rights* 1
Zuniga, Carmela, Thompson, Terri-Ann, and Blanchard, Kelly, 'Abortion as a Catastrophic Health Expenditure in the United States' (2020) 30(6) *Women's Health Issues* 416
Zwingel, Susanne, 'How Do Norms Travel? Theorizing International Women's Rights in Transnational Perspective' (2012) 56 *International Studies Quarterly* 115
Zwingel, Susanne, 'International Feminist Strategies: Strengths and Challenges of the Rights-Based Approach' (2013) 9(3) *Politics and Gender* 344
Zwingel, Susanne, 'Women's Rights Norms as Content-in-motion and Incomplete Practice' (2017) 2(5) *Third World Thematics* 675

Books

Amery, Fran, *Beyond Pro-Life and Pro-Choice* (Bristol, Bristol University Press, 2020)
Baird, Barbara, *Abortion Care is Health Care* (Melbourne University Press, 2023)
Baxi, Upendra, *The Future of Human Rights*, 3rd edn (Oxford, Oxford University Press, 2006)
Bloomer, Fiona and Campbell, Emma (eds), *Decriminalizing Abortion in Northern Ireland: Legislation and Protest* (Bloomsbury Publishing, 2022)
Bloomer, Fiona and Campbell, Emma (eds), *Decriminalizing Abortion in Northern Ireland: Allies and Abortion Provision* (Bloomsbury Publishing, 2022)
Bloomer, Fiona, Pierson, Claire, and Claudio, Sylvia Estrada, *Reimagining Global Abortion Politics: A Social Justice Perspective* (Policy Press, 2018)
Boyle, Mary, *Re-Thinking Abortion* (Routledge, 1997)
Browne, Kath and Calkin, Sydney (eds), *After Repeal: Rethinking Abortion Politics* (Bloomsbury Publishing, 2020)
Butler, Judith, *Gender Trouble* (Routledge, 1999, first pub 1989)
Calkin, Sydney, *Abortion Pills Go Global: Reproductive Freedom Across Borders* (University of California Press, 2023)
Chadwick, Rachelle, *Bodies That Birth: Vitalizing Birth Politics* (Routledge, 2018)
Chrisler, Joan C, (ed) *Reproductive Justice: A Global Concern* (Praeger, 2012)
Cooper, Davina, *Everyday Utopias* (Duke University Press, 2013)
Corrêa, Sonia, *Population and Reproductive Rights* (Zed Books, 2002)
Davis, Angela, *Are Prisons Obsolete?* (Seven Stories Press, 2003)
De Beauvoir, Simone, *The Second Sex* (Vintage Classics, 2015, first pub 1949)
De Búrca, Gráinne, *Reframing Human Rights in a Turbulent Era* (Oxford, Oxford University Press, 2021)
De Londras, Fiona and Enright, Máiréad, *Repealing the Eighth* (Policy Press, 2018)
Douzinas, Costas, *Human Rights and Empire* (Routledge-Cavendish, 2009)

Duffy, Deirdre, *Abortion Trail Activism: The Global Infrastructures for Abortion Access* (Bloomsbury Publishing, 2024)
Ely Yamin, Alicia, *When Misfortune Becomes Injustice* (Stanford University Press, 2020)
Engberg-Pederen, Lars, Fejerskov, Adam, and Cold-Ravnkilde, Signe Marie, *Rethinking Gender Equality in Global Governance: The Delusion of Norm Diffusion* (Palgrave Macmillan, 2019)
Engle Merry, Sally, *Human Rights and Gender Violence* (The University of Chicago Press, 2006)
Fernández Anderson, Cora, *Fighting for Abortion Rights in Latin America* (Routledge, 2020)
Fernandez Lynch, Holly, *Conflicts of Conscience in Health Care: An Institutional Compromise* (Massachusetts Institute of Technology Press, 2020)
Fissell, Mary, *Abortion: A History* (C Hurst & Co Publishers, 2025)
Freeman, Cordelia, *Magic Misoprostol: Reproductive Justice and Abortion Liberation in Latin America* (Bristol, Bristol University Press, 2025)
Gago, Verónica, *Feminist International* (Verso, 2020)
Gewirth, Alan, *The Community of Rights* (The University of Chicago Press, 1996)
Gilligan, Carol, *In A Different Voice* (Harvard University Press, 1993, first pub 1982)
Goodwin, Michele, *Policing the Womb* (Cambridge, Cambridge University Press, 2020)
Green, Alex and Hendry, Jennifer, *Legal Pluralism: New Trajectories in Law* (Routledge, 2024)
Hadley, Janet, *Abortion: Between Freedom and Necessity* (Virago, 1996)
Heikes, Deborah K, *Rationality and Feminist Philosophy* (Continuum, 2010)
Hennebel, Ludovic and Tigeoudja, Hélenè, *The American Convention on Human Rights: A Commentary* (Oxford, Oxford University Press, 2022)
Herzog, Dagmar, *Unlearning Eugenics* (University of Wisconsin Press, 2018)
Hill Collins, Patricia and Bilge, Sirma, *Intersectionality*, 2nd edn (Routledge, 2020)
Hill Collins, Patricia, *Black Feminist Thought* (Routledge, 2022, first pub 1990)
hooks, bell, *Feminist Theory: From Margin to Center* (Routledge, 2015, first pub 1984)
Hunt Botting, Eileen, *Wollstonecraft, Mill, and Women's Human Rights* (Yale University Press, 2016)
Jackson, Emily, *Regulating Reproduction* (Hart Publishing, 2001)
Jaffary, Nora E, *Reproduction and Its Discontents in Mexico: Childbirth and Contraception from 1750 to 1905* (University of North Carolina Press, 2016)
Kapur, Ratna, *Gender, Alterity and Human Rights* (Edward Elgar Publishing, 2020)
Keck, Margaret E and Sikkink, Kathryn, *Activists Beyond Borders* (Cornell University Press, 2014)
Klein, Naomi, *The Shock Doctrine: The Rise of Disaster Capitalism* (Henry Holt, 2007)
Levitas, Ruth, *Utopia as Method* (Palgrave Macmillan, 2013)
Luna, Zakiya, *Reproductive Rights as Human Rights* (New York University Press, 2020)
Mackenzie, Catriona and Stoljar, Natalie, *Relational Autonomy* (Oxford, Oxford University Press, 2000)
McLeod, Carolyn, *Conscience in Reproductive Health Care: Prioritizing Patient Interests* (Oxford, Oxford University Press, 2020)
McNeilly, Kathryn, *Human Rights and Radical Social Transformation* (Routledge, 2018)
Millar, Erica, *Happy Abortions* (Zed Books, 2017)
Mohanty, Chandra Talpade, *Feminism Without Borders* (Duke University Press, 2006)
Monticelli, Lara, *The Future Is Now: An Introduction to Prefigurative Politics* (Bristol, Bristol University Press, 2022)
Morgan, Lynn M and Michaels, Meredith W, *Fetal Subjects, Feminist Positions* (University of Pennsylvania Press, 1999)
Moyn, Samuel, *Not Enough: Human Rights in an Unequal World* (Harvard University Press, 2018)
Mullally, Siobhán, *Gender, Culture and Human Rights* (Hart Publishing, 2006)
Naish, Camille, *Death Comes to the Maiden: Sex and Execution 1431–1933* (Routledge 2013, first pub 1991)
Nash, Meredith, *Making 'Postmodern' Mothers* (Palgrave Macmillan, 2012)
Nnaemeka, Obioma (ed), *Female Circumcision and the Politics of Knowledge* (Praeger, 2005)
Ó Néill, Clayton, *Religion, Medicine and the Law* (Routledge, 2019)

Parsons, Jordan A and Romanis, Elizabeth Chloe, *Early Medical Abortion, Equality of Access, and the Telemedical Imperative* (Oxford, Oxford University Press, 2021)
Pattinson, Shaun D, *Influencing Traits Before Birth* (Ashgate, 2002)
Petchesky, Rosalind Pollack, *Abortion and Woman's Choice: The State, Sexuality, and Reproductive Freedom* (Northeastern University Press, 1984)
Pickles, Camilla and Herring, Jonathan (eds), *Childbirth, Vulnerability, and Law* (Routledge, 2019)
Pierson, Claire, *Women's Troubles: Gender and Feminist Politics in Post-Agreement Northern Ireland* (Manchester University Press, 2025)
Raekstad, Paul and Gradin, Sofa Saio, *Prefigurative Politics: Building Tomorrow Today* (Polity Press, 2020)
Reilly, Niamh, *Women's Human Rights* (Polity Press, 2009)
Renteln, Alison Dundes, *International Human Rights: Universalism Versus Relativism* (Sage, 1990)
Rich, Adrienne, *Of Woman Born* (first pub 1976, Norton, 1995)
Romanis, Elizabeth Chloe, *Biotechnology, Gestation, and the Law* (Oxford, Oxford University Press, 2025)
Ross, Loretta J and Solinger, Rickie, *Reproductive Justice: An Introduction* (University of California Press, 2017)
Sangari, Kumkum, *Solid:Liquid A (Trans)national Reproductive Formation* (Tulika Books, 2015)
Schwaller, John Frederick, *The History of the Catholic Church in Latin America* (New York University Press, 2011)
Scott, Rosamund, *Rights, Duties, and the Body* (Hart Publishing, 2002)
Sheldon, Sally, *Beyond Control* (Pluto Press, 1997)
Shi, Leiyu and Singh, Douglas A, *Essentials of the US Health Care System*, 6th edn (Jones & Bartlett Learning, 2023)
Sifris, Ronli, *Reproductive Freedom, Torture, and International Human Rights* (Routledge, 2013)
Sommer, Udi and Forman-Rabinovici, Aliza, *Producing Reproductive Rights* (Cambridge, Cambridge University Press, 2019)
Sumner, LW, *Abortion and Moral Theory* (Princeton University Press, 1981)
Warren, Mary Anne, *Gendercide: The Implications of Sex Selection* (Rowman & Allanheld, 1985)
Weinbaum, Alys Eve, *The Afterlife of Reproductive Slavery* (Duke University Press, 2019)
Whyte, Jessica, *The Morals of the Market* (Verso, 2019)
Wollstonecraft, Mary, *Vindication of the Rights of Woman* (first pub 1792, Vintage Classics, 2015)

Book Chapters

An-Na'im, Abdullahi Ahmed, 'State Responsibility Under International Human Rights Law to Change Religious and Customary Laws' in Rebecca J Cook (ed), *Human Rights of Women* (University of Pennsylvania Press, 1994)
Baird, Barbara, 'Tales of Mobility: Women's Travel and Abortion Services in a Globalized Australia' in Christabelle Sethna and Gayle Davis (eds), *Abortion Across Borders* (John Hopkins University Press, 2019)
Berer, Marge, 'The Cairo "Compromise" on Abortion and Its Consequences for Making Abortion Safe and Legal' in Laura Reichenbach and Mindy Jane Roseman (eds), *Reproductive Health and Human Rights* (University of Pennsylvania Press, 2011)
Bergallo, Paola, 'Argentina – Courts and the Right to Health: Achieving Fairness Despite "Routinization" in Individual Coverage Cases?' in Alicia Ely Yamin and Siri Gloppen (eds), *Litigating Health Rights: Can Courts Bring More Justice to Health?* (Harvard University Press, 2011)
Bergallo, Paola, 'The Struggle Against Informal Rules on Abortion in Argentina' in Rebecca J Cook, Bernard M Dickens, and Joanna N Erdman (eds), *Abortion Law in Transnational Perspective* (University of Pennsylvania Press, 2014)

Buss, Doris Elisabeth, 'Going Global: Feminist Theory, International Law, and the Public/Private Divide' in Susan B Boyd (ed), *Challenging the Public/Private Divide: Feminism, Law, and Policy* (University of Toronto Press, 1997)
Cabal, Luisa and Phillips, Suzannah, 'Reproductive Rights Litigation: From Recognition to Transformation' in Malcolm Langford, César Rodrígues-Garavito, and Julieta Rossi (eds), *Social Rights Judgments and the Politics of Compliance* (Cambridge, Cambridge University Press, 2017)
Colen, Shellee, '"Like a Mother to Them": Stratified Reproduction and West Indian Childcare Workers and Wmployers in New York' in Faye Ginsburg and Rayna Rapp (eds), *Conceiving the New World Order* (University of California Press, 2015)
Cook, Rebecca J, 'Stigmatized Meanings of Criminal Abortion Law' in Rebecca J Cook, Joanna N Erdman, and Bernard M Dickens (eds), *Abortion Law in Transnational Perspective* (University of Pennsylvania Press, 2014)
Cook, Rebecca J, 'Women's International Human Rights Law: The Way Forward' in Rebecca J Cook (ed), *Human Rights of Women* (University of Pennsylvania Press, 1994)
Corradi, Giselle, 'Human Rights and Legal Pluralism: Four Research Agendas' in Giselle Coradi, Eva Brems, and Mark Goodale (eds), *Human Rights Encounter Legal Pluralism* (Hart Publishing, 2017)
Cross, Judith, O'Rourke, Catherine, and Simpson, Audrey, 'The Request for an Inquiry under the CEDAW Option Protocol' in Fiona Bloomer and Emma Campbell (eds), *Decriminalizing Abortion in Northern Ireland: Legislation and Protest* (Bloomsbury Publishing, 2022)
De Barros, Juanita, 'Embodied Sources: Abortion, Medicine, and the Law in Early Twentieth-Century British Guiana' in Cassia Roth and Diana Paton (eds), *Intimate Politics: Fertility Control in Global Historical Perspective* (Routledge, 2024)
De Schutter, Olivier and Sant'Ana, Matthias, 'The European Committee of Social Rights (the ECSR)' in Gauthier de Beco (ed), *Human Rights Monitoring Mechanisms of the Council of Europe* (Routledge, 2012)
Engle Merry, Sally and Levitt, Peggy, 'The Vernacularization of Women's Human Rights' in Stephen Hopgood, Jack Snyder, and Leslie Vinjamuri (eds), *Human Rights Futures* (Cambridge, Cambridge University Press, 2017)
Erdman, Joanna N, 'Abortion in International Human Rights Law' in Sam Rowlands (ed), *Abortion Care* (Cambridge, Cambridge University Press, 2014)
Erdman, Joanna N, 'The Procedural Turn: Abortion at the European Court of Human Rights' in Rebecca J Cook, Joanna N Erdman, and Bernard M Dickens (eds), *Abortion Law in Transnational Perspective* (University of Pennsylvania Press, 2014)
Greasley, Kate, 'Abortion, Feminism, and 'Traditional' Moral Philosophy' in Andelka M Phillps, Thana C de Campos, and Jonathan Herring (eds), *Philosophical Foundations of Medical Law* (Oxford, Oxford University Press, 2019)
Greasley, Kate, 'In Defense of Abortion Rights' in Kate Greasley and Christopher Kaczor, *Abortion Rights: For and Against* (Cambridge, Cambridge University Press, 2017)
Hanckock, Ange-Marie, 'Overcoming Willful Blindness: Building Egalitarian Multicultural Women's Coalitions' France' in Obioma Nnaemeka (ed), *Female Circumcision and the Politics of Knowledge* (Praeger, 2005)
Hansbury, Griffin, 'Don't Take Up Space: How the Patriarchy Works to Undermine Trans Communities from Within' in Jean Petrucelli, Sarah Schoen, and Naomi Snider (eds), *Patriarchy and Its Discontents* (Routledge, 2022)
Harris, Lisa, 'The Moral Agency of Abortion Providers: Conscientious Provision, Dangertalk, and the Lived Experience of Doing Stigmatized Work' in Lori d'Agincourt-Canning and Carolyn Ells (eds), *Ethical Issues in Women's Healthcare: Practice and Policy* (Oxford, Oxford University Press, 2019)

Heinsen, Laura Louise, 'Moral Adherers: Pregnant Women Undergoing Routine Prenatal Screening in Denmark' in Ayo Wahlberg and Tine M Gammeltoft (eds), *Selective Reproduction in the 21st Century* (Palgrave Macmillan, 2018)

Herring, Jonathan, Jackson, Emily, and Sheldon, Sally, 'Would Decriminalisation Mean Deregulation?' in Sally Sheldon and Kaye Wellings (eds), *Decriminalising Abortion in the UK* (Policy Press, 2020)

Hopgood, Stephen, 'Human Rights on the Road to Nowhere' in Stephen Hopgood, Jack Snyder, and Leslie Vinjamuri (eds), *Human Rights Futures* (Cambridge, Cambridge University Press, 2017)

Ilumoka, Adetoun O, 'African Women's Economic, Social, and Cultural Rights – Towards a Relevant Theory and Practice' in Rebecca J Cook (ed), *Human Rights of Women* (University of Pennsylvania Press, 1994)

Kelly, Lisa M, 'Reckoning with Narratives of Innocent Suffering in Transnational Abortion Litigation' in Rebecca J Cook, Joanna N Erdman, and Bernard M Dickens (eds), *Abortion Law in Transnational Perspective* (University of Pennsylvania Press, 2014)

Kjærgård, Jonas Ross, 'The Inequality of Common Utility: Active/Passive Citizenship in French Revolutionary Human Rights' in Karen-Margrethe Simonsen and Jonas Ross Kjærgård (eds), *Discursive Framings of Human Rights* (Birkbeck Law Press, 2016)

Lee, Ellie, 'Psychologizing Abortion: Women's "Mental Health" and the Regulation of Abortion in Britain' in Anne Morris and Susan Nott (eds), *Well Women* (first pub 2002, Routledge, 2018)

Levitt, Peggy and Engle Merry, Sally, 'Making Women's Human Rights in the Vernacular: Navigating the Culture/Rights Divide' in Dorothy L Hodgson (ed), *Gender and Culture at the Limit of Rights* (University of Pennsylvania Press, 2011)

Lionnet, Françoise, 'Women's Rights, Bodies, and Identities: The Limits of Universalism and the Legal Debate around Excision in France' in Obioma Nnaemeka (ed), *Female Circumcision and the Politics of Knowledge* (Praeger, 2005)

Marks, Susan, 'Four Human Rights Myths' in David Kinley, Wojciech Sadurski, and Kevin Walton (eds), *Human Rights: Old Problems, New Possibilities* (Edward Elgar, 2013)

Millns, Susan, '"Bringing Rights Home": Feminism and the Human Rights Act 1998' in Susan Millns and Noel Whitty (eds), *Feminist Perspectives on Public Law* (Cavendish Publishing, 1999)

Numerato, Dino, Čada, Karel, and Honová, Petra, 'Citizenship, Neoliberalism and Healthcare' in Jonathan Gabe, Mario Cardano, and Angela Genova (eds), *Health and Illness in the Neoliberal Era in Europe* (Emerald Publishing, 2020)

O'Dowd, Kellie, Cross, Judith and Bloomer, Fiona, 'Alliance for Choice New Beginnings' in Fiona Bloomer and Emma Campbell (eds), *Decriminalizing Abortion in Northern Ireland: Legislation and Protest* (Bloomsbury Publishing, 2022)

Phillips, Anne, 'Multiculturalism, Universalism, and the Claims of Democracy' in Maxine Molyneux and Shahra Razavi (eds), *Gender Justice, Development, and Rights* (Oxford, Oxford University Press, 2002)

Pollis, Adamantia and Schwab, Peter, 'Human Rights: A Western Construct with Limited Applicability' in Adamantia Pollis and Peter Schwab (eds), *Human Rights: Cultural and Ideological Perspectives* (Praeger, 1979)

Polónia, Amélia and Capelão, Rosa, 'Women and Gender in the Portuguese Overseas Empire. Society, Economy, and Politics, 16th–17th Centuries' in Francisco Bethencourt (ed), *Gendering the Portuguese-Speaking World* (Brill, 2021)

Rao, Arati, 'The Politics of Gender and Culture in International Human Rights Discourse' in Julie Peters and Andrea Wolper (eds), *Women's Rights Human Rights* (Routledge, 1995)

Riedel, Eibe, Giacca, Gilles, and Golay, Christophe, 'The Development of Economic, Social, and Cultural Rights in International Law' in Eibe Riedel, Gilles Giacca, and Christophe Golay (eds), *Economic, Social, and Cultural Rights in International Law* (Oxford, Oxford University Press, 2014)

Saxon, Marsha, 'Disability Rights and Selective Abortion' in Lennard J Davis (ed), *The Disability Studies Reader*, 5th edn (Routledge, 2016)

Song, Sarah, 'Feminists Rethink Multiculturalism: Resisting Essentialism and Cross-Cultural Hypocrisy' in Margaret Davies and Vanessa E Munro (eds), *The Ashgate Research Companion to Feminist Legal Theory* (Ashgate, 2013)

Tongue, Zoe L, 'Abortion is Healthcare': The Promise and Pitfalls of Framing Abortion Under the Right to Health' in Elizabeth Wicks and Nataly Papadopoulou (eds), *Research Handbook on Human Rights Law and Health* (Edward Elgar Publishing, 2025)

Tongue, Zoe L, 'Ectogestation as Emancipation: A Feminist Science Fiction' in Alex Green, Mitchell Travis, and Kieran Tranter (eds), *Cultural Legal Studies of Science Fiction* (Routledge, 2024)

True, Jacqui, 'Feminist Problems with International Norms: Gender Mainstreaming in Global Governance' in J Ann Ticklet and Laura Sjoberg (eds), *Feminism and International Relations* (Routledge, 2013)

Tyler, Imogen, 'Reframing Pregnant Embodiment' in Sara Ahmed and others (eds), *Transformations* (Routledge, 2000)

Human Rights Documents

African Commission on Human and Peoples' Rights, 'General Comment No 2 on Article 14.1 (a), (b), (c), and (f) and Article 14.2 (a) and (c) of the Protocol to the African Charter on Human and People's Rights on the Rights of Women in Africa' (28 November 2014) https://achpr.au.int/index.php/ar/node/854 accessed 9 January 2026

African Union, 'List of Countries Which Have Signed, Ratified/Acceded to the Protocol to the African Charter on Human and People's Rights on the Rights of Women in Africa' (16 October 2019) https://au.int/en/treaties/protocol-african-charter-human-and-peoples-rights-rights-women-africa accessed 9 January 2026

African Union, 'List of Countries Which Have Signed, Ratified/Acceded to the Protocol on the Statute of the African Court of Justice and Human Rights' (18 June 2020) https://au.int/en/treaties/protocol-court-justice-african-union accessed 9 January 2026

Anand Grover, 'Interim Report of the Special Rapporteur on the Right of Everyone to the Enjoyment of the Highest Attainable Standard of Physical and Mental Health' (3 August 2011) UN Doc A/66/254

CEDAW, 'Assessment of the Follow-up Procedure under Article 18 of the CEDAW Convention' (6 November 2019) tbinternet.ohchr.org/_layouts/15/TreatyBodyExternal/FollowUp.aspx?Treaty=CEDAW&Lang=en accessed 9 January 2026

CEDAW, 'Concluding Observations on the Combined Eighth and Ninth Periodic Reports of Brazil' (6 June 2024) UN Doc CEDAW/C/BRA/CO/8-9

CEDAW, 'Concluding Observations on the Combined Fifth and Sixth Periodic Reports of Morocco' (12 July 2022) UN Doc CEDAW/C/MAR/CO/5-6

CEDAW, 'Concluding Observations on the Combined Fifth and Sixth Periodic Reports of Slovakia' (25 Nov 2015) UN Doc CEDAW/C/SVK/CO/5-6

CEDAW, 'Concluding Observations on the Combined Seventh and Eighth Periodic Report of Poland' (14 Nov 2014) UN Doc CEDAW/C/POL/CO/7-8

CEDAW, 'Concluding Observations on the Combined Seventh and Eighth Periodic Reports of Romania' (24 Jul 2017) UN Doc CEDAW/C/ROU/CO/7-8

CEDAW, 'Concluding Observations on the Combined Seventh and Eighth Periodic Reports of Germany' (9 March 2017) UN Doc CEDAW/C/DEU/CO/7-8

CEDAW, 'Concluding Observations on the Combined Seventh to Tenth Periodic Reports of Nicaragua' (14 February 2024) UN Doc CEDAW/C/NIC/CO/7-10

CEDAW, 'Concluding Observations on the Combined Third and Fourth Periodic Reports of Saudi Arabia' (14 March 2018) UN Doc CEDAW/C/SAU/CO/3-4

CEDAW, 'Concluding Observations on the Eighth Periodic Report of Chile' (31 October 2024) UN Doc CEDAW/C/CHL/CO/8

CEDAW, 'Concluding Observations on the Eighth Periodic Report of Ethiopia' (14 March 2019) UN Doc CEDAW/C/ETH/CO/8

CEDAW, 'Concluding Observations on the Eighth Periodic Report of Panama' (1 March 2022) UN Doc CEDAW/C/PAN/CO/8, para 38(c)

CEDAW, 'Concluding Observations on the Eighth Report of the Dominican Republic' (1 March 2022) UN Doc CEDAW/C/DOM/C/8

CEDAW, 'Concluding Observations on the Fourth Periodic Report on Andorra' (13 November 2019) UN Doc CEDAW/C/AND/CO/4

CEDAW, 'Concluding Observations on the Ninth Periodic Report of Japan' (30 October 2024) UN Doc CEDAW/C/JPN/CO/9

CEDAW, 'Concluding Observations on the Seventh Periodic Report of Gabon' (1 March 2022) UN Doc CEDAW/C/GAB/CO/7

CEDAW, 'Concluding Observations on the Sixth Periodic Report of Namibia' (12 July 2022) UN Doc CEDAW/C/NAM/CO/6

CEDAW, 'Concluding Observations on the Sixth Periodic Report of the Central African Republic' (20 February 2024) UN Doc CEDAW/C/CAF/CO/6

CEDAW, 'Declarations, Reservations, Objections and Notifications of Withdrawal of Reservations Relating to the Convention on the Elimination of All Forms of Discrimination Against Women' (10 April 2006) UN Doc CEDAW/SP/2006/2

CEDAW, 'General Recommendation No 24 on Article 12 (Women and Health)' (1999) UN Doc CEDA/A/54/38/Rev.1

CEDAW, 'General Recommendation No 33 on Women's Access to Justice' (23 July 2015) UN Doc CEDAW/C/GC/33

CEDAW, 'General Recommendation No 35 on Gender-Based Violence Against Women, updating General Recommendation No 19' (26 July 2017) UN Doc CEDAW/C/GC/35

CEDAW, 'Inquiry concerning the United Kingdom of Great Britain and Northern Ireland under Article 8 of the Optional Protocol to CEDAW' (6 March 2018) UN Doc CEDAW/C/OP.8 /GBR/1

CESCR, 'Concluding Observations on the Fifth Periodic Report of Nicaragua' (11 November 2021) UN Doc E/C.12/NIC/CO/5

CESCR, 'Concluding Observations on the Fourth Periodic Report of Kyrgyzstan' (11 October 2024) UN Doc E/C.12/KGZ/CO/4

CESCR, 'Concluding Observations on the Fourth Periodic Report of Ecuador' (14 November 2019) UN Doc E/C.12/ECU/CO/4, paras 51–52

CESCR, 'Concluding Observations on the Initial Report of Bahrain' (4 August 2022) UN Doc E/C.12/BHR/CO/1

CESCR, 'Concluding Observations on the Initial Report of South Africa' (29 November 2018) UN Doc E/C.12/ZAF/COF/1, paras 65–66

CESCR, 'Concluding Observations on the Initial Report of Uganda' (8 July 2015) UN Doc E/C.12/UGA/CO/1

CESCR, 'Concluding Observations on the Second Periodic Report of Indonesia' (14 March 2024) UN Doc E/C.12/IDN/CO/2

CESCR, 'Concluding Observations on the Sixth Periodic Report of Poland' (26 Oct 2016) UN Doc E/C.12/POL/CO/6

CESCR, 'Concluding Observations on the Sixth Periodic Report of Spain' (25 April 2018) UN Doc E/C.12/ESP/CO/6

CESCR, 'Concluding Observations on the Sixth Periodic Report of the Democratic Republic of the Congo' (28 March 2022) UN Doc E/C.12/COD/CO/6

CESCR, 'Concluding Observations on the Third Periodic Report of Honduras' (22 October 2024) UN Doc E/C.12/HND/CO/3
CESCR, 'Concluding Observations on the Third Periodic Report of Slovakia' (14 November 2019) UN Doc E/C.12/SVK/CO/3
CESCR, 'Concluding Observations on the Third Periodic Report of the Plurinational State of Bolivia' (5 November 2021) UN Doc E/C.12/BOL/CO/3
CESCR, 'General Comment No 12 on the Right to Adequate Food (Article 11)' (12 May 1999) UN Doc E/C.12/1999/5
CESCR, 'General Comment No 14: The Right to the Highest Attainable Standard of Health (Article 12 of the ICESCR)' (11 August 2000) UN Doc E/C.12/2000/4
CESCR, 'General Comment No 16: The Equal Right of Men and Women to the Enjoyment of All Economic, Social and Cultural Rights (Art 3 of the ICESCR)' (11 August 2005) UN Doc E/C.12/2005/4
CESCR, 'General Comment No 22 on the Right to Sexual and Reproductive Health (Article 12 of the ICESCR)' (2 May 2016) UN Doc E/C.12/GC/22
CESCR, 'General Comment No 25 on Science and Economic, Social and Cultural Rights' (30 April 2020) UN Doc E/C.12/GC/25
CESCR, 'General Comment No 26 on Land and Economic, Social, and Cultural Rights' (24 January 2023) UN Doc E/C.12/GC/26
CESCR, 'General Comment No 9 on the Domestic Application of the Covenant' (3 December 1998) UN Doc E/C.12/1998/24
CESCR, 'General Comment No 3: The Nature of States Parties' Obligations (Art 2, para 1 of the Covenant)' (14 December 1990) UN Doc E/1991/23
CESCR, 'Working methods concerning the Committee's follow-up to Views under the Optional Protocol to the International Covenant on Economic, Social, and Cultural Rights' (2017) UN Doc. E/C.12/62/4
CESCR, 'General Comment No 23 on the Right to Just and Favourable Conditions of Work (Article 7 ICESCR)' (27 April 2016) UN Doc E/C.12/GC/23
Comisión Inter-Americana de Derechos Humanos, 'Resolución 22/2015 Medidas Cautelares No 178/15, Asunto niña Mainumby respecto de Paraguay' (8 June 2015) www.oas.org/es/cidh/decisiones/pdf/2015/MC178-15-ES.pdf accessed 9 January 2026
Council of Europe, *Additional Protocol to the European Social Charter Providing for a System of Collection Complaints* (adopted 9 June 1995, entered into force 1 July 1998) ETS No 158
CRPD and CEDAW, 'Joint Statement by CRPD and CEDAW: Guaranteeing Sexual and Reproductive Health and Rights for All Women, in Particular Women with Disabilities' (29 August 2019) https://tbinternet.ohchr.org/Treaties/CEDAW/Shared%20Documents/1_Global/INT_CEDAW_STA_8744_E.docx accessed 9 January 2026
European Court of Human Rights, 'HUDOC' https://hudoc.echr.coe.int/eng accessed 9 January 2026
European Social Charter, 'HUDOC' https://hudoc.esc.coe.int/eng accessed 9 January 2026
HRC, 'General Comment No 28: Article 3 (The Equality of Rights Between Men and Women)' (29 March 2000) UN Doc CCPR/C/21/Rev.1/Add.10
HRC, 'Concluding Observations on the Fourth Periodic Report of India' (2 September 2024) UN Doc CCPR/C/IND/CO/4
HRC, 'Concluding Observations on the Fourth Periodic Report of the Plurinational State of Bolivia' (2 June 2022) UN Doc CCPR/C/BOL/CO/4
HRC, 'Concluding Observations on the Seventh Periodic Report of Colombia' (17 Nov 2016) UN Doc CCPR/C/COL/CO/7
HRC, 'Concluding Observations on the Seventh Periodic Report of El Salvador' (9 May 2018) UN Doc CCPR/C/SLV/CO/7
HRC, 'Concluding Observations on the Seventh Periodic Report of Germany' (30 November 2021) UN Doc CCPR/C/DEU/CO/7

HRC, 'Concluding Observations on the Third Periodic Report of Armenia' (25 November 2021) UN Doc CCPR/C/ARM/CO/3

HRC, 'General Comment No 22 on Article 18 of the ICCPR' (27 September 1993) UN Doc CCPR/21/Rev.1/Add.4

HRC, 'General Comment No 36: Article 6 (Right to Life)' (3 September 2019) UN Doc CCPR/C /GC/36

HRC, 'Legal Analysis of the Conduct of Israel in Gaza Pursuant to the Convention on the Prevention and Punishment of the Crime of Genocide' (16 September 2025) UN Doc A/HRC/60/CRP.3

HRC, 'Note by the Human Rights Committee on the procedure for follow-up to concluding observations' (23 December 2021) UN Doc CCPR/C/161

HRC, 'Visit to the United Kingdom of Great Britain and Northern Ireland: Report of the Special Rapporteur on Extreme Poverty and Human Rights' (23 April 2019) UN Doc A/HRC/41/39 /Add.1

Inter-American Court of Human Rights, '*Beatriz et al v El Salvador* Press Release (English)' https://corteidh.or.cr/docs/comunicados/cp_92_2024_eng.pdf accessed 9 January 2026

OHCHR, 'Detention in the Context of the Escalation of Hostilities in Gaza (October 2023 – June 2024)' (31 July 2024) www.ohchr.org/sites/default/files/documents/countries/opt/20240731 -Thematic-report-Detention-context-Gaza-hostilities.pdf accessed 9 January 2026

OHCHR, 'Human Rights Committee Holds Twelfth Informal Meeting with States Parties, Discusses Challenges Relating to the Work of the Committee' (18 July 2022) www.ohchr.org/en /press-releases/2022/07/human-rights-committee-holds-twelfth-informal-meeting-states-parties accessed 9 January 2026

OHCHR, 'Indiscriminate and Disproportionate Attacks During the Conflict in Gaza (October – December 2023)' (19 June 2024) www.ohchr.org/sites/default/files/documents/countries/opt /20240619-ohchr-thematic-report-indiscrim-disprop-attacks-gaza-oct-dec2023.pdf accessed 9 January 2026

OHCHR, 'Protecting Human Rights in the DRC Amid Escalating Conflict' (10 September 2025) www.ohchr.org/en/stories/2025/09/protecting-human-rights-drc-amid-escalating-conflict accessed 9 January 2026

OHCHR, 'Report on the Human Rights Situation in Ukraine: 1 June – 30 November 2025' (9 December 2025) https://ukraine.ohchr.org/en/reports/periodic-reports-on-the-human-rights -situation-in-ukraine accessed 9 January 2026

OHCHR, 'Six-month Update Report on the Human Rights Situation in Gaza: 1 November 2023 to 30 April 2024' (8 November 2024) www.ohchr.org/sites/default/files/documents/countries/opt /20241106-Gaza-Update-Report-OPT.pdf accessed 9 January 2026

OHCHR, 'Status of Ratification' https://indicators.ohchr.org/ accessed 9 January 2026

Philip Alston, 'Statement on Visit to the USA, by Professor Phillip Alston, United Nations Special Rapporteur on Extreme Poverty and Human Rights' (15 December 2017) www.ohchr .org/en/statements/2017/12/statement-visit-usa-professor-philip-alston-united-nations-special -rapporteur?LangID=E&NewsID=22533 accessed 9 January 2026

Tlaleng Mofokeng, 'Report of the Special Rapporteur on the Right of Everyone to the Enjoyment of the Highest Attainable Standard of Physical and Mental Health – Sexual and Reproductive Health Rights: Challenges and Opportunities During the COVID-19 Pandemic' (16 July 2021) UN Doc A/76/172

Tlaleng Mofokeng, 'Report of the Special Rapporteur on the Right of Everyone to the Enjoyment of the Highest Attainable Standard of Physical and Mental Health – Violence and its Impact on the Right to Health' (14 April 2022) UN Doc A/HRC/50/28

Tlaleng Mofokeng, 'Report of the Special Rapporteur on the Right of Everyone to the Enjoyment of the Highest Attainable Standard of Physical and Mental Health – Racism and the Right to Health' (20 July 2022) UN Doc A/77/197

United Nations General Assembly, 'Overall Review and Appraisal of the Implementation of the Programme of Action of the International Conference on Population and Development' (2 July 1999) UN Doc A/S-21/PV.9

United Nations General Assembly, 'Report of the Independent International Commission of Inquiry on the Occupied Palestinian Territory, Including East Jerusalem, and Israel' (11 September 2024) UN Doc A/79/232

United Nations, 'Beijing Declaration and Platform for Action, Adopted at the Fourth World Conference on Women, 4–15 September 1995' (1995) UN Doc A/CONF.177/20/Rev.1

United Nations, '*Programme of Action of the International Conference on Population and Development, Cairo,* 5–13 September 1994' (1994) UN Doc A/CONF.171/13

United Nations, 'Report of the World Conference of the International Women's Year, Mexico City, 19 June – 2 July 1975' (1976) UN Doc E/CONF.66/34

United Nations, 'Report of the World Conference of the United Nations Decade for Women: Equality, Development and Peace, Copenhagen, 14–30 July 1980' (1980) UN Doc A/COF.94/35

United Nations, 'Report of the World Conference to Review and Appraise the Achievements of the United Nations Decade for Women: Equality, Development and Peace, Nairobi, 15 – 26 July 1985' (1985) UN Doc A/CONF.116/28/Rev.1

United Nations, 'World Conference on Human Rights – Vienna Declaration and Programme of Action' (12 July 1993) UN Doc A/CONF.157/23

News Articles

Al Jazeera, 'Israel launches deadly strikes in Gaza in new ceasefire violations' (4 January 2026) www.aljazeera.com/news/2026/1/4/israel-launches-deadly-strikes-in-gaza-in-new-ceasefire-violations accessed 9 January 2026

Alsaafin, Linah and Amer, Ruwaida, 'No privacy, no water: Gaza women use period-delaying pills amid Israel war' (*Al Jazeera*, 31 October 2023) www.aljazeera.com/news/2023/10/31/no-privacy-no-water-gaza-women-use-period-delaying-pills-amid-war accessed 9 January 2026

Amnesty International, 'Poland: Decision to retry activist prosecuted for aiding an abortion gives hope that charges against Justyna can be withdrawn' (13 February 2025) www.amnesty.org/en/latest/news/2025/02/poland-decision-to-retry-activist-prosecuted-for-aiding-an-abortion-gives-hope-that-charges-against-justyna-can-be-withdrawn/ accessed 9 January 2026

Bhattacharya, Suryatapa, 'India Targets Illicit Sex-Selective abortions' (*The Wall Street Journal,* 31 January 2016) www.wsj.com/articles/india-targets-illicit-sex-selective-abortions-1454280280 accessed 9 January 2026

Brown, Cate, 'These countries no longer arm Israel. It's not making much difference.' (*The Washington Post*, 16 October 2025) www.washingtonpost.com/world/2025/10/16/israel-weapons-ban-gaza-arms/ accessed 9 January 2025

Dey, Sneda and Brooks Harper, Karen, 'Transgender Texas kids are terrified after governor orders that parents be investigated for child abuse' (*The Texas Tribune,* 28 February 2022) www.texastribune.org/2022/02/28/texas-transgender-child-abuse/ accessed 9 January 2026

Easton, Adam, 'Doctors found guilty over death of pregnant woman in Poland' (*BBC News*, 17 July 2025) www.bbc.co.uk/news/articles/c1lj145jy5zo accessed 9 January 2026

Gwyn Jones, Mared, 'Why is the EU mostly silent on South Africa's genocide case against Israel' (*Euro News,* 10 January 2024) www.euronews.com/my-europe/2024/01/12/where-do-eu-countries-stand-on-south-africas-genocide-case-against-israel accessed 9 January 2026

Heneghan, Tom, 'Monaco rejects abortion bill after prince asserts 'place of Catholicism'' (*The Tablet,* 2 December 2025) www.thetablet.co.uk/news/monaco-rejects-abortion-bill-after-prince-asserts-place-of-catholicism/ accessed 9 January 2026

Hines, Sally, 'Trans and feminist rights have been falsely cast in opposition' (*The Economist*, 13 July 2018) www.economist.com/open-future/2018/07/13/trans-and-feminist-rights-have-been-falsely-cast-in-opposition accessed 9 January 2026

Koerth, Maggie and Thomson-DeVeaux, Amelia, 'Overturning Roe Has Meant At Least 10,000 Fewer Legal Abortions' (*FiveThirtyEight*, 30 October 2022) https://fivethirtyeight.com/features/overturning-roe-has-meant-at-least-10000-fewer-legal-abortions/ accessed 9 January 2026

Lee, Matthew, 'US has given at least $21.7 billion in military aid to Israel since war in Gaza began, report says' (*AP News*, 7 October 2025) https://apnews.com/article/israel-gaza-war-military-aid-83cebb16b3e504f70112e374a0c74bfc accessed 9 January 2026

LeVine, Marianne, Martinez, Emmanuel, and Valiño, Álvaro, 'ICE shift in tactics leads to soaring number of at-large arrests, data shows' (*The Washington Post*, 28 December 2025) www.washingtonpost.com/immigration/2025/12/28/ice-deportations-data-trump-arrests/ accessed 9 January 2026

Malkin, Elisabeth, 'They Were Jailed for Miscarriages. Now, Campaign Aims to End Abortion Ban.' (The New York Times, 9 April 2018) www.nytimes.com/2018/04/09/world/americas/el-salvador-abortion.html accessed 9 January 2026

Mitchell, Archie, 'Nigel Farage calls for parliament to debate stricter abortion limits' (*Independent*, 28 November 2024) www.independent.co.uk/news/uk/politics/farage-abortion-limit-reform-b2655446.html accessed 9 January 2026

Najmabadi, Shannon, 'Gov Greg Abbott signs into law one of the nation's strictest abortion measures, banning procedure as early as six weeks into pregnancy' (*The Texas Tribune*, 19 May 2021) www.texastribune.org/2021/05/18/texas-heartbeat-bill-abortions-law/ accessed 9 January 2026

News, BBC, 'Italy Abortion Row as Woman Dies after Hospital Miscarriage' (20 October 2016) www.bbc.co.uk/news/world-europe-37713211 accessed 9 January 2026

Petriczko, Ada, 'We are done waiting': Inside Poland's First Abortion Centre' (*Context*, 5 May 2025) www.context.news/socioeconomic-inclusion/we-are-done-waiting-inside-polands-first-abortion-centre accessed 9 January 2026

Reuters, 'El Salvador Woman's 50-year Jail Sentence Outrages Abortion Rights Group' (4 July 2022) www.reuters.com/world/americas/el-salvador-womans-50-year-jail-sentence-outrages-abortion-rights-group-2022-07-04/ accessed 9 January 2026

Sancha, Natalia, 'UNRWA Chief: 'Gaza is Becoming the Graveyard of International Humanitarian Law' (*El País*, 1 September 2025) https://english.elpais.com/international/2025-09-01/unrwa-chief-gaza-is-becoming-the-graveyard-of-international-humanitarian-law.html accessed 9 January 2026

Singh, Kanishka, 'US Criticizes ICJ Opinion on Israeli Occupation of Palestinian Territories' (*Reuters*, 20 July 2024) www.reuters.com/world/us-criticizes-icj-opinion-israeli-occupation-palestinian-territories-2024-07-20/ accessed 9 January 2026

Singh, Maanvi, Murphy Marcos, Coral, and Simmonds, Charlotte, '2025 was ICE's Deadliest Year in Two Decades. Here are the 32 People Who Died in Custody' (*The Guardian*, 4 January 2026) www.theguardian.com/us-news/ng-interactive/2026/jan/04/ice-2025-deaths-timeline accessed 9 January 2026

Surana, Kavitha and Presser, Lizzie, '"Ticking Time Bomb": A Pregnant Mother Kept Getting Sicker. She Died After She Couldn't Get an Abortion in Texas' (*ProPublica*, 19 November 2025) www.propublica.org/article/texas-abortion-ban-tierra-walker-preeclampsia accessed 9 January 2026

Times of Malta, 'Activists Call for Abortion Law Reform Ahead of Valletta Rally' (20 September 2025) https://timesofmalta.com/article/activists-call-abortion-law-reform-ahead-valletta-rally.1116528 accessed 9 January 2026

Other

Zurawski v Texas (2024), dir Maisie Crow and Abbie Perrault, Together Films, US

Reports

Amnesty International UK, 'Legal But Not Local: Barriers to Accessing Abortion Services in Northern Ireland' (December 2023) www.amnesty.ie/wp-content/uploads/2023/12/Legal-but-not-local-barriers-to-abortion-access-in-Northern-Ireland.pdf accessed 9 January 2026

Berry, Charlie and Thompson, Mike, 'Shelter Briefing: Cost of Living Crisis and the Housing Emergency' (*Shelter*, 7 September 2022) https://england.shelter.org.uk/professional_resources/policy_and_research/policy_library/shelter_briefing_cost_of_living_crisis_and_the_housing_emergency accessed 9 January 2026

Boobis, Sophie and Albanese, Francesca 'The Impact of COVID-19 on People Facing Homelessness and Service Provision Across Great Britain' (*Crisis*, 19 November 2020) www.crisis.org.uk/media/244285/the_impact_of_covid19_on_people_facing_homelessness_and_service_provision_across_gb_2020.pdf accessed 9 January 2026

Department of Health and Social Care, 'Abortion Statistics, England and Wales: 2021' www.gov.uk/government/statistics/abortion-statistics-for-england-and-wales-2021/abortion-statistics-england-and-wales-2021 accessed 9 January 2026

Department of Health and Social Care, 'The Abortion Act 1967 – Approval of a Class of Places' (30 March 2020) https://assets.publishing.service.gov.uk/government/uploads/system/uploads/attachment_data/file/876740/30032020_The_Abortion_Act_1967_-_Approval_of_a_Class_of_Places.pdf accessed 9 January 2026

Dirección Nacional de Salud Sexual y Reproductiva, 'Implementar IVE-ILE: Ley 27.610: informe annual 2021' (Ministerio de Salud de Argentina, July 2022) https://bancos.salud.gob.ar/recurso/implementar-ive-ile-ley-27610-informe-anual-2021 accessed 9 January 2026

Felker, Allison and others (eds), 'Saving Lives, Improving Mothers' Care: Lessons learned to inform maternity care from the UK and Ireland Confidential Enquiries into Maternal Deaths and Morbidity 2021–23' (MBRRACE-UK, 11 September 2025) www.npeu.ox.ac.uk/mbrrace-uk/reports/maternal-reports/maternal-report-2021-2023 accessed 9 January 2026

FIGO, 'Conscientious objection: a barrier to care' (19 October 2021) www.figo.org/resources/figo-statements/conscientious-objection-barrier-care accessed 9 January 2026

Guttmacher, 'Fact Sheet: Abortion in the United States' (April 2025) www.guttmacher.org/fact-sheet/induced-abortion-united-states accessed 9 January 2026

Gunja, Munira Z, Gumas, Evan D, and Williams II, Reginald D, 'The U.S. Maternal Mortality Crisis Continues to Worsen: An International Comparison' (*The Commonwealth Fund*, 1 December 2022) www.commonwealthfund.org/blog/2022/us-maternal-mortality-crisis-continues-worsen-international-comparison accessed 9 January 2026

Hoyert, Donna L, 'Maternal Mortality Rates in the United States, 2023' (*National Centre for Health Statistics*, 1 May 2025) www.cdc.gov/nchs/data/hestat/maternal-mortality/2023/Estat-maternal-mortality.pdf accessed 9 January 2026

Jones, Rachel K, Gibson, Candace, and Philbin, Jesse, 'The Number of Brick-and-Mortar Abortion Clinics Drops, as US Abortion Rate Rises: New Data Underscore the Need for Policies that Support Providers' (*Guttmacher*, June 2024) www.guttmacher.org/report/abortion-clinics-united-states-2020-2024 accessed 9 January 2026

Ministro della Salute, 'Relazione del Ministro della Salute sulla attuazione della legge contenente norme per law tutela sociale della maternitá e per l'interruzione volontoria di gravidanza (legge 194/78) – dati definitivi 2020' (2022) www.salute.gov.it/imgs/C_17_pubblicazioni_3236_allegato.pdf accessed 9 January 2026

Ministro della Salute, 'Relazione del Ministro della Salute sulla attuazione della legge contenente norme per law tutela sociale della maternitá e per l'interruzione volontoria di gravidanza (legge 194/78) – dati definitivi 2022' (2024) www.salute.gov.it/new/sites/default/files/imported/C_17_pubblicazioni_3493_allegato.pdf accessed 9 January 2026

Ministry of Health and Social Development of the Russian Federation, *Guidelines on Psychological Pre-Abortion Counselling*, 15-0/10/2-9162 (13 October 2010) https://abortion-policies.srhr.org/documents/countries/02-Russian-Federation-Methodical-Letter-Pre-Abortion-Counseling-Ministry-of-Health-and-Social-Development-2010.pdf accessed 9 January 2026

Partners for Law in Development and SAMA Resource Group, *Sexual Health and Reproductive Health Rights in India* (*SAMA Women's Health*, 1 April 2018) https://samawomenshealth.in/srhr-country-assessment-report/ accessed 9 January 2026

Peter Matejic and Tom Clark, 'From Disability to Destitution' (*Joseph Rowntree Foundation*, 2022) www.jrf.org.uk/deep-poverty-and-destitution/from-disability-to-destitution accessed 9 January 2026

Scottish Government Chief Medical Officer, 'Abortion – COVID-19 – approval for mifepristone to be taken at home and other contingency measures' (31 March 2020) www.sehd.scot.nhs.uk/cmo/CMO(2020)09.pdf accessed 9 January 2026

UNFPA, 'From natural process to nightmare: How Gaza's women and girls cope with periods in a war zone' (2 June 2025) www.unfpa.org/news/natural-process-nightmare-how-gaza%E2%80%99s-women-and-girls-cope-their-periods-war-zone accessed 9 January 2026

UNFPA, 'UNFPA warns of catastrophic birth outcomes in Gaza amid starvation, psychological trauma and collapsing healthcare' (*UNFPA in Palestine*, 23 July 2025) https://palestine.unfpa.org/en/news/unfpa-warns-catastrophic-birth-outcomes-gaza-amid-starvation-psychological-trauma-and accessed 9 January 2026

United Nations Office for South-South Cooperation, 'Climate change and its impact on the countries of the Global South' (2025) https://southsouth-galaxy.org/wp-content/uploads/2025/07/Climate-change-and-its-impact-on-the-countries-of-the-Global-South.pdf accessed 9 January 2026

WHO, 'WHO guideline on self-care interventions for health and well-being, 2022 revision' (28 June 2022) www.who.int/publications/i/item/9789240052192 accessed 9 January 2026

WHO, 22nd *Model List of Essential Medicines* (WHO, 30 September 2021) www.who.int/publications/i/item/WHO-MHP-HPS-EML-2021.02 accessed 9 January 2026

WHO, *Abortion Care Guideline* (8 March 2022) www.who.int/publications/i/item/9789240039483 accessed 9 January 2026

WHO, *Safe Abortion: Technical & Policy Guidance for Health Systems* (WHO, 29 June 2015) https://wkc.who.int/resources/publications/i/item/safe-abortion-technical-policy-guidance-for-health-systems accessed 9 January 2026

Websites

ACLU, 'Mapping Attacks of LGBTQ Rights in US State Legislatures in 2025' (29 December 2025) www.aclu.org/legislative-attacks-on-lgbtq-rights-2025 accessed 9 January 2026

Arango Olaya, Mónica 'The Fundamental Right to Abortion in Colombia' (*Oxford Human Rights Hub*, 10 Mar 2022) https://ohrh.law.ox.ac.uk/the-fundamental-right-to-abortion-in-colombia/ accessed 9 January 2026

BDS Movement https://bdsmovement.net/ accessed 9 January 2026

British Pregnancy Advisory Service, 'Pills by Post – Abortion Pill treatment at home' www.bpas.org/abortion-care/abortion-treatments/the-abortion-pill/remote-treatment/ accessed 9 January 2026

Campaña Nacional por el Derecho al Aborto Legal, Seguro y Gratuito www.abortolegal.com.ar accessed 9 January 2026

Causa Justa, 'Quiénes Somos' https://causajustaporelaborto.org/quienes-somos-2/ accessed 9 January 2026

Center for Reproductive Rights, 'European Abortion Laws: A Comparative Overview' (December 2020) https://reproductiverights.org/wp-content/uploads/2020/12/European-abortion-law-a-comparative-review.pdf accessed 9 January 2026

Center for Reproductive Rights, 'Landmark Cases' https://reproductiverights.org/our-work/landmark-cases/ accessed 9 January 2026

Center for Reproductive Rights, 'The Plaintiffs and Their Stories: Zurawski v State of Texas' (14 November 2023) https://reproductiverights.org/news/zurawski-v-texas-plaintiffs-stories-remarks/ accessed 9 January 2026

Center for Reproductive Rights, 'The World's Abortion Laws' https://reproductiverights.org/maps/worlds-abortion-laws/? accessed 9 January 2026

Commonwealth of Australia, 'Bringing Them Home: Report of the National Inquiry into the Separation of Aboriginal and Torres Strait Islander Children from Their Families' (1997) https://bth.humanrights.gov.au/sites/default/files/documents/bringing_them_home_report.pdf accessed 9 January 2026

Constitute Project, 'Colombia's Constitution of 1991 with Amendments through 2015' www.constituteproject.org/constitution/Colombia_2015.pdf?lang=en accessed 9 January 2026

Constitute Project, 'Cuba 2019' www.constituteproject.org/constitution/Cuba_2019 accessed 9 January 2026

Culture WA, 'Perth's Prohibited Area' https://culture.wa.gov.au/feature/perths-prohibited-area accessed 9 January 2026

ESCR-Net, 'Judgment T-760/08 July 31, 2008' www.escr-net.org/sites/default/files/English_summary_T-760.pdf accessed 9 January 2026

Gianella, Camila, 'Despite Legal Exceptions, Access to Abortion Denied in Peru' (*Bill of Health* Blog, 23 October 2023) https://petrieflom.law.harvard.edu/2023/10/23/despite-legal-exceptions-access-to-abortion-denied-in-peru/ accessed 9 January 2026

Leal-Neri, Hugo, '*F, AL* Unofficial Translation' www.law.utoronto.ca/sites/default/files/documents/reprohealth/Case-Argentina_abortion_rape_English.pdf accessed 9 January 2026

Linfield, Aimee, 'Reducing cervical screening inequalities for trans people' (Public Health England Screening, 10 April 2019) https://phescreening.blog.gov.uk/2019/04/10/reducing-cervical-screening-inequalities-for-trans-people/ accessed 9 January 2026

Palestinian Feminist Collective, 'The Palestinian Feminist Collective Condemns Reproductive Genocide in Gaza' https://palestinianfeministcollective.org/the-pfc-condemns-reproductive-genocide-in-gaza/ accessed 9 January 2026

Police Brutality Center, 'Policing Killings Surpass 1,000 in 2025' (10 October 2025) https://policebrutalitycenter.org/news/police-killings-surpass-1000-in-2025/ accessed 9 January

Samsara, 'Samsara Hotline' https://samsara.or.id/samsara-hotline/ accessed 9 January 2026

SisterSong, 'What is Reproductive Justice?' www.sistersong.net/reproductive-justice accessed 9 January 2026

Socorristas en Red, '¿Cómo hacerse un aborto seguro con medicamentos?' http://socorristasenred.org/ accessed 9 January 2026

Steininger, Silvia, 'Sex Work Can't Buy Human Rights' (*Verfassungsblog*, 3 October 2024) https://verfassungsblog.de/ecthr-sex-work-intersectionality/ accessed 9 January 2026

The Eleanor Roosevelt Papers Project, https://erpapers.columbian.gwu.edu/struggle-human-rights-1948 accessed 9 January 2026

Tongue, Zoe L and Graham, Lewis, 'YP v Russia: Sterilisation Without Consent, Article 3, and Weak Reproductive Rights at the ECTHR' (*Strasbourg Observers*, 30 September 2022) https://strasbourgobservers.com/2022/09/30/y-p-v-russia-sterilisation-without-consent-article-3-and-weak-reproductive-rights-at-the-ecthr/ accessed 9 January 2026

University of Toronto, 'Concurring and Partially Dissenting Opinion of Judge Humberto Antonio Sierra Porto – Unofficial English Translation' www.law.utoronto.ca/sites/default/files/documents/reprohealth/iacthr_beatriz_opinion_sierra_porto_eng.pdf accessed 9 January 2026

Varon, Joana and others, 'On the blocking of abortion rights websites: Women on Waves & Women on Web' (OONI, 29 Oct 2019) https://ooni.org/post/2019-blocking-abortion-rights-websites-women-on-waves-web/ accessed 9 January 2026

Women on Waves, 'Who Are We? www.womenonwaves.org/en/page/650/who-are-we accessed 9 January 2026

Women on Web, 'Abortion with pills' www.womenonweb.org/en/abortion-pill accessed 9 January 2026

Women on Web, 'Spain censors information about abortion amid Covid-19 lockdown' (17 Jun 2020) www.womenonweb.org/en/page/20230/spain-censors-information-about-abortion-amid-covid-19-lockdown accessed 9 January 2026

World Bank Data Team, 'New World Bank country classifications by income level: 2022-2023' (*World Bank Blogs*, 1 July 2022) https://blogs.worldbank.org/opendata/new-world-bank-country-classifications-income-level-2022-2023 accessed 9 January 2026

Index

www.ingramcontent.com/pod-product-compliance
Ingram Content Group UK Ltd.
Pitfield, Milton Keynes, MK11 3LW, UK
UKHW022205220926
475873UK00003B/67

9 781509 989966